AF674728

DIGITAL PROTECTION

Protective Relaying from Electromechanical to Microprocessor

DIGITAL PROTECTION

Protective Relaying from Electromechanical to Microprocessor

SECOND EDITION

L P SINGH
Former Professor
Department of Electrical Engineering
Indian Institute of Technology, Kanpur
Uttar Pradesh

NEW AGE REFERENCE

An Imprint of

NEW AGE INTERNATIONAL (P) LIMITED, PUBLISHERS
LONDON • NEW DELHI • NAIROBI
Bangalore • Chennai • Cochin • Guwahati • Hyderabad • Kolkata • Lucknow • Mumbai
Visit us at www.newagepublishers.com

Copyright © 1997, 1994, New Age International (P) Ltd., Publishers
Published by New Age International (P) Ltd., Publishers
First Edition: 1994
Second Edition: 1997
Reprint: 2018

All rights reserved.
No part of this book may be reproduced in any form, by photostat, microfilm, xerography, or any other means, or incorporated into any information retrieval system, electronic or mechanical, without the written permission of the publisher.

GLOBAL OFFICES

- **New Delhi** **NEW AGE INTERNATIONAL (P) LIMITED, PUBLISHERS**
  7/30 A, Daryaganj, New Delhi-110002, (INDIA)
  Tel.: (011) 23253771, 23253472, **Telefax:** 23267437, 43551305
  E-mail: contactus@newagepublishers.com • Visit us at www.newagepublishers.com
- **London** **NEW AGE INTERNATIONAL (UK) LTD.**
  27 Old Gloucester Street, London, WC1N 3AX, UK
  E-mail: info@newacademicscience.co.uk • Visit us at www.newacademicscience.co.uk
- **Nairobi** **NEW AGE GOLDEN (EAST AFRICA) LTD.**
  Ground Floor, Westlands Arcade, Chiromo Road (Next to Naivas Supermarket)
  Westlands, Nairobi, KENYA, **Tel.:** 00-254-713848772, 00-254-725700286
  E-mail: kenya@newagepublishers.com

BRANCHES

- **Bangalore** 37/10, 8th Cross (Near Hanuman Temple), Azad Nagar, Chamarajpet, Bangalore- 560 018
  Tel.: (080) 26756823, **Telefax:** 26756820, **E-mail: bangalore@newagepublishers.com**
- **Chennai** 26, Damodaran Street, T. Nagar, Chennai-600 017, **Tel.:** (044) 24353401
  Telefax: 24351463, **E-mail: chennai@newagepublishers.com**
- **Cochin** CC-39/1016, Carrier Station Road, Ernakulam South, Cochin-682 016
  Tel.: (0484) 2377303, **Telefax:** 4051304, **E-mail: cochin@newagepublishers.com**
- **Guwahati** Hemsen Complex, Mohd. Shah Road, Paltan Bazar, Near Starline Hotel
  Guwahati-781 008, **Tel.:** (0361) 2513881, **Telefax:** 2543669
  E-mail: guwahati@newagepublishers.com
- **Hyderabad** 105, 1st Floor, Madhiray Kaveri Tower, 3-2-19, Azam Jahi Road, Near Kumar Theater
  Nimboliadda Kachiguda, Hyderabad-500 027, **Tel.:** (040) 24652456, **Telefax:** 24652457
  E-mail: hyderabad@newagepublishers.com
- **Kolkata** RDB Chambers (Formerly Lotus Cinema) 106A, 1st Floor, S N Banerjee Road
  Kolkata-700 014, **Tel.:** (033) 22273773, **Telefax:** 22275247
  E-mail: kolkata@newagepublishers.com
- **Lucknow** 16-A, Jopling Road, Lucknow-226 001, **Tel.:** (0522) 2209578, 4045297, **Telefax:** 2204098
  E-mail: lucknow@newagepublishers.com
- **Mumbai** 142C, Victor House, Ground Floor, N.M. Joshi Marg, Lower Parel, Mumbai-400 013
  Tel.: (022) 24927869, **Telefax:** 24915415, **E-mail: mumbai@newagepublishers.com**
- **New Delhi** 22, Golden House, Daryaganj, New Delhi-110 002, **Tel.:** (011) 23262368, 23262370
  Telefax: 43551305, **E-mail: sales@newagepublishers.com**

ISBN: 978-81-224-1053-2
C-17-04-10424

Printed in India at Glorious Printers, Delhi.
Typeset at Grover DTP Systems, Delhi.

NEW AGE INTERNATIONAL (P) LIMITED, PUBLISHERS
7/30 A, Daryaganj, New Delhi-110002
Visit us at **www.newagepublishers.com**
(CIN: U74899DL1966PTC004618)

DEDICATED TO
THE LOVING MEMORY OF
OUR DEAREST AND THE YOUNGEST
BROTHER
LATE BRIG. B.P. SINGH

FOREWORD

Power Systems in general have become complex to operate in view of their increased size both with respect to the area and capacity. To improve the reliability and economy in operation the individual systems have been interconnected. The formation of state, region and national grids have given rise to the concept of hierarchical control to provide reliable and quality power supply at the consumers' end. Protection of such large system from any type contingency or faults is essential to realise the benefits of inter connection. An ideal protective relaying scheme should isolate only the faulted area in the minimum possible time so that the rest of the system can function normally.

These relaying systems comprise schemes for protecting generating equipment, transmission lines, substations, VAR sources and distribution equipment. These schemes have gone through a tremendous change in the last few decades. Electromechanical relays have given place to electronic, digital systems and now computer aided relaying has become the latest technology. These developments in protective relays are mainly due to the requirement of specific characteristics for the protection system, with regard to speed of operation, improved characteristics, higher reliability and accuracy. These features have become necessary due to the complexity of the modern power systems. It is therefore essential that the present day power engineer should be aware of the conventional systems so that he can adopt the latest technology in the system whenever he gets an opportunity. There are a number of text books on this subject which are available to students specialising in electric power engineering. The present book is a valuable addition to this literature on power system protection. The coverage by this book is quite wide and includes essentials of conventional relaying systems and also details of computer aided of conventional relaying systems and also details of computer aided relaying. The material presented is helpful to the graduate student to carry on further research in the field of power system protection. The author is well known in this field and has used this material for the graduate and under-graduate courses at IIT Kanpur. It proves the usefulness of this book to the student community. I compliment the author for his efforts in bringing out a good book.

Bangalore

26 March 1993 M. RAMAMOORTY

PREFACE TO THE SECOND EDITION

First of all, the author expresses his gratitude and thanks to the readers and well-wishers who have welcomed the first edition of the book. Now the second edition is before you. Proper care has been taken to remove all the errors of the first edition. In addition, the second edition contains an additional chapter viz. Chapter 10 on Distance (Impedance) and Overcurrent Relay Setting and Coordination using Computer Graphics and an Appendix - II on Ultra High Speed Protective Relays for High Voltage Long Transmission Line. By the addition of these two chapters, the present book becomes complete in all respects. In the preparation of the manuscript of the second edition, the research work carried out by his graduate students, namely Dr. K.V. Desikachar, Dr. A.J. Kellog, Dr. K.K.Islam, Dr. A.K. Gupta, V.P. Singh and Nitin Bhagat have been often refered to.

The autor is thankful to all his faculty colleagues, students, staff and members of his family, relations and freinds for the cooperation shown and encouragement given by them from time to time.

February, 1996 L.P. SINGH
I.I.T. Kanpur

PREFACE

For the proper operation of a power system, an effective, efficient and reliable protection scheme is desirable. Power system components are designed to operate under normal operating conditions. However, if due to any reason say a fault, there is an abnormality, it is necessary that there should be a device which senses these abnormal conditions and if so, the element or component where such abnormality has taken place is removed, i.e. deleted from the rest of the system as soon as possible. This is necessary because the power system component can never be designed to withstand the worst possible conditions due to the fact that this will make the whole system highly uneconomical. And therefore, if such an abnormality takes place in any element or component of the power system network, it is desirable that the affected element/component is removed from the rest of the system reliably and quickly in order to restore power in the remaining system under the normal condition as soon as possible. This is why an appropriate protection scheme for the proposed system is decided right at the planning stage.

The protection scheme includes both the protective relays and switching circuits, i.e. circuit breakers. The protective relay which functions as a brain is a very important component. The protective relay is a sensing device, which senses the fault, determines its location and then sends command to the proper circuit breaker by closing its trip coil. The circuit breaker after getting command from the protective relay, disconnectes only the faulted element. This is why the protective relay must be reliable, maintainable and fast in operation. The relay must operate if there is a fault and must not operate if there is no fault.

In early days, there used to be electromechanicals relay of induction disk-type. However, very soon the disk was replaced by inverted cup, i.e. hollow cylinder and the new relay obtained was known as an induction cup or induction cylinder relay. This relay, which is still in use, possesses several important features such as higher speed, higher torque for a given power input and more uniform torque.

However, with the advent of electronic tubes, electronic relays having distinct features were developed during 1940s. With the discovery of solid state components during 1950s, static relays with numerous advantages were developed. The use of digital computers for protective relaying purposes has been engaging the attention of research and practising engineers since late 1960s and since 1980, the microprocessor/mini computer-based relaying scheme, because of its numerous advantages such as self checking feature and flexibility, is becoming more and more popular.

The present book is the result of the author's teaching at the under-graduate and post-graduate level and supervising several doctoral and master thesises and graduate level projects in the area of power system protection, at the Indian Institute of Technology, Kanpur for nearly two decades. The content of the present volume has been class-tested for several years at the under-graduate and post-graduate level classes at I.I.T. Kanpur. It has also been tested in several intensive courses offered by the author under QIP and other schemes to the teachers of academic institutions and also engineers working with utilities.

The book, which contains in all nine main chapters and an appendix, starts with the chapter on Introduction and includes chapters on fundamental and basic theory of protection schemes, definition of various terms, different types of protective relaying schemes, generalized mathematical theory of protective relay, relay as a comparator, different types and arrangement of protection schemes for various components and detailed studies of electromechanical, static and digital relaying schemes. The digital protection of synchronous machines, transformer and transmission line based both on fundamental and travelling wave phenomena, is dealt with in detail. Also included in the present volume, are the related topics such as theory and design of dynamic test bench, and P.C-based short circuit studies. The book which contains almost all the topics of current interest in the area of protective relaying will certainly be very useful to the teachers, students and engineers working with the utilities.

In the preparation of the manuscript of the book, the author gratefully acknowledges the financial assistance received from the Continuing Education Programme Cell, Indian Institute of Technology, Kanpur and also the assistance and facilities received from the administration of the Indian Institute of Technology, Kanpur. The author is thankful to all his friends and colleagues and staff of the Department of Electrical Engineering, IIT Kanpur, in particular to Drs. M. Ramamoorty, K. Parathasarthy, H.P. Khincha, V. Rajaraman, K.R. Padiyar, S.K. Basu, S.C. Srivastava, P.K. Kalra, V.P. Sinha, Sachchidanand, G.K. Dubey, M.M. Hasan, K.R. Sarma and R.N. Biswas and also to his graduate students Drs. K.V. Desikachar, A.J. Kellog and K.K. Islam for providing encouragement and moral support during the process of preparing the manuscript. The author is thankful to the Mr. L.S. Bajpai for typing the manuscript in an excellent format and to the Mr. S.Q. Hussain and Mr. Triveni Tewari for finely drawing the illustrations and xeroxing work respectively.

As a matter of fact, all the staff, students and faculties of the Indian Institute of Technology, Kanpur in general and Electrical Engineering Department in particular deserve special thanks.

Finally the author expresses his indebtness and gratitude to the members of his family, his father, brothers, sister-in-laws and his wife Smt. Tara Singh and children, Alok, Poonam, Ashok, Ajit, Anita and the youngest and dearest Nishant Kashyap for patiently providing encouragement and moral support without which the book would not have come to its present form.

I.I.T. Kanpur

December 2, 1991. L.P. SINGH

CONTENTS

1

INTRODUCTION

1.1 NEED FOR POWER SYSTEM PROTECTION

Power system protection is one of the most important and exciting topics which has been attracting the attention of both academic institutions and utilities ever since Power Systems came into being. For the proper operation of the power system, an effective, efficient and reliable protection scheme is desirable. The power system components, which include synchronous machines, bus bar, transformer, transmission line and distribution system consisting of complex and composite loads, are designed to operate under normal conditions of voltage, frequency, power factor, etc. However, due to any reason, say some fault, if any of these quantities become abnormal—say voltage becomes very high or very low, current becomes very high, power factor becomes very poor or line flows become abnormally very high—it is necessary that there should be a device which senses these abnormal conditions and if so, the element or component where such abnormality has taken place is removed, i.e. deleted from the rest of the system as soon as possible. This is necessary because the power system components can never be designed to withstand the worst possible conditions, as it will make the whole system highly uneconomical. Therefore, if such abnormal condition takes place in any element or component of the power system network, it is desirable that the affected component is removed from the rest of the system reliably and quickly so as to restore power to the remaining system under normal conditions as soon as possible.

1.2 DIGITAL PROTECTION: STATE OF ART

In early days, there used to be isolated thermal plants for each locality known as urban system. However, with the growth in the demand of electricity for different purposes such as industrial, agricultural, public places and domestic consumers, the need arises to have both the thermal as well as hydroelectric plants interconnected to supply common loads. Such systems are known as grid systems which have both thermal plants operating as base load plant and hydel plant operating as peak load plant for supplying electric power at normal operating condition to the complex load system. For such complex power system, the protection scheme required must be highly sensitive, efficient and reliable in operation. The protection scheme includes both the protective relay as well as the switching circuit, i.e. the circuit breaker. The protective relay which functions as a brain is a very important component. In the early days, there were electromechanical relays, especially of induction disk-type. However, very soon the disk was replaced by an inverted cup, i.e. hollow cylinder, and the new relay is known as induction cylinder relay or induction cup relay. This relay which is in use even now, possesses several important features such as higher speed, higher torque for a given power input and more uniform torque.

However, with the advent of electronic tubes, electronic relays were developed during 1940s which had several distinct features. With the advent of solid state devices during 1950s, static relays using these solid state components with numerous advantages, were developed. The digital computer was developed during the 1950s and the first planning studies on the digital computer were completed by the year 1957. In the following paras, a brief literature survey indicating the state of art in the area of digital protection is presented.

The use of digital computers and microprocessors for protective relaying purposes has been engaging the attention of research and practising engineers since late 1960s. The first serious proposals for using digital computers came from Rockefeller. The algorithms proposed till now can be classified into two categories; distance relay algorithms and travelling wave relay algorithms. The distance relay algorithms involve the determination of the fundamental-frequency impedance to fault from the fundamental components of voltages and currents which are extracted from the complex post-fault waveforms by analog and/or digital filters. Slemon *et al.*, described the determination of the fundamental components in phasor form from an ensemble of samples collected over one full cycle by using Fourier analysis techniques. Ramamoorty described the determination of the impedance from the peak values of voltage and current and phase angle between them from the fundamental phasor components of voltage and current. Both these methods require samples collected over one full cycle. Mann and Morrison described the predictive calculation of the peak values of and the phase angle between the voltage and current from a much fewer number of samples and their time derivatives and also discussed, in another paper, the relaying of a three-phase line using this technique. The predictive technique was presented also by Gilcrest *et al.*, who proposed the use of first and second time derivatives of the samples, and by Gilbert and Shovlin who proposed the use of samples and the sampling interval. Carr and Jackson described the use of two digital orthogonal notch filters with sine characteristics to determine the magnitude and phase angle of the fundamental components from samples taken at four equally spaced time intervals over the fundamental period, and the use of an analog low pass RC filter with a cutoff frequency of 85 Hz to band-limit the voltage and current signals prior to sampling.

The use of Fourier analysis techniques for extracting the fundamental components in phasor form has been reported by several authors, besides Slemon *et al.*, and Ramamoorty. Hope and Umamaheswaran described the use of odd and even square waves, besides sine and cosine functions, for the extraction of the fundamental components. Hope *et al.*, and Tirupathaiah *et al.*, have also employed Fourier analysis techniques with one cycle data window, whilst Phadke *et al.*, and Wiszniewski have employed these techniques with half a cycle data window. Horton described the use of Walsh functions to extract the fundamental components.

Quite a few authors have proposed the modelling of the line by a series R–L circuit, and solving the resultant differential equations to obtain the values of R and L between the relaying and fault points. Mc Innes and Morrison proposed the integration of the differential equations over two successive sampling intervals to generate adequate number of equations to solve for R and L, and used the trapezoidal rule to evaluate the integrals. Poncelet and Barnard and Bastide treated the deficiency in this modelling as an error and solved for R and L subjected to the minimization of the sum of squares of these errors over a certain number of successive sampling intervals. Smolinski modelled the line by a single Pi section and solved the resultant differential equations by replacing them by finite differences and using four sample sets to obtain the values of R and L. Ranjbar and Cory presented a novel digital harmonic filter in which the integration is carried out over a certain number of overlapping subintervals with present limits while the above differential equations are being solved by the numerical integration method. In this way, any unwanted harmonics and their multiples can be eliminated. Sakaguchi and Uemura defined the inverse Laplace transform of $1/(sL+R)$ as a weighting function and discussed a numerical solution technique to determine it. They showed that the weighting function is greater than zero only for a fault ahead of the relaying point.

Sachdeva and Baribeau assumed the post-fault waveform to be consisting of a decaying d.c. offset, the fundamental and a certain number of harmonics and determined the unknown parameters of the fundamental by applying the least square error method. After expanding the exponential term associated with the d.c. offset in a series, they considered three terms of this series and only the third harmonic for elimination. Following the same method, Luckett *et al.*, considered the d.c. offset and two harmonics for elimination, whilst Brooks represented the complex post-fault waveform by a constant plus the fundamental frequency term. Johns and Martin presented a finite transform method by which the fundamental frequency impedance can be determined by carrying out the filtering process in the frequency domain. Girgis and Brown developed two-state and three-state Kalman filters to extract the fundamental voltage and current phasors respectively, and reported that the error involved is less than 1 per cent after half a cycle. Sanderson and Wright have dealt with series compensated lines. They modelled the line by a series RLC circuit and solved the resultant differential equations by integrating them over three successive sampling intervals.

Vitin's correlation method based on travelling wave theory is suitable for computer application also. Takagi and Yamakosi described the microcomputer application of the differential current relay whose operation is based on the travelling wave theory.

Dasgupta *et al.*, also reported the use of filtering techniques to power system protection. Sachedev *et al.*, described the Kalman technique to implement the filter as an estimator for the real and imaginary components of a power system component phasor. Dash *et al.*, presented digital impedance protection of power transmission line using a spectral observer. Desikachar *et al.*, described a digital algorithm for the implementation of travelling wave relay based on amplitude comparison to find direction of fault. They proposed a fault locating algorithm by considering derivatives and Islam *et al.* proposed microprocessor-based relaying schemes for the protection of EHV/UHV transmission line based upon fundamental components and travelling wave phenomena.

1.3 MERITS OF MICROPROCESSOR (MINI COMPUTER)-BASED RELAYING SCHEME

The advantages of the mircoprocessor based relays are as follows:

1. *Self-checking capability.* With the proper software control, most of the hardware faults can be diagnosed and properly checked.
2. *Flexibility.* A variety of protection functions can be accomplished with suitable modifications in the software only either with the same hardware or with slight modifications in the hardware.
3. *Reliability.* A significant improvement in the relay reliability is obtained because the use of fewer components results in less interconnections and reduced component failures.
4. *Obtaining different types of relay characteristics.* Given the system requirements, it is possible to provide better matching of protection characteristics since these characteristics are stored in the memory of the microprocessor.
5. *Arithmetical and logical function simulation ability.* The simulation of logical functions and mathematical equations is feasible.
6. *Digital communication.* The micorprocessor based relay furnishes easy interface with digital communication equipments.
7. *Modular frame.* The relay hardware consists of standard modules resulting in ease of service.
8. *Low burden.* The microprocessor based relays impose minimum burden on the instrument transformers.
9. *Cost reduction.* The total cost and day to day expenditure of the microprocessor hardware is progressively decreasing. In the near future, the software development cost will also reduce as large number of manufacturers will come forward with such relays.

1.4 POWER SYSTEM COMPONENTS

The electric power system contains the following major components: (a) Synchronous Machines, (b) Bus Bar, (c) Transformer, (d) Transmission Line, and (e) Distribution System Including Complex Load.

For each of these components, a distinct and reliable protection scheme is needed.

From the network point of view, the power system network basically consists of three sub-networks, viz. generation sub-network, transmission sub-network and distribution sub-network. The generation sub-network, consisting of mostly three-phase synchronous generators, is designed and constructed to generate three-phase balanced voltages, i.e. voltages equal in magnitude and displaced in phase by 120°. In other words, the three-phase generation network is balanced and symmetric. The transmission network is either arranged symmetrically on the supporting structure or transposed at regular intervals to balance electrical characteristics, with the result that the three-phase transmission network is also balanced and symmetric. Because of the proper load survey, the distribution network is also balanced and symmetric. From this we conclude that during steady state operation, the three-phase power system network is balanced and hence, for the purpose of analysis, it can be treated as a single-phase system because whatever voltage, current, power factor and power flow are obtained for one-phase will be the same for the remaining phases as well. Here comes the use of one-line diagram which is actually the single-phase representation of the three-phase system in which the neutral return is suppressed.

However, during fault — especially unbalanced fault — the voltage per phase may change in magnitude or phase; similarly current, power factor may also be different for different phases. This is the case of three-phase unbalanced excitation with three-phase balanced network. Such cases cannot be represented by single-phase equivalent circuit, i.e. one-line diagram. Here all the three coupled equations of the three-phase power system network have to be solved. However, with the help of linear, power-invariant transformation such as symmetrical component transformation, the phasor quantities can be transformed to the component quantities. By doing so we arrive at a set of uncoupled equations, i.e. the new coefficient matrix in the field of component is a diagonal matrix while it was a full matrix in the field of phasor. For the purpose of designing protection scheme fault analysis is needed. And hence, transformation of phasor quantities to component quantities with the help of linear and power-invariant transformation becomes desirable since, during fault, even though the three-phase network elements are balanced and symmetric, the three-phase excitation is unbalanced.

1.5 CONCLUDING REMARKS

The content of the present volume has been class tested for several years at the graduate level classes at the Indian Institute of Technology, Kanpur. It has also been tested in several intensive courses offered by the author under Quality Improvement Scheme to the teachers of academic institutions and also to the engineers working in utilities.

The book, which contains in all nine main chapters and an appendix, starts with the chapter on Introduction and includes chapters on fundamental basic theory of protection schemes, definition of various terms, generalized mathematical theory of protective relay, different types of relaying schemes and detailed studies of Electromechanical, Static and Digital Relaying schemes. The digital protection of synchronous machines, bus bar, transformer, feeder and transmission lines are dealt with in detail. Other related and important topics such as theory and application of analog and digital filter, Microprocessor and its application to protective relays and P.C. based short circuit studies for designing adequate protection scheme have also been included in the present volume. The book which contains almost all the topics of current interests in the area of protection scheme, will certainly be very useful to the teachers, students and engineers working in utilities.

REFERENCES

1. Bornard, P., and J.C. Bastide, 'A Prototype of Multiprocessor Based Distance Relay', *IEEE Trans. Pwr. Apparat. & Syst.*, Vol. PAS-101, Feb. 1982, pp. 491–498.
2. Brooke (Jr.), A.W., 'Distance Relaying Using Least-Square Estimates of Voltage, Current and Impedance', *Proceedings of PICA Conference, IEEE Publication* No. 77 CH 1131–2 PWR, May 1977, pp 394–402.
3. Carr, J., and R.V. Jackson, 'Frequency Domain Analysis Applied to Digital Transmission Line Protection', *IEEE Trans. Pwr. Apparat. & Syst.*, Vol. PAS-94, July/Aug. 1975, pp. 1157–1166.
4. Dasgupta, K.S., O.P. Malik and G.S. Hope, 'Kalman Filtering Approach to Impedance Protection', *Trans. Can. Electr. Assoc.*, March 1983, pp 1–14.
5. Dash, P.K., and D.K. Panda, 'Digital Impedance Protection of Power Transmission Line using Spectral Observer', *IEEE Trans. Pwr. Delivery*, Vol. 3, No. 1, Jan. 1988, pp. 121–129.
6. Desikachar, K.V., and L.P. Singh, 'Fault Analysis of Multinode Power Systems for Designing Ultra High Speed Protective Relays along with a Proposed Relaying Scheme', *Electr. Pwr. syst. Res.*, Vol. 6, No. 1, Mar-May, 1983, pp. 13–26.
7. Gilbert, J.G., and R.J. Shovlin, 'High Speed Transmission Line Fault Impedance Calculation Using a Dedicated Minicomputer', *IEEE Trans. Pwr. Apparat. & Syst.*, Vol. PAS-94, May/June 1975, pp 872–883.
8. Gilcrest, G.B., G.D. Rockefeller and E.A. Udren, 'High-Speed Distance Relaying Using a Digital Computer: Part I—System Description', *IEEE Trans. Pwr. Apparat. & Syst.*, Vol. PAS-91, May/June 1972, pp. 1235–1242.
9. Girgis, A.A., and R.G. Brown, 'Application of Kalman Filtering in Computer Relaying', *IEEE Trans. Pwr. Apparat. & Syst.*, Vol PAS-100, July 1981, pp. 3387–3395.
10. Girgis, A.A., 'A New Kalman Filtering Based Digital Distance Relay', *IEEE Trans. Pwr. Apparat. & Syst.*, Vol. PAS-101, Sept. 1982, pp. 3471–3480.
11. Hope, G.S., and V.S. Umamaheswaran, 'Sampling for Computer Protection of Transmission Lines', *IEEE Trans. Pwr. Apparat. & Syst.*, Vol. PAS-93, Sept./Oct. 1974, pp. 1522–1534.
12. Hope, G.S., O.P. Malik and M.E. Rasmy, 'Digital Transmission Line Protection in Real Time', *Proc IEE*, Vol. 123, December 1976, pp. 1349–1354.
13. Horton, J.W., 'Walsh Functions for Digital Impedance Relaying for Power Lines', *IBM J. Res. & Dev.*, No. 10, 1976, pp. 530–541.
14. Humpage, W.D., K.P. Wong., T.T. Nguyen and D. Sutanto, 'Z-Transform Electromagnetic Transient Analysis in Power System', *Proc. IEE.*, Part C, Vol. 127, June 1980, pp. 370–378.
15. Islam, K.K., and L.P. Singh, 'Microprocessor: Application to Power System Protection', *Proceedings of Conference 52nd R&D of CBIP* held at Aurangabad, Vol. 3, Feb. 1985, pp. 7–12.
16. Islam, K.K., S.K. Bose and L.P. Singh, 'On Line Microprocessor Based Relaying Scheme', *Proceedings of the Platinum Jubilee Conference on Systems and Signal Processing*, held at I.I.Sc. Bangalore, Dec. 1986, pp. 241.
17. Islam, K.K., S.K. Bose and L.P. Singh, 'On Line Microprocessor Based Relaying Scheme for EHV/UHV Transmission Line: An Existing 400 KV Transmission Line', *Electr. Machines & Pwr. Syst.*, Vol. 12, 1987, pp. 313–324.

18. Islam, K.K., S.K. Bose and L.P. Singh, 'Digital Protection of EHV/UHV Transmission Line Based upon Travelling Wave Phenomena', *Electr. Machines & Pwr. Syst.*, Vol. 14, 1988, pp. 413–431.
19. Johns, A.T., and M.A. Martin, 'Fundamental Digital Approach to the Distance Protection of E.H.V. Transmission Lines', *Proc. IEE,* Vol. 125, May 1978, pp. 377–384.
20. Luckett, R.G., P.J. Munday and B.E. Murray, 'A Substation Based Computer for Control and Protection', Conference on Modern Developments in Protection, Institution of Electrical Engineers, London, 1975, *Conference Publication* No. 125, pp. 252–260.
21. Mann, B.J. and I.F. Morrison, 'Digital Calculation of Impedance for Transmission Line Protection', *IEEE Trans. Pwr. Apparat. & Syst.,* Vol. PAS-90, Jan./Feb. 1971, pp. 270–279.
22. Mann, B.J. and I.F. Morrison, 'Relaying a Three-phase Transmission Line with a Digital Computer', *IEEE Trans. Pwr. Apparat. & Syst.,* Vol. PAS-90. March/April 1971, pp. 2742–2750.
23. Mc Innes, A.D. and I.F. Morrison, 'Real Time Calculation of Resistance and Reactance for Transmission Line Protection by Digital Computer', *IEE Trans.*, Institution of Engineers, Australia, EE7, No. 1, 1971, pp. 16–23.
24. Phadke, A.G., T. Hlibka and M. Ibrahim, 'A Digital Computer System for EHV Substations: Analysis and Field Tests', *IEEE Trans. Pwr. Apparat. & Syst.,* Vol. PAS-95, Jan./Feb. 1976, pp. 291–301.
25. Phadke, A.G., M. Ibrahim and T. Hlibka, ' Fundamental Basis for Distance Relaying with Symmetrical Components', *IEEE Trans. Pwr. Apparat. & Syst.*, Vol. PAS-96, March/April 1977, pp 635–646.
26. Poncelet, R., 'The Use of Digital Computers for Network Protection'. CIGRE, Paris, 1972, paper No. 32–08
27. Ramamoorty, M., 'A Note on Impedance Measurement Using Digital Computers', *IEE-IERE Proc. (India)*, Vol. 9, Nov./Dec. 1971 pp. 2143–2147.
28. Ranjbar, A.M. and B.J. Cory, 'An Improved Method for the Digital Protection of Transmission Lines', *IEEE Trans. Pwr.,* Vol. PAS-94, March/April 1975, pp. 544–550.
29. Rockefeller, G.D., 'Fault Protection with a Digital Computer', *IEEE Trans. Power. Applications and Systems*, Vol. PAS-88, April 1969, pp. 438–464.
30. Sachdev, M.S. and M.A. Baribeau, 'A New Algorithm for Digital Impedance Relay', *IEEE Trans. Pwr. Apparat. & Syst.,* Vol. PAS-98, May/June 1979, pp. 2232–2240.
31. Sachdev, M.S., J.C. Wood and N.G. Johnson, Kalman Filtering Applied to Power System Measurements for Relaying', *IEEE, Trans. Pwr. Apparat. & Syst.,* PAS, Vol. PAS-104, Dec. 1985.
32. Sakaguchi, T. and K. Uemura, 'A New Directional Protection Based on Laplace Transformation with Special Reference to Computer Relaying', Second International Conference on Developments in Power System Protection, London, June 10–12, 1980, *Conference publication* No. 185 Institution of Electrical Engineers, London, 1980, pp. 146–150.
33. Sanderson, J.V.H. and A. Wright, 'Protective Scheme for Series-Compensated Transmission Lines', *Proc. IEE,* Vol. 121, Nov. 1974, pp. 1377–1384.
34. Siyaram and L.P. Singh, "Digital Protection of Transmission Line", *Proceedings of the* 53rd CBIP, *R & D Conference* held at Bhubaneswar, Vol. VII, May, 1986, pp. 85–98.
35. Slemon, G.R., S.D.T. Robertson and M. Ramamoorty, 'High Speed Protection of Power Systems Based on Improved System Models', CIGRE, Paris, 1969, Paper No. 31–09.
36. Smolinski, W.J., 'An Algorithm for Digital Impedance Calculation Using a Single Pi Section Transmission Line', *IEEE Trans. Pwr. Apparat. & Syst.,* Vol. PAS-98, Sept./Oct. 1979, pp. 1546–1551.
37. Sunnak, V.P., and L.P. Singh, "Microprocessor Based Protection Scheme for EHV/UHV Transmission Line", *J. Inst. Engrs. (India)*, (1) Vol. 65, Parts EL2 and EL3, Oct-Dec. 1984, pp. 89–96.
38. Takagi, T., and Y. Yamakosi, 'Digital Differential Relaying System for Transmission Line Primary Protection Using Travelling Wave Theory—Its Theory and Field Experience', Paper presented at the IEEE PES Winter Meeting, 1979, Paper No. A79–096–9.

39. Thirupathaiah, G., A. Varshney and L.P. Singh, 'On-Line Digital Protection Using a Microcomputer—A Decentralized Approach', *Technical Proceedings, National Conference on Planning, Operation and Control of Large Scale Power Systems,* Annamalai University, India, June 24–25, 1982, Paper No. S5.3.
40. Wiszniewaski, A., 'How to Reduce Errors of Distance Fault Locating Algorithms'. *IEEE Trans. Pwr. Apparat. & Syst.*, Vol. PAS-100, Dec. 1981, pp. 4815–4820.

2

PROTECTION SCHEME

2.1 INTRODUCTION

In Chap. 1, the essential need for providing a protection scheme for any power system network is detailed. The fundamental principle and basic theory of protection schemes, classification of protection schemes, types of protective relay based upon different criteria, protective relay as a comparator, different components and definition of various terms are discussed in this chapter.

2.2 BASIC PHILOSOPHY OF PROTECTION SCHEME

Any protection scheme, which is required to safeguard the power system components against abnormal conditions such as faults, consists basically of two elements: (i) Protective relay and (ii) Circuit breaker. The protective relay functions as a sensing device. It senses the fault, determines its location and finally it sends the command to the circuit breaker by closing its trip coil. The circuit breaker after getting the trip command from the protective relay, disconnects the faulted elements from the rest of the system. Thus it is seen that the protective relay which is primarily the brain behind the whole scheme plays a very important role. Therefore proper care should be taken in selecting an appropriate protective relay which is reliable, efficient and fast in operation. The protective relay must satisfy the following requirements:

1. Since faults on a well designed and healthy system are normally rare, the relays are called upon to operate only occasionally. This means that the relaying scheme is normally idle and must operate whenever fault occurs. In other words, it must be reliable.
2. Since the reliability partly depends upon the maintenance, the relay must be easily maintainable.
3. The maloperation of the relay can be in two ways. One is the failure to operate in case a fault occurs and second is the relay operation when there is no fault.

As a matter of fact, relay must operate if there is a fault and must not operate if there is no fault.

4. Relaying scheme must be sensitive enough to distinguish between normal and the faulty system.

2.3 SECTIONS OF SYSTEM PROTECTION

The overall protection is divided into following sections:

(i) Generator protection
(ii) Transformer protection
(iii) Bus protection
(iv) Feeder protection
(v) Transmission line protection

For each of these systems, distinct and reliable protection schemes are used.

2.4 CIRCUIT BREAKER

Circuit breaker after getting the command from the protective relay, disconnects only the faulty element, reliably and promptly. The following types of circuit breakers are in common use: (i) Air circuit breaker, (ii) Oil circuit breaker, (iii) Minimum oil circuit breaker, (iv) Air blast circuit breaker, (v) SF_6 breaker and (vi) Vacuum switches.

The air circuit breaker is normally used for apparatus protection. The oil circuit breaker which was very common earlier even for transmission system, is now used for feeder protection only. The minimum oil circuit breaker and air blast circuit breaker are very common for EHV/UHV transmission lines. However, the air blast circuit breaker on EHV/UHV lines has become standard practice. In place of air, SF_6 is used and these SF_6 breakers which have a bright future have several advantages such as optimal size and quick arc quenching. Nowadays, SF_6 bus bar and SF_6 cable are also being used very often. Vacuum switches which seem to have bright future are not still used in the case of EHV/UHV lines because of high cost. These breakers have clearing time of less than one cycle with the result, they produce current chopping and therefore switching resistances are normally used with these breakers. For important lines, the circuit breakers are provided with reclosing feature. The circuit breaker after opening the circuit, closes again after a prescribed time. The reclosing time is nearly 20 cycles. The reason for this practice is that the major percentage of faults on lines are transient in nature. They are due to conductor swinging when there is a strong wind or rain fall. These faults, therefore, are cleared automatically. Even though the fault is not cleared automatically, the arc gets extinguished when the line is opened.

2.5 PROTECTIVE RELAY

The function of the protective relay, as stated earlier, is to sense the fault and energize the trip coil of the circuit breaker. These days, the protecting relays are designed in such a way that they sense the fault, determine the location of the fault and then send the trip command to the proper circuit breaker by closing its trip coil and finally, the circuit breaker after getting the command from the protective relay disconnects only the faulted elements.

2.5.1 Types of Protective Relays

The following types of protective relays are used for the apparatus such as synchronous machines, bus bar, transformer and other apparatus and transmission line protection.

(i) Overcurrent relays
(ii) Undervoltage relays
(iii) Underfrequency relays
(iv) Directional relays
(v) Thermal relays
(vi) Phase sequence relays such as (a) negative sequence relays and (b) zero sequence relays
(vii) Differential relays and percentage differential relays
(viii) Distance relays such as (a) plane impedance relays (b) angle impedance relays, i.e. Ohm or reactance relays (c) angle admittance relays, i.e. Mho relays and (d) offset and restricted relays
(ix) Pilot relays such as (a) wire pilot relays (b) carrier channel pilot relays and (c) microwave pilot relays.

All the existing relaying schemes use either one or more of these relays with slight modifications. Figure 2.1 shows the basic connection of relay. There are two ways in which the circuit breaker trip coil is energized. In one method, the station battery is used to supply the current in the trip coil after the relay contacts are closed

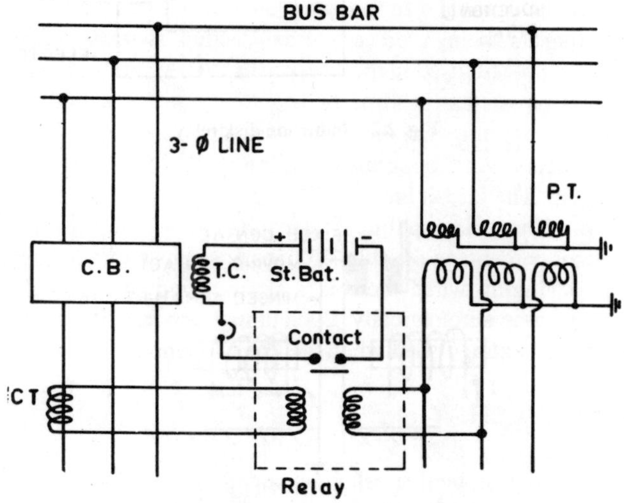

Fig. 2.1 Relay connection

by the operation of protective relay. In the second method, as soon as the relay operates the CT secondary current flows through the trip coil and energizes it. This does not need a station battery and it is used for feeder protection.

2.5.2 Relaying Scheme Based upon Construction

The various types of the relaying schemes, based upon construction, are described in the following.

(i) *Electromechanical type.* In this type of relays the torque on the moving member is produced by electromagnetic action. In the beginning, induction disk type of relay was used. This is shown in Fig. 2.2. Here the disk rotates with the production of electromagnetic torque when the element current flows in the operating coil or current proportional to voltage flows in the operating coil. Later on, the disk was replaced by an inverted cup, i.e. hollow cylinder and induction cup, i.e. induction cylinder relay was obtained with this modifications. The induction cup relay has higher torque because of reduced inertia, more uniform torque and is faster in operation. The next type of electromagnetic relay developed is the attracted armature type, i.e. hinged armature or hinged beam type. This relay is shown in Fig. 2.3. It is certainly faster than the other types of electromechanical relays. These are discussed in detail in the next chapter.

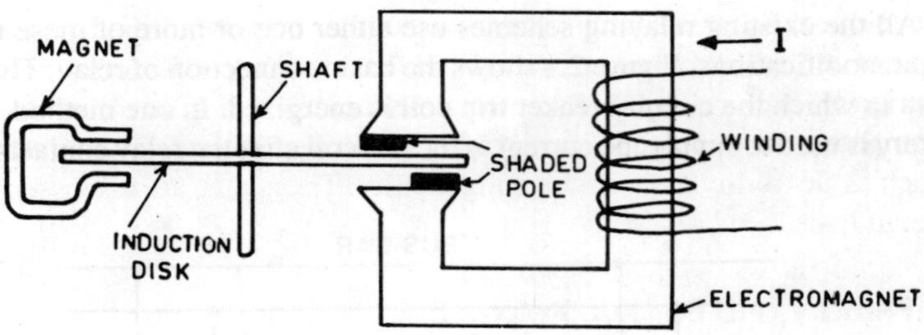

Fig. 2.2 Induction disk relay

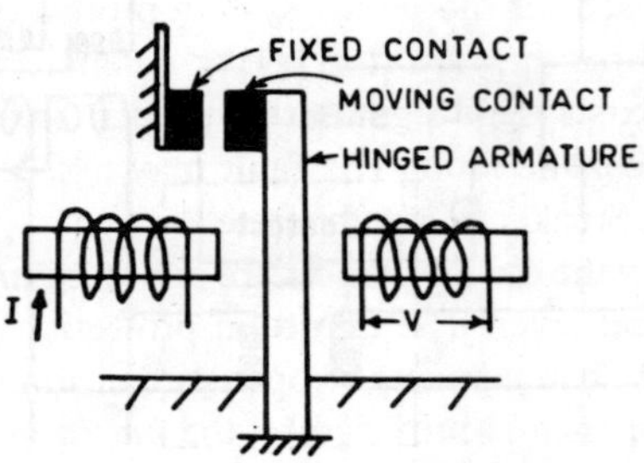

Fig. 2.3 Hinged armature relay

(ii) *Thermal relays.* These relays use bimetallic strips and the relay operation is based on unequal expansion of the two strips. These are used for apparatus protection. They are not as sensitive as the induction cup relays discussed earlier. These relays also have got a very low dropout because of large thermal constant.

(iii) *Transductor relays.* These relays use the non-linear B-H curve of the magnetic core. Transductor implies variable inductance. When the core is not saturated, the coil offers a very high impedance and when the core is saturated the coil is almost short circuited.

(iv) *Rectifier bridge relay.* These relays also use electromagnetic action for the production of torque. The signals to these relay coils are obtained after full wave rectification. These relays can be used both as an amplitude as well as a phase comparator.

(v) *Electronic relays.* These relays were developed during the 1940s and they have no moving parts. These have several merits which will be discussed later.

(vi) *Static relays.* After the advent of semiconductor devices during the 1950s, static relays were developed incorporating these semiconductor components. These relays are known as solid state relays and they have numerous advantages and they are used also for EHV/UHV lines. These are discussed in the next chapter in detail.

(vii) *Digital relaying schemes.* With the advent of digital computer during 1950s, protection engineers started using the digital computer for the purpose of protection. However, in the beginning only software packages were developed. But this could not become popular because of high cost and large size of dedicated computer. With the advent of microprocessor/mini computer during 1980s, on the line protection schemes using microprocessor/mini computers are developed increasingly because of their numerous advantages such as flexibility and selfchecking facility. These also are discussed in great detail later.

2.5.3 Primary and Backup Relays

The protective relay which functions as a sensing device must be reliable, maintainable and sensitive enough to distinguish between normal and faulty conditions. The relay must operate if there is a fault and must not operate if there is no fault. A number of relays are used for the power system protection, some of them are *primary relays,* meaning that they are first line of defence. These primary relays sense the fault and, if it exists, send signal to the proper circuit breaker by closing its trip coil and hence clear the fault. The fault may not be cleared if the relay maloperates or the circuit breaker fails to operate.

The causes of failure in the circuit breaker are either failure of supply to its trip coil or a struck mechanical lever. The failure in protective relay are because of wrong setting of the relay, bad contacts or open circuit in the relay coil. In such cases, a second line of defence is provided by the *backup relays*. These backup relays have longer operating time even though they sense the fault along with the primary relays. *Relay operating time* is defined as the time interval between sensing of fault by the relay and sending the trip signal to the proper circuit breaker. Backup relays are arranged in two ways, viz. they may be located at the same place as the primary relay, i.e. local backup and operate the same breaker. In the other case, they are located at different stations, i.e. remote backup, and operate different circuit breaker. The remote backup is preferred because it is more reliable even though it disconnects a longer section of the line. In order to attain the desired reliability, the power system network is divided into different protection zones.

2.5.4 Merits of Fast Fault Clearing

In the beginning, there used to be only electromechanical relays which were very slow in operation. However, with the passage of time, the operating time of the relay was reduced and today we have the relay based upon travelling wave phenomena which can operate within a quarter cycle. The main merits of the fast fault clearing with the help of fast acting protective relay and associated circuit breakers are as follows:

(i) By clearing the fault fast, the permanent damage to the apparatus and components such as burning of conductors or cracking of insulators, is reduced.
(ii) By clearing the fault fast, chances of fire and other hazards are reduced.
(iii) By clearing the fault fast, risk to the life of personnel is also reduced.
(iv) By quickly removing the particular faulted section or elements, the continuity of electric supply is maintained in the remaining healthy section.
(v) By clearing the fault fast, fault arising time is reduced and, therefore, the power system can be brought back to the normal state sooner.
(vi) By clearing the fault fast, the transient state stability limit of the power system is greatly improved.
(vii) Permanent damage to the apparatus is avoided.
(viii) By clearing the fault fast, the possibility of developing the simplest but the most common fault such as single-phase to ground fault into more severe fault, such as two-phase to ground fault, is avoided.

2.5.5 Protective Relay as a Comparator

To recognize fault in any element or component of the power system network, the relay monitors one quantity—usually the current entering the element—and compares it with another quantity with which it has got certain amplitude or phase angle relation. Another quantity can be local bus voltage or current leaving the element at the other end or some constant quantity which might be gravitational force or pull of a spring. From this, it follows that the protective relay is basically a comparator which must be able to carry out addition, subtraction, multiplication or division of some scalar or some vector quantities as desired. Based upon this principle, the protective relay as a comparator is classified into various types, as detailed in the following.

(a) *Single input comparator.* These relays have only one input signal. They are also known as level detectors. Such a relay monitors one quantity and compares it with certain constant quantity, i.e. a reference or base quantity which may be the pull of a spring or gravitational force. An example of this relay is an overcurrent relay where the relay measures the current entering the circuit and compares it with certain reference or base quantities. These relays, though simple in theory and construction, have several drawback such as: (i) they are non-directional, (ii) their action depends upon a single quantity which may be highly unreliable and (iii) failure to attain the desired reliability. These features will be discussed later in detail.

(b) *Dual input comparator.* These relays have two input signals. In such relays the relay, measures one quantity and compares it with another quantity with which it has normally a certain magnitude or phase angle relation. The typical examples are distance relaying scheme and differential relaying scheme. Here the relay measures the current entering the circuit and compares it in magnitude or in phase angle with the local bus voltage in the case of distance relaying scheme and with the current leaving the circuit at the other end in the case of differential relaying scheme, i.e. in the unit protection scheme. Several threshold characteristics such as straight line and circle can be obtained with the help of dual input comparator. Dual input comparators are of two types, viz. *amplitude comparator* where only the amplitude of the input signal is compared irrespective of phase angle between the two input signals and *phase comparator* where only the phase angle between the input signals is used for tripping purpose. Both, amplitude and phase comparators are dual in nature, i.e. if the signals are given as an amplitude comparator, signals as a phase comparator can be found by adding or subtracting signals as amplitude comparator. These relays have several advantages and wide applications.

(c) *Multi-input comparator.* In order to obtain characteristics other than straight line or circle, multi-input comparators are used. Here the number of signals to the protective relay is more than two. In case the phase angle criterion is used for the purpose of tripping, we obtain quadrilateral characteristics and in case amplitude criterion is used, we obtain conic characteristics such as elliptical or hyperbolic characteristics. In the case of multi-input relay, there is no duality between phase and amplitude comparator.

2.6 DEFINITION

The basic terminology used in connection with the protective relays are as follows:

Pick up. Minimum value of operating quantity for which the relay operates, i.e pick up.

Drop out. Maximum value of operating quantity for which the relay resets after it has operated.

Sensitivity. Ability of the relay to discriminate between healthy and faulted conditions.

Selectivity. Ability to select fault only within the desirable zone of protection.

Reliability. Ability of the relay to perform its function when desired.

Reach. The set maximum distance to fault from the relay location which the relay can detect.

Overreach. Ratio of the maximum distance of fault from the relay location to the set distance for the relay.

Underreach. Ratio of the minimum distance of fault from the relay location to the set distance for the relay.

Set impedance. Impedance of the line up to the reach of the relay.

Fault impedance. Impedance of the fault (i.e. arcing resistance).

Instantaneous. No time delay involved in the relay operation.

Time delay. Time interval between the sensing of the fault by the relay and the instant the relay contacts close.

Inverse time. Time delay inversely proportional to the operating quantity.

Primary relay. Main relays, i.e. first line of defence.

Backup relay. Supporting or supervisory relays, i.e. second line of defence.

Comparator. Another name for relay.

Phase comparator. Relay comparing only the phase angles between input quantities.

Amplitude comparator. Relay comparing the amplitudes of input quantities.

Instantaneous comparator. Relay comparing instantaneous values of input signals.

Blocking relay. Relay operation which produces blocking.

Blinders. Make the relay immune for certain faults.

Dual input comparator. Has two input signals.

Multi-input comparator. Has more than two input signals.

Seal in relay. Relay contacts are bypassed after the seal in relay operates.

Flag indicator. Indicator to show that the relay has operated.

Burden. VA product of the relay coil (i.e. volt ampere)

Transactor. Air core coil which converts a current signal to voltage.

Transducer. Which produces the proper relay signals from the power system.

N.C. contacts. Normally closed contacts.

N.O. contacts. Normally opened contacts.

Auxiliary contact. Contacts other than the main contacts in circuit breakers.

Threshold operation. Relay is about to operate. Net torque is close to zero. The fault has occurred at the balance point, i.e. at the reach of the relay.

2.7 SUMMARY

The protection scheme, which plays a vital and an important role for the normal operation, i.e. steady state operation of different components of the power system network, must be reliable, efficient and fast in operation. In order to achieve all these features, it is essential that there should be proper care in designing and choosing an appropriate and efficient protection scheme. In this chapter, the basic philosophy and fundamental principle of the protection scheme along with its classifications based upon different criterion, have been outlined. In addition, the protective relay which functions as a brain behind the whole scheme along with its types, and definitions of different terms have also been discussed.

EXERCISES

1. (a) Discuss briefly the basic philosophy of protection scheme.
   (b) What is the function of a circuit breaker? Mention different types of circuit breaker you are familiar with. State also their applications.
2. (a) Discuss briefly the function of a protective relay. Name different types of protective relays you are familiar with.
   (b) What do you understand by primary and back up relays? Discuss briefly. Why a power system network is divided into different protection zones? Discuss with the help of a neat diagram.
3. (a) Write short notes on different types of protection schemes based upon construction.
   (b) Discuss the distinct merits of fast fault clearing.
4. (a) Justify the statement "protective relay is a sensing device"
   (b) Comment on the statement "protective relay is a comparator". Discuss briefly (a) single input comparator, (b) dual input comparator and (c) multi-input comparator.
5. Define the following terms: (i) Pick up, (ii) Drop out, (iii) Sensitivity, (iv) Reach, (v) Overreach and underreach, (vi) Set impedance and set distance, (vii) Balance point, (viii) Phase comparator and amplitude comparator, (ix) Blocking relay, (x) Blinder, (xi) Seal-in-relay, (xii) Flag indicator, (xiii) Blinder, (xiv) Burden, (xv) Threshold operation.

REFERENCES

1. Kimbark, E.W., *Power System Stability*, Vol. II, John Wiley & Sons. New York, 1965.
2. Mason, C.R., *The Art and Science of Protective Relaying*, Wiley Eastern Ltd., 1979.
3. Singh, L.P., *Advanced Power System Analysis and Dynamics*. 3rd Edition, Wiley Eastern Ltd., 1992.
4. Warrington, A.R., Van, C. *Protective Relays, Their Theory and Practice*, Vol. I, Chapman and Hall Ltd., London, 1976.
5. Warrington, A.R., Van, C. *Protective Relays, Their Theory and Practice*, Vol. II, Chapman and Hall Ltd., London, 1974.

3

ELECTROMECHANICAL RELAY

3.1 INTRODUCTION

Overcurrent relays of electromechanical type were used for the protection of the transmission line and also equipment in the early days. However, they were found to be unsuitable for the protection of transmission lines because of their inherent drawbacks such as the shifting of balance point (i.e. reach) with the type of fault, variation in generation capacity and switching operation. These overcurrent relays are used only on distribution systems where the minimum fault current exceeds the maximum (normal) current and only up to 33 kV transmission systems. However, the directional overcurrent relays are still used for ground fault relaying at sub-transmission and transmission levels. Distance relays have been developed to overcome the problems associated with the overcurrent relays. The requirement of UHS (Ultra High Speed) fault clearance for the accomplishment of improved transient stability is met by developing protective relays whose operation is based upon travelling wave phenomena.

In the evolution of relays for the protection of transmission lines, the electromechanical relays were developed first, and in the evolution of distance relays, the plain impedance relay was the first one that was conceived and developed. In 1923, Chrichton reported about an impedance relay which employed an induction disc actuating structure and operated in a time proportional to the impedance between the relay and the fault point. In 1928, McLaughlin and Erickson reported about a directional impedance-time relay built with an induction disc actuating structure. They presented the constructional details, and described the principle of operation, methods of obtaining proper voltage for the restraining elements and methods of compensating for the voltage drop in power transformers and for the secondary neutral shift. In 1930, Crichton reported about a high speed impedance relay, the high speed of operation having been obtained with a balanced beam structure. He described a three-step directional impedance relaying scheme and discussed the effect of fault resistance on the operating speed of the relay. The development of a high speed impedance relay with a balanced beam structure was also reported by Goldsborough and Lewis. In 1944, Goldsborough reported about a modified impedance relay built with a balanced beam structure and described how a circular pickup characteristic of any desired radius and with any desired location of the centre could be obtained with a voltage proportional to the system current added to or subtracted from the relay voltage and with a current proportional to the system voltage added to or subtracted from the relay current.

In 1928, Warrington designed an induction disc type reactance relay for an American company. In 1931, George presented the performance records of normal speed as well as high speed reactance relays installed at two hydroplants of Tennesse Electric Power Company of America, and reported that, although they had performed satisfactorily on long lines with wide variations in short circuit conditions, certain difficulties had arisen on interconnectors operating near stability. In 1933, Warrington reported about a high speed reactance relay which was built with a four-pole induction cup actuating structure carrying current coils on one pair of opposite poles, and current and voltage coils on each of the other poles. Dewey and Mc Glynn as well as Warren C. New have reported about three-step directional reactance relaying schemes with zones 1 and 2 protected by the combination of reactance and mho units, and zone 3, by mho units. Both the reactance and mho relays has employed 4-pole induction cup structures.

Though the mho relay was first used in 1933 as the directional unit for an early type reactance relay, its independent use for the protection of heavily loaded and long transmission lines was first recommended in 1943 by Warrington with its merits lucidly brought out. In 1944, Cordrey and Warrington described its actual use in a carrier current scheme. Later, Hutchinson described its use in a three-step distance relaying scheme in which protection for zones 1 and 2 was provided by normal mho units, and for zone 3, by an offset mho unit. He presented also the test results in the form of transient overreach of zone 1 unit, and the operating time of each unit as a function of the ratio of the impedance to fault to the setting impedance.

In 1962, Skuderna put forth the mathematical development of how offset conic and limicon characteristics could be produced with a four-pole induction cup structure. He presented also detailed circuitry needed to obtain the various winding inputs and described the setting procedure with a numerical example for getting an offset elliptical characteristic.

3.2 INDUCTION RELAYS

Induction type relays are the most common type of electromechanical relays. In the induction relays, there, may be one or more exciting coil wound on magnetic core. Due to flow of the current in the exciting coil, electromagnetic torque is produced which tries to rotate the rotor (i.e. armature). The rotation of the rotor, closes the relay contacts thus energizing the trip coil of the circuit breaker. Three types of induction relays are commonly used, viz. Induction disk Relays, Induction cup relays and Hinged armature, i.e. beam type relays.

3.2.1 Induction Disk Relay

This relay is very much similar in construction to that of watt hour meter. It has a magnetic core carrying the operating (or exciting) winding. Between the poles of the magnetic core, an induction disk mounted on shaft is placed (Fig. 3.1). The current of the element which is being protected or the current proportional to the voltage flows through the operating i.e. exciting winding placed on the magnetic core. In order to produce torque to rotate the disk, part of pole face is shaded with copper strips, thus converting it similar to a single phase shaded pole type induction motor. Thus due to flow of current in the operating coil, an electromagnetic torque is produced which tries to rotate the disk placed in between the poles. The rotation of the disk closes the relay contact thus energizing the trip coil of the circuit breaker. Normally, a weight or spring is attached to the disk. The gravitational force due to the weight or pull of the spring attached to the disk opposes the rotation of the disk; hence the disk can only rotate if the operating torque overcomes the restraining torque due to gravitational force due to weight or pull of the spring attached to the disk. The relay is quite slow in operation. In another type of induction disk relay, there are two electromagnets and the disk is placed in between these electromagnets. The upper electromagnet carries an exciting (primary) winding in which element current flows. The secondary winding which is short circuited is placed on the lower electromagnet. The flux produced due to the current in the primary winding in the upper electromagnet induces a voltage in the short circuit secondary winding on the lower electromagnet, with the result, the induced current flows in this winding also. Because of the interaction of fields due to the currents in these two windings, an electromagnetic torque is produced which, in turn, tries to rotate the induction disk placed between the poles of these two electromagnets. This is a faster type of induction disk relay.

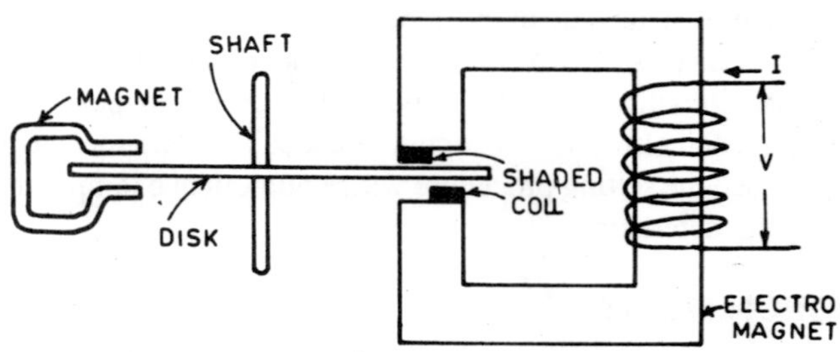

Fig. 3.1 Induction disk relay

3.2.2 Induction Cup Relay

The induction disk relay discussed in the previous section is relatively slow and also not very efficient. In order to improve the efficiency as well as to make the relay faster, in the first attempt, the disk was replaced by an inverted cup, i.e. hollow cylinder, and the resulting relay is known as induction cup relay or induction cylinder relay. The speed of the relay improves considerably, i.e. the relay becomes very fast, due to the reduced inertia. In the next improvement, multi-polar construction with short air gap was introduced. Because of these modifications, the induction cup (cylinder) relay is very fast in operation, it has higher torque for a given power input and more uniform torque and less contact chatter. This relay which is shown in Fig. 3.2 is still very popular and is used also in H.V. transmission lines.

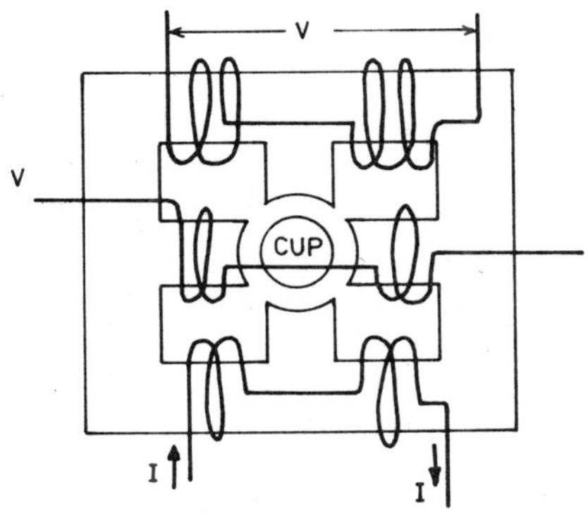

Fig. 3.2 Induction cup relay

3.2.3 Hinged (or Attracted) Armature (Beam) Relay

This relay has still higher torque and is also faster in operation. It has a hinged armature (i.e. beam) which is attracted by the pull of two electromagnets (Fig. 3.3) placed on either side of the beam. Due to flow of currents in these electromagnets, an electromagnetic torque is produced. One of the electromagnets produces an operating torque and tries to attract the beam while the other electromagnet produces a restraining torque which opposes the operating torque. And hence only if the operating torque exceeds the restraining torque, the beam is attracted thus closing the relay contacts. This relay is also called an attracted armature or beam relay.

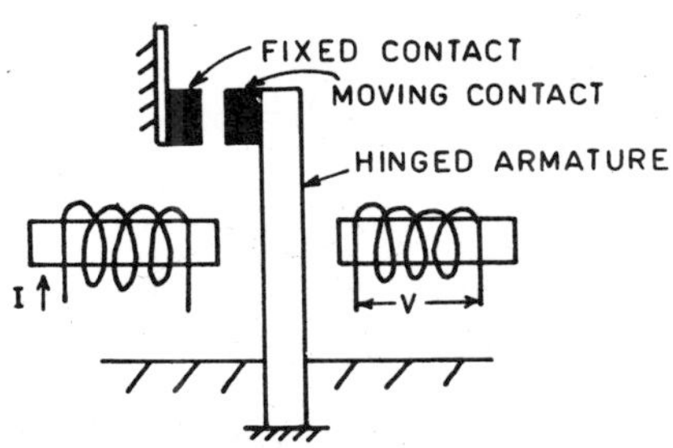

Fig. 3.3 Hinged armature relay

3.2.4 Relay Currents and Voltages

The relay currents or voltages are not taken directly from the line. These are taken through the instrument transformers. Actually with the help of instrument transformers both the current as well as voltage are reduced to a very low value in order to design the relay coil economically and also to provide safety to the personnel working at the protection bus bar. The current is obtained through current transformer (CT) which reduces current to a very low value. Normally with 3-ϕ system, 3 CTs are used with their primaries in series with each line and secondaries connected in Y, i.e. in star. Only one set of 3-PTs connected to the bus bar or cap potential devices is enough to supply reduced voltage to all the relays for all the three phase lines emerging from the bus. The potential transformers (PTs) are connected in Y. This is necessary in case we want line to ground (i.e. phase) voltages. However, in case we want only line to line voltages, only two PTs connected in V, i.e. in open delta, is sufficient.

In the case of 3-ϕ lines, we normally use the three lines i.e. phase (i.e. Y) currents and three line to ground i.e. phase (i.e. Y) voltages. We also use delta voltage, i.e. line to line voltages, and delta currents, i.e. difference of line currents. Sometimes we use also component quantities, especially negative sequence or zero sequence currents and voltages.

3.2.5 Drawbacks of Electromechanical Relays

The electromechanical relays discussed earlier have moving parts and also contacts. Because of this, such relays have several drawbacks which are listed below in order of severity.

(i) High burden on instrument transformers (i.e. high burden on CTs and PTs)

(ii) High operating time due to inertia of moving parts and hence slow in operation.

(iii) Contact pitting. Because of this contacts get spoiled and the relay maloperates.

(iv) Contact racing. This defect results from the inertia of moving parts. Due to this, the relay coordination becomes quite difficult.

(v) Requires frequent maintenance because of moving parts and opening and closing of relay contacts.

(vi) Affected by vibrations and shocks caused by external sources.

The electromechanical relays may as well be actuated by external causes such as vibrations and shocks caused by movement of diesel or electric locomotives or tram cars in the nearby localities or due to vibrations caused by earthquakes, etc.

3.2.6 Problems in Electromechanical Relays and Remedies

The induction relays have several drawbacks as listed above. Some of the additional problems and their remedies are discussed in the following.

(a) *Damping in relays.* Damping is necessary in electromagnetic relays to avoid overshooting of moving contacts. This overshooting sometimes results in the relay maloperation because the relay contacts may remain closed even though the fault is cleared, due to inertia of moving parts. Damping is usually provided by permanent magnet. Mechanical damping is also used occasionally. Dash pots consist of a magnetically operated plunger which is retarded by fluid flowing through an adjustable orifice.

(b) *Contacts.* Contacts performance is probably the most important item affecting the reliability of protective relays. Corrosion of contacts or dust collected on contacts can prevent the relay from tripping. Consequently, the material and shape of contacts are very important for reliable relay operation. The maintenance of contacts can be considerably minimized by high contact pressure, hard smooth contact surface, bounce proof contact design and use of dust proof relay cases. Normally, these days silver contacts are used and these contacts are enclosed in dust proof cases. A thin coating of petroleum on the contacts has been found to reduce metal transfer and corrosion of contacts without increasing contact resistances appreciably. The short time current carrying capacity of contacts depends upon their weight, thermal conductivity, electrical conductivity and surface resistance. For modern silver contact design, the short term current rating is about four times the continuous rating. Spark quenching across relay contacts is another very important requirement in the proper operation of the relay. When relay contacts make or break, due to inductive nature of control circuitry, there will be sparking at the relay contacts. This results in contact pitting and the relay maloperates. Therefore, arc quenching circuit consisting of RC circuit is provided across contacts. The major sources of contact failure such as contact corrosion, contact erosion and increase in contact resistance can be taken care of with these measures.

(c) *Relay currents and voltages.* Normally, relay coil currents are 1 A or 5 A and coil voltages are 220 V or 110 V. However, the relay coil insulation is designed to withstand at least 4 kV and the conductor size of the relay coil is chosen such that it can carry at least fifteen times normal current for one second. This is because the fault current may be many times the normal load current. From the mechanical strength point of view, the conductor diameter must not be less than 0.05 cm even if the above considerations are satisfied.

3.3 OVERCURRENT RELAYS

Normally, when fault occurs in any element or component of the power system network, the current becomes very high, much more than normal load current. And hence it is not surprising that this aspect of detecting fault was considered earlier by protection engineers. The overcurrent (OC) relay utilizes this aspect. In the case of induction disk relay (Fig. 3.1), the current in the element which is being protected is passed through the operating coil of the relay. The current is obtained through CT. The electromagnetic torque produced by the current is proportional to the square of the current and this torque in turn, rotates the induction disk. However, the induction disk is provided with gravitational force by attaching a weight with the disk or pull of a spring by attaching a spring with the disk. And when the operating torque due to the current in the operating coil exceeds the restraining torque due to the gravitational force or the pull of the spring, the disk rotates and closes the relay contacts. Such relays are slow in operation. In the faster type of overcurrent relay, the relay pick up is decided by the fault current at the reach (i.e. at the balance point) of the relay. And hence if the current exceeds this value, it clearly indicates that the fault is internal, i.e. in the line, and hence, the relay will give trip command if the relay current exceeds the pick up current. The following types of this relay are normally used.

3.3.1 Types of Overcurrent Relays

The following types of overcurrent relays are in common use:

(a) Definite time overcurrent (i.e. DTOC) relay.
(b) Inverse definite minimum time overcurrent (i.e. IDMTOC) relay.

In the case of DTOC relays, the relay operating time is the least at the farthest end and increases as we proceed towards the generating station. At the generating station, the relay operating time is the largest. This is the serious drawback of this relay because for a fault at the generating station where the fault current is maximum, the relay operating time is also maximum. In other words large fault current at the generating station for a fault at the generating station is cleared last. This is shown in Fig. 3.4. However, such relays are preferred for short lines fed from only one end. However, if the line is long and it is fed from both the ends, IDMTOC relay is the only solution. Here relay operating time is made inversely

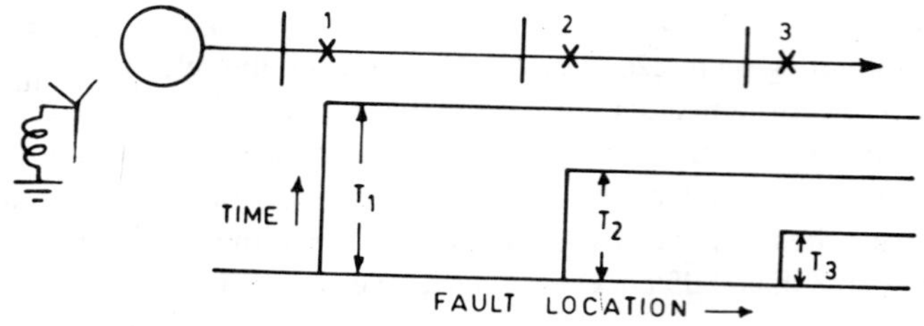

Fig. 3.4 DTOC relay

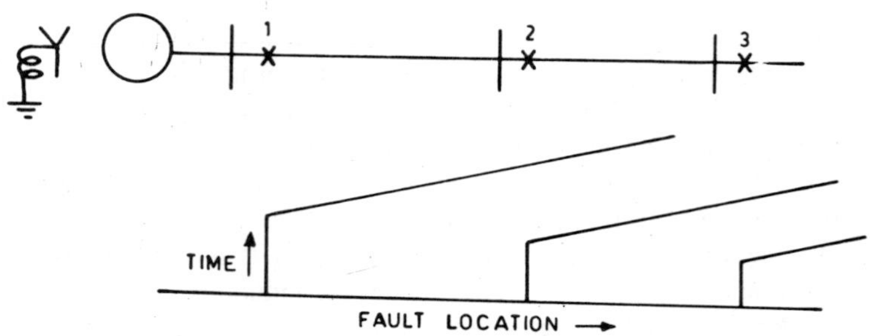

Fig. 3.5 IDMTOC relay

proportional to fault current i.e. more is the fault current, less is the time for the relay to operate. We know as the fault travels farther from the bus, the fault current decreases because of increase in line impedance between the bus and the fault location and hence the relay operating time increases as we proceed further from the bus bar as seen in Fig. 3.5. The curve between fault current and time of operation of this relay is shown in Fig. 3.6. Here both time and current setting are adjustable.

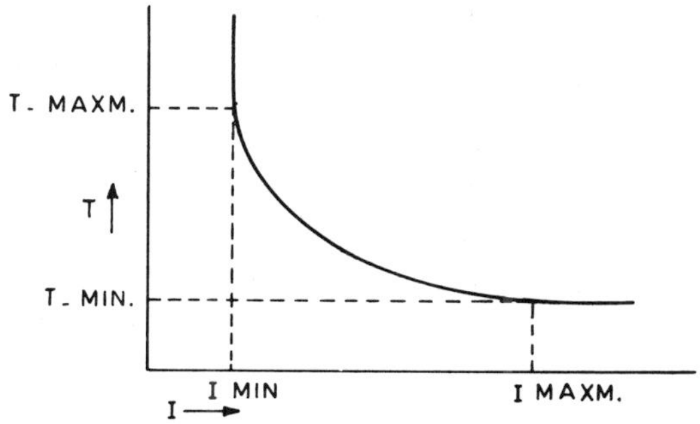

Fig. 3.6 IDMTOC relay time vs. fault current

3.3.2 Protection of 3-ϕ Line by *OC* Relay

The current magnitude is widely used as a means of detecting and clearing fault on distribution system only but seldom on high voltage transmission line. This is because of the fact that both the operating time and reach of the OC relays very much depend upon the generation behind the relay and type of fault. Because of this, OC relays are normally used for distribution system and transmission line up to 33 kV only.

For protecting 3-ϕ lines, there are two alternatives as shown in Figs. 3.7 and 3.8. In Fig. 3.7, relays have been used in three lines. We will see later that in the single line to ground fault, i.e. LG fault, the relay may not opertae as the fault current due to LG fault, may be even less than the normal line current. Normally pick up

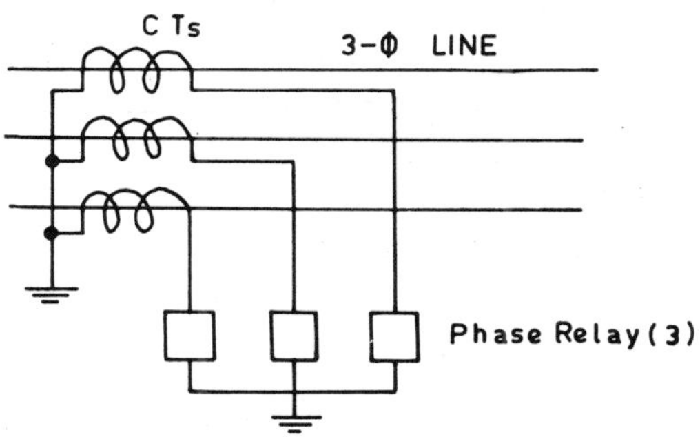

Fig. 3.7

of the relay is much higher than the normal load current to ensure that the relay does not operate during momentary overload conditions. This is why the arrangement shown in Fig. 3.8 is certainly better where two relays are connected in the secondary CTs to take care of faults involving two or more lines (i.e. phases) and the relay in the neutral circuit takes care of only LG fault. Here also we need only three OC relays as earlier but this scheme is certainly better. We will discuss later phase relays which take care of faults involving two or more phases and ground relays which take care of only LG fault.

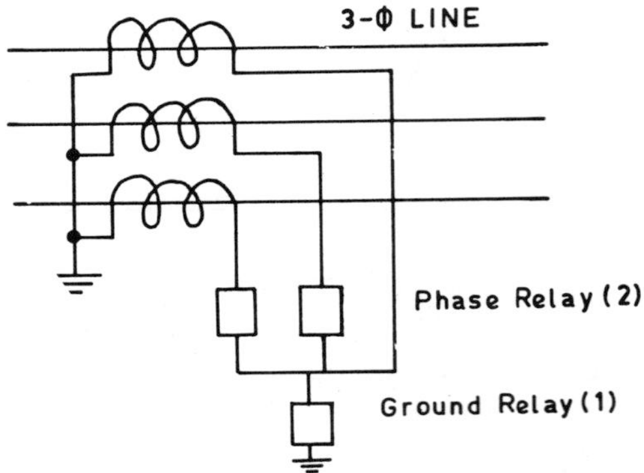

Fig. 3.8

3.3.3 Problems and Limitations of *OC* Relay

The main problems associated with OC relays are the shifting of its balance point, i.e. the reach of the relay with the change in type of fault at the same location, change in generation capacity and switching operation. The OC relay 'sees' its reach only by monitoring the current. In other words, to decide its reach, a fault is created at its reach and if the current exceeds this current, it means that fault is internal and hence the relay must give the tripping command. Therefore, if the reach has been decided based upon 3-ϕ fault which is the severemost and which causes maximum fault current, for single phase to ground fault to have the same current as that of 3-ϕ fault, single phase to ground fault must occur earlier, i.e. its reach becomes shorter. Similarly, if the reach has been decided based upon LG fault, the 3-ϕ fault must take place later, i.e. its reach becomes longer. Similarly, with the increase in generation capacity or switching operation, the reach of OC relay shifts. This is why OC relay is not normally used in the case of transmission line exceeding 33 kV. We use distance relaying scheme for the protection of EHV/UHV lines. In addition, the OC relay is a single input comparator where only one signal, i.e. current, is used for tripping purposes which is not a reliable decision. Moreover, the over current relay is also non-directional, i.e. the relay gives tripping command for a fault both in the forward and also in the reverse direction and, therefore, directional relay is needed along with the over current relay so that the relay trips only for fault in the forward direction.

3.4 DIRECTIONAL RELAY

Wherever power flows in both the directions, for example, in the present day grid system having sources normally at both ends of the transmission line, directional relays are needed. The directional relay is connected in series with the OC relay so that the trip command is only given if there is a fault and also flow of power due to the fault in the forward direction, i.e. away from the bus. Directional relay is supplied with the current as well as the voltage. Torque produced by directional relay is given by

$$T = KVI \cos(\phi - \theta) \tag{3.1}$$

where K is a relay constant, V is the voltage applied to the voltage winding of the relay, I is the relay current, ϕ is the phase angle and θ is the relay setting, i.e. it is the value of ϕ at which the relay develops maximum torque in the contact closing direction for a fault in the forward direction.

There are three ways of connecting current and voltage windings of relay, viz. 90° connection, 60° connection and 30° connection. In 90° connection, the voltage winding of the relay is supplied with line to line voltage and current winding of the relay is supplied with line current. Here, under the condition of unity p.f., the relay current leads the voltage by 90° as shown in Fig. 3.9. In 60° connection, the voltage

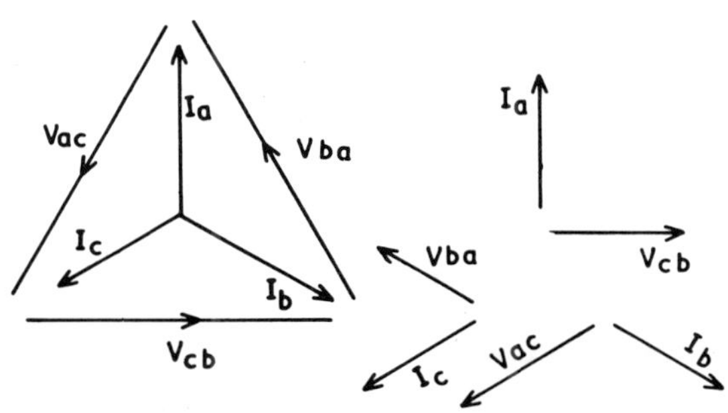

Fig. 3.9 90° Connection

winding receives delta voltage, i.e. line to line voltage and current winding receives also delta current, i.e. difference of line currents. However, in the case of 30° connection, Y-current, i.e. line current, is supplied to the current winding and Δ-voltage, i.e. line to line voltage, to the voltage winding. These connections are illustrated in the Fig. 3.10.

30° Connection 60° Connection

Fig. 3.10

3.4.1 Types of Directional Relays

There are two types of directional relays, viz. single phase directional relay and poly phase directional relay. In the case of single phase directional relay, we need three single phase directional relays and also three OC relays. Both the directional relay and OC relay are connected in series with every line so that trip circuit is only complete if there is a fault and also power flow due to fault in the forward direction. In the case of poly phase directional relay, while we use three OC relays, one with each line, we use only one poly phase directional relay. This is shown in Fig. 3.11. Directional relay may fail to operate if fault takes place at the bus itself because at that time bus voltage may become zero and thus the voltage coil of the relay may not get any voltage. However, in actual practice normally fault takes place through arcing resistance and at least one percent of voltage is available because of voltage drop across arcing resistance which is sufficient to operate the relay. In some fast operating directional relay, by providing memory action, the torque of the directional relay is improved. This is actually a resonant LC circuit formed by connecting capacitance across the voltage circuit of the relay. This will also retard the decay of bus voltage during fault at the bus.

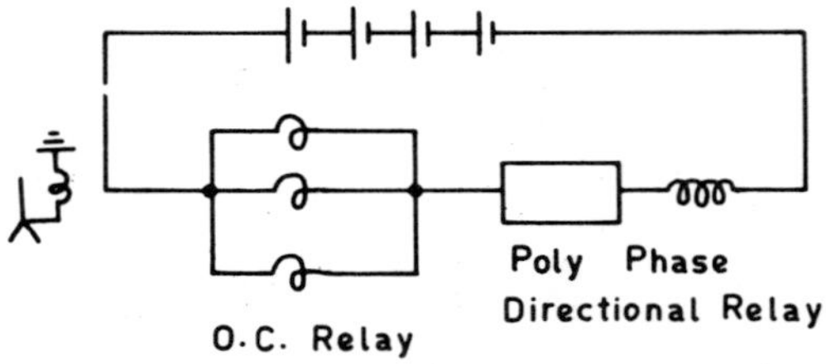

Fig. 3.11

3.4.2 Protection of Loop Line

This is illustrated in Fig. 3.12. Here except at the bus where source is connected, at all other buses both directional relay as well as OC relay are used. This is because at the bus where the source is connected, power always flows away from the bus.

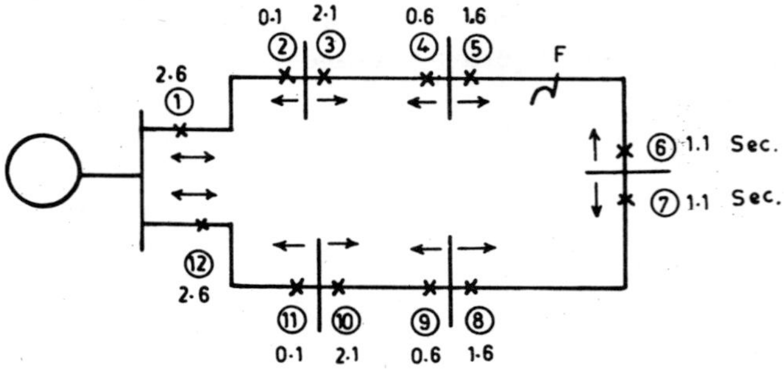

Fig. 3.12

However, at the other buses so as to give trip command only for internal fault, both OC and directional relays are used. The OC relay has graded time setting. It is clear from the figure that the proper selectivity is obtained by the use of graded time setting OC relay and directional relay. Here minimum length is disconnected in the event of fault as it is clear from Fig. 3.12 where for a fault at F, only relays 5 and 6 operate and the line segment 5 – 6 is only removed.

3.4.3 Zero Sequence Relay

Zero sequence relay is used only for the LG fault by the OC relay. The connection diagram for the zero sequence relay is shown in Fig 3.13.

We use two types of relays, one of them is known as a phase relay and it is meant for phase fault involving two or more phases and the second is known as ground relay and it is meant for ground fault i.e. single phase to ground fault. This is due to the fact that the fault current after LG fault may be less than even normal load current because the source, i.e. three phase synchronous generator which is Y-connected, has its neutral grounded through reactance and also because the single phase to ground fault normally takes place through fault impedance, i.e. arcing resistance. And hence it is clear that because of these two impedances, viz. reactance in the neutral circuit and arcing resistance due to fault, the fault current may be less than the normal load current as these impedances are in series in the circuit of LG fault. This is why separate relay, known as ground relay, is used for LG fault referred to as ground fault.

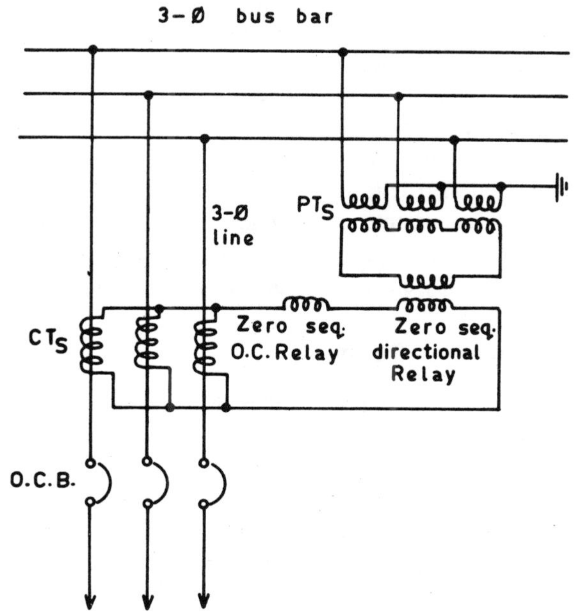

Fig. 3.13 Zero sequence relay

The zero sequence current for the OC relay is obtained by connecting the relay in the neutral circuit of Y-connected transformer (i.e. CT) as shown in Fig. 3.13. The zero sequence current and zero sequence voltage may also be given to the directional relay. Here zero sequence current is obtained in a similar fashion by connecting the relay in the neutral circuit of 3-ϕ Y-connected transformer, but zero sequence voltage is obtained by connecting the potential transformer primary windings in Y and secondary winding in series, i.e. in open delta. Since, the zero sequence current (or power) flows from fault towards the bus, the relay sensing this quantity for tripping may be set to trip only if there is current (or power) flow towards the bus which may be quite less and the relay is set not to trip for higher current or power flowing in the proper direction which is away from the bus.

The zero sequence relay is only possible as an OC relay and not as a distance relay. This is because the distance relaying scheme, which calculates the impedance to the fault by comparing the bus voltage with the fault current, gives only impedance in this case from the bus to the point of grounding and not from the bus to the point of fault. This is because, the zero sequence current flows in the opposite direction, i.e. from the fault towards the bus, and hence the ratio between the bus voltage and zero sequence current is the impedance between the bus and point of grounding, i.e. neutral grounding of the synchronous generator and not between the bus and the point of fault.

3.5 DISTANCE RELAYS

The distance relaying scheme is a dual input comaprator. Here the relay is supplied with the line current through CT and bus voltage through PT. The current winding of the relay receives the line current and the voltage winding of the relay is supplied with the bus voltage. The reach of the distance relay does not shift with the type of fault or with the change in generation capacity or switching operation. To attain this feature, the phase relay which responds to the phase fault involving two or more phases is supplied with delta voltage, i.e. line to line voltage and delta current, i.e. the difference of line currents and ground relay for ground fault, i.e. LG fault, is supplied with Y-voltage, i.e. phase voltage and Y-current, i.e. phase current. In this chapter we discuss only electromechanical type of distance relaying scheme.

3.5.1 Plane Impedance Relay

The plane impedance relay is supplied with both line current obtained through CT and bus voltage obtained through PT. The relay computes the impedance to the fault by comparing the bus voltage with the line current as the impedance to the fault is the ratio between the bus voltage and the line current. Hinged armature (i.e. hinged beam) type relay is used as a plane impedance relay. Here the beam carries a moving contact and it is attracted by the pull of two electromagnets placed on either side of the beam. The electromagnet which is supplied with the line current attracts the beam in the contact closing direction and the electromagnet supplied with the bus voltage (i.e. current proportional to the bus voltage) pulls the beam in the contact opening direction. Hence for tripping, the operating torque due to current (i.e. $K_1 I^2$) should exceed the restraining torque due to the voltage (i.e. $K_2 V^2$) (Fig. 3.3), i.e.

$$K_1 I^2 > K_2 V^2 \quad (3.2)$$

or

$$\frac{K_1}{K_2} > \frac{V^2}{I^2}$$

or

$$\sqrt{K_1/K_2} > \frac{V}{I}$$

or

$$\frac{V}{I} < \sqrt{\frac{K_1}{K_2}} \quad (3.3)$$

Now $\sqrt{K_1/K_2} = Z_R$ (i.e. the relay setting) and $V/I = Z$, i.e. impedance to the point of fault.

From the above, we get the condition for tripping as

$$Z < Z_R \quad (3.4)$$

In other words, the relay contacts are closed (i.e. tripping takes place) if $Z < Z_R$.

And at threshold, i.e. when the fault takes place at the balance point or at the reach of the relay, the pulls of the two electromagnets are equal and the beam is balanced, which means

$$Z = Z_R$$

3.5.2 Angle Impedance Relay

This relay measures certain angular component of the impedance up to the point of fault. If the angle of the replica impedance is made 90°, the relay is known as Reactance Relay. The reactance relay, known as OHM unit is preferred as ground relay for LG fault. In the case of LG fault, normally fault takes place through fault impedance, i.e. arcing resistance which is quite significant and which affects the reach of the relay. As in the case of reactance relay, this relay measures only reactance upto the point of fault and compares it with the relay setting to give trip command, the reach of the relay is immune to arcing resistance. The reactance relay is a 4-pole induction cup, i.e. induction cylinder relay with windings arranged as shown in Fig. 3.14. The front, back and right hand side poles are excited by line current and hence, the flux produced by these poles is proportional to the current. However, the flux in the right hand side pole is out of phase with the flux produced by front and back poles as on the right hand pole; there is also a short circuited winding closed through phase shifting impedance. The interaction of these fluxes produces operating torque proportional to the square of the current tending to close the relay contacts. The voltage winding on the left hand side pole produces flux which interacts with the flux due to front and back poles, tending to open the relay contacts, i.e. it produces restraining torque.

Hence, we have for the tripping condition, operating torque ($= K I^2$) > restraining torque ($= VI \cos(\phi - \theta)$), i.e.

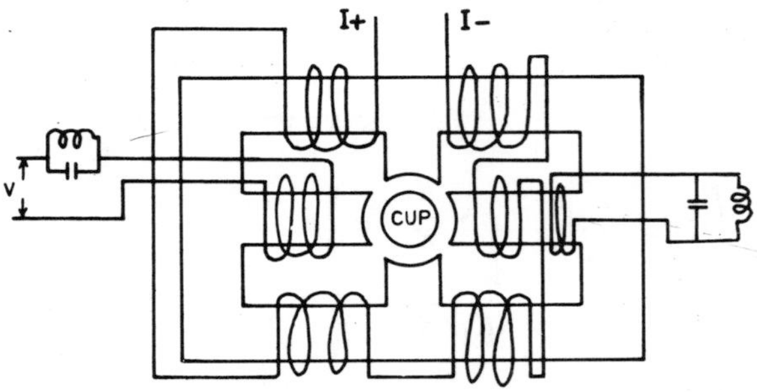

Fig. 3.14 Angle impedance relay

$$K I^2 > V I \cos(\phi - \theta) \tag{3.5}$$

For reactance relay, $\theta = 90°$ and hence

$$K I^2 > V I \cos(\phi - 90°)$$

$$K I^2 > V I \sin\phi$$

or
$$K > \frac{V I}{I^2} \sin\phi$$

i.e.
$$K > Z \sin\phi \; (= X)$$

or
$$K > X \tag{3.6}$$

Hence
$$X < K \tag{3.7}$$

The relay trips if the reactance up to the fault is less than the relay setting.

3.5.3 Angle Admittance (i.e. MHO's) Relay

This relay is also realized by 4-pole induction cup relay. Here the side poles are excited by voltage to produce polarizing flux and memory action is provided by series capacitor to retard the decay of voltage when bus fault takes places. The front pole is excited by the current and the back pole by voltage. The operating torque is due to current and polarizing flux (Fig. 3.15) and it is equal to $K_1 \; V I \cos(\phi - \theta)$.

The restraining torque is due to restraining field proportional to voltage and polarizing field also proportional to voltage and hence it is proportional to $K_2 V^2$.

For tripping

$$K_1 \, V I \cos(\phi - \theta) > K_2 \, V^2$$

i.e.
$$\frac{K_1}{K_2} \cos(\phi - \theta) > \frac{V^2}{VI}$$

i.e.
$$Z_R \cos(\phi - \theta) > Z$$

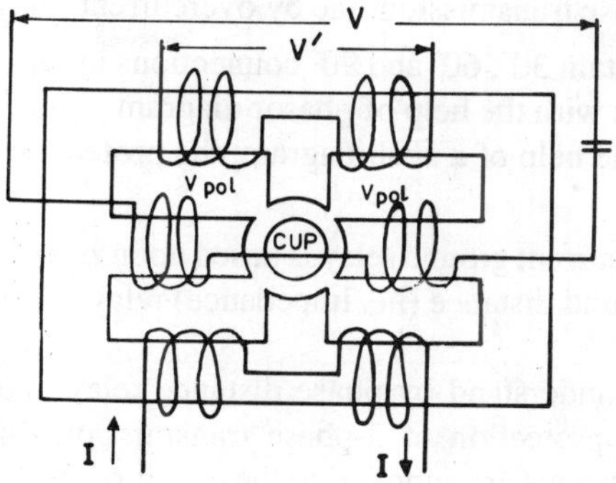

Fig. 3.15 Angle admittance relay

(Here $\dfrac{K_1}{K_2} = Z_R$ which is relay setting.)

i.e.
$$Z < Z_R \cos(\phi - \theta) \tag{3.9}$$

This relay which is known as MHO's relay has numerous advantages which will be discussed in the next chapter in detail.

EXERCISES

1. (a) What are the different types of electromechanical relays you are familiar with? Discuss with the help of a neat diagram, the theory and principle of operation of an induction disk relay.
   (b) How is an induction cup relay obtained? State its merits. Also discuss with the help of a neat diagram, the working principle of an induction cup relay.
2. (a) For the purpose of protective relay, what types of currents and voltages are used? Discuss also the methods to obtain desired relay voltage and currents.
   (b) Mention in the order of their severity, the drawbacks of electromechanical relays.
3. (a) What are the main problems associated with electromechanical relays? Discuss the measures to rectify these problems.
   (b) What are the different types of faults in a 3-phase over head transmission line? State in the order of their severity. Which fault is the most common and which fault is most severe?
4. (a) Why an overcurrent relay is used only up to 50 kV line. Write the demerits of an overcurrent relay.
   (b) Discuss what you understand by phase and ground relay. For what types of fault these are used?
5. (a) Name different types of overcurrent relays.

(b) With the help of a neat diagram, discuss the protection scheme of an overhead 3-phase transmission line by overcurrent relays.

6. (a) How do you obtain 30°, 60° and 90° connections in the case of directional relays? Discuss with the help of phasor diagram.
   (b) Discuss with the help of a neat diagram, the protection scheme of a loop line.
7. (a) Why only overcurrent ground relay is based upon zero sequence quantities and not the ground distance (i.e. impedance) relay? Discuss with the help of a diagram.
   (b) What do your understand by phase distance relay and ground distance relay? For the protection of 3-phase transmission line, what types of voltages and currents are supplied to these two relays?
8. (a) Discuss with the help of a neat diagram, the theory and principle of operation of a hinged beam type of plane impedance relays. Write the main shortcommings of the plane impedance relays.
   (b) For the protection of long, heavily loaded transmission line, what types of relaying scheme you recommend? Discuss the reasons for your recommendations.
9. (a) With the help of a neat diagram, explain the theory and working principle of an induction cup type of an angle admittance (i.e. MHO's) relay. State the merits of MHO's relays.
   (b) Why we prefer angle impedance relay as a ground relay, for the protection against ground fault? Discuss with the help of a neat diagram, the theory and principle of operation of an induction cup type of reactance relays. What are the main shortcommings of these relays?
10. Prove that the balance point of a distance (i.e. an impedance) relay for a 3-phase (i.e. LLL or LLG) fault is nearly 15% farther from the relay than the balance point for the line to line (i.e. LL) fault, if the relay operates on line current and adjacent line to line voltage. Assume no fault impedance and single circuit system.

REFERENCES

1. Cordrey, and A.R. Van C. Warrington, "The MHO Carrier Relaying Scheme", *AIEE Trans.*, Vol. 63, 1944, pp. 228–235
2. Crichton, L.N., "The Distance Relay for Automatically Sectionalizing Electrical Networks" *AIEE Trans.*, Vol 42., 1923, pp. 527–537.
3. Crichton, L.N. "High Speed Protective Relays", *AIEE Trans.*, Vol. 49, 1930, pp. 1232–1242.
4. Dewey, C.G. and J.R. Mc Glynn, "A New Reactance Distance Relay" *AIEE Trans.*, Vol. 67, Part I, 1948, pp. 743–746.
5. George, E.E., "Operating Experience with Reactance-type Distance Relays", *AIEE Trans.*, Vol. 50, 1931, pp. 288–293.
6. Goldborough, S.L., and W.A. Lewis, "New High Speed Distance Relay". *Elect. Engng.*, Vol. 51, March 1932, pp. 157–160.
7. Goldsborough, S.L., "A Distance Relay with Adjustable Phase-Angle Discrimination". *AIEE Trans.*, Vol. 63, 1944, pp. 835–838.
8. Hutchinson, R.M., "The MHO Distance Relay" *AIEE Trans.*, Vol. 65, June 1946, pp. 353–359.

9. IEEE Committee Report, "Review of Recent Practices and Trends in Protective Relaying", *IEEE Trans*. on Power Apparatus and Systems, Vol. PAS-100, Aug. 1981, pp. 4054–4063.
10. Kimbark, E.W., "*Power System Stability*" Vol. II, John Wiley & Sons Inc., New York, 1965.
11. McLaughlin, H.A. and E.O. Erickson, "The Impedance Relay", *AIEE Trans*., Vol. 47, 1928, pp. 776–782.
12. Singh, L.P., "*Advanced Power System Analysis and Dynamics*", 3rd Ed., Wiley Eastern Ltd., New Delhi, 1992.
13. Skuderna, J.E., "A Mathematical Basis for a Protective Relay with Conic Pick up Chracteristics", *AIEE Trans*., Vol. 81, Part III, 1962, pp. 81–88.
14. New Warren, C., "Combined Phase and Ground Distance Relaying", *AIEE Trans*., Vol. 69, Part I, 1950, pp. 37–44.
15. Warrington, A.R. Van C., "A High Speed Reactance Relay", *Elect. Engng*., Vol. 52, April 1933, pp. 248–252.
16. Warrington, A.R. Van C., "Prospective Relaying for Long Transmission Lines", *AIEE Trans*., Vol. 62, 1943, pp. 261–268.
17. Warrington, A.R. Van C., *Protective Relays—Their Theory and Practice*, Vol. I, Chapman and Hall Ltd., London, 1976.

4

STATIC RELAYS

4.1 INTRODUCTION

Protective relays incorporating static components were developed after the year 1950. Since then, there had been gradual development and improvement in the static relaying scheme. During the year 1956, the earliest distance relay was introduced by Adamson and Wedepohl which used phase comparator principle giving mho characteristics using transistorized circuits. In their first paper, they presented the mathematical background required for developing various threshold characteristics such as directional, ohm, offset impedance and mho by the use of 2-input phase comparator using the transient overreach in their coincidence block average phase comparator principle.

In their second paper, Adamson and Wedepohl proposed dual comparators to minimize this transient overreach present in their coincidence block average phase comparator. Adamson and Talkham, Dewey and Hodges described a phase comparison carrier relaying scheme using transistors. Dewey and Caleca *et al.*, in 1963, described in their two companion papers, the design principles, typical circuits based upon block-spike phase comparison technique giving mho characteristics.

Mathews and Nellist outlined a general procedure for drawing characteristics by using geometrical methods. This drawback of relays having no proper solid mathematical background has been overcome now and methods have been developed to predict relay performance well in advance for close up faults with good results.

A polarized mho relay which overcame the problem of non-operation for close in faults and which gave a better performance was reported by Wedepohl in 1965. In the same year, Humpage and Sabberwal developed a general technique for a two-input phase comparator by suitable logic and also for several 2-input comparators. They also developed multi-input phase comparators to generate quadrilateral characteristics. The problem of the time co-ordination of several 2-input comparators was surmounted by introducing improved composite characteristics having 3 zones of protection as reported by Hans *et al.,* However, in 1966, Parthasarathy developed a three-step quadrilateral distance relay using transistor circuits for measuring, discriminating and performing logic functions and employing the multi-signal block-spike phase comparison technique. The relay gave good performance for all types of shunt faults and was also immune to power swing.

Anil Kumar and Parthasarathy, in 1967, reported mathematical formulation for multi-input sine phase comparators to produce conventional and quadrilateral characteristics. They reported about a three-step transistorized circuit giving quadrilateral characteristic and also, proposed modification necessary for using it with carrier-blocking and carrier-tripping schemes. In 1968, Jackson *et al.*, discussed the parameters and the limits of optimum dynamic design of block-average scheme of static relay comparators. A new sampling technique was proposed by McLaren in the same year, which permits a comparison of instantaneous values of relay inputs at different instants of time and dispenses with the need for phase shifting and mixing circuits. Maleev proposed a polyphase relay based upon phase-sequence detection of four input signals. Vitanov reported a complete relaying scheme for quadrilateral characteristics using transistorized circuitry.

In 1969, Gupta described polyphase relaying schemes using phase-sequence detection of selected input signals. In 1970, Ramamoorty and Wani published a paper describing the fabrication and test results of solid-state quadrilateral distance relay. Khincha *et al.,* developed a new amplitude comparison technique, in which the signals were derived from the primary line quantities. This removes the zero-crossing detector, delay units, sampling gates and amplitude-pulse duration convertors. They extended this philosophy to produce directional parallelogram and directional quadrilateral characteristics. Anil Kumar reported the production of quadrilateral characteristics with phase sequence detectors, which used ferrite core logic and semiconductor flip-flops. In 1972, Johns described a generalized phase comparison principle in which a comparison period of fixed duration and related to either positive-going or negative-going zero crossings is assigned to each relaying signal. The coincidence of the comparison periods of all the relaying signals provides the criterion for the relay operation. This method is described for the setting of two-input comparators. However, in 1973, he extended this idea to multi-input comparators and showed the procedure to determine the settings, with an example worked out for a 4-input comparator. He also gave a method to show how quadrilateral characteristics could be obtained with a 3-input comparator employing this technique. In the same year, he described generalized techniques to obtain variable characteristics for distance protection which involve varying the resistive reach of a replica impedance by adding an extra current-derived component to the appropriate relay input. Here, the input component to the protective relay is a linear function of all the line currents and is arranged to be zero under all balanced conditions and finite during unbalanced faults. He also reported how to get a variable quadrilateral characteristic whose area will be minimal during power swings and heavy overload conditions. Later, he presented the extension of this principle to the distance protection of a double circuit line and also to lines with selective pole autoreclosure. A polyphase ground distance relay based upon phase coincidence detection of three compensated line to ground voltages was reported by Choudhury *et al.* Paithanker *et al.,* proposed a very simple and foolproof polyphase relay based on phase-sequence detection of four selected input voltage signals, responding to all ten types of shunt faults, but the tolerance to arc resistance was found to be very marginal.

However, Jackson in 1974 described a comparator with automatically variable angular limits of phase comparison to get near-quadrilateral characteristics. A multi-input amplitude comparator is proposed by Paithanker and Ingole which incorporated any desired quadrilateral characteristic with fast response. Basu *et al.,* described a polyphase relay based upon phase sequence detection of any three compensated voltages or combination of compensated and phase voltages by using four pulse sequence comparators.

Patra *et al.,* reported an improved version of the polyphase relay based on detection of phase sequence of four selected input signals by using transistorized zero crossing detectors and flip-flops to realize the complete relay for all the ten types of shunt faults. In 1979, Ramamoorthy and Lall described a phase comparator using digital circuits which employed the coincidence block average principle. They used a digital up/down counter, and asymmetrical angular limits of comparison which can easily be attained by having clocks of different frequencies during coincidence and anti-coincidence periods. In 1980, Parthasarathy *et al.,* reported an adaptable distance relay which has a narrow tripping of the pickup characteristics during the power swing conditions of a long, heavily loaded, EHV transmission line and which expands automatically during unbalanced fault conditions. A multi-input phase comparator using digital ICs was reported by Ramamoorthy and Lall in the same year to produce a quadrilateral characteristic whose reach in X and Y directions can be changed at will. Ramamoorty extended the same idea to produce elliptical characteristic using an operational amplifier chip as an amplitude comparator. In the same year, Paithanker and Thoke described an earth-fault quadrilateral distance relay capable of producing a characteristic which is also suitable for double-end infeed lines. Weller *et al.,*, also in 1980, proposed a new technique of phase comparison. The relay inputs are converted to a binary square wave ANDed. The states of the AND gate output will have a particular sequence over the operating angular range, which is totally different from that over the blocking range. The tripping sequence is provided by the aid of a counter. Desikachar and Singh reported a single phase, 3-zone distance relay using TTL logic and many pulsing circuits which made the circuit complicated and thus prone to spurious signals. In 1983, Basu *et al.,* developed a simple and effective method for the protection of series compensated lines. They provided a 4-input phase sequence detector to produce 2-quadrilateral characteristic by use of transistorized logic gates. In 1984, Kellong *et al.,* described a relaying scheme using digital circuit and CMOS logic, capable of producing any desired threshold characteristics. The phase comparator reported by them can be used as either cosine or sine comparator. They also extended the technique to get modified mho and quadrilateral characteristics with 3-input signals only for 3-zone polyphase relaying. The paper includes the results of a dynamic test bench with respect to operating time, accuracy, transient reach versus switching angle fault, current and range.

4.2 STATIC RELAY

The function of the protective relay in an electric power system is to sense the fault, determine its location and initiate prompt removal of the faulty element. This action permits the remaining system to continue operation under normal conditions thereby assuring continuity of supply to the users. Protective relay is an important part of the electrical system and, therefore, it must be considered early in system planning and design to optimize the system performance. In the continual development of improved relaying scheme, the major targets have been increased speed and improved reliability. Of these, speed of course offers greater economic contribution to the system. Studies have shown that a given electric power system can transmit a larger amount of power without loss of synchronism when fault is cleared quickly. This is the reason for resorting to static relay, which because of its very fast speed, clears the fault quickly and thus maximize the system power transfer capability.

The semiconductor components which have wide range of applications are transistors (NPN and PNP), unijunction transistor and silicon controlled rectifier (SCR). These semiconductor devices along with the familiar resistors, capacitor, reactors, transformers and diodes, i.e. rectifier connected in an appropriate manner, are used to produce a variety of distance relaying schemes.

Static distance relays are commonly used for the protection of EHV/UHV transmission lines due to their high speed of operation, accuracy and reliability. Practically, no maintenance is needed once the relay is put into service except for checking VT fuse, transactor, and simulated fault clearing by relay. The relays generally use analog devices which give delayed operation at threshold condition. The operating time is a function of phase displacement and becomes infinity at the boundary conditions. This creates a serious relay co-ordination problem. This drawback was overcome by Ramamoorthy and Lal by developing a comparator in which the response time was kept constant. The authors used digital techniques and TTL logic gates (circuits). This relay was capable of generating many important characteristics such as ohms, directional, mho, restricted ohms and elliptical characteristics, using variable angular criteria for operation. They also obtained a quadrilateral characteristic, based upon multi-input coincidence principle, but rather in a different way. The digital relay appeared to be good at first sight; however, a detailed study showed the following general drawbacks:

1. TTL gates used are sensitive to spurious signals due to low, noise immunity, thus the relay could be prone to transients and line disturbances.
2. The basic comparator circuit appears to be more complicated, using more components, hence less reliable, and also, uneconomical and slow in operation (1 cycle to 2 cycles).
3. The same relay (comparator) cannot be used to obtain quadrilateral characteristic.
4. The same comparator cannot function both as cosine and sine comparator.

These drawbacks of existing digital relays could be eliminated by using CMOS IC' and simple relay circuit. This chapter presents the theory, design and development of improved digital relays and technique for obtaining different types of threshold characteristics. Efforts have been made to keep the hardware to a minimum, so as to give economy and reliability with fast operating time. Flexibility is provided so that the same relay could be used both as cosine and sine comparator and can cater to additional requirements like power swing blocking etc.

4.2.1 Operating Principle

The two-input or multi-input phase comparator developed is symmetrical. In general, two-input phase comparator initiates relay tripping when the phase angle α between input signals S_1 and S_2 satisfies the following conditions:

$$-\beta \leq \alpha \leq \beta$$

The phase angle α is positive when signal S_1 leads S_2; otherwise it is negative. Normally, the angular limit of phase comparator β is 90°. Such comparators are called 90° phase comparator or cosine comparator. Here, if the phase difference between signals S_1 and S_2 (*viz.* $180-\alpha$) is more than 90°, relay tripping is initiated. As the tripping level is nearly set to zero, the response time is more or less the same up to ± 90° of phase displacement.

The same tripping characteristics can be obtained by taking signals $-S_1$ and S_2 and measuring the anti-coincidence α' between the signals S_1 and S_2. Here the tripping occurs when

$$\beta' \geq \alpha' \geq \beta$$

If $\beta = 90°$ then β' becomes 270° and hence we have $270° \geq \alpha \geq 90°$.

Hence the same comparator functions as sine comparator in which tripping occurs when the signals $-S_1$ leads S_2 by more than 90° over a range of 0 to 180°.

4.2.2 Gradual Development in Relaying Scheme

We have discussed in the previous chapter electromechanical relays and also the problems associated with such relays. Due to these problems (i.e. drawbacks) development work in the area of static relay was started during 1940–50, initially utilizing thermionic valves. The relays using thermionic tubes are known as electronic relays and they have several advantages as follows:

(a) Low burden on CTs and PTs
(b) No moving parts or contacts and hence all the problems associated with the movement and also with the contact do not exist. This is primarily because of the absence of inertia of rotating parts; hence problems associated with inertia, such as high operating time, contact pitting and contact racing, are avoided.
(c) They need much less maintenance.
(d) They are not affected by external causes, i.e. they do not operate i.e. trip due to vibrations caused by the movement of diesel or electric locomotives in nearby localities, earthquakes, etc.

However, with the advent of transistors and other solid state components during the period 1950–60, the static relay development incorporated these devices and the thermionic tubes were abandoned due to their inherent limitations. Solid state relays have all the advantages of electronic relays and, in addition, they are compact, more reliable and do not need high voltage power supply. In the initial stages, the static circuits were mere substitutes of their electromechanical counterparts. In the later stages, new principles have been developed employing hybrid and other non-conventional devices to obtain different types of threshold characteristics. Phase and amplitude comparators gave place to instantaneous sampling comparators.

4.2.3 Merits of Static Relays

The following are the main advantages of static relays:

(a) *Reliability.* Due to the elimination of mechanical motion and contacts, servicing and maintenance problems have been reduced and operational reliability has been greatly increased. There are no shock and vibration problems, especially where the relays are located in areas exposed to railways and other heavy vehicles, in diesel power stations, in earthquake prone zones and many such areas. The reliability of any electrical equipment is a function of reliability of the components as well as the reliability of the circuit. However, in recent years, there has been considerable improvement in the components and also in the circuit, e.g. printed circuit and integrated circuit technology.

(b) *Sensitivity.* Greater sensitivity and high pickup ratio.

(c) *Speed.* With static relays, tripping time of 1/2 cycle or even less can be obtained. Resetting is also fast.

(d) *Selectivity.* The static relays have much improved selectivity and low power consumption. The burden (i.e. *VA* product) is also very low.

(e) *Versatility.* With the static relays, several new and hybrid threshold characteristics are possible.

4.3 OVERCURRENT RELAY

The overcurrent (OC) relay based upon electromagnetic induction principle has been discussed in detail in the previous chapter. The OC relay is a single input comparator and also it is non-directional. The line/element current is obtained through CT and passed through a triggering circuit in such a way that if the current exceeds its reference (i.e. base) voltage, a voltage pulse is generated. This pulse is applied to the gate of SCR. The reference current is actually the pickup current which is obtained in the case of transmission line by creating a fault at the reach of the relay. And hence current exceeding this current clearly indicates an internal fault, a condition for which the relay must give tripping command to the circuit breaker.

The OC relays are normally used as a backup protection in the case of feeder or apparatus. Their use is also limited in the case of transmission line protection. The main drawbacks of OC relays are: (i) their lack of reliability as these are single input comparators (ii) their non-directional feature and hence, except for radial system, they must be supplemented by directional relay and (iii) the change of its reach with the change in type of fault, change in generation or switching which actually changes the fault level. Because of these problems, the OC relay is used for the protection of feeder, distribution system and transmission system not exceeding 33 kV. For high voltage transmission system exceeding 33 kV, distance relaying scheme is preferred. Because of the non-directional feature of the OC relay, it is always supplemented with directional relay wherever there are sources at both the ends of the line. The directional relay of electromechanical type has been discussed in the previous chapter. As a static relay, the directional relay is supplied with both the line current obtained through CT and bus voltage obtained through PT. For a direct short circuit at the bus which may make the bus voltage very low, memory action is provided by shunting the voltage coil of the relay by a capacitor. Sometimes to ensure proper relay operation, the voltage coil of the relay is supplied by PT connected on different bus. Normally, fault takes place through fault impedance, i.e. arcing resistance, and at least one per cent voltage is available across the arc which is sufficient to operate the relay. The scheme of protection of 3-ϕ line and also loop system by OC relay and directional relay is discussed in detail in the previous chapter.

4.4 DISTANCE RELAY

Distance relay is a dual input comparator, i.e. it receives two input signals from the element being protected. The relay operates if these two input quantities change in magnitude or in phase relation. Normally the relay receives the current entering the circuit and compares it in magnitude or in phase relation with another quantity which may be the current leaving the circuit at the far end in the case of differential relaying scheme or local bus voltage in the case of distance relaying scheme. Distance relays are very popular for providing primary protection to the transmission line.

4.4.1 Relay Threshold Characteristics

It is known that the threshold characteristic of a dual input comparator, i.e. relay which compares any two quantities, viz. A and B, is a circle on the coordinate axes which are the real and imaginary coordinates of the ratio of the two quantities, A and B which are being compared. Here A and B are current and voltage respectively in the case of distance relaying scheme and both are currents in the case of differential relaying scheme. Such diagrams are applicable to linear system and in these diagrams, amplitude and phase angle relations are clearly indicated. Thus we have two types of representations, viz. β-plane and α-plane. In the β-plane, the two coordinate axes are marked as real $|B/A|$ and imaginary $\left|\frac{B}{A}\right|$. Say if A is the current (element current obtained through CT) and B is the voltage (local bus voltage obtained by PT), then clearly ratio $\left|\frac{B}{A}\right|$ is equal to ratio $\left|\frac{V}{I}\right|$, i.e. impedance. Now in this case the real axis is real $\left|\frac{V}{I}\right|$, i.e. real $Z = Z \cos \phi = R$ and imaginary axis imaginary $\left|\frac{V}{I}\right|$, i.e. imaginary $Z = Z \sin \phi = X$. Therefore, complex β-plane in this case is complex Z-plane whose axes are R axis and X axis. Similarly, in the case of α-plane, we use inverse relation, i.e. real $\left|\frac{I}{V}\right|$ and imaginary $\left|\frac{I}{V}\right|$. Therefore, clearly α-plane is a complex admittance plane whose axes are $\left|\frac{I}{V}\right| \cos \phi = Y \cos \phi = G$ and $\left|\frac{I}{V}\right| \sin \phi = Y \sin \phi = B$. In this way, we have two sets of coordinates for plotting the relay threshold characteristics, *viz.* complex β-plane (i.e. complex Z-plane) and complex α-plane (i.e. complex Y-plane).

4.4.2 Plane Impedance Relay

This is the earliest type of distance relaying scheme based upon the principle of amplitude comparison. Its theory as well as the static circuit to obtain this relay is simple and straight-forward. The relay measures the impedance Z up to the point of fault and gives trip signal if this impedance is less than the relay setting Z_R. The relay setting Z_R is actually the replica impedance which is proportional to set impedance, i.e. impedance of the line up to the reach of the relay. As usual, the relay monitors continuously the line current I through CT and bus voltage V through PT. The line current I is passed through an air core transformer, known as transactor, having its equivalent impedance Z_R. Thus by passing line current I through the transactor having impedance equal to replica impedance Z_R, a signal IZ_R is realized. Thus signal to the relay (as an amplitude comparator) becomes,

$$S_1 = I Z_R$$

This is the operate signal and

$$S_2 = V \tag{4.1}$$

This is the restraint signal.

For a fault in the line at any point F (Fig. 4.1), we have

$$V = I Z \tag{4.2}$$

Here Z is the impedance of the line up to the point of fault F and the fault is assumed to be direct short circuit with zero fault impedance.

Substituting from Eq. (4.2) in Eq. (4.1), we get

$$S_1 = I Z_R ; \quad S_2 = V = I Z \tag{4.3}$$

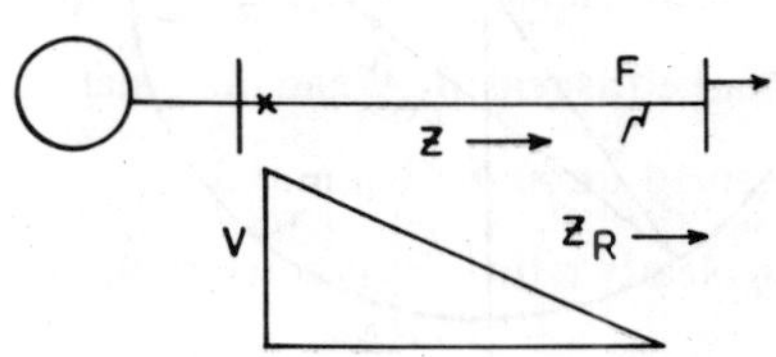

Fig. 4.1

Dividing both the signals in Eq. (4.3) by the common current I, we get the final signals as

$$S_1' = Z_R; \quad S_2' = Z \tag{4.4}$$

Hence the relay computes impedance Z up to the point of fault and compares it with the relay setting Z_R. For tripping

$$Z < Z_R$$

and at threshold, i.e. for the fault at the reach of the relay

$$S_1 = S_2, \text{ i.e. } S_1' = S_2'$$

Hence, $$Z = Z_R$$

We will show later that there is a duality between amplitude comparator and phase comparator, i.e. if signals are available as an amplitude comparator, the signals as phase comparator can be obtained by finding sum and difference of signals as amplitude comparator. Hence signals as phase comparator are obtained by finding sum and difference of signals S_1 and S_2 [Eq. 4.3]. Therefore, signals as phase comparator are:

$$\left.\begin{aligned} S_3 &= IZ_R - V = IZ_R - IZ \\ S_4 &= IZ_R + V = IZ_R + IZ \end{aligned}\right| \angle\alpha \tag{4.5}$$

Dividing the above signals by common current I, we get

$$\left.\begin{aligned} S_3' &= Z_R - Z \\ S_4' &= Z_R + Z \end{aligned}\right| \angle\alpha \tag{4.6}$$

Here α is the phase angle between signals S_3' and S_4. For tripping, we have the criterion

$$-90 < \alpha < 90 \tag{4.7}$$

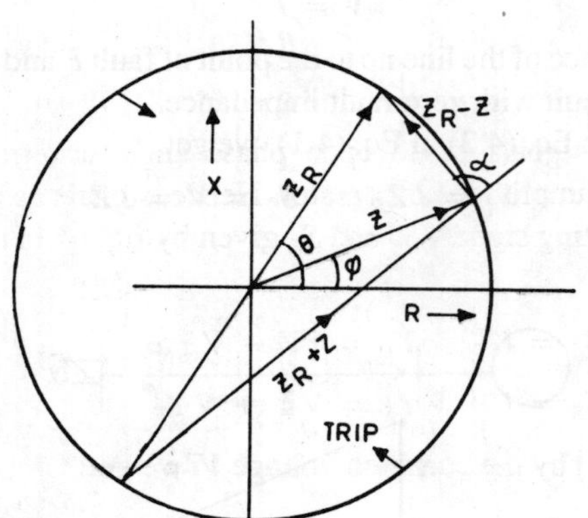

Fig. 4.2 Plane Impedance Relay *Z*-plane

and at threshold, i.e. if the fault occurs at the reach of the relay, we have,

$$\alpha = \pm 90 \tag{4.8}$$

The threshold characteristics of the relay plotted in β-plane, i.e. complex Z-plane with the real axis marked as R and with imaginary axis marked X, will be a circle of radius Z_R with the centre at the origin (Fig. 4.2). It is clear that to satisfy the conditions given by Eqs. (4.7) and (4.8), the tripping will be within the limits of the circle. This relay is a cosine comparator where at threshold, $\alpha = \pm 90°$. It is clear from the above signals that in complex β-plane (or complex Z-plane) signals are voltages or impedances. We will see later that in complex α-plane, i.e. in complex Y-plane, signals are currents or admittances.

The signals in complex α-plane, i.e. in complex Y-plane, are obtained by dividing the signals in complex β-plane by Z_R, i.e. by multiplying the above signals by Y_R, where $Y_R = \frac{1}{Z_R}$. Thus signals in complex Y-plane are as shown in the following.

Amplitude comparator

$$\left.\begin{array}{ll}\text{Operate signal} & S_5 = I \\ \text{Restrained singal} & S_6 = V Y_R\end{array}\right\} \tag{4.9}$$

For a fault at any point F, we have,

$$I = YV \tag{4.10}$$

Here Y is the admittance up to the point of fault ($Y = \frac{1}{Z}$ where Z is the impedance up to the point of fault). Substituting from Eq. (4.10) in Eq. (4.9), we get

$$S_5 = I = YV \quad \text{and} \quad S_6 = V Y_R \tag{4.11}$$

Dividing Eq. (4.11), by the common voltage V, we get

$$S_5' = Y; \quad S_6' = Y_R \tag{4.12}$$

Here the relay computes the admittance Y up to the point of fault and compares it with the set admittance Y_R,

For tripping $\quad Y > Y_R$,

and at threshold $\quad Y = Y_R$.

Here also we obtain signals based upon phase angle criterion by adding and subtracting signals as amplitude comparator. Hence, signals as phase comparator, by adding and subtracting signals S_5 and S_6 given by Eq. (4.11), will be as shown

Phase comparator

$$\left.\begin{array}{l}S_7 = I - V Y_R = YV - V Y_R \\ S_8 = I + V Y_R = VY + V Y_R\end{array}\right\} \angle\alpha \tag{4.13}$$

Dividing the Eq. (4.13) by the common voltage V, we get

$$\left.\begin{aligned} S_7 &= Y - Y_R \\ S_8 &= Y + Y_R \end{aligned}\right\} \angle\alpha \tag{4.14}$$

For tripping as cosine comparator

$$-90 < \alpha < 90$$

and at threshold

$$\alpha = \pm 90$$

This is a cosine comparator whose threshold characteristic is also a circle of radius Y_R with the centre at the origin as shown in the Fig. 4.3. The tripping is outside the circle.

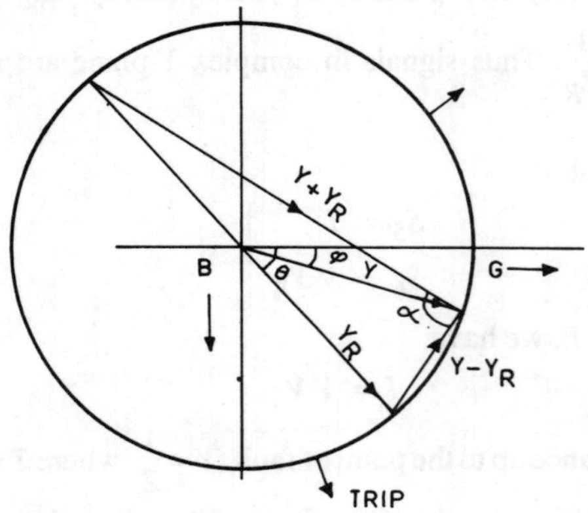

Fig. 4.3 Plane Impedance Relay *Y*-plane

The plane impedance relay which was developed first, is certainly simple in theory and construction. However, it has certain drawbacks. This relay computes only the impedance up to the point of fault and compares it with the set impedance for tripping. In other words, it is non-directional, i.e. it can operate for fault in either direction. Hence, a directional relay has to be incorporated with the plane impedance relay in order that the relay operates only for a fault in the forward direction. The relay threshold characteristic is also bulky as its radius is Z_R (i.e. replica impedance) and it becomes very large for long lines. Because of this bulky characteristics, the relay has the tendency to trip due to external causes such as power swing. During power swing which is caused by severe fault, the relay sees a fictitious impedance and if this impedance becomes less than the relay setting, the relay may operate. If the fault takes place near the reach of the relay with fault impedance, i.e. with arcing resistance, there is a possibility of the relay not operating and not tripping the breaker, because the total impedance seen by the relay may be more than the relay setting. This is especially true for LG fault with arcing resistance near the reach of the relay. In this way the reach of the plane impedance relay is also affected by arcing resistance. Plane impedance relay is basically an amplitude comparator.

4.4.3 Directional Relay

This relay is the dual of plane impedance relay. Its signals are dual in the sense that the signals as an amplitude comparator in the case of plane impedance relay become signals as a phase comparator in the case of directional relay and vice versa. While plane impedance relay is an amplitude comparator, the directional relay is a phase comparator.

Its signals are obtained directly from the plane impedance relay as follows.

Complex impedance plane

Amplitude comparator

$$\begin{aligned} S_1 &= I Z_R + V \propto Z_R + Z \\ S_2 &= I Z_R - V \propto Z_R - Z \end{aligned} \tag{4.15}$$

Phase comparator

$$\left.\begin{aligned} S_3 &= I Z_R \propto Z_R \\ S_4 &= V \propto Z \end{aligned}\right| \angle\alpha \tag{4.16}$$

For tripping

$$-90^\circ < \alpha < 90^\circ$$

and at threshold, $\alpha = \pm 90^\circ$.

The threshold characteristic of the relay is a straight line passing through the origin and tripping direction is as shown in Fig. 4.4.

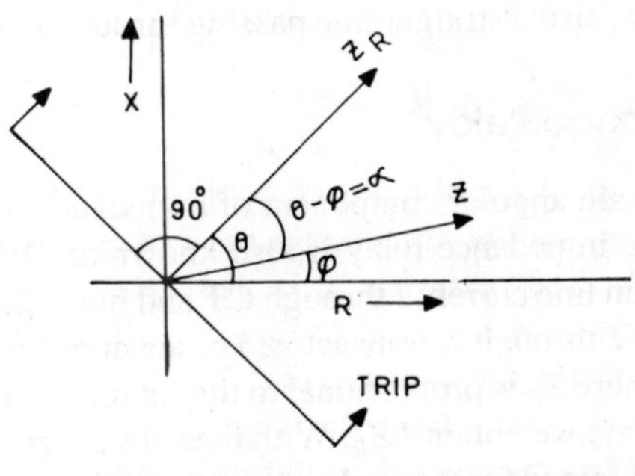

Fig. 4.4 Directional Relay Z-plane

The signals in Y-plane are obtained in a similar fashion by dividing the signals in Z-plane by Z_R or multiplying it by Y_R (where $Y_R = \frac{1}{Z_R}$).

Complex Y-plane

Amplitude comparator

$$\begin{aligned} S_5 &= I + V Y_R = Y V + V Y_R \propto Y + Y_R \\ S_6 &= I - V Y_R = V Y - Y_R V \propto Y - Y_R \end{aligned} \tag{4.17}$$

Phase comparator

$$\left.\begin{aligned} S_5 &= I = VY \propto Y \\ S_6' &= VY_R \propto Y_R \end{aligned}\right| \angle\alpha \tag{4.18}$$

For tripping $-90° < \alpha < 90°$

and at threshold, $\alpha = \pm 90°$.

The threshold characteristic in this case also is a straight line passing through the origin and the tripping direction is as shown in Fig. 4.5.

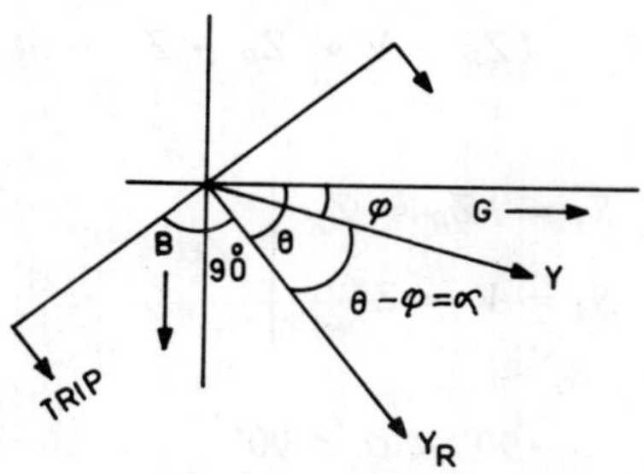

Fig. 4.5 Directional Relay *Y*-plane

It is clear from the above that if the threshold characteristic is a circle with the centre at the origin in *Z*-plane, it is also a circle with the centre at the origin in *Y*-plane. However, if the threshold characteristic is a straight line passing through the origin in *Z*-plane, it is also a straight line passing through the origin in *Y*-plane.

4.4.4 Angle Impedance Relay

This relay measures certain angular component of impedance of the line up to the point of fault. The angle impedance relay is also known as OHM relay or OHM unit. Here, also, we obtain line current I through CT and bus voltage V through PT. By passing line current I through a transactor, i.e. air cored transformer having replica impedance Z_R where Z_R is proportional to the set impedance i.e. impedance up to the reach of the relay, we obtain $I\,Z_R$. With these two signals viz. $I\,Z_R$ and V, appropriate signals are obtained for the angle impedance relay with the help of logic circuit. Final signals are as follows:

Z-plane

Amplitude comparator

$$\begin{aligned} &\text{Operate signal} &&= S_1 = 2\,I\,Z_R - V, \quad \text{i.e. } 2\,Z_R - Z \\ &\text{Restraining signal} &&= S_2 = V, \quad \text{i.e. } Z \end{aligned} \tag{4.19}$$

Phase comparator

$$\left.\begin{aligned} S_3 &= I\,Z_R - V, \quad \text{i.e } Z_R - Z \\ S_4 &= I\,Z_R, \quad \text{i.e. } Z_R \end{aligned}\right| \angle\alpha \tag{4.20}$$

For tripping $\qquad -90° < \alpha < 90°$

and at threshold, $\qquad \alpha = \pm 90°$

Here also for a fault at any point F, we have $V = I\,Z$ where Z is the impedance up to the point of fault F and fault is a direct short circuit with zero fault impedance. Signals as amplitude and phase comparators are dual as usual. The threshold characteristic is a straight line normal to Z_R and thus offset from origin by the length Z_R. The tripping direction is shown in the Fig. 4.6.

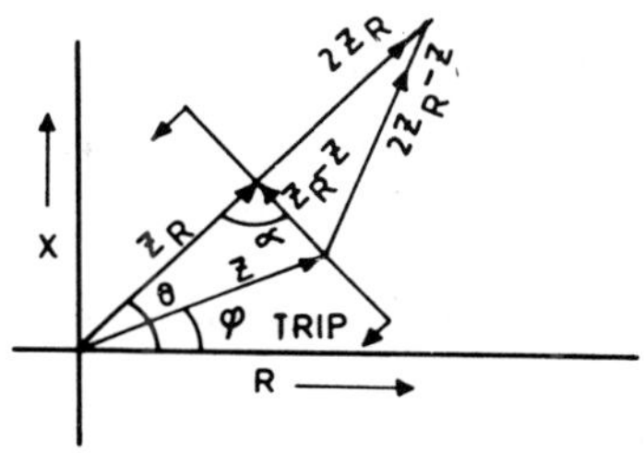

Fig. 4.6 Angle Imp. Relay *Z*-plane

In a similar fashion, signals are obtained in *Y*-plane by dividing signals in *Z*-plane by Z_R (or multiplied by Y_R where $Y_R = \frac{1}{Z_R}$).

Y-plane

Amplitude comaprator

$$\begin{aligned} &\text{Operate signal} & S_3 &= 2I - VY_R \propto 2Y - Y_R \\ &\text{Restraining signal} & S_4 &= VY_R \propto Y_R \end{aligned} \qquad (4.21)$$

Phase comparator

$$\left.\begin{aligned} S_3' &= I - VY_R \propto Y - Y_R \\ S_4' &= I \propto Y \end{aligned}\right| \angle\alpha \qquad (4.22)$$

As usual $I = YV$ where Y is the admittance to the point of fault and it is equal to $\frac{1}{Z}$.

For tripping, $\qquad -90° < \alpha < 90°$

and at threshold, $\qquad \alpha = \pm 90°$

The threshold characteristic is a circle with diameter Y_R and passing through the origin. The tripping is outside the circle, as indicated in Fig. 4.7.

By setting angle θ of the replica impedance Z_R equal to 90°, we obtain a special type of relay known as a reactance relay. Its signals are the same as that of the angle impedance relay except that the angle for the relay setting Z_R is 90°. Its threshold characteristics are shown in Fig. 4.8 and Fig. 4.9. This relay which only computes

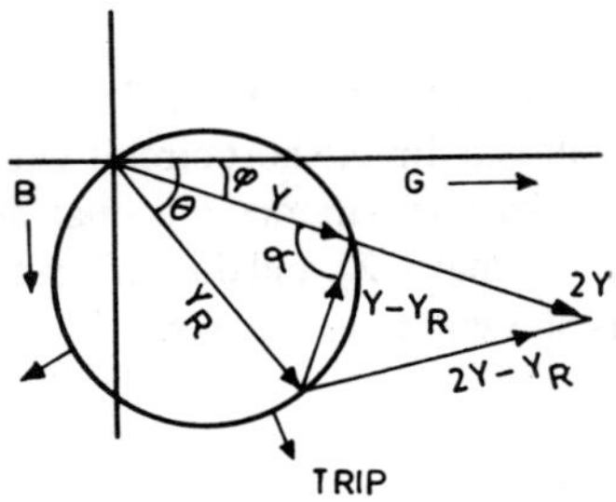

Fig. 4.7 Angle Imp. Relay *Y*-plane

$Z \angle \theta$ i.e. $Z \angle 90 = X$ to the point of fault is very suitable as a ground relay to take care of LG fault since its reach is not affected by arcing resistance. However, it is non-directional and also during normal load condition at high p.f., the reactance seen by this relay may be less than the relay setting and thus the relay may give trip signal even though there is no fault. Therefore this relay is never allowed to trip by itself; its operation is governed by directional starting i.e. MHO's relay.

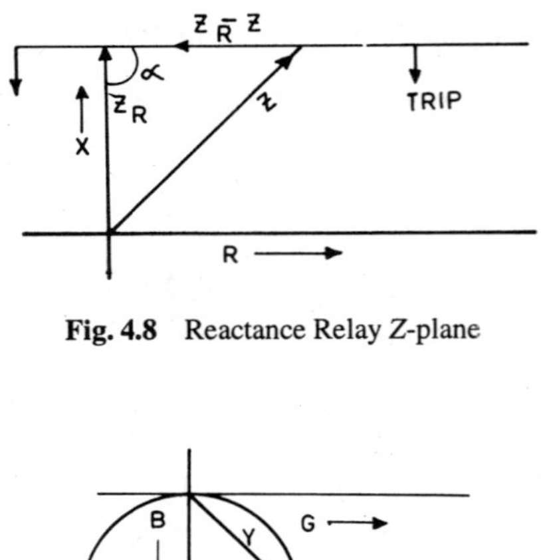

Fig. 4.8 Reactance Relay *Z*-plane

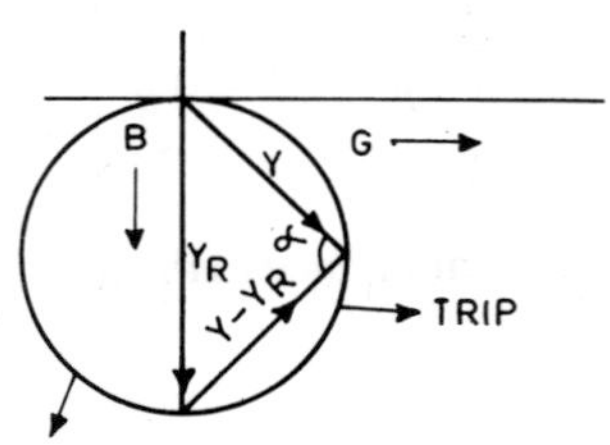

Fig. 4.9 Reactance Relay *Y*-plane

4.4.5 Angle Admittance (MHO's) Relay

The angle admittance relay is also called MHO's relay. This relay is the *dual* of angle impedance relay, i.e. OHM relay as it is clear from their name. The angle admittance relay is known as MHO's relay while angle impedance relay is known as OHM relay. Their characteristics are also dual. The threshold characteristic of angle admittance relay is a circle passing through origin in Z-plane and it is a straight line offset from the origin and normal to Y_R in Y-plane; in the case of angle impedance, it is just the reverse, i.e. a straight line offset from origin and normal to Z_R in Z-plane and a circle passing through the origin in Y-plane.

As usual the line current I is monitored continuously by CT and bus voltage V by PT and passing the current I through a transactor having replica impedance Z_R, the signal $I\,Z_R$ is obtained. After this, through appropriate logic circuit, the signals both for Z-plane and Y-plane are obtained as follows:

Z-plane

Amplitude comparator:

$$\begin{aligned} &\text{Operate signal} && S_1 = I\,Z_R, \text{ i.e. } Z_R \\ &\text{Restraining signal} && S_2 = 2\,V - I\,Z_R = 2I\,Z - I\,Z_R, \text{ i.e. } 2\,Z - Z_R \end{aligned} \tag{4.23}$$

The signals as phase comparator which are sum and difference of signals as an amplitude comparator are as follows.

Phase comparator;

$$\left.\begin{aligned} S_3 &= I\,Z_R - V \\ &= I\,Z_R - I\,Z, \quad \text{i.e. } Z_R - Z \\ S_4 &= V = I\,Z \quad \text{i.e. } Z \end{aligned}\right| \angle\alpha \tag{4.24}$$

Here α is the angle between signals S_3 and S_4. For tripping as cosine comparator,

$$-\,90^\circ < \alpha < 90^\circ$$

and at threshold, $\alpha = \pm\, 90^\circ$

The threshold characteristic, as shown in Fig. 4.10, is a circle passing through the origin with diameter Z_R and tripping is inside the circle where α is less than 90°.

The signals in Y-plane are obtained in the similar fashion by dividing the above signals by Z_R i.e. multiplying by Y_R where $Y_R = \dfrac{1}{Z_R}$.

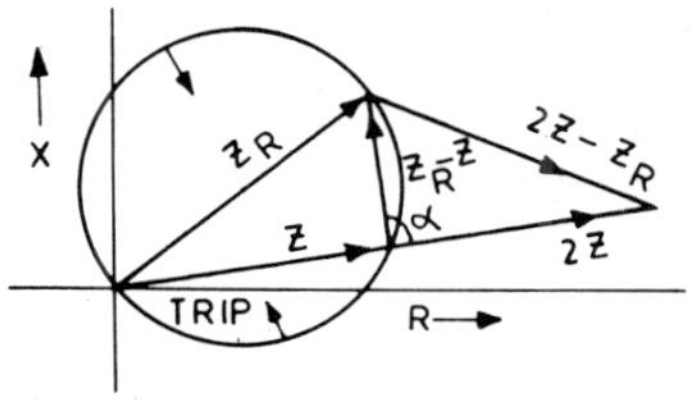

Fig. 4.10 Angle Adm. Relay Z-plane

Y-plane

Amplitude comparator:

$$\begin{aligned} &\text{Operate signal} && = S_5 = I = Y\,V, \quad \text{i.e. } Y \\ &\text{Restraining signal} && = S_6 = 2\,V\,Y_R - I = 2V\,Y_R - Y\,V, \end{aligned} \tag{4.25}$$

i.e. $$2\,Y_R - Y \qquad (4.26)$$

The signal in *Y*-plane as phase comparator are obtained by finding sum and difference of the above signals, as follows.
Phase comparator:

$$\left.\begin{aligned} S_5 &= I - VY_R = YV - VY_R, \quad \text{i.e. } Y - Y_R \\ S_6 &= VY_R, \quad \text{i.e. } Y_R \end{aligned}\right| \angle\alpha \qquad (4.27)$$

Here α is the phase angle between signals. Now for tripping,

$$-90° < \alpha < 90°$$

and at threshold, $\alpha = \pm 90°$.

The threshold characteristic as shown in Fig. 4.11 is a straight line offset from the origin and at right angles to the replica admittance Y_R.

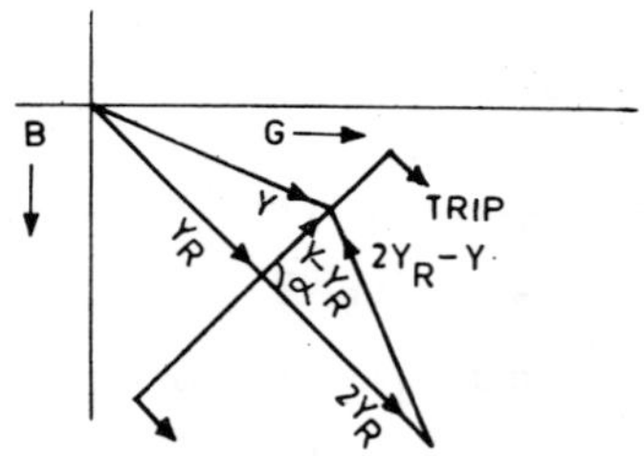

Fig. 4.11 Angle Adm. Relay *Y*-plane

The MHO's relay is suitable for the protection of long and heavily loaded transmission line because the threshold characteristic of this relay is a circle of diameter Z_R and passing through the origin in *Z*-plane. Thus the threshold characteristic becomes quite compact and the relay is also directional. Because of this on one hand, the fault area is enclosed compactly and thus there is much less chance to operate during power swing. During power swing caused by severe fault, the relay sees a fictitious impedance and if this impedance becomes less than the relay setting, the relay may operate. This chance is reduced in the case of MHO's relay because of compact characteristic and, as the relay is directional, there is no need to use an additional directional relay in this case.

4.4.6 Restricted Relay

The restricted relay characteristic is obtained by restricting the limit of phase angle α of signals as phase comparator, i.e.

$$-\beta < \alpha < B$$

where β is not equal to 90°. When $\beta = 90°$, it is called cosine comparator. Here β may be more than or less than 90°. Restricted relay characteristics can be obtained for directional relay, angle impedance (i.e. reactance) relay and angle admittance (i.e. MHO's) relay.

Restricted directional relay. Let us take its signals as phase comparator in Z-plane, i.e.

$$\left.\begin{aligned} S_1 &= I Z_R, \quad \text{i.e. } Z_R \\ S_2 &= V = I Z, \quad \text{i.e. } Z \end{aligned}\right| \angle\alpha$$

Here α is the phase angle between signals S_1 and S_2. As a normal relay as shown earlier, the tripping will occur if

$$-90^\circ < \alpha < 90^\circ$$

but now as restricted relay, for tripping, we have

$$-\beta_1 < \alpha < \beta_2$$

where $$\beta_1 < \beta_2 < 90^\circ.$$

The threshold characteristic is shown in Fig. 4.12. Normally $\beta_1 = \beta_2 = \beta$, thus we have for tripping,

$$-\beta < \alpha < \beta$$

and $$\beta < 90^\circ.$$

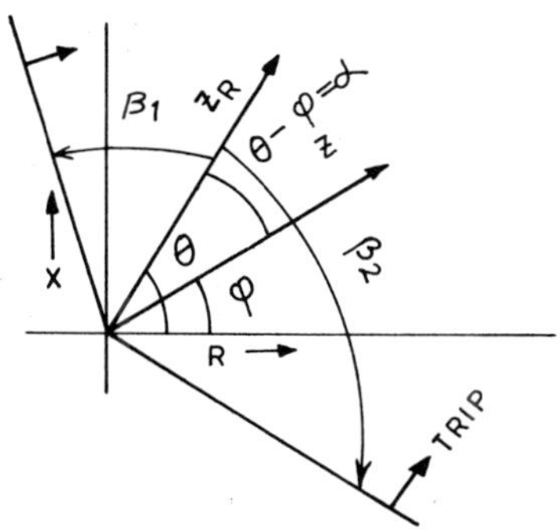

Fig. 4.12 Restricted directional relay

Such characteristics are preferred as they limit the zone of tripping.

Restricted reactance (i.e. OHM Relay). Here also taking signals in Z-plane as phase comparator,

$$\left.\begin{aligned} S_1 &= I Z_R - V, \quad \text{i.e. } Z_R - Z \\ S_2 &= I Z_R, \quad \text{i.e. } Z_R \end{aligned}\right| \angle\alpha$$

and restricting the phase angle α as shown, we get restricted reactance relay characteristic, i.e.

$$-\beta < \alpha < \beta \text{ and } \beta < 90^\circ$$

The same thing can also be done in *Y*-plane. The restricted relay characteristic is shown in Fig. 4.13 and is the preferred characteristic as it restrictes the zone of tripping.

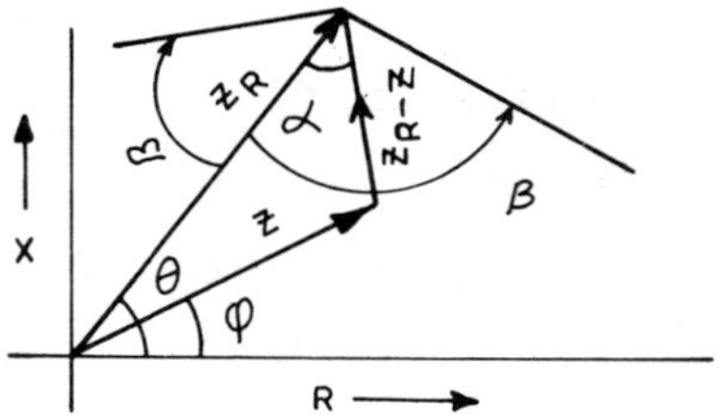

Fig. 4.13 Restricted reactance relay

Restricted MHO's relay. Let us take signals of MHO's relay as phase comparator in Z-plane as follows.

$$\left.\begin{aligned} S_1 &= I Z_R - V, \quad \text{i.e. } Z_R - Z \\ S_2 &= V, \quad \text{i.e. } Z \end{aligned}\right| \angle\alpha$$

Now as restricted relay, we have the criterion for tripping

$$-\beta < \alpha < \beta$$

Now for $\beta < 90°$, we have the threshold characteristic as shown in Fig. 4.14. As seen from the diagram, the characteristic is very similar to that of elliptical characteristics which considerably, restricts the zone of tripping. Hence such relays are preferred for blocking relay operation during power swing. This is why this relay is chosen as third zone MHO's relay element when power swing phenomena is quite significant. Now if $\beta > 90°$, we get a characteristic as shown in Fig. 4.15. This characteristic is quite large and bulky as it is the sum of two large semicircles which is preferred for ground fault with high arcing resistance. This relay is also preferred as blocking relay. The threshold characteristic in Y-plane is shown in Fig. 4.16. All these characteristics are in fact dual of the characteristics of reactance relay.

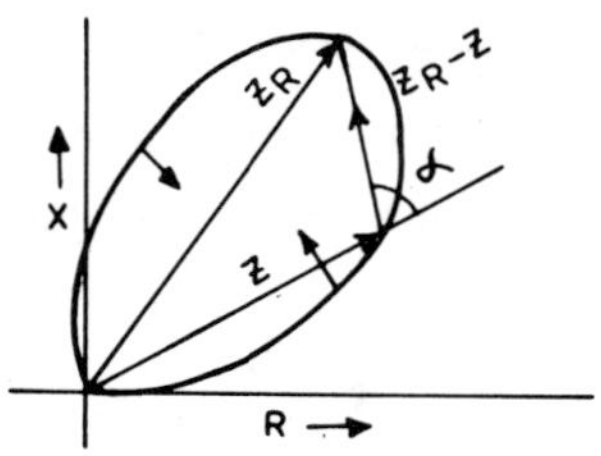

Fig. 4.14 Restricted Mho's Relay

The restricted relay characteristics are obtained by changing the clock frequency. Say f_0 is the normal clock frequency corresponding to 90° and corresponding angle is β_0. To obtain the angle β_1 or β_2, the clock frequency is changed from f_0 to f_1 or f_0 to f_2. Hence, we have

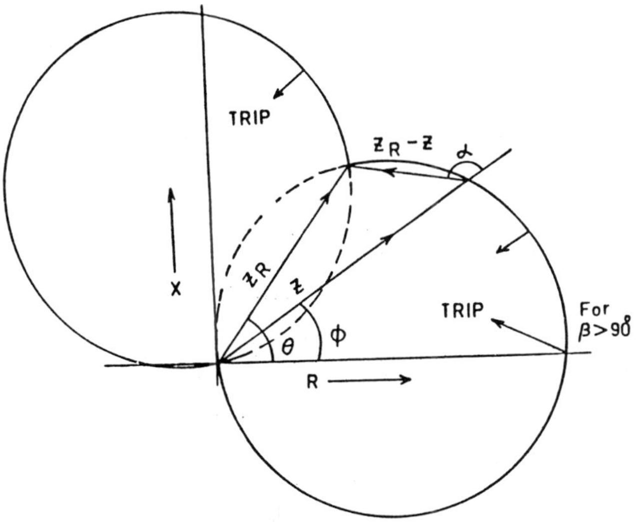

Fig. 4.15 Restricted Mho's Relay

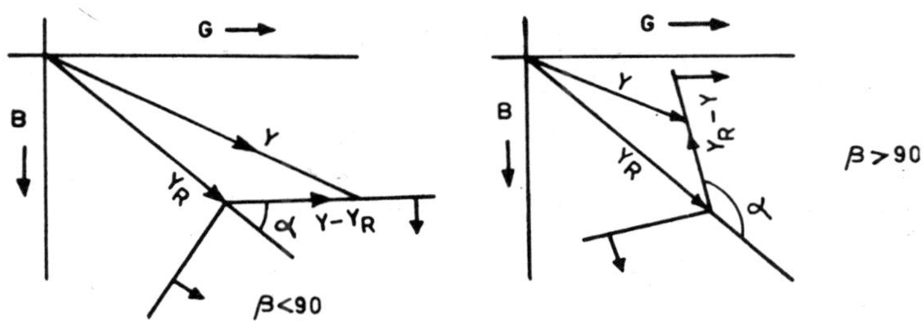

Fig. 4.16

$$\frac{f_1}{f_0} = \frac{180 - \beta_0}{180 - \beta_1} = \frac{90}{180 - \beta_1}$$

i.e.

$$f_1 = \frac{f_0}{2 - \dfrac{\beta_1}{90°}} \text{ and } f_2 = \frac{f_0}{2 - \dfrac{\beta_2}{90°}}$$

Thus by varying clock frequency we get,

$$\beta_1 = 90\ [2 - f_0/f_1] \text{ and } \beta_2 = 90\ [2 - f_0/f_2]$$

Any type of restricted relay characteristic can be obtained by changing clock frequency from its normal value of f_0 to f_1 or f_2 to obtain β_1 or β_2.

4.4.7 Offset Characteristics

Offset characteristics can be obtained by adding to the voltage coil, a voltage proportional to the line current. Signals for offset angle admittance, i.e. MHO's relay in Z-plane and Y-plane as phase comparators which are obtained by adding to the voltage coil, voltage proportional to line current, are as follows

Z-plane

$$S_1 = I Z_R - V$$

$$S_2 = V - K I Z_R = V - I K Z_R = V - I Z_0 \text{ i.e. } K Z_R = Z_0$$

where $K < 1$

Y-plane

$$S_3 = I - V Y_R$$

$$S_4 = V Y_0 - I \quad \text{where } Y_0 = \frac{1}{Z_0}$$

The threshold characteristics are shown in Fig. 4.17 and Fig. 4.18. These relays are preferred as starting element, i.e. 3rd zone element.

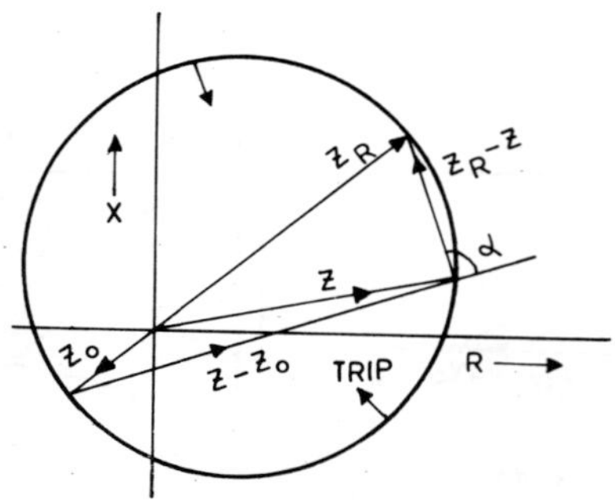

Fig. 4.17 Offset Mho's relay : Z-plane

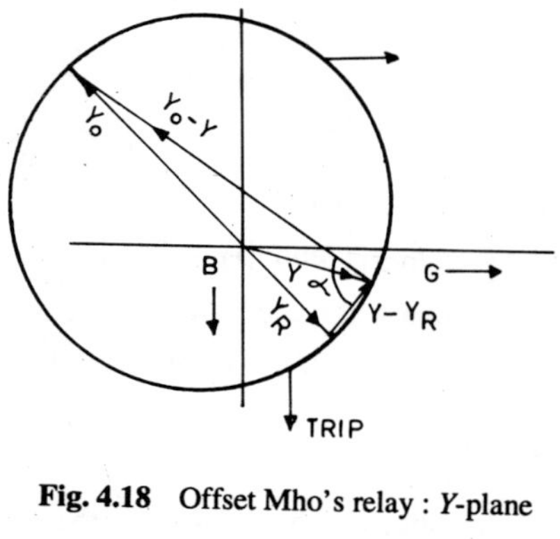

Fig. 4.18 Offset Mho's relay : Y-plane

4.5 PROTECTION SCHEME FOR TRANSMISSION LINE

The protection of transmission line, especially overhead line is both interesting and challenging. This is because of great length of the line with its consequent exposure to lightning and other atmospheric hazards. It is a fact that the number of faults on transmission lines are much more than those in apparatus.

4.5.1 Faults on Transmission Line

Following types of faults take place in a transmission line. They are listed in the order of severity.

(i) 3-ϕ fault (LLL fault) or 3-ϕ to ground fault (LLLG fault) with or without fault impedance. This fault which is most severe but least common is only one in number.

(ii) Double line to ground (LLG) fault with or without fault impedance. This fault is less severe but more common than 3-ϕ fault. However, this type of faults are three in number.

(iii) Line to line (LL) fault. This fault is more common but less severe than the above faults. These faults are also three in number.

(iv) Single phase to ground (LG) fault. This fault is the least severe but the most common. These faults are also three in number.

From the above, we conclude that there are four types of faults which are ten in number. The first three faults such as LLL or LLLG, LLG and LL faults involving two or more phases are known as phase fault while the fourth fault, namely, LG fault, is called ground fault. We use phase relay for phase fault involving two or more phases and ground relay for ground fault. Main reasons of using separate relay for ground faults are: (i) after this fault, the fault current may be less than the normal load current because the neutral of 3-phase synchronous generator is grounded through reactance, (ii) this fault normally takes place with finite fault impedance (i.e. arcing resistance) and since the reactance and the arcing resistance are in series in the circuit of LG fault, certainly the fault current after LG fault may be less than the normal load current. Hence, it is obvious that the normal phase relays for phase fault, will not be able to operate for ground fault.

We use 3 phase relays for phase faults and 3 ground relays for ground, i.e. LG fault at any location. The phase relays are supplied with line to line voltage (delta voltage) and difference of line currents (delta currents). The ground relays, on the other hand, are supplied with phase voltage (Y), phase current and some residual currents.

4.5.2 Measuring Elements

Every relay, as shown in Fig. 4.19, has three measuring elements. The first measuring element which is the fastest, protects nearly 80–90% of the line which is being protected. The second measuring element reaches nearly half of the next line, thus clearing the end zone fault of the line which is being protected with delay and provides backup protection to half of the adjacent line. The third measuring element reaches the end of the next line, thus providing backup protection for the

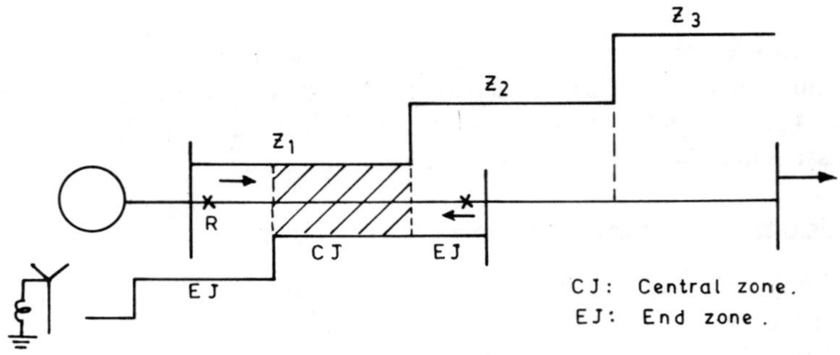

Fig. 4.19 Measuring elements

complete next line. This measuring element is normally used as a starting element to start the carrier.

4.5.3 Protection Scheme

The scheme for providing proper protection of a 3-ϕ transmission line is shown in Fig. 4.20. For a fault at any point F with finite fault impedance R_F along the area of the fault is shown in Fig. 4.21. Actually the arc resistance is assumed constant

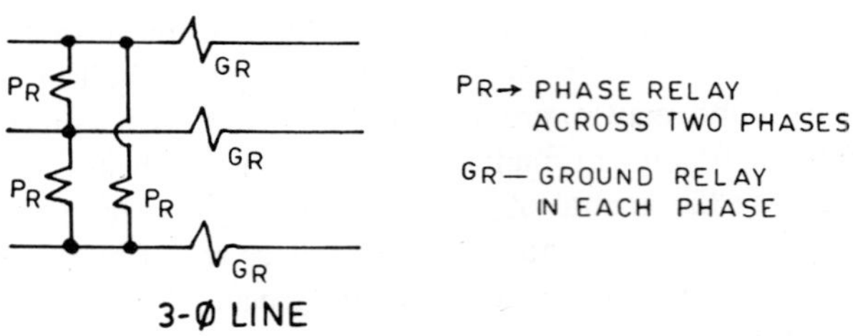

Fig. 4.20

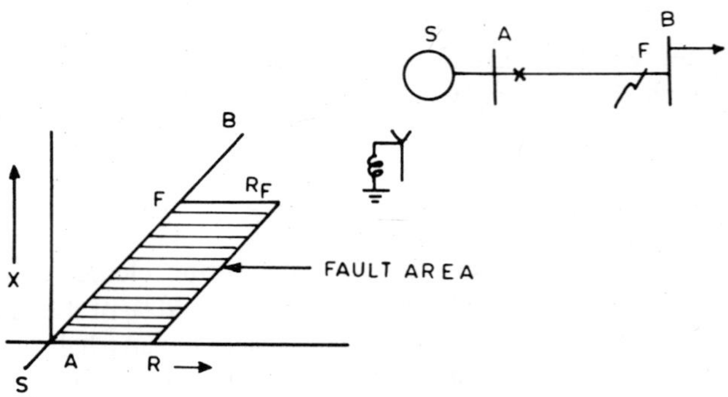

Fig. 4.21

here though in actual practice, it decreases slightly as we approach the relay location. As explained earlier at any bus we use three phase relays for phase faults and three ground relays for ground fault. The phase relays are supplied with line to line i.e. delta voltage and delta current which is the difference of line current. The ground relays are supplied with phase voltage, phase current and residual currents. The relays are provided to protect the line against internal faults and hence they see in the forward direction as shown in Fig. 4.21. It is clear from the figure, that the faults in the central zone are cleared promptly with simultaneous operation of relays at both ends while faults in the end zones are cleared sequentially, i.e. the relay close to fault operates quickly but the relay at the far end operates with delay. Hence to clear the fault even in the end zones promptly and simultaneously, carrier channel is required.

The main reason of setting the first zone measuring element of the relay to reach only 80% to 90% of the protected length is to ensure that in no case, the next bus is tripped by the first measuring element. Because of this and also because the relay is not very sensitive to distinguish between internal and external faults, the relay setting of the first measuring element is less than the next bus i.e. only upto 80% to 90% of the protected length. Similarly, the second zone measuring element which clears the end zones fault with delay (if there is no carrier) and provides backup protection to half of the adjoining line, must include the next bus but must never include the remote bus. It is set to include, at the maximum, half of the adjoining line. If more than one line branch from the next bus, then the second measuring element should only include the half length of the shortest line. However, if any of the line is very short, such that half length of this shortest line amounts to less than 15% length of the longest line, then it is better to exclude this shortest line and this length is protected by unit protection scheme. In the same way, the third measuring unit (M_3) must include the remote bus (Fig. 4.22).

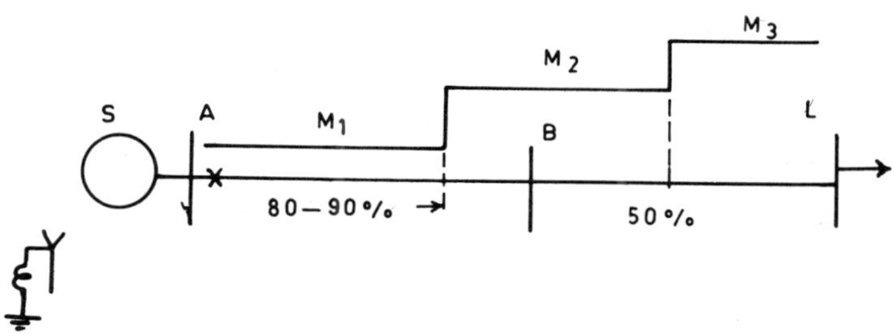

Fig. 4.22

In the case of long and heavily loaded lines, the protection against phase faults is provided by MHO's relay M_1, M_2 and OM_3 as shown in Fig. 4.23. The third measuring element OM_3 which is a starting element to start the carrier may use offset elliptical characteristic to avoid tripping because of power swing. Power swing caused by severe fault, being an electromechanical transient, is slow and hence its effect is felt only during the operation of third measuring element. For

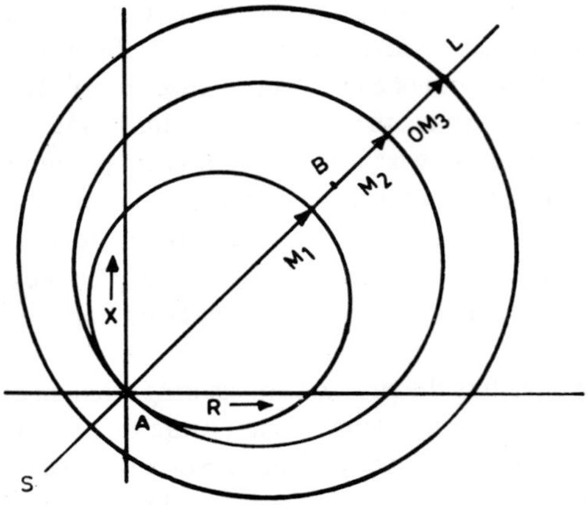

Fig. 4.23

ground fault, reactance relays X_1, X_2 and X_3 are used. However, since reactance relay is non-directional and since it can also operate during normal load with high power factor, its action is always supervised by directional starting, i.e. MHO's relay. Therefore, the tripping area is between the first reactance element X_1 and second MHO's element M_2 (Fig. 4.24).

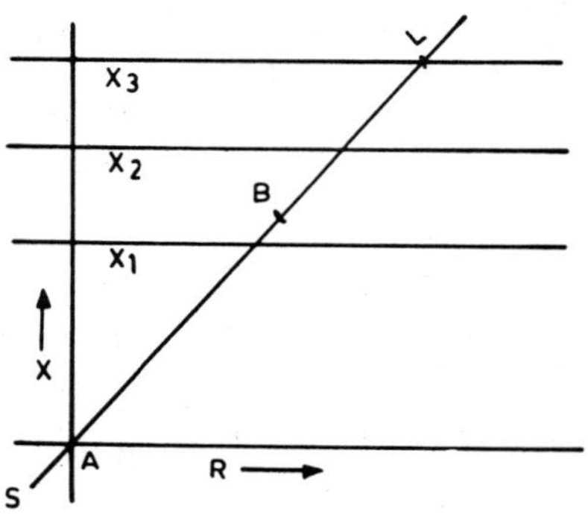

Fig. 4.24

4.6 SWITCHED DISTANCE RELAYS

We have seen, in Sec. 4.5.1, that at any bus we need 3 phase relays for phase faults, each relay with three measuring units and 3 ground relays for ground fault again each relay with three measuring elements. That is, we need a total of eighteen measuring elements (i.e. relays), four fault detectors and also a logic unit. In addition, there may be other relaying schemes as well. Thus it is clear that it is a costly affair and also needs lot of panel space. To economize the number of relaying schemes to be used at any bus, in the first step, only three phase relays and three ground relays are used at any bus. However, with the change in the fault location, the logic circuit changes the reach of the relay from the first zone (which is 80% to 90% of the protected line), to the second or the third zone. In the second step of switching, instead of using separate relays for phase and ground faults, only a total of three relays are used at any location. The relays are delta connected, i.e. they receive delta current and delta voltage and thus only clear quickly the phase fault which is quite severe. However, if ground fault takes place, the switching device changes the delta connection to star connection thus providing phase current and phase voltage to the relay, thus the relay becomes the ground relay and clears ground fault. In this scheme, the phase fault which is severe is cleared quickly and ground fault which is less severe is cleared with delay. As a general practice, transmission lines exceeding 100 kV are provided with three phase and three ground relays with a provision for changing the reach of the relay with the change in fault location. Below 100 kV, only three relays both for phase and ground faults are used. The reach of the relays is changed from zone 1, 2 or 3 depending upon fault location.

4.7 POLYPHASE RELAYS

The polyphase relaying scheme also optimizes the number of relays at any bus. Here, instead of using at least three relays as mentioned above, only one relay is used. The block diagram of the relay is shown in Fig. 4.25. As shown in the diagram, the outputs of phase modules *A*, *B* and *C* are OR-gated to give final trip signal. The

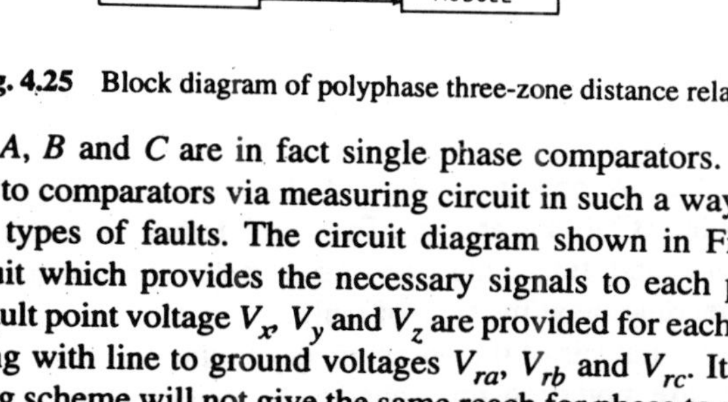

Fig. 4.25 Block diagram of polyphase three-zone distance relay

phase modules *A*, *B* and *C* are in fact single phase comparators. Suitable input signals are sent to comparators via measuring circuit in such a way that the relay responds to all types of faults. The circuit diagram shown in Fig. 4.26 is the measuring circuit which provides the necessary signals to each phase module. Compensated fault point voltage V_x, V_y and V_z are provided for each phase module *A*, *B* and *C* along with line to ground voltages V_{ra}, V_{rb} and V_{rc}. It is known that such a measuring scheme will not give the same reach for phase to phase fault and phase to ground faults owing to different short circuit line currents I_a, I_b, and I_c.

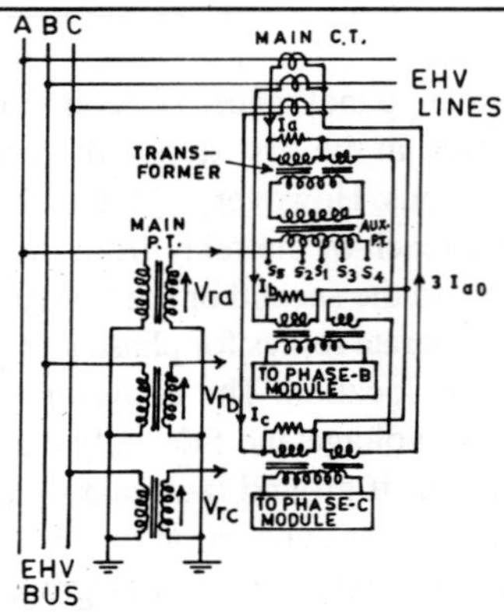

Fig. 4.26 Measuring circuit of polyphase relay

But if zero sequence current is taken into account, the measuring circuits will give the correct measurement both for phase fault as well as line to ground fault. The compensated fault point voltages are derived as explained in the following.

The line to neutral fault point voltage of phase '*a*' during any type of short circuit with zero fault impedance, is

$$V_{fa} = V_{ra} - I_a Z_L$$

Now converting I_a into its sequence components and changing Z_L likewise, we get

$$V_{fa} = V_{ra} - I_{a1} Z_{L1} - I_{a2} Z_{L2} - I_{a0} Z_{L0}$$

$$= V_{ra} - (I_a + K I_{a0}) Z_{L1}$$

where $k = n - 1$ and $n = L_{L0}/Z_{L1}$ and assuming $Z_{L1} = Z_{L2}$ for transmission lines.

Hence, the three compensated voltages are:

$$V_x = V_{ra} - (I_a + K I_{a0}) Z_R = V_{x1} + V_{x2} + V_{x0}$$

$$V_y = V_{rb} - (I_b + K I_{a0}) Z_R = \alpha^2 V_{x1} + \alpha V_{x2} + V_{x0}$$

$$V_z = V_{rc} - (I_c + K I_{a0}) Z_R = \alpha V_{x1} + \alpha^2 V_{x2} + V_{x0}$$

where $Z_{L1} = Z_R$ is replica impedance, and α is an operator.

$$V_{x1} = V_{ra1} - I_{a1} Z_R$$

$$V_{x2} = V_{ra2} - I_{a2} Z_R$$

$$V_{x0} = V_{ra0} - I_{a0} Z_R$$

The signals sent to phase A module are V_{ra} and $-V_x$, to phase module B are V_{rb} and $-V_y$ and to phase module C are V_{rc} and $-V_z$. The characteristic of each phase module will be MHO's type and final characteristic will be a combination of these characteristics, depending upon the type of fault.

The mathematical analysis of the operation is as follows.

The signals to phase module A for second zone operation are,

$$S_1 = V_{ra}$$

and
$$S_2 = -V_x = (I_a + K I_{a0})\, Z_R - V_{ra}$$

$$\frac{-V_x}{V_{ra}} = \frac{(I_a + K I_{a0})\, Z_R - V_{ra}}{V_{ra}}$$

$$= \frac{Z_R}{V_{ra}/(I_a + K I_{a0})} - 1 = \frac{Z_R - Z_L}{Z_L}$$

if
$$\frac{-V_x}{V_{ra}} = \alpha = \frac{Z_R - Z_L}{Z_L},$$

then criterion for tripping is $-90° < \alpha < 90°$. Thus characteristic will be that of a MHO relay passing through the origin, which will satisfy the above condition. The criterion for a line to ground fault for different phases will be the same as above.

4.8 SUMMARY

Static distance relays are commonly used for the protection of EHV/UHV transmission lines. Due to their high speed of operation, accuracy and reliability, practically no maintenance is needed once it is put into service. The relay generally uses analog devices which give delayed operation at threshold condition. Here, the operating time is a function of phase angle displacement and becomes infinite at boundary condition. This creates a serious relay coordination problem. This drawback can be overcome by using digital circuits and TTL logic in which response time is kept constant. As TTL logic gates are sensitive to spurious signals due to their low noise immunity, digital relays with CMOS logic are developed. The static relays discussed in this chapter use CMOS logic and simple logic circuits. Static relays because of their numerous advantages are still very common. However, the days are not very far when digital protection will be used for the protection of both apparatus and transmission line. We will discuss in detail digital protection in the succeeding chapters.

EXERCISES

1. (a) What do you understand by static relays? Name different components used in a typical static relaying scheme.
   (b) State, in the order of importance, the merits of static relaying scheme.
2. (a) Discuss what do you understand by complex β-plane (i.e. complex *Z*-plane) and complex α-plane (i.e. complex *Y*-plane). Why is it preferred to plot the relay threshold characteristics on these planes?
   (b) Give signals of the plane impedance relay as an amplitude comparator and also as a phase comparator in the complex *Z*-plane and draw the corresponding threshold characteristics in the complex *Z*-plane. What will be the signals of the plane impedance relay in the complex α-plane (i.e. complex *Y*-plane) both as an amplitude comparator as well as a phase comparator? Draw also its threshold characteristics in the complex *Y*-plane.

3. What is the dual of plane impedance relay? Derive its signals both as an amplitude comparator as well as a phase comparator in the complex *Z*-plane and draw the corresponding threshold characteristics in the complex *Z*-plane. Obtain the relation between signals as an amplitude comparator and as a phase comparator, give also its signals both as an amplitude comparator as well as a phase comparator in the complex *Y*-plane and draw the corresponding threshold characteristics. Derive also the relation between signals in the complex *Z*-plane and corresponding signals in the complex *Y*-plane.
4. Obtain the signals both as an amplitude comparator as well as a phase comparator of an angle admittance (i.e. MHO's) relay in the complex β-plane and complex α-plane and draw the corresponding threshold characteristics in the two planes. For a long, heavily loaded line, why is an angle admittance (i.e. MHO's) relay preferred? State the merits of this relay.
5. Why an angle impedance (i.e. Ohm) relay is called a dual of an angle admittance relay (i.e. MHO's) relay? Obtain the signals both as an amplitude comparator as well as a phase comparator of the angle impedance relay in the complex *Z*-plane and complex *Y*-plane and draw the corresponding threshold characteristics in the two planes. State briefly the demerits of an angle impedance relay.
6. Comment on the statement "Reactance relay is realized by setting the set angle θ of the angle impedance relay equal to 90°". Draw the threshold characteristics of the reactance relay both in the complex *Z*-plane and complex *Y*-plane. Why this relay is used as a ground relay for ground fault. Discuss principal shortcommings of this relay.
7. Draw the threshold characteristics of the angle admittance (i.e. MHO's) relay both in the complex β-plane as well as in the complex α-plane for phase angle β between relay signals equal to 90° (i.e. cosine comparator) and less than 90° and more than 90° (i.e. restricted characteristics). Under what situations these restricted MHO's relays are used and why?
8. How do you obtain OFFSET threshold characteristics of an angle admittance (i.e. MHO's) relay. Obtain the signals of the OFFSET MHO's characteristics as a phase comparator both in the complex *Z*-plane and complex *Y*-plane and draw the corresponding threshold characteristics in both the planes. Where these relays are preferred and why?
9. What do you understand by phase relays and ground relays. State for what types of-faults these relays are used giving reasons. Discuss with the help of a neat diagram the protection scheme for 3-phase overhead transmission line using static distance relays. How many phase relays and ground relays covering all the three zones of protection of the transmission line are used at any bus?
10. What do you understand by switched distance relays? Why these relays are preferred over conventional phase and ground relays for transmission line protection? Discuss the working principle of a switched distance relay with the help of a neat diagram.

11. What are the advantages of using polyphase relays for transmission line protection? Discuss with the help of a neat diagram the theory and principle of operation of a polyphase relay.

REFERENCES

1. Adamson, C. and L.M. Wedepohl, "A Dual-Comparator Mho-type Distance Relay Utilizing Transistors", *Proc. IEE*, Vol. 103-A, Sept. 1956, pp. 509–517.
2. Adamson, C. and E.A. Talkhan, "The Application of Transistors to Phase-Comparison Carrier Protection", *Proc. IEE*, Vol. 106, Part A, Feb. 1959, pp. 51–63.
3. Anil Kumar, N.M. and K. Parathasarathy, "A Mathematical Basis for Multi-Input Sine Comparators", *J. Instn. Engrs. (India)*, Vol. 48, Part EL1, Oct. 1967, pp. 9–21.
4. Anil Kumar, N.M., K. Parathasarathy and K.K. Thakkar, "A 3-Step Transistorized Distance Relay with A Quadrilateral Polar Characteristic", *J. Inst. Engrs. (India)*, Vol. 48, Part EL2, Dec. 1967, pp. 189–204.
5. Anil Kumar, N.M., "New Approach to Distance Relays with Quadrilateral Polar Characteristic for EHV Line Protection", *Proc. IEEE*, Vol. 117, Oct. 1970, pp. 1986–1992.
6. Basu, S.K., S. Chaudhuri, R. Chakrabarti, "Polyphase Distance Relaying by Phase Sequence Detection", *J.I.E. (India)*, Vol. 54, Part EL-4, 1974, pp. 135–141.
7. Basu, K.P., G. Mahboob and B.H. Khan, "Distance Relay Characteristics for Protection of Series Compensated transmission Lines", *J. Instn. Engrs. (India)*, 63, Pt. EL-4, Feb. 1983, pp. 203–205.
8. Caleca, V., S.H. Horowitz, A.J. Mc Connell nad H.T. Seeley, "Static Mho Distance and Pilot Relaying: Application and Test Results", *IEEE Trans*: Power Apparatus and Systems, Vol. PAS-82, Aug. 1963, pp. 424–436.
9. Chandra, A. and L.P. Singh, "Fault Studies on Six-phase Systems and a Proposed Ultra High Speed Relaying Scheme". *Proc. All India Seminar Multiphase (High Phase order) System*, Kanpur, March 17–19, 1989, pp. 124–134.
10. Chandra, A., Sachchidanand and L.P.Singh, "Proposed Ultra High Speed Relaying Scheme for High Phase Order (HPOT) System", *Proc.* 16th *Ann. Conf.* of IEEE *Industrial Electronic Society* (IECON'90), held at Pacific Grove, California, USA, November 27–30, 1990.
11. Choudhury, S., S.K. Basu and S.P. Patra, "Polyphase Ground Distance Relaying by Phase Coincidence Principle", Transaction Paper No. T-72, 4281, Presented at IEEE Summer Power Meeting, 1972, *IEEE Trans.*, PAS-92, 1972, pp. 626–634.
12. Desikachar, K.V. and L.P. Singh, "Protection of EHV/UHV Transmission Lines Using Travelling Wave Phenomena", Paper presented to the National Power Systems Conference (India) Dec. 1981, pp. S4.4.1.
13. Desikachar, K.V., Y. Asthana and L.P. Singh, "New Relay Scheme for EHV/UHV Transmission Lines", *J. Instn. Engrs. (India)*, Vol. 63, Pt. EL3, Dec. 1982, pp. 159–164.
14. Desikachar, K.V. and L.P. Singh, "Fault Analysis of Multinode Power Systems for Designing U.H.S. Protective Relays along with a Proposed Relaying Scheme", *Electr. Pwr. Syst. Res.*, Vol. 6, 1983, pp. 13–25.
15. Desikachar, K.V. and L.P. Singh, "A Novel Protective System for Transmission Line Protection Based on Travelling Wave Phenomena", Paper presented to 2nd National Power Systems Conference, Hyderabad (India), Sept. 1983.
16. Desikachar, K.V. and L.P. Singh, "Digital Travelling Wave Protection of Transmission Lines", *Electr. Pwr. Syst. Res.*, Vol. 7, (1984), pp. 19–28.
17. Desikachar, K.V. and L.P. Singh, "A Proposed Ultra High Speed Relaying Scheme for the protection of an Existing 400 kV Line", *Proc. Int. (IEEE) Conf. Computers* etc., held at Bangalore, Dec. 9–12, 1984, Proc.3, pp. 1359–1363.
18. Desikachar, K.V. and L.P. Singh, "Application of FFT to the Computation of Electrical Transients", *Proc. Natl. Conf. Computer and Society* held at Annamalai University, Chidambaram, Aug. 1986, p. 27.

19. Dewey, C.G., C.A. Mathews and W.C. Morris, "Static Mho Distance and Pilot Relaying: Principles and Circuits", *IEEE Trans*: Power Apparatus and Systems, Vol. PAS-82, June 1963, pp. 391–400.
20. Dewey, C.G. and M.E. Hodges, "Transistorized Phase-Comparison Relaying: Principles and Circuits", *AIEE Trans.*, Vol. 79, Part III, Aug. 1960, pp. 373–380.
21. Gupta, S.C. "Static Polyphase Distance Relay Schemes for the Protection of Transmission Lines", *Ph.D. Thesis*, Roorkee University, Nov. 1969.
22. Hoel Hans, W.D. Humpage and C.P. Chapman, "Composite Polar Characteristics in Multi-zone Systems of Phase-Comparison Distance Protection", *Proc. IEEE*, Vol. 113, Oct. 1966, pp. 1631–1642.
23. Humpage, W.D. and S.P. Sabberwal, "Developments in Phase-Comparison Techniques for Distances Protection", *Proc. IEEE*, Vol. 112, July 1965, pp. 1383–1394.
24. Islam, K.K., S.K. Bose and L.P. Singh, "On-Line Microprocessor Based Relaying Scheme", *Proc. Platinum Jubilee Conf. Systems and Signal Processing*, I.I.Sc., Bangalore, Dec. 1986, p. 241.
25. Jackson, L., J.B. Patrickson and L.M. Wedepohl, "Distance Protection: Optimum Dynamic Design of Static Relay Comparators", *Proc. IEEE*, Vol. 115, Feb. 1968, pp. 280–287.
26. Jackson, L., "Distance-Protection Comparator with Signal Dependent Phase-Angle Criterion", *Proc. IEEE*, Vol. 121, Aug. 1974, pp. 817–825.
27. Johns, A.T., "Generalised Phase Comparator Techniques for Distance Protection-Basis of their Operation and Design", *Proc. IEEE*, Vol. 119, July 1972, pp. 833–841.
28. Johns, A.T., "Generalised Phase Comparator Techniques for Distance Protection–Theory and Operation of Multi-input Devices", *Proc. IEEE*, Vol. 119, Nov. 1972, pp. 1595–1603.
29. Johns, A.T., "Vibrable-Characteristic Generalised Techniques for Distance Protection: Theory and Initial Performance Studies", *Proc. IEEE*, Vol. 120, Aug. 1973, pp. 891–89.
30. Johns, A.T., "Vibrable-Characteristic Generalised Techniques for Distance Protection: Double-Circuit Application Studies", *Proc. IEEE*, Vol. 121, Dec. 1974, pp
31. Johns, A.T., "New Discriminative Distance-Protective Relays for Selective-Pole Autoreclosure Applications", *Proc. IEEE*, Vol. 126, Feb. 1979, pp. 159–161.
32. Kellog, A.J., L.P. Singh and G.K. Dubey, "Protection of EHV Transmission Lines by Using Static Relays", *Proc. Conf. Power System Protection*, Madras, April 1980, Vol. 1, Institution of Engineers (India), Calcutta p. B5.
33. Kellog, A.J., L.P. Singh and G.K. Dubey, "General Purpose Static Relay Using Digital Techniques", *J. Instn. Engrs. (India)*, Vol. 63, Part EL2, August 1982, pp. 5–11.
34. Kellog, A.J., L.P. Singh and G.K. Dubey, "3-phase Polyphase Distance Relay Using Digital Circuits", Paper presented to 2nd National Power Systems Conference, Hyderabad (India), Sept. 1983.
35. Kellog, A.J., L.P. Singh and G.K. Dubey, "A High Speed 3-Zone Distance Relay Using Digital Circuit", *Int. IEEE Conf. Computers etc.*, Bangalore, Dec. 1984, *Proceedings III*, pp. 1349–1353.
36. Kellog, A.J., L.P. Singh and G.K. Dubey, "A High Speed Three-Zone Distance Relay Using Digital Circuits", *Electr. Pwr. Syst. Res.*, Vol. 8, 1984/85, pp. 187–195.
37. Khincha, H.P., K. Parthasarathy and B.S. Ashok Kumar, "Developments in Amplitude-Comparator Techniques for Distance Relays", *Proc. IEEE*, Vol. 117, June 1970, pp. 1118–1124.
38. Khincha, H.P., K. Parthasarathy, B.S. Ashok Kumar and C.G. Arun, "New Possibilities in Amplitude-and Phase-Comparison Techniques for Distance Relays", *Proc. IEEE*, Vol. 117, Nov. 1970, pp. 2133–2141.
39. Kimbark, E.W., *Power System Stability*, Vol. 2, John Willey and Sons Inc., New York, 1965.
40. Maleev, A.M., "Three-phase Impedance Relay Responding to the Phase-Sequence of Four Electrical Quantities", *Electrihertvo, USSR*, 1968, p. 1.
41. Mathews, P. and B.D. Nellist, "Transients in Distance Protection", *Proc. IEEE*. Vol. 110, 1963, pp. 407–418.
42. Mc Laren, P.G., "Static Sampling Distance Relays", *Proc. IEEE*, Vol. 115, March 1968, pp. 418–424.

43. Paithankar, Y.G., and M.V. Deshpande, "Polyphase Distance Relay", *Proc. IEEE,* Vol. 120(9), 1973, pp. 1013–1015.
44. Paithankar, Y.G., and V.T. Ingole, "New Techniques in Multi-Input Amplitude Comparators to Generate Quadrilateral Distance Relay", *J. Instn. Engrs. (India),* Vol. 54, Part EL3, Feb. 1974, pp. 79–85.
45. Paithankar, Y.G. and A.S. Thoke, "Variable Characteristic Earth-Fault Quadrilateral Distance Relay Suitable for Double-End-Infeed Lines: A New Technique", *Conference Paper*: Vol. 1, *Conf. Power System Protection,* Madras (India), April 16–19, 1980, Paper No. A6.
46. Parthasarathy, K., "New Static 3-Step Distance Relay", *Proc. IEEE,* Vol.113, April 1966, pp. 633–640.
47. Parthasarathy, K., H.P. Khincha and B.L. Mathur, "An Adaptive Distance Relay for the Protection of Transmission Lines", *Conference Papers* : Vol. 1, *Conf. Power System Protection,* Madras (India), April 16–19, 1980, Paper No. A3.
48. Patra, S.P., S.K. Basu, S. Chaudhuri and R Chakrabarti, "A Single Unit Distance Relay for Three-Phase Transmission Lines", *Electr. India,* March, 1974.
49. Ramamoorty, M. and N.S. Wani, "Static Distance Relay with Quadrilateral Characteristic", Presented at the *IEEE Summer Meeting,* 1970, Paper No. 70C571.
50. Ramamoorty, M. and S.N. Lall, "A Versatile Phase Comparator Relay Using Digital Circuits", *J.I.E. Engrs. (India),* Vol. 59, Part El6, June 1979, pp. 309–314.
51. Ramamoorty, M. and S.N. Lall, "Digital Multi-Input Phase Comparator", *Conference Papers*: Vol. 1, *Conf Power System Protection,* Madras (India), April 16–19, 1980, Paper No. A5.
52. Ramamoorty, M. and M.N. Gandhi, R.J. Phansalkar and P.J. Durkal, "Static Distance Relay with Conic Characteristics", *Conference Papers*: Vol., *Conf. Power System Protection,* Madras (India), April 16–19, 1980, Paper No. A7.
53. Singh, L.P., "Advanced Power System Analysis and Dynamics". 3rd Edition, Wiley Eastern Ltd., New Delhi 1992.
54. Singh, L.P. and V.P. Singh, "Coordination and Setting of Relays: A Case Study of Chukha Transmission System", *Proc. Int. Sysp. EHV/UHV A.C. HVDC Transmission Systems,* Bangalore 1987, SIV-27.
55. Vitanov, A., "Quadrilateral-Characteristic: Transistor Distance Protection", *CIGRE, Paris,* 1968, Paper No. 31–03.
56. Van, A.R., Warrington, C., *Protective Relays,* Vol. 2, Chapman and Hall, London, 1976.
57. Van, A.R., Warrington, C., *Protective Relays,* Vol. 2, Chapman and Hall, London, 1974.
58. Wedepohl, L.M., "Polarised Mho Distance Relay–A New Approach to the Analysis of practical Characteristics", *Proc. IEEE,* Vol. 112, March 1965, pp. 525–535.
59. Weller, G.C., A. Newbould and R.B. Miller, "New Principles for Distance Protective Relays", Second Int. Conf. Developments in Power System Protection, London, June 10–12, 1980, *Conf. Publ.* No. 185, Institution of Electronics Engineers, 1980, pp. 284–288.

5

GENERAL MATHEMATICAL THEORY OF RELAY AS A COMPARATOR

5.1 INTRODUCTION

Protective relay is actually a comparator because it operates when an electrical quantity of protection section changes from its normal value or changes its ratio or phase relation with respect to another quantity with which it has normally a certain magnitude or phase angle relation. In actual practice, normally the relay measures one quantity which may be the current entering the circuit and compares it with some constant quantity, which may be in the case of overcurrent relay the base current obtained by biasing the SCR. The relay operates only if the current entering the circuit exceeds the base current. Such relays are single input comparators because there is only one input signal. These relays are known as level detectors. Because of difficulties in obtaining proper selectivity on the basis of single input quantity alone and also because this relay is non-directional and also the reach of the relay is not fixed, these relays (single input comparators) are not used for the protection of EHV/UHV transmission line.

For EHV/UHV transmission line, the dual input comparator is preferred. This type of relay monitors normally the current entering the circuit and compares it in magnitude or in phase relation with another quantity such as current leaving the circuit at the other end in the case of differential relaying scheme or local bus voltage in the case of distance relaying scheme. From this we conclude, that the relay must be capable of carrying out addition, subtraction, multiplication or division of some scalar or vector quantities as desired.

5.2 DUAL INPUT COMPARATOR

In the case of dual input comparator the relay receives two input signals and the relay operates when one of the two input signals changes in magnitude or in phase relation with respect to the other. Distance relaying schemes are dual input comparators. Here the relay monitors through CT, the line current entering the circuit and compares it in magnitude or phase relation with local bus voltage obtained thorough PT. Dual input comparators are classified as an *amplitude comparator* where only amplitude of input signals are compared and the relay gives trip command if the amplitude (i.e. magnitude) of one signal changes with respect to the amplitude of other signal. The second category is *phase comparator* where only the change in the phase relation between input signals is the basis for relay operation.

There is a perfect duality between amplitude comparator and phase comparator which is evident from Fig. 5.1. In an amplitude comparator, we compare the mods of two input signals and the relay gives trip signal if $|S_1| < |S_2|$. At threshold, i.e. for a fault at the reach of the relay, $|S_1| = |S_2|$ and for external fault outside the protected section $|S_1| > |S_2|$ and there is no tripping. Now, if we obtain sum and difference of these signals, we automatically arrive at phase angle criterion for relay tripping. Say, if we convert the signal S_1 and S_2 into their sum and difference, viz. $S_2 - S_1$ and $S_2 + S_1$ and determine the phase angle between $S_2 - S_1$ and $S_2 + S_1$, then we arrive at the following very important conclusion, as seen from Fig. 5.1.

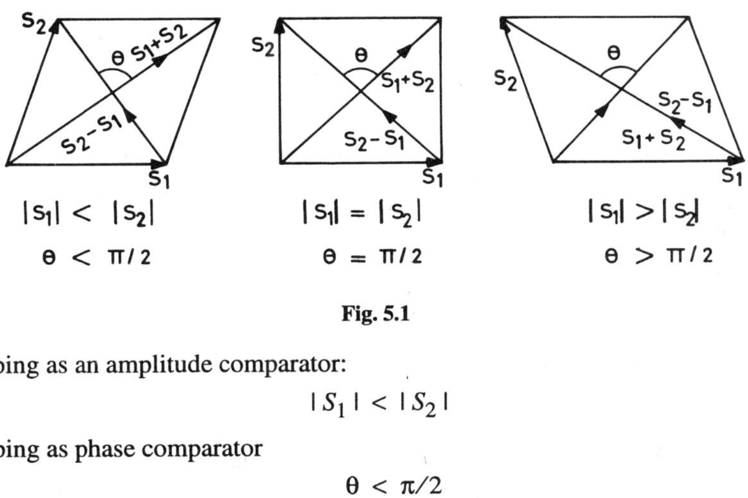

Fig. 5.1

Tripping as an amplitude comparator:

$$|S_1| < |S_2|$$

Tripping as phase comparator

$$\theta < \pi/2$$

At threshold,

$$|S_2| = |S_1|$$

$$\theta = \pi/2$$

For blocking operation when there is an external fault,

Amplitude comparator, $|S_1| > |S_2|$

Phase comparator, $\theta > \pi/2$

From the above, we conclude that there is a perfect duality between amplitude and phase comparator. If we know signals as phase comparator or vice versa, by finding their sum and difference, we obtain signals as amplitude comparator. In inherent amplitude comparator, the two signals are opposed and the relay operates whenever operating signal exceeds the restraining signal only in magnitude irrespective of their phase relations. Similarly, in inherent phase comparator, the relay operation depends solely upon the phase relations between input signals irrespective of their magnitude.

5.2.1 Dual Input Amplitude Comparator

Threshold characteristics of dual input comparator can be obtained both in β-plane and in α-plane. Let us assume that A and B are two quantities which are obtained from the element that is being protected. In the case of distance relaying scheme, A is the line current obtained through CT and B is the local bus voltage obtained through PT. The protective relay with the help of proper logic circuit converts the input quantities A and B in the following form:

$$S_1 = L_1 |A| + L_2 |B| \qquad \angle(\phi - \theta)$$

$$S_2 = L_3 |A| + L_4 |B| \qquad \angle(\phi - \theta) \tag{5.1}$$

Here L_1, L_2, L_3 and L_4 are design (i.e. circuit) constants. In most of the cases, at least one of them is zero and two of them are normally equal; θ is the reference or set angle, i.e. angle made by the reference signal A from the reference axis and ϕ is the angle made by B from the reference axis. Hence, the phase angle between A and B will be $\phi - \theta$. Equation (5.1) can be expressed in the following form (Fig. 5.2):

$$S_1 = L_1 |A| + L_2 |B| \,[\cos(\phi - \theta) + j \sin(\phi - \theta)]$$

$$S_2 = L_3 |A| + L_4 |B| \,[\cos(\phi - \theta) + j \sin(\phi - \theta)] \tag{5.2}$$

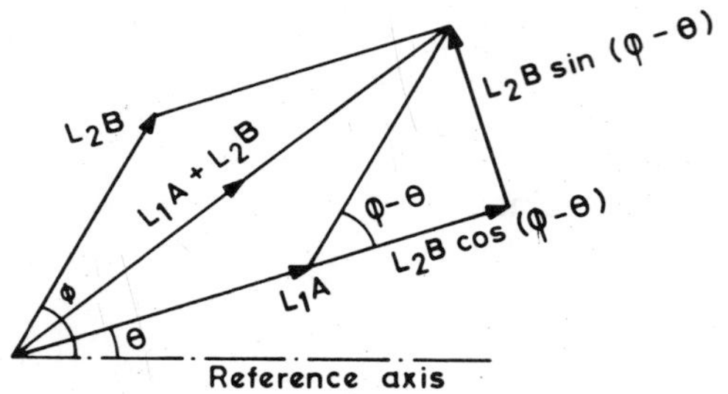

Fig. 5.2

At threshold, the moduli of signals S_1 and S_2 will be equal for any phase angle between them and hence its locus will be the relay threshold characteristic. Thus

$$|S_1| = |S_2|$$

or

$$|S_1|^2 = |S_2|^2 \tag{5.3}$$

Substituting for S_1 and S_2 from Eq. (5.2) into (5.3), we get

$$\left|\left[L_1 |A| + L_2 |B| (\cos(\phi - \theta) + j \sin(\phi - \theta))\right]\right|^2$$

$$= \left|\left[L_3 |A| + L_4 |B| \cos(\phi - \theta) + j \sin(\phi - \theta)\right)\right]\right|^2$$

Expanding the above equation, we get,

$$[L_1 |A| + L_2 |B| (\cos(\phi - \theta))]^2 + [L_2 |B| \sin(\phi - \theta)]^2$$

$$= [L_3 |A| + L_4 |B| (\cos(\phi - \theta)]^2 + [L_4 |B| \sin(\phi - \theta)]^2$$

i.e. $[L_1 |A|]^2 + [L_2 |B| \cos(\phi - \theta)]^2 + 2 L_1 |A| L_2 |B| \cos(\phi - \theta)$

$$+ [L_2 |B| \sin(\phi - \theta)]^2 = [L_3 |A|]^2 + [L_4 |B| \cos(\phi - \theta)]^2$$

$$+ 2 L_3 |A| L_4 |B| \cos(\phi - \theta) + [L_4 |B| \sin(\phi - \theta)]^2$$

i.e. $[L_1 |A|]^2 + 2 L_1 L_2 |A||B| \cos(\phi - \theta) + [L_2 |B|]^2$

$$= [L_3 |A|]^2 + 2 L_3 L_4 |A||B| \cos(\phi - \theta) + [L_4 |B|]^2$$

i.e. $(L_1 |A|)^2 - (L_3 |A|^2) + 2 L_1 L_2 |A||B| \cos(\phi - \theta)$

$$+ (L_2 |B|)^2 - (L_4 |B|)^2 - 2 L_3 L_4 |A||B| \cos(\phi - \theta) = 0$$

i.e. $(L_1^2 - L_3^2) |A|^2 + 2 (L_1 L_2 - L_3 L_4) |A||B| \cos(\phi - \theta)$

$$+ (L_2^2 - L_4^2) |B|^2 = 0 \tag{5.4}$$

To obtain the threshold characteristic in the complex β-plane, we divide Eq. (5.4) by $(L_2^2 - L_4^2) |A|^2$ and hence, we get

$$\frac{L_1^2 - L_3^2}{L_2^2 - L_4^2} + \frac{2 (L_1 L_2 - L_3 L_4)}{L_2^2 - L_4^2} \left|\frac{B}{A}\right| \cos(\phi - \theta) + \left|\frac{B}{A}\right|^2 = 0 \tag{5.5}$$

Equation (5.5) is converted into the form of the following standard equation for circle.

$$\left|\frac{B}{A}\right|^2 - 2C \left|\frac{B}{A}\right| \cos(\phi - \theta) + C^2 = r^2 \tag{5.6}$$

where C represents coördinates and r the radius of the circle. Hence, we obtain from Eq. (5.5).

$$\left|\frac{B}{A}\right|^2 + \frac{2 (L_1 L_2 - L_3 L_4)}{L_2^2 - L_4^2} \left|\frac{B}{A}\right| \cos(\phi - \theta) + \left[\frac{L_1 L_2 - L_3 L_4}{L_2^2 - L_4^2}\right]^2$$

$$= \left[\frac{L_1 L_2 - L_3 L_4}{L_2^2 - L_4^2}\right]^2 - \frac{L_1^2 - L_3^2}{L_2^2 - L_4^2}$$

$$= \left[\frac{L_1 L_4 - L_2 L_3}{L_2^2 - L_4^2}\right]^2$$

i.e.
$$\left|\frac{B}{A}\right|^2 + \frac{2(L_1 L_2 - L_3 L_4)}{L_2^2 - L_4^2}\left|\frac{B}{A}\right| \cos(\phi - \theta) + \left[\frac{L_1 L_2 - L_3 L_4}{L_2^2 - L_4^2}\right]^2 = \left[\frac{L_1 L_4 - L_2 L_3}{L_2^2 - L_4^2}\right]^2 \quad (5.7)$$

Comparing the coefficients of the similar Eqs. (5.6) and (5.7), we get

$$C = -\frac{L_1 L_2 - L_3 L_4}{L_2^2 - L_4^2} \angle\theta$$

and
$$r = \frac{L_1 L_4 - L_2 L_3}{L_2^2 - L_4^2}$$

Equation (5.7) represents a circle whose coordinates in complex β-plane are,

$-\dfrac{L_1 L_2 - L_3 L_4}{L_2^2 - L_4^2} \cos\theta$ is the horizontal component

and $-\dfrac{L_1 L_2 - L_3 L_4}{L_2^2 - L_4^2} \sin\theta$ is the vertical component, with the radius

$$r = \frac{L_1 L_4 - L_2 L_3}{L_2^2 - L_4^2} \quad (5.8)$$

In order to obtain the coordinates of the circle and its radius in the complex α-plane, we divide Eq. (5.4) by $(L_1^2 - L_3^2)\,|B|^2$ and hence, we get

$$\left|\frac{A}{B}\right|^2 + \frac{2(L_1 L_2 - L_3 L_4)}{L_1^2 - L_3^2}\left|\frac{A}{B}\right| \cos(\phi - \theta) + \frac{L_2^2 - L_4^2}{L_1^2 - L_3^2} = 0 \quad (5.9)$$

This equation is also transformed to the standard equation by adding to both sides of Eq. (5.9),

$\left[\dfrac{L_1 L_2 - L_3 L_4}{L_1^2 - L_3^2}\right]^2$ and transferring the term

$\dfrac{L_2^2 - L_4^2}{L_1^2 - L_3^2}$ on the right hand side. Thus we obtain

$$\left|\frac{A}{B}\right|^2 + \frac{2(L_1 L_2 - L_3 L_4)}{L_1^2 - L_3^2}\left|\frac{A}{B}\right| \cos(\phi - \theta) + \left[\frac{L_1 L_2 - L_3 L_4}{L_1^2 - L_3^2}\right]^2 = \left[\frac{L_1 L_2 - L_3 L_4}{L_1^2 - L_3^2}\right]^2 - \frac{L_2^2 - L_4^2}{L_1^2 - L_3^2}$$

i.e. $$\left|\frac{A}{B}\right|^2 + \frac{2\,(L_1 L_2 - L_3 L_4)}{L_1^2 - L_3^2}\left|\frac{A}{B}\right| \cos\,(\phi - \theta) + \left[\frac{L_1 L_2 - L_3 L_4}{L_1^2 - L_3^2}\right]^2$$

$$= \left[\frac{L_1 L_4 - L_2 L_3}{L_1^2 - L_3^2}\right]^2 \qquad (5.10)$$

From this equation, we obtain coordinates of the circle and its radius in the complex α-plane as follows,

$$C = -\frac{L_1 L_2 - L_3 L_4}{L_1^2 - L_3^2} \angle\theta$$

and hence its horizontal and vertical coordinates are

$$H = -\frac{L_1 L_2 - L_3 L_4}{L_1^2 - L_3^2} \cos\,\theta$$

$$V = -\frac{L_1 L_2 - L_3 L_4}{L_1^2 - L_3^2} \sin\,\theta$$

and radius is

$$r = \frac{L_1 L_4 - L_2 L_3}{L_1^2 - L_3^2}$$

5.2.2 Dual Input Phase Comparator

Here also we obtain similar equations as those for amplitude comparison scheme, except that the constants are different. Hence Eq. (5.2) for the phase comparator becomes

$$S_1 = L_1' \,|A| + L_2' \,|B|\,[\cos\,(\phi - \theta) + j\,\sin\,(\phi - \theta)]$$

$$S_2 = L_3' \,|A| + L_4' \,|B|\,[\cos\,(\phi - \theta) + j\,\sin\,(\phi - \theta)] \qquad (5.11)$$

The Eq. (5.11) can be expressed in terms of its magnitude and phase angle as shown,

$$S_1 = |S_1| \angle\alpha = |L_1' \,|A| + L_2' \,|B|\,[\cos\,(\phi - \theta) + j\,\sin\,(\phi - \theta)]| \angle\alpha$$

$$S_2 = |S_2| \angle\beta = |L_3' \,|A| + L_4' \,|B|\,[\cos\,(\phi - \theta) + j\,\sin\,(\phi - \theta)]| \angle\beta \qquad (5.12)$$

Hence the phase difference between signals S_1 and S_2 will be $\alpha - \beta$. As a cosine comparator, the phase difference between signal S_1 and S_2 should be $\pm$ 90° at threshold, i.e. $\alpha - \beta = \pm 90°$.

Thus $\tan\,(\alpha - \beta) = \pm\,\infty$,

i.e. $$\frac{\tan\alpha - \tan\beta}{1 + \tan\alpha\,.\,\tan\beta} = \pm\,\infty$$

i.e. $$1 + \tan\alpha\,.\,\tan\beta = 0$$

or
$$\tan \alpha = -\frac{1}{\tan \beta} \tag{5.13}$$

From Eq. (5.12), we get

$$\tan \alpha = \frac{L_2' |B| \sin(\phi - \theta)}{L_1' |A| + L_2' |B| \cos(\phi - \theta)}$$

and
$$\tan \beta = \frac{L_4' |B| \sin(\phi - \theta)}{L_3' |A| + L_4' |B| \cos(\phi - \theta)} \tag{5.14}$$

Substituting from Eq. (5.14) in Eq. (5.13), we get

$$\frac{L_2' |B| \sin(\phi - \theta)}{L_1' |A| + L_2' |B| \cos(\phi - \theta)} \times \frac{L_4' |B| \sin(\phi - \theta)}{L_3' |A| + L_4' |B| \cos(\phi - \theta)} = -1$$

i.e. $L_2' L_4' |B|^2 \sin^2(\phi - \theta) = -(L_1' L_3' |A|^2$

$+ L_1' L_4' |A||B| \cos(\phi - \theta) + L_2' L_3' |A||B| \cos(\phi - \theta)$

$+ L_2' L_4' |B|^2 \cos^2(\phi - \theta)) = 0$

i.e.
$$L_2' L_4' |B|^2 + L_1' L_3' |A|^2 + (L_1' L_4' + L_2' L_3') |A||B| \cos(\phi - \theta)) = 0 \tag{5.15}$$

Equation (5.15) is divided by $L_2' L_4' |A|^2$ to obtain the threshold characteristic in β-plane; thus we get

$$\left|\frac{B}{A}\right|^2 + \frac{(L_1' L_4' + L_2' L_3')}{L_2' L_4'} \left|\frac{B}{A}\right| \cos(\phi - \theta) + \frac{L_1' L_3'}{L_2' L_4'} = 0 \tag{5.16}$$

The Eq. (5.16) is arranged in the form of the equation for a circle by adding C^2, i.e.

$$\left[\frac{L_1' L_4' + L_2' L_3'}{2 L_2' L_4'}\right]^2$$

to both the sides of Eq. (5.16) and transferring the term $\frac{L_1' L_3'}{L_2' L_4'}$ to the right hand side.

Thus we get

$$\left|\frac{B}{A}\right|^2 + \frac{2(L_1' L_4' + L_2' L_3')}{2 L_2' L_4'} \left|\frac{B}{A}\right| \cos(\phi - \theta) + \left[\frac{L_1' L_4' + L_2' L_3'}{2 L_2' L_4'}\right]^2$$

$$= \left[\frac{L_1' L_4' + L_2' L_3'}{2 L_2' L_4'}\right]^2 - \frac{L_1' L_3'}{L_2' L_4'} = \left[\frac{L_1' L_4' - L_2' L_3'}{2 L_2' L_4'}\right]^2 \tag{5.17}$$

From Eq. (5.17), the coordinates of the centre and the radius of the circle in complex β-plane can be seen as follows

$$C = -\frac{L_1' L_4' + L_2' L_3'}{2L_2' L_4'} \angle\theta \text{ and } r = \frac{L_1' L_4' - L_2' L_3'}{2 L_2' L_4'}$$

In order to obtain the coordinates of the centre and radius of the circle in complex α-plane, we divide Eq. (5.15) by $L_1' L_3' | B |^2$ and get

$$\left|\frac{A}{B}\right|^2 + 2\frac{(L_1' L_4' + L_2' L_3')}{2L_1' L_3'} \left|\frac{A}{B}\right| \cos(\phi - \theta) + \frac{L_2' L_4'}{L_1' L_3'} = 0 \tag{5.18}$$

Again adding C^2, i.e.

$$\left[\frac{L_1' L_4' + L_2' L_3'}{2 L_1' L_3'}\right]^2$$

to both sides of Eq. (5.18) and transferring the term $L_2' L_4'/L_1' L_3'$ to the right hand side, we get

$$\left|\frac{A}{B}\right|^2 + 2\frac{(L_1' L_4' + L_2' L_3')}{2 L_1' L_3'} \left|\frac{A}{B}\right| \cos(\phi - \theta) + \left[\frac{L_1' L_4' + L_2' L_3'}{2 L_1' L_3'}\right]^2$$

$$= \left[\frac{L_1' L_4' + L_2' L_3'}{2 L_1' L_3'}\right]^2 - \frac{L_2' L_4'}{L_1' L_3'} = \left[\frac{L_1' L_4' - L_2' L_3'}{2 L_1' L_3'}\right]^2 \tag{5.19}$$

Thus from Eq. (5.19), we have the coordinates of the circle and its radius as follows;

$$C = -\frac{L_1' L_4' + L_2' L_3'}{2 L_1' L_3'} \angle\theta \text{ and } r = \frac{L_1' L_4' - L_2' L_3'}{2 L_1' L_3'}$$

5.3 RELAY CHARACTERISTICS BY COMPARISON OF CONSTANTS

In the previous section, the coordinates of centre of the circle and also its radius are determined both as an amplitude comparator as well as a phase comparator in the complex β-plane and complex α-plane. Using these generalized equations for threshold characteristics and by comparison of constants of similar equations, coordinates of the centre and radius of the circle are determined. We will now take up distance relaying schemes and also differential relaying scheme which is used for short line or feeder protection.

5.3.1 Differential Relaying Scheme

The unit protection scheme is probably the most effective and efficient protection scheme for the protection of short line, feeder and apparatus. The relay compares the magnitude or direction of current entering protected circuit with that of current leaving the protected circuit. For short lines, feeders or apparatus the magnitude or phase of the current leaving the component being protected will be the same as that of the current entering the component during normal steady state operation.

However, during an internal fault in the component, the current leaving the component will be different from the current entering the component. Any difference between these currents is an indication of internal fault. In the most simplified scheme shown in Fig. 5.3, there is an operating coil in which the differential current $I_1 - I_2$ flows. This difference is only finite if there is an internal fault in the component. Such scheme is known as differential relaying scheme. However, even during external short circuit, i.e. fault close to the component being protected, even though the primary current is the same in both the CTs connected on the two sides of the component (Fig. 5.3), the secondary current may differ because of different level of saturation of the CTs and hence even though there is no internal fault, still the CTs, secondary currents I_1 and I_2 may differ and thus a finite current $I_1 - I_2$ may flow in the operating coil thus giving a trip command. To avoid this problem, in addition to the operating coil, a restraining coil is also added to the relay. This relay is known as percentage differential relay. Here in the operating coil, current is $I_1 - I_2$ and in the restraining coil, mean through current flows (Fig. 5.4). Say operating coil has N_1 turns and restraining coil has N_2 turns. Then the relay operates, if the operating quantity exceeds the restraining quantity.

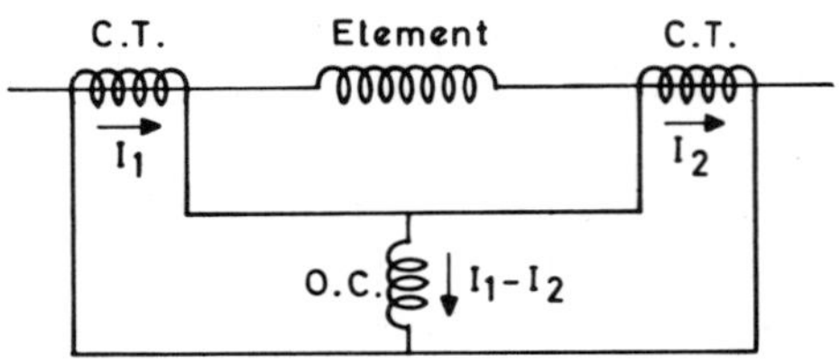

Fig. 5.3

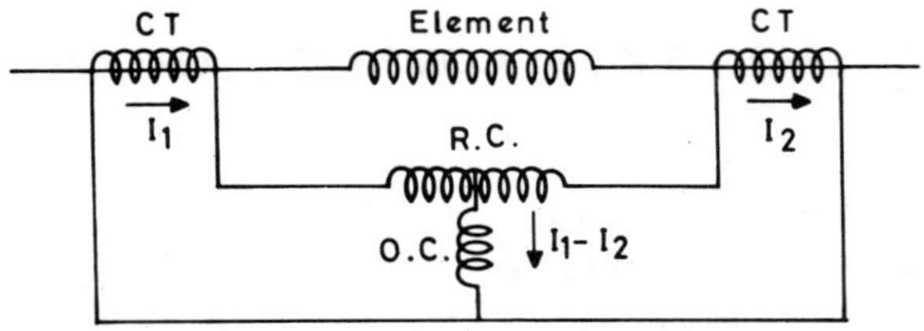

Fig. 5.4 Percentage differential relay

Hence as an electromechanical relay, we have for tripping

$$N_1 \ (I_1 - I_2) > \left(\frac{N_2}{2} I_1 + \frac{N_2}{2} I_2\right)$$

i.e.

$$N_1 \ (I_1 - I_2) > \frac{N_2}{2} (I_1 + I_2)$$

or

$$N_1 \ (I_1 - I_2) > N_2 \left(\frac{I_1 + I_2}{2}\right)$$

or
$$|I_1 - I_2| > \frac{N_2}{N_1}\left|\frac{I_1 + I_2}{2}\right|$$

i.e.
$$|I_1 - I_2| > S\left|\frac{I_1 + I_2}{2}\right|$$

where
$$S = N_2/N_1$$

Normally $N_1 >> N_2$ and hence, S is a fraction. Therefore, we have for tripping

$$|I_1 - I_2| > S\left|\frac{I_1 + I_2}{2}\right|$$

i.e. difference current $(I_1–I_2)$ exceeds S times the mean through current $(I_1 + I_2)/2$.

S is a fraction. In static relay, S is a bias and for relay operation

$$|I_1 - I_2| > S\left|\frac{I_1 + I_2}{2}\right| \tag{5.20}$$

For comparison of constants, let us take Eq. (5.2)

Operating quantity for a differential relay = $S_1 = |I_1 - I_2|$

$$= |[L_1 |A| + L_2 |B| [\cos(\phi - \theta) + j\sin(\phi - \theta)]| \tag{5.21}$$

Now for differential relaying scheme,

$$A = I_1 \text{ and } B = I_2 \text{ and } \theta = 0$$

Thus we have from Eq. (5.21), with above substitutions,

$$S_1 = |I_1 - I_2| = |[L_1 |I_1| + L_2 |I_2| (\cos\phi + j\sin\phi)]|$$

and restraining quantity for a differential relay using Eq. (5.2)

$$S_2 = \frac{S\,|I_1 + I_2|}{2} = L_3 |I_1| + L_4 |I_2| (\cos\phi + j\sin\phi) \tag{5.22}$$

Comparing the coefficients on both sides in Eq. (5.22), we get

$$L_1 = 1 = -L_2$$
$$L_3 = S/2 = L_4$$

With the help of Eq. (5.8), the coordinates of the centre and radius of the circle in complex β-plane are obtained as

$$r = \frac{L_1 L_4 - L_2 L_3}{L_2^2 - L_4^2} = \frac{S/2 + S/2}{1 - (S/2)^2} = \frac{S}{1 - \frac{S^2}{4}}$$

and
$$C = -\frac{L_1 L_2 - L_3 L_4}{L_2^2 - L_4^2}\angle\theta = \frac{1 + S^2/4}{1 - \frac{S^2}{4}}\angle 0$$

The relay characteristic is shown in Fig. 5.5, which is a circle on the horizontal axis.

Plane impedance relay. Operating quantity, as an amplitude comparator, in β-plane = $I Z_R$ and the restraining quantity = V. Comparing the above with the Eq. (5.2), which is the general equation of the relay at threshold as an amplitude comparator in β– plane, we get

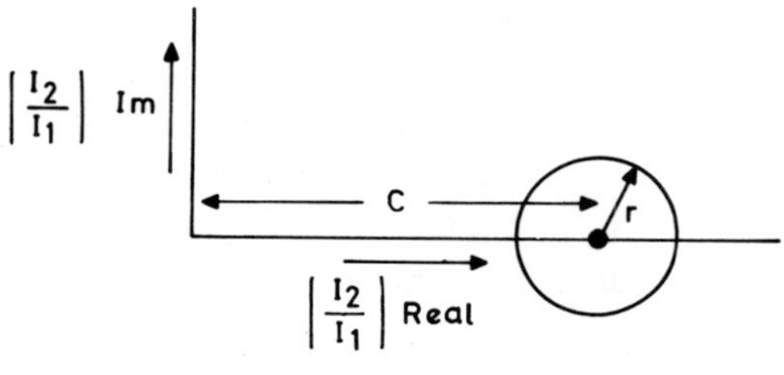

Fig. 5.5

$$I\,Z_R = L_1\,|A| + L_2\,|B|\,(\cos(\phi - \theta) + j\sin(\phi\ \theta))$$

$$V = L_3\,|A| + L_4\,|B|\,(\cos(\phi - \theta) + j\sin(\phi - \theta)) \quad (5.23)$$

Here $A = I$ and $B = V$ and again $\theta = 0$. With these substitutions, Eq. (5.23) becomes,

$$I\,Z_R = L_1\,|I| + L_2\,|V|\,(\cos\phi + j\sin\theta)$$

$$V = L_3\,|I| + L_4\,|V|\,(\cos\phi + j\sin\phi)$$

From the above equation, we get

$$L_1 = Z_R \quad L_2 = 0$$

$$L_3 = 0 \quad L_4 = 1$$

In order determine the coordinates of the centre and the radius of circle for an amplitude comparator in the complex β-plane, the above constants are substituted in Eq. (5.8), and we get

i.e.
$$r = \frac{L_1\,L_4 - L_2L_3}{L_2^2 - L_4^2} = \frac{Z_R}{1} = Z_R$$

and
$$C = -\frac{L_1\,L_2 - L_3\,L_4}{L_2^2 - L_4^2} = 0$$

Hence the same result is obtained for this relay also. The threshold characteristic is a circle of radius Z_R with the centre at the origin.

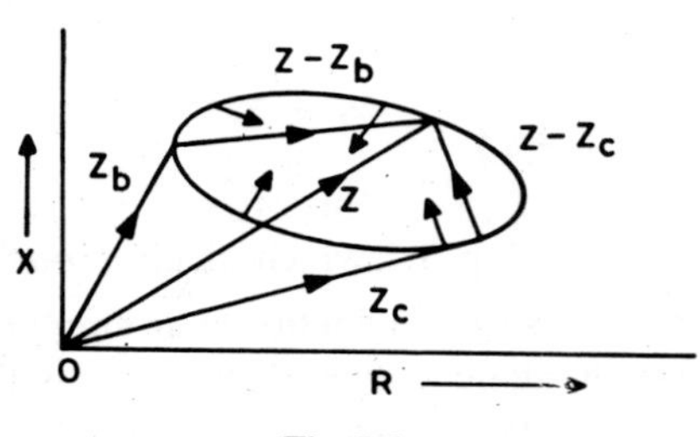

Fig. 5.6

Angle Impedance relay. Similarly, for angle impedance relay, the signals in the complex β-plane as an amplitude comparator with substitution $A = I$, $B = V$ and $\theta = 0$, will be,

$$2I\,Z_R - V = L_1\,|I| + L_2\,|V|\,(\cos\phi + j\sin\phi)$$

$$V = L_3\,|I| + L_4\,|V|\,(\cos\phi + j\sin\phi)$$

Hence

$$L_1 = 2Z_R \quad L_2 = -1$$

$$L_3 = 0 \quad L_4 = 1$$

$$C = -\frac{L_1 L_2 - L_3 L_4}{L_2^2 - L_4^2} = \frac{2Z_R}{0} = \infty$$

$$r = \frac{L_1 L_4 - L_2 L_3}{L_2^2 - L_4^2} = \frac{2Z_R}{0} = \infty$$

The threshold characteristic is a straight line, as obtained earlier.

Angle admittance (MHO's) relay. For angle admittance, i.e. MHO's relay, the signals in β-plane as an amplitude comparator with the same substitution, i.e. $A = I$, $B = V$ and $\theta = 0$, will be,

$$I\,Z_R = L_1\,|I| + L_2\,|V|\,(\cos\phi + j\sin\phi)$$

$$-I\,Z_R + 2V = L_3\,|I| + L_4\,|V|\,(\cos\phi + j\sin\phi)$$

Comparing coefficients,

$$L_1 = Z_R \quad L_2 = 0$$

$$L_3 = -Z_R \quad L_4 = 2$$

Thus

$$C = -\frac{L_1 L_2 - L_3 L_4}{L_2^2 - L_4^2} = \frac{2Z_R}{4} = \frac{Z_R}{2}$$

$$r = \frac{L_1 L_4 - L_2 L_3}{L_2^2 - L_4^2} = \frac{2Z_R}{4} = \frac{Z_R}{2}$$

Hence, the threshold characteristic is the same as derived earlier, i.e. it is a circle of diameter Z_R and passing through the origin. The same result can also be derived as a phase comparator.

5.4 MULTI-INPUT COMPARATOR

The multi-input comparator means that the number of signals given to the relay is more than two. Actually speaking with the help of dual input comparator, only circular or straight line characteristics can be obtained. In case we want other types of threshold characteristics such as conic or quadrilateral, multi-input comparator is necessary. In the case of multi-input comparator, there is no duality between phase and amplitude scheme which exists only in the case of dual input comparator.

Multi-input comparator can broadly be divided into two categories, viz. multi-input amplitude comparator and multi-input phase comparator. With the help of multi-input amplitude comparator, conic—such as elliptical or hyperbolic—characteristics are obtained while with the help of multi-input phase comparator, quadrilateral characteristics are obtained.

5.4.1 Multi-input Amplitude Comparator

Rectifier bridge relays are normally used for multi-input amplitude comparator. Here only amplitudes of input signals are compared and based upon the comparison, trip signal is given.

There are two varieties of rectifier bridge amplitude comparator. In one scheme, the relay comprises a number of coils. Some coils are connected to give operating torque and others to give restraining torque. Each coil is energized by fully rectified signals. Hence for tripping.

$$|S_1| + |S_2| + \ldots > |S_3| + |S_4| + \ldots.$$

This comparator is called linear comparator because here net operating or restraining torque is directly related with the input signals. Here coils giving signals S_1 and S_2 are connected to provide operating torque and coils giving signals S_3 and S_4 are connected to provide restraining torque.

In the other form of amplitude comparison scheme, there is only one coil in which all the operating as well as the restraining signals are given after rectification with the help of full wave rectifier bridge. Again, the relay operates when operating torque exceeds the restraining torque, i.e.

$$|S_1| + |S_2| + \ldots > |S_3| + |S_4| + \ldots$$

Here again S_l and S_2 are connected in operate mode and S_3 and S_4 are connected in restrain mode. This comparator is non-linear because here output current is not a function of input current.

We know that the power system characteristics indicating normal, faulted or other operating conditions are defined as a complex ratio of the voltage V_R and the current I_R at the relay location. Since the relay is required to respond to power system conditions, the input signals to the relay must be a function of V_R and I_R. In practice they are realized through a linear mixing circuit or with the use of operational computer elements. Thus, in general, the input to the multi-input comparator having say n input signals can be expressed as,

$$S_1 = K_1 V_R + K_2 I_R$$

$$S_2 = K_3 V_R + K_4 I_R$$

$$S_3 = K_5 V_R + K_6 I_R$$

$$S_n = K_{2n-1} V_R + K_{2n} I_R \tag{5.24}$$

where K_1 ...... K_{2n-1} are complex multipliers realizable through practical logic circuit.

As an amplitude comparator, the magnitude (i.e. amplitude) of the algebraic sum of signals connected in operate mode and restrain mode must be zero, i.e.

$$\pm |S_1| \pm |S_2| \pm |S_3| \pm .... \pm |S_n| = 0 \qquad (5.25)$$

Here plus sign indicates the signals connected in operate mode and minus sign indicates the signals connected in restrain mode. Substituting from Eq. (5.24) in Eq. (5.25), we get

$$\pm |K_1 V_R + K_2 I_R| \pm |K_3 V_R + K_4 I_R| \pm |K_5 V_R + K_6 I_R| \pm ..... \pm$$
$$\pm |K_{2n-1} V_R + K_{2n} I_R| = 0 \qquad (5.26)$$

Dividing Eq. (5.26) by I_R and substituting $V_R/I_R = Z$ (i.e. impedance up to point of fault), we get

$$\pm |K_1 Z + K_2| \pm |K_3 Z + K_4| \pm |K_5 Z + K_6| \pm ..... \pm$$
$$\pm |K_{2n-1} Z + K_{2n}| = 0$$

i.e. $$|K_1| \left| Z + \frac{K_2}{K_1} \right| \pm K_3 \left| Z + \frac{K_4}{K_3} \right| \pm K_5 \left| Z + \frac{K_6}{K_5} \right| \pm .....$$

$$\pm K_{2n-1} \left| Z + \frac{K_{2n}}{K_{2n-1}} \right| = 0 \qquad (5.27)$$

Let $$\frac{K_2}{K_1} = -Z_a, \; \frac{K_4}{K_3} = -Z_b, \; \frac{K_6}{K_5} = -Z_c$$

and $$\frac{K_{2n}}{K_{2n-1}} = -Z_n$$

Substituting these relations in Eq. (5.27), we get

$$\pm K_1 |Z - Z_a| \pm K_3 |Z - Z_b| \pm K_5 |Z - Z_c| \pm ....\pm$$
$$\pm K_{2n-1} |Z - Z_n| = 0 \qquad (5.28)$$

Points Z_A, Z_B, Z_C .... Z_N are extremities of the vectors Z_a, Z_b, Z_c .... Z_n respectively representing, on the complex β-plane (i.e. complex Z-plane), system conditions under which the corresponding input signals vanish to zero and every term in Eq. (5.28) represents the distance of a moving point Z (which is actually the line impedance up to the point of fault) from the fixed points Z_A, Z_B, Z_C .... Z_N multiplied by constants. Thus at the threshold condition, for linear multi-input amplitude comparator, the sum of distances corresponding to inputs connected in positive (i.e. operate mode) manner is equal to the sum of distances corresponding to inputs connected in the negative (i.e. restrain mode) manner. Hence, in the complex Z-plane, the locus of Z which is the impedance up to the point of fault ($Z = (V_R / I_R)$) is the relay threshold characteristic.

Elliptical characteristic. This is a special type of conic characteristic and it is used as a third measuring element to avoid the possibility of relay operation during power swing. During power swing caused by severe fault, the relay sees a fictitious impedance and if this impedance is less than relay setting, the relay operates. Only three input signals are required to obtain elliptical characteristics. Thus using Eq. (5.24).

$$S_1 = K_1 V_R + K_2 I_R$$
$$S_2 = K_3 V_R + K_4 I_R$$
$$S_3 = K_5 V_R + K_6 I_R$$

Here K_1 is zero, thus

$$S_1 = K_2 I_R$$
$$S_2 = K_3 V_R + K_4 I_R$$
$$S_3 = K_5 V_R + K_6 I_R \tag{5.29}$$

Dividing Eq. (5.29) by I_R, substituting $\frac{V_R}{I_R} = Z$ and also substituting

$$\frac{K_4}{K_3} = -Z_b, \quad \frac{K_6}{K_5} = -Z_c,$$

we get

$$+|S_1| - |S_2| - |S_3| = 0$$
$$|K_2| - |K_3||Z - Z_b| - |K_5||Z - Z_c| = 0 \tag{5.30}$$

Here signals S_1 is connected in operate mode and signals S_2 and S_3 in restrain mode. Choosing constants $K_3 = K_5$ and rearranging, the Eq. (5.30) takes the following form,

$$|Z - Z_b| + |Z - Z_c| = \frac{K_2}{K_3} \tag{5.31}$$

Equation (5.31) represents the locus of point Z (i.e. fault impedance which is variable), sum of whose distances from two fixed points, viz. Z_B and Z_C, are constant. This locus is consequently an ellipse with Z_B and Z_C as foci and the major axis which is aligned along $\overline{Z_B Z_C}$ is equal to $|K_2/K_3|$. This is shown in Fig. 5.6. A set of ellipses as shown in the figure are obtained by varying K_2 and keeping K_3 to K_6 constant. Here the inner part of the ellipse is in operate zone.

Hyperbolic characteristic. Here, again just as in the case of elliptic characteristic, three signals are used. However, signals S_1 and S_2 are connected in operate mode and only S_3 is connected in restrain mode. Hence, Eq. (5.30) becomes

$$|K_2| + |K_3||Z - Z_b| - |K_5||Z - Z_c| = 0$$

Choosing again $K_3 = K_5$, the final equation will take the following form,

$$|Z - Z_c| - |Z - Z_b| = \frac{K_2}{K_3} \tag{5.32}$$

Equation (5.32) represents locus of point Z, the difference of whose distances from two fixed points, viz. Z_B and Z_C, is constant. Thus the locus is consequently a hyperbola with Z_B and Z_C as foci (Fig. 5.7). The operate zone is to the left of the characteristic. By varying K_2 and keeping K_3 to K_6 constant, a set of hyperbolas is obtained. For upper limit when $|K_2/K_3| = \overline{Z_B Z_C}$, the characteristic is a straight line radiating from Z_B to infinity along $\overline{Z_B Z_C}$ and for lower limit, where $|K_2/K_3| = 0$, the characteristic becomes a straight line which is the perpendicular bisector of $\overline{Z_B Z_C}$.

In practice, the elliptical characteristic is obtained by a multi-input amplitude comparator having three signals.

$$\begin{aligned} S_1 &= V - I Z_R \\ S_2 &= V - I K Z_R \\ S_3 &= I (Z_R + K Z_R) \end{aligned} \tag{5.33}$$

Here Z_R and $K Z_R$ are replica impedance with K as a scalar. I is the line current obtained through CT and V is the bus voltage obtained through PT. Substituting $V = I Z$, where Z is the impedance up to the point of fault, Eq. (5.33) becomes

$$\begin{aligned} S_1 &= I Z - I Z_R \\ S_2 &= I Z - I K Z_R \\ S_3 &= I (Z_R + K Z_R) \end{aligned} \tag{5.34}$$

Here S_1 and S_2 provide restraining signals and S_3 operating signal. Thus, for tripping, Eq. (5.34) will be

$$|S_1| + |S_2| < |S_3|$$

i.e. $$|I Z - I Z_R| + |I Z - I K Z_R| < I \, |Z_R + K Z_R|$$

Dividing the above equation by the common current I, we get

$$|Z - Z_R| + |Z - K Z_R| < |Z_R + K Z_R| \tag{5.35}$$

Equation (5.35) represents an ellipse passing through the origin. In order to obtain offset elliptical characteristic which is desired as a third zone starting element, the signals will be as follows:

$$\begin{aligned} S_1 &= V - I Z_R \\ S_2 &= V \\ S_3 &= I (Z_R + 2 K Z_R) \end{aligned}$$

The final equation for the offset elliptical characteristic relay for tripping is

$$|S_1| + |S_2| < |S_3|$$

$$|Z - Z_R| + |Z| < |Z_R + 2 K Z_R| \tag{5.36}$$

Similarly, for hyperbolic characteristic passing through the origin, signal S_1 is in restrain mode and signals S_2 and S_3 are in operate mode. Thus for tripping,

$$|S_1| - |S_2| < |S_3|$$

$$|V - I Z_R| - |V - I K Z_R| < I \, |Z_R + K Z_R|$$

i.e. $$|Z - Z_R| - |Z - K Z_R| < |Z_R + K Z_R| \tag{5.37}$$

5.4.2 Multi-Input Phase Comparator

With the help of multi-input phase comparator, quadrilateral characteristic is obtained. This is the best characteristic as it encloses the fault area compactly (Fig. 5.8). However, there is no duality between the multi-input amplitude and phase comparators; the multi-input phase comparator works on the principle of duration of coincidence of all the signals. Let us take the example of three-input phase

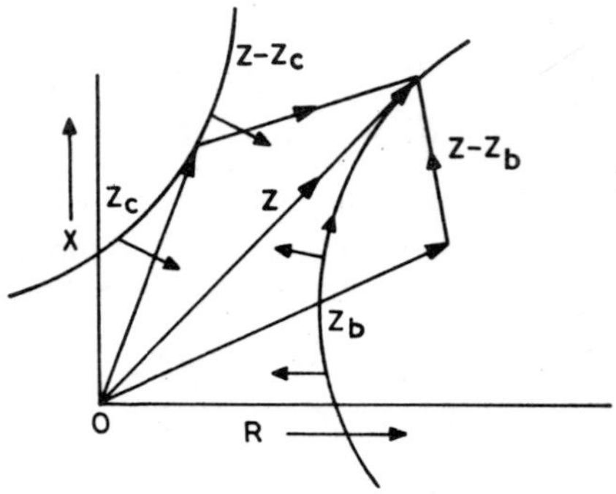

Fig. 5.7

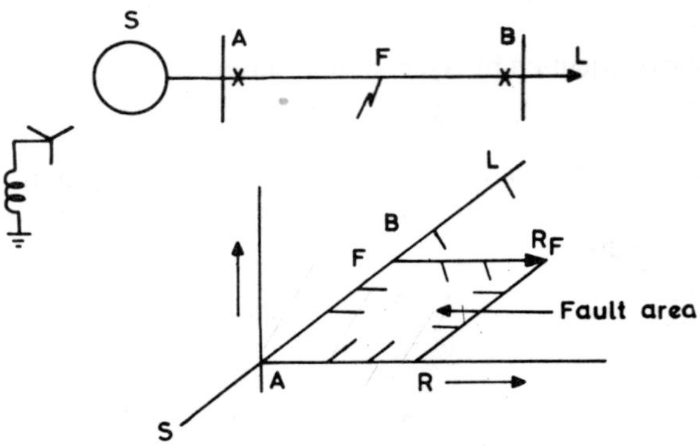

Fig. 5.8

comparator shown in Fig. 5.9. The relay measures the duration of coincidence of the three input signals and gives the tripping command if this duration is more than 90°. If this criterion is satisfied, then automatically, the phase angle between any two input signals will be less than 90°. Therefore, a multi-input phase comparator is in fact equal to a set of two-input comparator whose outputs are all connected to an AND logic circuit. The characteristic of the individual two-input comparator defines the boundaries of multi-input phase comparator characteristic.

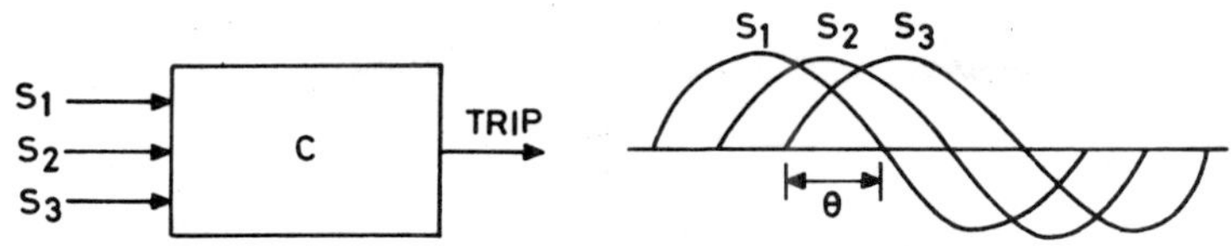

Fig. 5.9

In the simplest manner, multi-input phase comparator with the following four signals (Fig. 5.10) may be used to obtain the quadrilateral characteristic

$$S_1 = I\,Z_R - V$$
$$S_2 = V$$
$$S_3 = I\,R_R$$
$$S_4 = I\,X_R$$

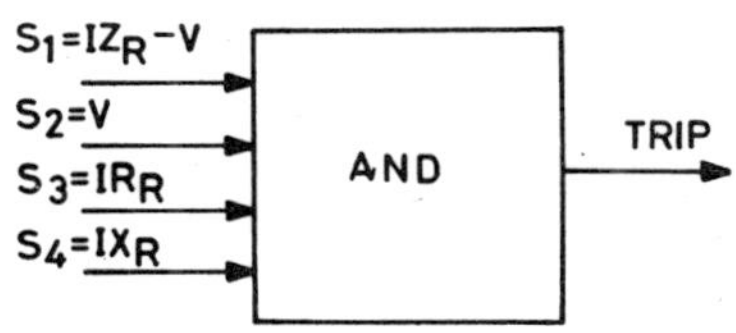

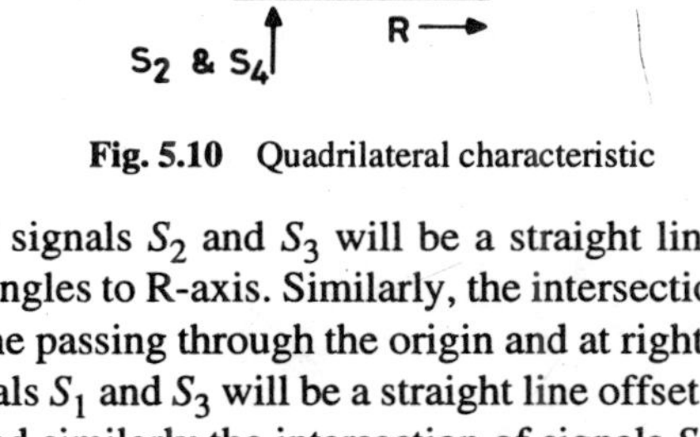

Fig. 5.10 Quadrilateral characteristic

The intersection of signals S_2 and S_3 will be a straight line passing through the origin and at right angles to R-axis. Similarly, the intersection of signals S_2 and S_4 will be a straight line passing through the origin and at right angles to X-axis. The intersection of signals S_1 and S_3 will be a straight line offset from the origin, i.e. at right angle to R_R and similarly the intersection of signals S_1 and S_4 will also be a straight line offset from the origin and at right angles to X_R. The tripping occurs if all the above criteria are simultaneously satisfied. In other words, if all the four signals are given to the relay, the resulting threshold characteristic will be a quadrilateral. But in order that the signals S_1 and S_2 do not interact to produce MHO's characteristic, they should be applied in the form of pulses. Several types of quadrilateral characteristic can be obtained by modifying the above signals. Even with the help of restricted reactance relay and restricted directional relay and giving their output to an AND logic circuit, a quadrilateral characteristic determined by the following relations can be obtained:

$$S_1 = I\,Z_R - V$$
$$S_2 = I\,Z_R$$
$$S_3 = I\,Z_R$$
$$S_4 = V$$

Since signals S_2 and S_3 are the same, only three signals S_1, S_2 and S_4 are sufficient to produce quadrilateral characteristic as shown in Fig. 5.11.

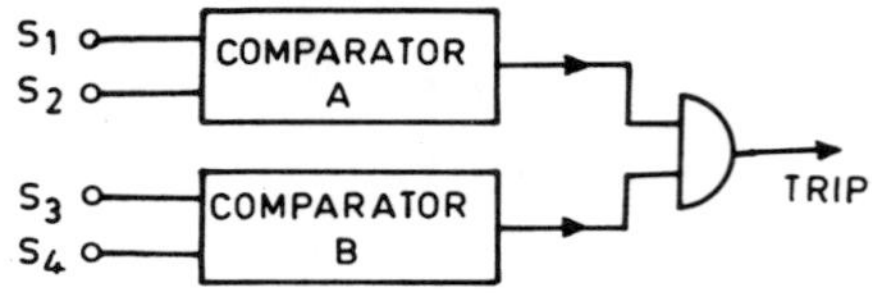

Multi-comparator Relay

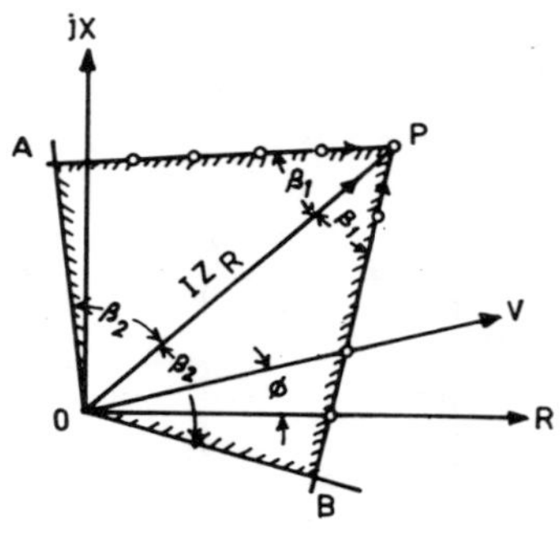

Normal Characteristics

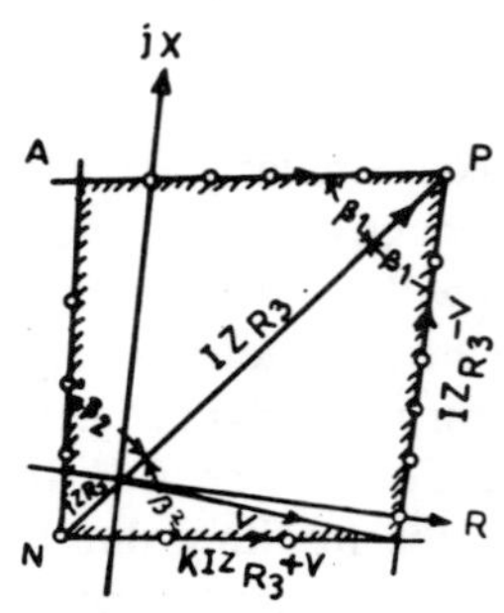

Fig. 5.11 Starting characteristics

5.5 PILOT RELAYING SCHEME

Pilot relaying schemes used are of three types:

(i) Wire pilot scheme
(ii) Carrier current pilot scheme
(iii) Microwave pilot scheme.

Actually, the term pilot means that there exists a communication channel of any of the three types as mentioned above between the two ends of the transmission over which information may be exchanged.

The wire pilot scheme consists of a two-wire circuit similar to the telephone line, either overhead wire or underground cable. Frequently, these are rented from the telephone department. In the case of carrier current pilot, a low power, low voltage, high frequency (50–500 kHz) signal is transmitted on the same conductor of the transmission line; usually ground forms the return circuit. However, in the case of microwave pilot, an ultra high frequency signal in the range of 900 to 6000 MHz is transmitted from one end of the transmission line to the other end through the medium of space by erecting line of sight antenna at the two ends.

5.5.1 Wire Pilot Scheme

Wire pilot scheme is very similar to percentage differential relaying scheme used for apparatus protection. Due to economic reasons, it is used only for short transmission line not exceeding 20 km. Because of its inherent limitations, d.c. wire pilot scheme is not very popular. Normally, a.c. wire pilot scheme is used. Main reasons of the popularity of a.c. wire pilot schemes are: (i) use of transformer in a.c. system which reduces the magnitude of the current that flows in the pilot circuit to a very low value and (ii) the use of only two wire pilot. This may be achieved either by phase sequence filters connected at both ends of the line which convert the three phase current and ground current to single phase current, or by the use of mixing transformers at both the ends which convert the three phase quantity to equivalent single phase quantity for all types of faults. Wire pilot scheme has at both of its ends protective relays having operating coil and restraining coil. Wire pilot schemes may be classified into circulating current type and opposed voltage type.

Circulating current type a.c. wire pilot scheme is quite similar to percentage differential scheme used for apparatus protection. In this scheme, as shown in Fig. 5.12, the output currents I_1 and I_2 of CTs connected at the two-ends of the line are equal if there is no internal fault in the line. This current circulates in the wire pilot and there is no current flowing in the operating coil. However, if there is a fault in the line, the difference current flows in the operating coil and hence if the torque due to the current in the operating coil exceeds the restraining torque due mean through current in the restraining coil, the relay issues trip command. In the opposed voltage type, because of reversing the connection, normally there is no current flowing in the wire pilot and hence no current flows in the operating coil. However, if there is a fault in the line, the difference current flows in the wire pilot and thus current flows in the operating coil and hence relay issues trip signal (Fig. 5.13).

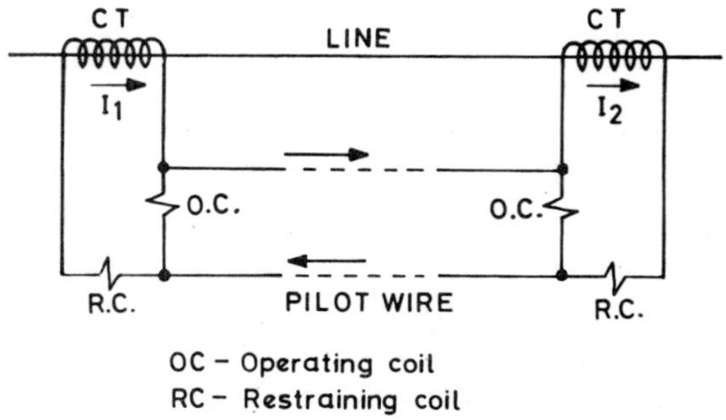

Fig. 5.12 Circulating current type

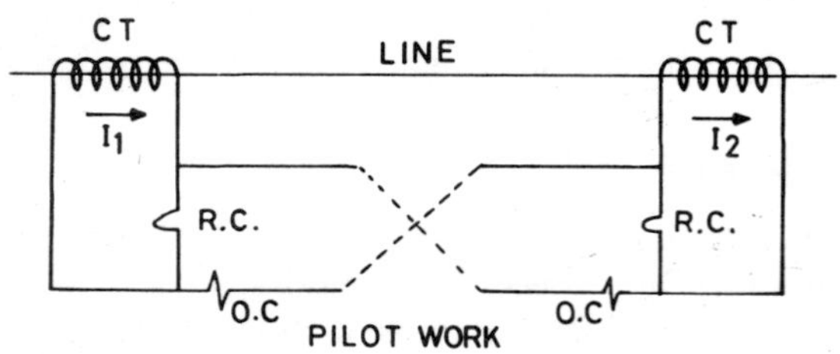

Fig. 5.13 Opposed voltage type

Short circuit and oen circuit has opposite effects on circulating current type and opposed voltage types of wire pilot scheme. While the short circuit in the wire pilot blocks tripping in the circulating current type, it causes tripping in the opposed voltage type. Similarly, while the open circuit in the wire pilot causes tripping in the circulating current type, it blocks tripping in the opposed voltage type. Both manual and automatic equipments are used for the supervision of wire pilot.

5.5.2 Carrier Current Pilot Scheme

For long lines, the carrier current pilot scheme is used even though the terminal equipments are expensive and complicated than those for wire pilot scheme. However, the cost component is not very effective because, in addition to relaying, the carrier is used also for the purpose of communication. Moreover, in the carrier current scheme there is no quantitative comparison between the currents which is done in the case of the wire pilot scheme. Instead, a simplified signal such as carrier is ON or OFF is transmitted, and hence signal attenuation does not affect very much the carrier transmission. Fig. 5.14 is the block diagram representation of carrier current scheme. As shown in the figure, at each end of the line there are transmitter-receiver unit, coupling capacitor and line trap. The carrier signal is generated by the transmitter, consisting of master oscillator and power amplifier unit with an output of 15–20 W at a frequency 50–500 kHz. This frequency range is chosen

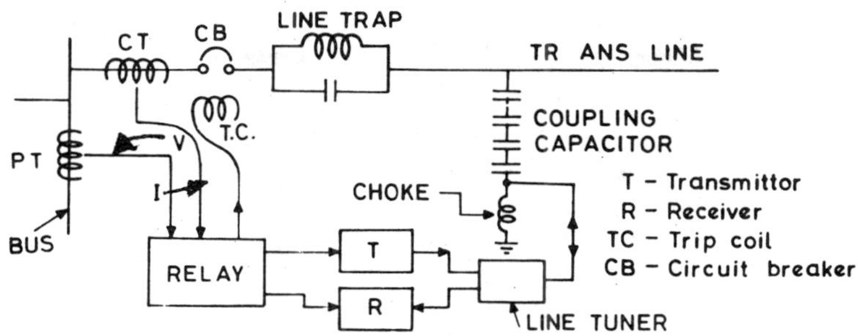

Fig. 5.14

because below 50 kHz the size and cost of terminal equipment is excessive and above 500 kHz, the signal attenuation is too high. Carrier current scheme is only possible in the case of overhead line and not in the case of underground cable because of the capacitance of the cable which attenuates the carrier signal to a very low value. The carrier signal is injected into the power line through coupling capacitor and is prevented from going outside the protected zone by the line trap, which is a parallel resonant circuit tuned to carrier frequency as shown in Fig. 5.14. The coupling capacitor consists of porcelain-clad, oil-filled stack of capaci-tors connected in series to withstand high voltage transmission line and is grounded through an inductance. The rating of inductance is normally 100 mH and that of capacitance stack 0.001 μF. The inductive coil offers a very high impedance to the carrier signal and low impedance to the normal supply of 50 Hz while coupling capacitor offers a very low impedance to the carrier signal and very high impedance to the normal 50 Hz supply. Hence, the carrier transmitter and receiver unit is effectively insulated from transmission line and grounded at 50 Hz while it is connected to transmission line and insulated from the ground at the carrier frequency. The line trap which consists of parallel combination of inductance and capacitance, is tuned to carrier frequency and connected in series at each end of the transmission line. By providing line trap the carrier is confined to its own zone, i.e. line only, and also the disturbances such as faults etc. outside the protected line, do not affect the carrier. The carrier may be injected into only one line with ground forming the return circuit or it may be injected between one line and another line which provides the return path. The single conductor scheme with ground providing return path is preferred because it is economical even though there is higher attenuation, higher interference level and stronger coupling. The two conductor system, though technically better is certainly more expensive because this needs two sets of coupling capacitors and two sets of line traps, one with each line.

The carrier current scheme is of two types viz. (a) blocking carrier scheme and (b) interdependent carrier scheme. In the blocking carrier scheme, normally there is no carrier; when fault takes place, as sensed by fault detector, the carrier starts. However, if the fault is internal as sensed by directional elements, the carrier stops and there is tripping. The presence of carrier blocks tripping of relays. However, for external fault, only one of the directional relays will stop the carrier while the other directional relay will maintain the carrier and there is no tripping. This is known as directional comparison scheme. Here in addition to usual carrier equipments, there is also a fault detector and a directional relay. Normally, there is no carrier; if fault takes place anywhere, i.e. internal or external, the fault detector relay starts the carrier. However, if fault is internal as sensed by the directional relays, which only operate if fault current flows away from the bus, the carrier stops and the relay trips. In other words, both the directional relays must stop the carrier. If any of the directional relays does not stop the carrier, say for external fault, the carrier appears in the line and the tripping is blocked.

In the case of carrier tripping known as interdependent tripping or intertripping (or transferred tripping), the presence of carrier gives trip signal while in the case of carrier blocking scheme as discussed in the previous section, the presence of carrier blocks tripping. Here, after the occurrence of fault, the zone one unit of the relay at the end nearest to the fault not only causes local tripping but also sends carrier to the other bus at the other end of the protected line. The relay at this bus after getting carrier signal causes immediate tripping even though the fault may be outside its zone one reach. An alternative to carrier intertripping, is carrier acceleration where after the receipt of carrier by the relay, the zone one unit is automatically extended to zone two unit and thus fault in the zone two unit of this relay is also cleared rapidly. Interdependent carrier scheme is shown in Fig. 5.15 (a). and carrier acceleration scheme is shown in Fig. 5.15 (b). In the carrier acceleration scheme, the zone two measuring unit is not necessary because after the receipt of carrier by the relay, the reach of zone one measuring unit is extended to include zone two measuring unit as well. Here, after the occurrence of fault, the relay close to fault not only gives trip command but also starts the carrier. The relay at the other end, after receiving the carrier, extends the reach of zone one measuring element to include zone two measuring element as well so that the fault in zone two is cleared quickly along with zone one measuring element. In the case of intertripping or interdependent tripping, the receipt of carrier causes immediate tripping. These schemes operate due to directional comparison.

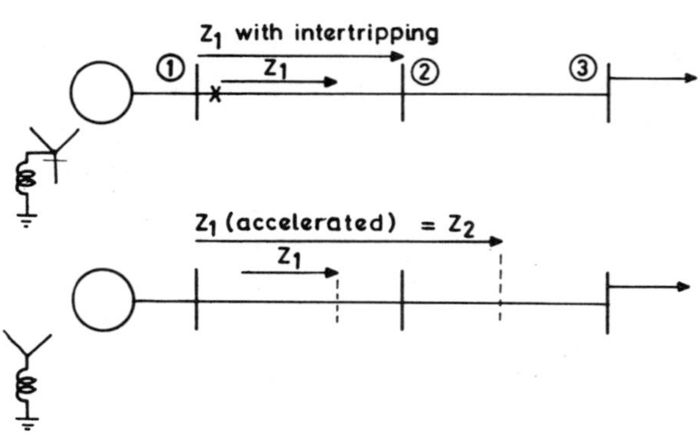

Fig. 5.15 **(a)** Carrier intertripping **(b)** Carrier acceleration

In the next scheme, the phase relation between current entering the circuit at one end and current leaving the circuit at the other end, provides criterion for relay operation. In this scheme current magnitude is not compared. Phase relaying scheme provides primary protection and is quite similar to the a.c. wire pilot relaying scheme. Here again with the help of appropriate logic circuit, single phase equivalent of three phase quantity is obtained. In this way, with the help of 3 CTs connected to the 3 phase transmission line, three line currents of the three phase system are monitored and then they are combined into a single equivalent current of appropriate form such as $I_1 - N I_2$ where N may be 4 or 5. This current is applied to a modulator which is associated with a carrier frequency oscillator. Therefore, if a fault occurs, carrier current at a very high frequency is produced and it is transmitted to the other end by injecting this carrier into the power line through coupling capacitor; normally ground forms the return circuit. With the help of line trap, the carrier signal is confined to its own zone, i.e. within the protected line. It is clear from Fig. 5.16 that for an external fault at any point B, the output voltage

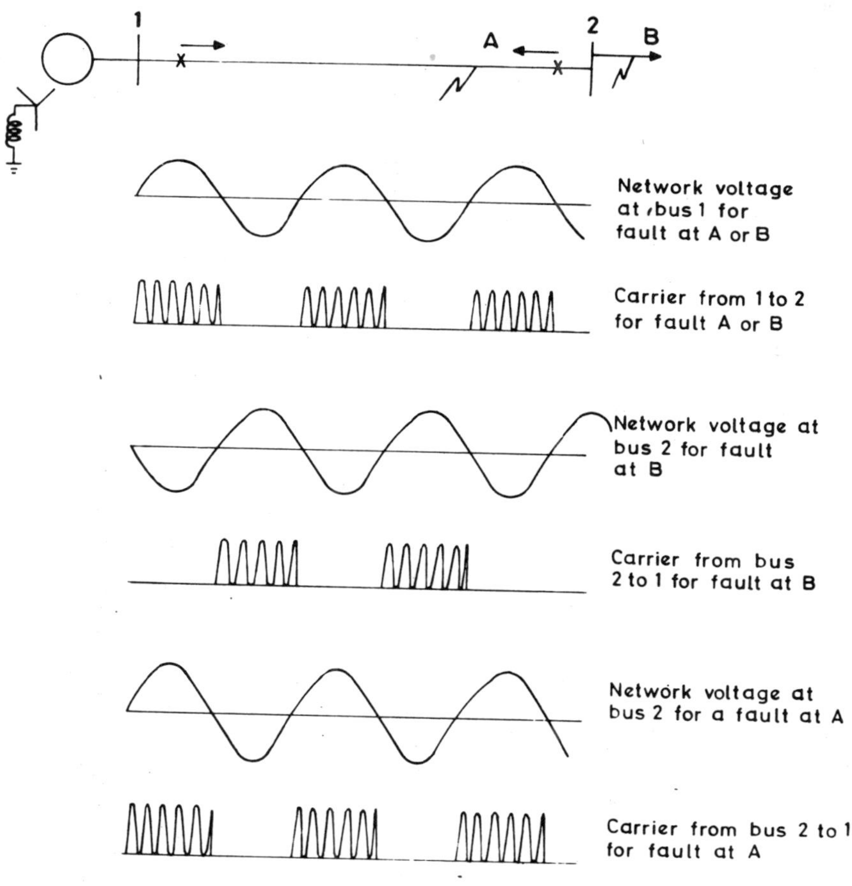

Fig. 5.16

at the buses 1 and 2 are out of phase by 180° as CTs at the two ends are connected in the reverse way. This voltage is applied to the transmitter which only transmits the carrier during the period when the voltage wave is positive. Therefore in this case, there is always a carrier and thus there is no relay operation because, being a blocking carrier, the presence of carrier will only block the relay operation. But when an internal fault say at any point A takes place, then the voltages at both the buses 1 and 2 become in phase. In this case as the carrier is only transmitted during positive half cycle of the voltage wave and since the two voltage are in phase, it is natural that there is carrier transmitted from both the ends i.e. both the buses during the same period and hence there is carrier for half cycle when both the voltages are positive and there is no carrier during next half cycle when both the voltages are negative. In this way, there is carrier only for half cycle and no carrier signal for next half cycle i.e. for 180°. If there is no carrier signal, naturally there will be relay operation which will cause tripping. From this we conclude that for external fault there is always a carrier but for internal fault, there is a carrier for half cycle and then there is no carrier for other half cycle which will cause relay tripping as absence of carrier means an internal fault and thus relay operation. In other words, the phase interval between carrier blocks is 180° for internal fault, i.e. there is a carrier for half the cycle and then there is no carrier for the other half cycle. For external fault, there is no interval between carrier blocks, i.e. zero interval between carrier blocks, in other words, there is always a carrier. However, in practice, 180° interval between carrier blocks for tripping during internal fault is reduced due to (i) phase angle displacement between the sources at both the ends and (ii) through normal load current which is added to fault current at one end and subtracted from the fault current at the other end. On the other hand, zero degree interval between carrier blocks during external fault for blocking the relay operation is increased considerably due to (i) carrier signal propagation time constant (ii) the response time of the carrier band pass filter and (iii) charging of the line, i.e. line capacitance. The phase comparison carrier current relaying is more economical and also convenient than directional comparison scheme.

5.5.3 Microwave Pilot Scheme

This is very similar to the carrier current pilot scheme except that the carrier signal in this case is not transmitted through the same power line as in the case of carrier current pilot scheme. Here, line of the sight antenna is erected at an interval of about 90 km. Carrier of very high frequency in the range of 900 MHz to 6000 MHz is generated and is transmitted in space with the help of line of sight antenna. Because of the high frequencies used, as many as 40 signals spaced at 10 kHz may be transmitted. In the case of microwave pilot, coupling capacitor and line traps are not required. However, there must be clear line of sight between stations. The microwave pilot scheme for relaying purposes are not very popular.

5.6 SUMMARY

The protective relay is a comparator which compares one quantity with another quantity with which it has certain magnitude or phase relation. On this basis the relaying scheme can be classified as single input, dual input or multi-input comparator. Generalized treatment based upon mathematical theory of the relay as a comparator has been dealt within this chapter. In addition, differential relaying scheme which provides unit protection to the apparatus and pilot relaying schemes have also been discussed.

EXERCISES

1. (a) Comment on the statement "Relay is basically a comparator". Classify different types of relays as a comparator and discuss them briefly.
   (b) Prove and show with the help of phasor diagram that there is a strict duality between a phase comparator and an amplitude comparator only as a dual input comparator.
2. Derive from the fundamentals the generalized expression of radius of the circle and coordinates of the centre of a dual input comparator both as an amplitude comparator as well as a phase comparator in the complex β-plane and draw also the corresponding threshold characteristics.
3. Derive from the fundamentals the radius of the circle and coördinates of its centre in the complex α-plane of a dual input amplitude comparator and draw also the corresponding threshold characteristics. Derive also the radius of the circle and coordinates of its centre of a dual input phase comparator in the complex α-plane and draw the corresponding threshold characteristics.
4. (a) Discuss briefly what you understand by multi-input comparators. What types of characteristics are obtained by using the principle of multi-input amplitude comparison and what type of characteristics are obtained by the principle of multi-input phase comparison?
   (b) Discuss with the help of neat diagram the principle of multi-input phase comparator based upon the principle of coincidence.
5. Derive from the fundamentals the signals to obtain elliptical characteristic. What modifications are done in the signals to obtain offset elliptical characteristics? Explain why we prefer to use elliptical characteristic as a third zone starting element.
6. Where do we use relay having quadrilateral characteristics? Derive signals to obtain quadrilateral characteristics and also offset quadrilateral characteristics.
7. What do you understand by pilot relaying scheme? Discuss briefly the various types of pilot relaying schemes with the help of neat diagrams?
8. Discuss with the help of neat diagrams, the opposed voltage type and circulating current type wire pilot schemes. What are the main constraints with the wire pilot scheme and up to what line length, this scheme is used?
9. What do you understand by carrier current pilot scheme and microwave pilot scheme? With the help of a detailed diagram, explain the working principle of the carrier current pilot scheme, showing CT and PT connections, line trap,

coupling capacitor, choke and line tuner, etc. What is the purpose of line trap? Discuss briefly.

10. (a) Explain with the help of neat diagrams, the carrier tripping and carrier blocking schemes.
    (b) Discuss with the help of neat sketches, the theory of carrier current scheme based upon phase angle comparison.

11. A normal carrier current scheme has a coupling capacitor unit consisting of a 0.0015 μF capacitor grounded through 150 mH choke coil. What portion of line to ground voltage appears across the choke coil (a) at the power frequency of 50 Hz and (b) at the carrier frequency of 159 kHz?

REFERENCES

1. Kimbark, E.W., *Power System Stability*, Vol. 2, John Wiley and Sons, New York, 1965.
2. Mason, C.R., *The Art and Science of Relay*, Wiley Eastern Ltd., New Delhi, 1979.
3. Singh, L.P., *Advanced Power System Analysis and Dynamics*, 3rd Edition, Wiley Eastern Ltd., New Delhi, 1992.
4. Warrington, A.R., Van, C., *Protective Relay*, Vol. I, Chapman & Hall Ltd., London, 1976.
5. Warrington, A.R., Van, C., *Protective Relay*, Vol. II, Chapman & Hall Ltd., London, 1974.

6

DIGITAL PROTECTION OF TRANSMISSION LINE

6.1 INTRODUCTION

The development of modern digital technology has resulted in fast, compact, reliable and efficient relaying schemes for the protection of transmission lines. In the past, overcurrent relays were used for protecting transmission lines. Because of the inherent demerits of these relays (e.g. shifting of balance point with the type of fault or with changes in generation or switching), they were replaced by distance relays such as plane impedance relays, angle impedance relays, angle admittance relays, etc.

In the beginning electromechanical relays were used. These had several drawbacks such as high burden on instrument transformers, long operating time, contact problems, etc. Solid-state relays which avoid most of these disadvantages are gradually replacing electromagnetic relays.

Static relays have also been increasingly used in recent years because of their inherent advantages of compactness, lower burden, less maintenance and high speed. Though successfully used, these suffer from a number of disadvantages, e.g. inflexibility, duplication of specification efforts, inadaptability to changing system conditions, complexity and cost. Software (digital) schemes avoid most of these disadvantages. Programmable equipment can respond fast and may be used to implement complex threshold characteristics at low cost. They can also be self-checking in nature thereby requiring less maintenance and providing greater reliability. Implementation of digital relaying was first proposed by G.D. Rockefeller in 1969. Efforts were made to predict the peak fault voltage and current. Fault impedance could then be calculated by taking a few samples at the initial stage of the fault (as reported by B.J. Mann *et al.*).

The bulk of recent literature on digital protection of transmission lines is devoted to utilizing on-line microcomputer to perform the protection, switching, monitoring and data collection functions of EHV/UHV transmission line by developing suitable algorithms. The microprocessor-based protection scheme is especially preferred for transmission lines since several types of threshold characteristics can be implemented with the same hardware or with a minimum change in hardware. The equipment is also self-checking in nature. With the advent of the microprocessor, the implementation of digital protection promises to be cost-effective.

Relays based on the travelling wave phenomenon have been proposed by a number of authors such as Deshikachar *et al.*, Most of these relays are very fast in operation and can detect fault in a few milliseconds (≤ 5 ms). However their long-term durability is yet to be established.

This chapter presents the design and development of a microprocessor-based distance relaying scheme along with other interfacing circuits. The steady state model of the transmission line with fundamental waveforms of voltage and current has been used. All harmonics have been suppressed with appropriate filter circuits. The hardware implemented has been optimized resulting in low cost and simplicity. In addition, novel relaying schemes based upon travelling wave phenomena along with its basic philosophy and mathematical theory, have also been discussed. This relaying scheme which is also referred to as ultra high speed protective relaying scheme has been found to operate within a quarter cycle.

6.2 PROTECTION SCHEME OF TRANSMISSION LINE

Earlier over current relays were used for transmission line protection. However, because of numerous shortcomings of over current relays, for transmission line exceeding 50 kV, only distance relaying schemes are used. The distance relaying schemes, which are of different types viz. plane impedance relay, angle impedance relay (i.e. OHM relay or reactance relay), angle admittance relay i.e. MHO's relay including restricted and offset relays, are very popular for transmission line protection. The main reasons of restricting the over current relays for the protection of feeders or transmission line only upto 50 kV are the shifting of balance point i.e. reach of the relay with the change in type of fault, change in generation capacity and switching operation. Moreover, the over current relays are non directional and hence so as to provide tripping only for internal fault, the over current relays are always supplemented by directional relays. The over current relay, being single input comparator, is certainly less reliable than distance relaying schemes.

For the protection of transmission line, distance relaying schemes are used. For phase faults involving two or more phases, phase relays are used and for ground fault i.e. LG fault, ground relays are used. The phase relays are supplied with delta voltage i.e. line to line voltage and delta current i.e. difference of line currents. The ground relays are supplied with star i.e. phase voltage and star i.e. phase current and also residual current. With such connections, the reach of distance relaying schemes do not shift with the change in types of faults, change in generation level or due to switching. MHO's relays are preferred for phase faults in a long and heavily loaded lines while OHM relays are preferred for ground fault. However, OHM relay (i.e. reactance relay) is always associated with a directional starting i.e.

MHO's relays and tripping is within second zone of MHO's relay and the first zone of OHM i.e. reactance relay.

The relaying schemes reported in the literature for EHV/UHV transmission lines may be classified into two major categories.

(i) Distance relaying schemes
(ii) Relaying scheme based upon travelling wave phenomena

Extensive simulation studies have been conducted to develop an optimal algorithm which had, both, high computation efficiency and excellent protection capability.

6.3 DISTANCE RELAYS

In these relays, the aim is to extract the fundamental power frequency components of voltage and current signals from the complex post-fault waveforms using suitable filters. From the fundamental components the apparent impedance seen by the relay is calculated. Based upon the magnitude of this impedance, the relaying decision whether to trip or block is taken. A number of algorithms for digital protection have been proposed by several authors which can be grouped into four categories described briefly in the following.

6.3.1 Fourier Analysis with a One-Cycle Data Window

This algorithm was proposed by Ramamoorthy and others. Here, the incoming samples for voltage and current are correlated over one cycle with the stored samples of reference (fundamental) sine and cosine waves in order to extract the complex value of the fundamental component in rectangular form. The general expressions for the sine and cosine components of voltage at a sample point K are,

$$V_s = \frac{1}{N}\left[2\sum_{L=1}^{N-1} V_{K-N+L}\sin\left(\frac{2\pi}{N}L\right)\right] \tag{6.1}$$

$$V_c = \frac{1}{N}\left[V_{K-N} + V_K + 2\sum_{L=1}^{N-1} V_{K-N+L}\cos\left(\frac{2\pi}{N}L\right)\right] \tag{6.2}$$

where V_i are the voltage samples and N is the number of samples taken per fundamental cycle. Similar expressions are evaluated for the corresponding current components I_s and I_c; these four relations are used to calculate the phase impedance value.

6.3.2 Predictive Calculation of Peak Values

The method of calculation of line impedance in this case, is based upon predicting the peak current (i_{PK}) and peak voltage (V_{PK}). The impedance is then calculated by dividing the peak voltage by the peak current.

Let v, the voltage sample data at any time t, be given by

$$v = V_{PK} \sin \omega t \tag{6.3}$$

whose derivative v' is given by

$$v' = \omega V_{PK} \cos \omega t \tag{6.4}$$

where v' is determined numerically. From Eqs. (6.3) and (6.4), we get

$$V_{PK}^2 = (v)^2 + \left(\frac{v'}{\omega}\right)^2 \tag{6.5}$$

For a point on the voltage cycle, the angle θ_V is given by,

$$\theta_V = \omega t = \tan^{-1}\left(\frac{\omega v}{v'}\right) \tag{6.6}$$

If the current waveform i is represented as

$$i = i_{PK} \sin(\omega t - \alpha) \tag{6.7}$$

then, in a manner analogous to deriving Eq. (6.5), we get

$$I_{PK}^2 = i^2 + (i'/\omega)^2 \tag{6.8}$$

$$\theta_i = \alpha + \tan^{-1}\left(\frac{\omega i}{i'}\right) \tag{6.9}$$

$$Z = \left[V_{PK}^2 / I_{PK}^2\right]^{1/2} \tag{6.10}$$

and the impedance angle as

$$\alpha = \tan^{-1}\left(\frac{\omega v}{v'}\right) - \tan^{-1}\left(\frac{\omega i}{i'}\right) \tag{6.11}$$

6.3.3 Solution of Differential Equation

In this method, the line is modelled by differential equations, the numerical solution of which yields the value of R_L and L_L. The differential equation describing the transmission line (neglecting shunt parameters) is

$$V = R_L i + L_L \frac{di}{dt} \tag{6.12}$$

A number of algorithms were proposed to solve Eq. (6.12) numerically over two successive time periods and solution of the resulting simultaneous linear equations.

If one takes samples of line voltage and current waveforms at uniform time increments $h = \Delta t$ and replaces derivatives suggested in central finite difference for each of two successive set of samples, one gets Eq. (6.13).

$$\begin{bmatrix} i_K \\ i_{K+1} \end{bmatrix} \begin{bmatrix} \dfrac{i_{K+1} - i_{K-1}}{2h} \\ \dfrac{i_{K+2} - i_K}{2h} \end{bmatrix} \begin{bmatrix} R_L \\ L_L \end{bmatrix} = \begin{bmatrix} V_K \\ V_{K+1} \end{bmatrix} \tag{6.13}$$

Equation (6.13) can be solved for R_L and L_L.

Similarly, McInnes *et al.*, proposed the algorithm in which integration was carried out over two successive time intervals. The final expression for R_L and L_L are:

$$R_L = \frac{(V_{K-1} + V_K)(i_{K-1} - i_{K-2}) - (V_{K-1} + V_{K-2})(i_K - i_{K-1})}{(i_{K-1} + i_K)(i_{K-1} - i_{K-2}) - (i_{K-1} + i_{K-2})(i_K - i_{K-1})} \tag{6.14}$$

$$L_L = \frac{h}{2} \frac{(V_{K-1} + V_{K-2})(i_{K-1} - i_{K-2}) - (V_{K-1} + V_{K-2})(i_K - i_{K-1})}{(i_{K-1} + i_K)(i_{K-1} - i_{K-2}) - (i_{K-1} + i_{K-2})(i_K - i_{K-1})} \tag{6.15}$$

The above equations assume a perfectly transposed transmission line and it does not account for the shunt capacitance or series compensation. The fault resistance and the effect of power flow on the transmission line at the moment of a fault are also ignored. The data window is one cycle.

In 1975, Rajbar and Cory proposed another techniques in which R and L parameters are calculated from the equations shown in the following by selecting overlapping limits of integration chosen to eliminate specific low order harmonics and their multiples.

For example, to eliminate harmonics, K, M and N, the authors suggest the following

$$L\left(\Sigma \int di\right) + R\left(\Sigma \int i\,dt\right) = \Sigma \int v\,dt \tag{6.16}$$

$$\Sigma \int v\,dt = \int_0^{2\pi/K} v\,dt + \int_{\pi/M}^{2\pi/K+\pi/M} v\,dt + \int_{\pi/N}^{2\pi/K+\pi/N} v\,dt + \int_{\pi/M+\pi/N}^{2\pi/K+\pi/M+\pi/N} v\,dt \tag{6.17}$$

The quantities $\Sigma \int di$ and $\Sigma \int i\,dt$ are calculated similarly.

In 1979, Smolinksi proposed an algorithm which accommodates both the d.c. transient and transient in high frequency component of line voltage and current signals, without any additional filtering for these transients. The transmission line model used in this algorithm is a single π equivalent section for the protection of the line from the relay location to the point of fault. The approach used in this algorithm is therefore one of including the sources of transient components of the line voltage and the line current signals in the impedance calculation algorithm, rather than one of filtering out the transient components and then calculating the line impedance from the filtered signals.

During post-fault conditions, this single π section model is described by the equations:

$$v = R_L\,(i - i_c) + L_L \frac{d(i - i_c)}{dt} \tag{6.18}$$

$$i_c = C \frac{dv}{dt} \tag{6.19}$$

So, Eq. (6.18) can be written in the form

$$v = R_L i + L_L \frac{di}{dt} - R_L C \frac{dv}{dt} - L_L C \frac{d^2v}{dt^2} \tag{6.20}$$

By selecting four successive sets of voltage and current samples and replacing the derivatives in Eq. (6.20) by corresponding finite differences, one gets the values of R_L and L_L by a matrix reduction technique, and as well the unknown line capacitance C is eliminated in the process.

6.3.4 Fourier Analysis with Sub-cycle Window

Here, the digital impedance determines the complex value of the physical quantity (viz. current or voltage) by sampling two orthogonal functions of the variable time. Two sets of such orthogonal functions, viz. cosine/sine functions and even/odd square functions are used.

If the extraction of the fundamental frequency components is done by means of correlating the signal with sine and cosine functions of the fundamental frequency, and the data window is shorter than one cycle, the presence of a periodic components in the signals gives rise to large errors. The author suggests that in order to reduce the errors, the signals ought to be correlated with sine/cosine functions which have periods equal to the data window length.

Let the current and voltage input signals be,

$$I(t) = I_1 \cos(\omega_1 t - \alpha) + I_a e^{-(t/T_a)} + I_p e^{-t/\tau_p} \cos(\omega_p t - \beta)$$

$$V(t) = V_1 \cos(\omega_1 t - \alpha) + V_a e^{-(t/T_a)} + V_p e^{-t/\tau_p} \cos(\omega_p t - \beta)$$

The first, second and third terms correspond to the steady state, aperiodic (i.e. dc) component decaying with time constant T_a and decaying oscillations induced by the fault.

The real and imaginary components of voltage and current are calculated for the angular frequency of ω_2 corresponding to a data window for which the spectrum of aperiodic component reaches minimum. It is known that,

$$V_1 = V_d + j V_q \tag{6.21}$$

and,

$$I_1 = I_d + j I_q \tag{6.22}$$

Let,

$$\tau = t - \left(t_1 + \frac{T_w}{2}\right)$$

where t_1 is the beginning of the data window T_w.

Following Fourier transform theory and correlating the signal with sine/cosine functions which have period equal to data window T_w, that is $\omega_2 = 2\pi/T_w$, we have,

$$V_d = \frac{K}{T_w} \int_{-T_w/2}^{T_w/2} V(\tau) \cos \omega_2 \tau \, d\tau \tag{6.23}$$

$$V_q = \frac{P}{T_w} \int_{-T_w/2}^{T_w/2} V(\tau) \sin \omega_2 \tau \, d\tau \tag{6.24}$$

$$I_d = \frac{K}{T_w} \int_{-T_w/2}^{T_w/2} I(\tau) \cos \omega_2 \tau \, d\tau \tag{6.25}$$

$$I_q = \frac{P}{T_w} \int_{-T_w/2}^{T_w/2} I(\tau) \sin \omega_2 \tau \, d\tau \tag{6.26}$$

where coefficients K and P are

$$K = \frac{\pi (1 - r)^2}{r \sin \pi r}, \quad P = \frac{-\pi (1 - r^2)}{\sin \pi r} \quad \text{and} \quad r = \frac{\omega_1}{\omega_2}$$

Here, ω_1 is the normal power frequency and ω_2 the angular frequency corresponding to data window.

Taking data window equal to half the period, or half cycle (i.e. $T_w = \pi/\omega_1$), the coefficients K and P can be written as,

$$K = \frac{3\pi}{2}, \quad P = \frac{-3\pi}{4}$$

Substituting the values of coefficients K and P in Eqs. (6.23)–(6.26) and using trapezoidal method of integration, the values of V_d, V_q, I_d and I_q are evaluated.

The impedance seen by the relay is obtained by dividing the peak of voltage by the peak of current, that is

$$Z = \frac{V_1}{I_1} = \frac{V_d + j V_q}{I_d + j I_q}$$

$$= \frac{V_d I_d + V_q I_q}{I_d^2 + I_q^2} + j \frac{V_q I_d - V_d I_q}{I_d^2 + I_q^2}$$

Since $Z = R + jX$, we get

$$R = \frac{V_d I_d + V_q I_q}{I_d^2 + I_q^2} \tag{6.27}$$

$$X = \frac{V_q I_d - V_d I_q}{I_d^2 + I_q^2} \tag{6.28}$$

Compared with the standard practice of extracting the fundamental components by means of correlating the signals with the sine/cosine functions of the fundamental frequency, the above method minimizes errors due to the presence of aperiodic components in the signal, but increases those errors which result from oscillatory components.

Girgis proposed the use of Kalman filters to estimate the fundamental frequency component from the corrupted voltage and current signals to determine apparent distance (i.e. impedance) as quickly as possible satisfying the security of the first zone demands. Here, Kalman filters, as recursive optimal estimators are used optimally to estimate the fundamental components of voltage and current.

Later, Phadke *et al.*, proposed microcomputer-based symmetrical component distance relay (SCDR) in the ultra high frequency mode using a single equation which was found to be adequate for handling all types of faults. The software program processed the sample data recursively in real time. Symmetrical components were calculated continuously at every sample time. These authors claim that the average operating time for zone 1 faults, was observed to be half cycle.

Miki *et al.*, proposed a study of high speed distance relay using microcomputer. Jeyasura *et al.*, described a method of digital distance relays and digital filter algorithm for transmission line protection. They proposed the possible combination of the 3rd order recursive low pass filter algorithm and distance relay algorithm to determine the transient apparent impedance based on the solution of differential equation representing the transmission line model. However, they had not considered in their formulation, the frequency dependance of line parameters. The operating time of 1st zone in this case is also equal to the half cycle.

The newly developed relay schemes using mini- and micro-computers for distance protection possess some important features such as modularity, flexibility accuracy, availability, reliability and security, compatibility and self checking capability.

6.4 TRAVELLING WAVE RELAYS

In recent years, there has been an increasing awareness of the benefits of ultra fast clearance of faults. The ultra high speed (u.h.s) clearing of faults improves the transient stability of a power system. The fault clearing time depends on the speed of both the protective relay and the associated circuit breaker.

Attention is now focussed on the development of u.h.s. protective relays because of the recent development of u.h.s. circuit breakers. This has been possible with the utilization of the concepts of the travelling wave phenomena.

The travelling wave relays can broadly be classified into following categories:

(i) Amplitude comparison relay
(ii) Directional comparison relay
(iii) Phase comparison (correlation technique) relay

6.4.1 Amplitude Comparison Relays

Several authors have reported the development of u.h.s. protective relays based on travelling wave phenomena. After the occurrence of a fault, the voltage and current at any point in a power system can be regarded as the sum of prefault and fault generated components. During the first few milliseconds after the occurrence of a fault, the fault generated components may be represented by the travelling waves.

The d'Alembert relay due to Takagi *et al.*, computes the travelling waves at the local and remote ends and then uses their difference to detect an internal fault.

This relaying signal is zero if no internal fault exists and is finite only if an internal fault takes place. For the protection of three-phase lines, the model components of voltages and currents and appropriate model surge impedances are used. Also, three relaying signals, one for each mode, are employed. Its main demerit is, that, it requires the exchange of quantitative information between the ends of the protected line.

Walker *et al.,* had established that the first and the most prominent high frequency (h.f.) fault component and the other frequency components are inversely proportional to the distance to a fault on a plain feeder. A directional comparison blocking scheme had been proposed by Johns which assesses the direction to the fault at both zone boundaries by determining the sequence in which the forward $(V + IZ)$ and reverse $(V - IZ)$ travelling wave signals exceed a pre-set threshold.

Dommel derived a travelling wave directional discriminant that is independent of fault initiation angle and line termination. In this relay, the fault discriminant has been derived from the sampled data available at the local end only. If the voltage and current changes produced by the fault point are ΔV_F and Δi_F, then,

$$\Delta V_F(t) - Z_c \Delta i_F(t) = \Delta V_A(t + \tau_F) - Z_c \Delta i_A(t + \tau_F) \tag{6.29}$$

For an L – L fault occurring at time $t = 0$,

$$\Delta V_F(t) - Z_C \Delta i_F(t) = V_F' \sin(\omega t + \phi) \tag{6.30}$$

where V_F' is the peak-fault line voltage.

Substitution from Eq. (6.29) in Eq. (6.30), we get,

$$\Delta V_F(t + \tau_F) - Z_c \Delta i_A(t + \tau_F) = -V_F' \sin(\omega t + \phi) \tag{6.31}$$

The above equation is valid at the end A from time τ_F to 3 τ_F. After 3 τ_F, successive reflections from the fault point will corrupt the equation. For a fault inception at the zero-crossing of the voltage ($\phi = 0°$), Eq. (6.31) becomes $-V_F' \sin \omega t$ and hence is difficult to detect in the time interval τ_F to 3 τ_F. To overcome this problem, the derivation of Eq. (6.31) is taken as,

$$\frac{d}{dt} \Delta V_A(t + \tau_F) - Z_c \frac{d}{dt} \Delta i_A(t + \tau_F) = -\omega V_F' \cos(\omega t + \phi) \tag{6.32}$$

From Eq. (6.31) and Eqn. (6.32), the fault discriminant D_F is derived as

$$D_F = [\Delta V_A(t + \tau_F) - Z_c \Delta i_A(t + \tau_F)]^2$$

$$+ \frac{1}{\omega^2}\left[\frac{d}{dt} \Delta V_A(t + \tau_F) - Z_c \frac{d}{dt} \Delta i_A(t + \tau_F)\right]^2 = V_F'^2 \tag{6.33}$$

for $\tau_F \le t \le 3\,\tau_F$.

The distribution of the fault discriminant following internal and external faults in a typical power system is shown in Fig. 6.1. The relay uses a transfer trip/block scheme.

The equation to evaluate the fault discriminant is quite complex and hence is not suitable for implementation with microprocessors. The results are also erratic for close-up faults where rapid build-up of multiple reflections occurs.

Mansour and Swift proposed the discriminant function based on travelling wave phenomena for both forward and backward waves. For a single-phase line, the discriminant function is defined to be the square root of an expression defined as

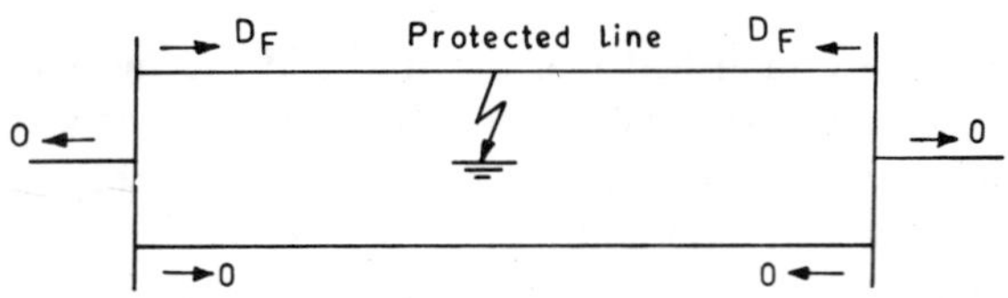

(a) Fault inside protected zone

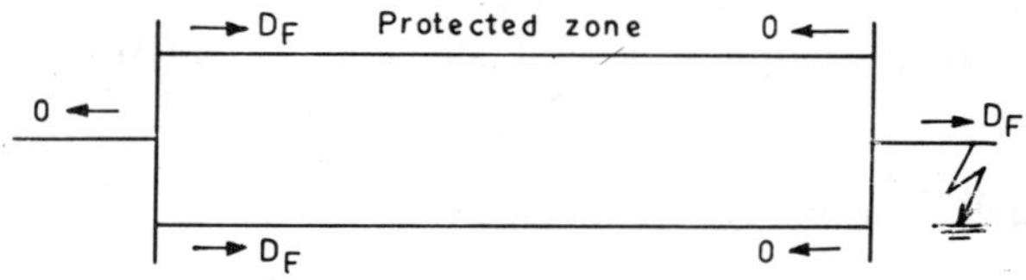

(b) Fault outside protected zone

Fig. 6.1 Distribution of fault discrimination D_F

$$D = \sqrt{[(d)^2 + (d'/\omega)^2]^{1/2}} \tag{6.34}$$

where, d is the wave characteristic at the relay point, d' is its derivative with respect to time, and ω is the power frequency.

$$d = \Delta V_R - Z \Delta i_R \tag{6.35}$$

for the forward wave characteristic, and

$$d = \Delta V_R + Z \Delta i_R \tag{6.36}$$

for the backward wave characteristic, where Z is line characteristic impedance and ΔV_R and Δi_R are the changes in the voltage and current respectively at the relay location.

From the forward discriminant components, the threshold value is compared to detect the existence of fault and its direction; then, if the fault is in the forward direction, selecting the faulted phase and/or classifying the type of fault. If none of the checked forward discriminant components exceeds the threshold, the backward components are checked. If any one exceeds the threshold, it indicates a backward fault.

The evaluation of Eqs. (6.33) and (6.34) using microprocessors is very difficult. It is suggested to use of four microprocessors at each end of the line, but this results in a very complex hardware and hence reduced reliability.

6.4.2 Phase Comparison Relay

Here, the relays perform correlation of a forward and backward travelling wave at the relay location. The correlation peak occurs at a time equal to twice the travel time to fault. The distance to fault is obtained from this time.

Paithankar and Sants proposed an algorithm for fault distance calculation based on auto-correlation of travelling wave transient signals. The wave signals are defined as,

$$a(t) = \frac{1}{2}[\Delta V_A(t) + Z_c \Delta i_A(t)] \tag{6.37}$$

$$b(t) = \frac{1}{2}[-\Delta V_A(t) + Z_c \Delta i_A(t)] \tag{6.38}$$

The forward travelling wave $a(t)$ gets reflected at the fault point and returns to the relaying location after a time $2\tau_F$.

Hence,

$$b(t) = r \cdot a(t - 2\tau_F) \tag{6.39}$$

where r is reflection coefficient at the fault point.

To find the time $2\tau_F$, the authors suggested auto-correlation of $a(t)$ with a time shifted $b(t)$ signal. The auto-correlation peak occurs when the time shift of $b(t)$ is equal to $2\tau_F$.

The algorithm implementation involves evaluation of the following integrals:

$$\text{First integral} = \int_{t=0}^{4\tau} a(t)\, b(t)\, dt \tag{6.40}$$

$$\text{Second integral} = \int_{t=0}^{4\tau} a(t)\, b(t-T)\, dt \tag{6.41}$$

and so on. The integration process is carried out until the value of Nth integral < the value of $(N-1)$th integral.

Now travel time to fault is

$$\tau_F = \frac{(N-2)\,T}{2} \tag{6.42}$$

The relay issues trip signal if

$$\tau_F < \tau$$

A similar algorithm for fault location based on auto-correlation of travelling waves has also been reported by Crossly and McLaren. The accuracy of both travelling wave distance algorithms using correlation technique is dependent on the voltage angle of fault inception, since there is no obvious travelling wave signal at really point in the case of fault inception at zero voltage.

Rajendra and McLaren also worked on similar lines and proposed an algorithm for the protection of double circuit lines and teed circuits. Results obtained through computer simulation indicate that in case of external faults the evaluated distance is not accurate and effect of fault inception angle is not discussed for the distance estimate.

Vitnis developed a method, by means of which the fault can be determined through a time delay equal to twice the travel time of the travelling waves between fault and relaying points. He proposed the application of a correlation technique for the determination of this time delay. Computer simulation results indicate a fault location time of about 10.0 ms and directional discrimination time of 6.16 ms. It is suggested that low pass and d.c. offset filters are necessary, though their requirements are minimum.

6.4.3 Directional Comparison Relay

These relays are extensions of the amplitude comparison relays discussed earlier and the signals which represent the forward and backward travelling waves are derived in a similar manner at the relay location.

Johns *et al.*, have reported the development of an u.h.s. directional comparison relaying scheme. They developed three pairs of relaying signals, one for each propagation mode. The signals of each pair are formed from the corresponding modal components of the fault-generated components of the relaying point voltages and currents. The direction of the fault is determined by the sequence in which the relaying signals of each mode exceed preset level. The qualitative information about the direction of the fault is exchanged through an ultra high frequency carrier communication channel.

The main features of this relay are:

(1) The relay is analog circuitry-based and does not involve extensive filtering of the input signals.
(2) Close-up faults are difficult to sense because of multiple reflection.
(3) The relay setting procedure is easy.
(4) Typical relay operating time of 4.0 ms on a 128 km long line has been reported.
(5) The relay does not identify the phase involved in a fault.
(6) The authors suggested the use of charge-coupled-device for the extraction of superimposed components.

To overcome the limitations of this relay, a microprocessor-based amplitude comparison relay has been proposed by Johns *et al.*, The important feature of this relay is the use of suitable filters to counter the poor (high frequency) response of the signal transducers.

The relaying decision is based upon the two signals represented as follows.

$$D_1 = |a(t)| - |b(t)|$$

$$D_2 = |a'(t)| - |b'(t)| \quad (6.43)$$

where $a'(t)$ and $b'(t)$ are time derivatives of $a(t)$ and $b(t)$ respectively. To take care of the possibility of fault occurring near voltage zero, the signal D_2 has been included. It is suggested that following a forward fault, both D_1 and D_2 would never simultaneously be negative. Similarly, following a reverse fault, both D_1 and D_2 would never simultaneously be positive.

A similar approach for determining the direction of the fault has been proposed by Vitnis. In this scheme, this direction is determined by the sequence in which two relaying signals exceed a threshold level. Here, pair of signals are formed from the fault-generated components of a phase voltage and corresponding line current.

Ramamoorthy and Verma described a relaying principle in which a discriminant is used to determine the direction of the fault. The discriminant is a function of fault-generated backward wave voltage and current. It exceeds a present value for an internal fault.

The implementation of amplitude comparison relay based on John's work has been extended by Desikachar and Singh. They also presented a digital algorithm for the location of fault. It has been shown that, following a forward fault when the first travelling wave arrives at the relay location, its maximum slope is $2\,\omega\,V_F'$, where V_F' is the peak pre-fault voltage at the fault point. After a time of $2\,\tau_F$, the wave arrives back with a maximum slope of $2\,\rho_S\,\omega\,V_F'$ where ρ_S is the reflection coefficient at the source. Based upon the above theory, the authors presented a fault locating scheme by taking derivatives of the super-imposed components and checking for their magnitude. Performance of the algorithm for fault occurring near voltage zero and close-up faults have not been discussed in detail. Only off-line computer simulation of the algorithm has been reported.

The directional comparison relay combined with a distance relay for remote and back-up protection has been developed by Giuliante *et al.*, Also, a neutral current monitor to identify very high resistance earth faults has been provided. The relay integrates multiple functions to provide better performance by mutual support where by the inherent strengths of each technique are used to improve the characteristics of the other.

6.4.4 Fault Location Scheme

This scheme is proposed by String field, Marihart and Stevens for overhead transmission lines. The various types of fault locators under this category are discussed in the following:

Type-A fault locator. In this type of fault locator, the time taken by the fault initiated travelling wave to travel from the relaying point to the fault location and back is recorded on an oscilloscope as shown in Fig. 6.2. Fault distance is evaluated from this time.

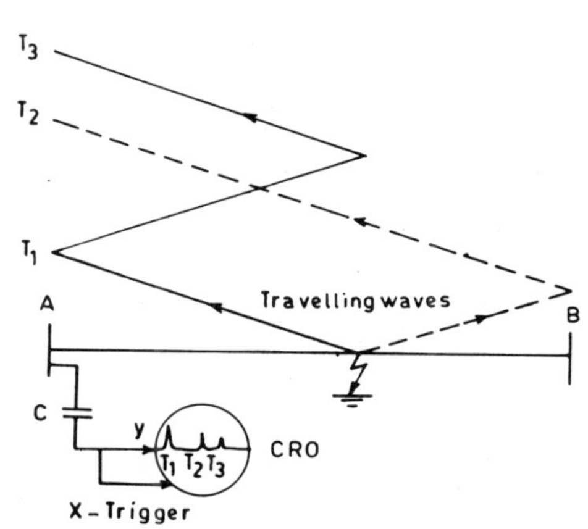

Fig. 6.2 Type-A fault locator

Type-B fault locator. The fault-initiated travelling wave, on reaching one end of the transmission line starts a counter and on reaching the other end, triggers a communication channel, as shown in Fig. 6.3. The counter is stopped on receiving the communication channel data. The time interval measured by the counter is used to calculate the fault distance.

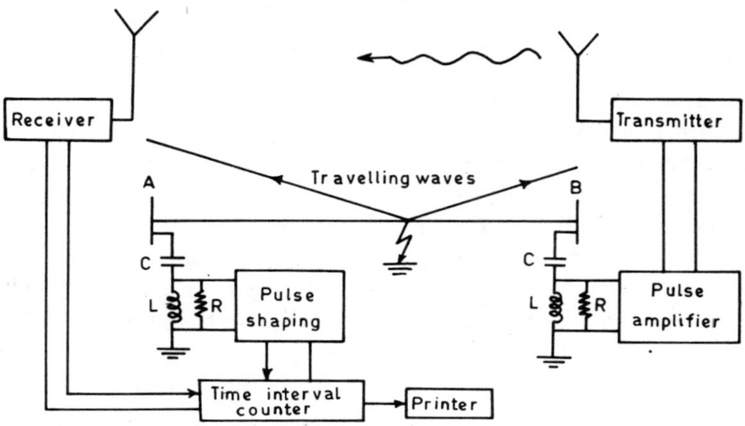

Fig. 6.3 Type-B fault locator

Type-D fault locator. Here, as shown in Fig. 6.4, the arrival of the travelling wave at the two ends of the line stops electronic counters at the ends which are previously running under synchronism. The difference in the counter readings at both the ends is used to locate the fault.

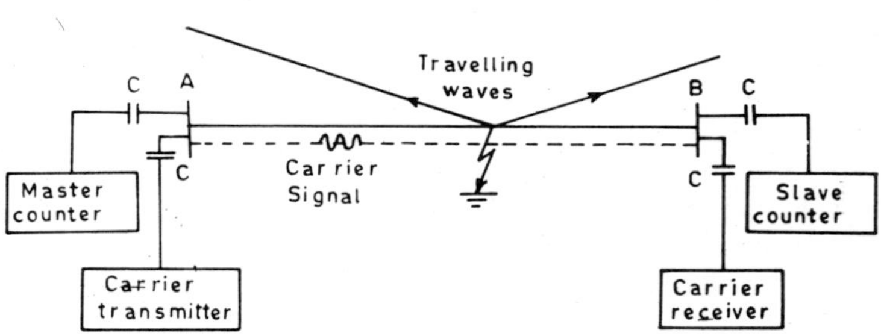

Fig. 6.4 Type-D fault locator

Relative Merits and Drawbacks. The type-A fault locators assume a definite discontinuity in the surge impedance of the line behind the fault locators at either end of the line. This may not be the case always. The type-B fault locators require a fast communication channel. The type-D fault locators overcome the above limitations but the main problem associated with this fault locator is the carrier signal transmitter.

6.5 DIGITAL PROTECTION SCHEME BASED UPON FUNDAMENTAL SIGNAL

In this scheme, the fundamental components of currents and voltages are used to obtain appropriate relay signals. The ratio of the fundamental component of voltage and the fundamental component of current is the impedance of the transmission line up to the point of fault. For homogeneous line, having same impedance per unit length and also having the same impedance angle, the impedance up to the point of fault is proportional to the distance of the line up to the point of fault. This is why this scheme is also known as distance relaying scheme.

6.5.1 Basic Philosophy

Before the occurrence of fault, the power system components and hence the entire network will be in steady state condition with normal sinusoidal excitation (i.e. bus voltage) and normal sinusoidal line current. However, after the occurrence of fault, transients are produced. Hence during post-fault condition, the bus voltage and the line current contains, in addition to the fundamental sinusoidal components, the transient components including d.c. offset as well. However, in this scheme, the transient and d.c. offset components in both bus voltage and line current, are eliminated with the help of analog/digital filtering techniques. In the case of static relays or electromechanical relays, the transients are eliminated by the use of replica impedance.

Hence in the case of digital distance relaying scheme, the line currents are continuously monitored through CT and bus voltages through PT. Since the impedance to the point of fault is the ratio of fundamental component of voltage and current, it is necessary to eliminate the transient components in voltage and current which appear after the occurrence of fault with the help of appropriate filter circuit. In the case of analog filter, the line current and bus voltage are passed through active bandpass filter, which rejects transients and hence bandpasses only the fundamental component. However, in the case of digital filter, by appropriate software programme, the transients are eliminated. Therefore, in the case of distance relaying scheme, by removing the transients from both the voltage and current waveform, only fundamental sinusoidal component of voltage and fundamental sinusoidal component of current are used to determine line impedance upto the point of fault. This is obvious because only the ratio of fundamental sinusoidal component of voltage and current is the impedance.

6.5.2 Mathematical Theory

Here, the transmission line is modelled by a linear differential equation. The differential equation of the transmission line (neglecting the shunt parameters) is assumed to be expressed as follows:

$$V = iR + L\frac{di}{dt} \tag{6.44}$$

The proposed algorithms for the calculation of impedance up to the point of fault are based on two methods : the first one involves the predictive calculation of peak voltage and peak current; the second one is the numerical solution of Eq. (6.44).

Predictive calculation of apparent impedance. The method of calculation of line impedance predicts the peak current and the peak voltage. The impedance is then calculated by dividing the peak voltage by the peak current. We assume that the signal contains only the fundamental component. Furthermore, the phase difference between the voltage and current waveforms is determined, enabling complete impedance determination, i.e. both its mod as well as its angle. Let v and v', the voltage sample and its derivative respectively at time t be given by

$$v = V_{PK} \sin \omega t \tag{6.45}$$

$$v' = \omega V_{PK} \cos \omega t \tag{6.46}$$

v' is determined numerically, From Eqs. (6.45) and (6.46), we get,

$$v_{PK}^2 = v^2 + [v'/\omega]^2 \tag{6.47}$$

For a point on the voltage cycle, the angle θ_V is given by

$$\theta_v = \omega t = \tan^{-1}\left(\frac{\omega v}{v'}\right) \tag{6.48}$$

If the current waveform is represented as

$$i = I_{PK} \sin (\omega t - \alpha) \tag{6.49}$$

then in a similar manner, we get

$$I_{PK}^2 = i^2 + (i'/\omega)^2 \tag{6.50}$$

$$\theta_i = \alpha + \tan^{-1} (\omega i/i') \tag{6.51}$$

From Eqs. (6.47)–(6.51), we get the apparent impedance magnitude as

$$Z = \left[\frac{V_{PK}^2}{I_{PK}^2}\right]^{1/2} \tag{6.52}$$

and the impedance angle as

$$\alpha = \tan^{-1}\left(\frac{\omega v}{v'}\right) - \tan^{-1}\left(\frac{\omega i}{i'}\right) \tag{6.53}$$

Solution of differential equation. The second formulation for the calculation of impedance is proposed by McInnes *et al.*, The equation is solved numerically by the finite difference method using successive set of samples. The final expressions for the calculation of impedance, i.e. the values of R and L up to the point of fault are as follows:

$$R = \frac{(V_{K-1} + V_K)(i_{K-1} - i_{K-2}) - (V_{K-1} + V_{K+2})(i_K - i_{K-1})}{(i_{K-1} + i_K)(i_{K-1} - i_{K-2}) - (i_{K-1} + i_{K-2})(i_K - i_{K-1})} \tag{6.54}$$

$$L = \frac{h}{2}\,\frac{(V_{K-1} + V_{K-2})(i_{K-1} + i_K) - (V_{K-1} + V_K)(i_{K-1} + i_{K-2})}{(i_{K-1} + i_K)(i_{K-1} - i_{K-2}) - (i_{K-1} + i_{K-2})(i_K - i_{K-1})} \tag{6.55}$$

where, h is the time interval between two consecutive samples.

6.5.3 Analog and Digital Filtering Scheme

The mimic impedance used in the CT secondary plays the role of an analog filter since it filters out the d.c. offset in the current signal. Complete suppression of the d.c. offset is, however, not possible owing to the fact that exact matching of the X/R ratios of the primary and secondary circuits are difficult to obtain because the X/R ratio of the primary circuit up to the point of fault is variable.

RC low pass filters, with a suitable cutoff frequency, have been used to eliminate the high frequency components in conjunction with some of the algorithms. The fact, that a single analog filter cannot suppress all the unwanted components and that these filters are slower than the digital ones, led to the development and preferential use of the digital filters. The various types of digital filters, which have been proposed so far, are described below.

Notch filters. Two orthogonal notch filters with sine characteristics have been used to extract the fundamental components after the high frequency components are eliminated by an analog low pass filter.

Selected harmonic filter. While the differential equations of the transmission line are being solved by numerical integration, the integration is carried out over a certain number of overlapping subintervals with appropriate limits. This leads to the elimination of certain harmonics and their multiples.

Least square error filters. In one type of these filters, the deficiency in the modelling of the line by differential equations is treated as an error, and solution for the parameters of the model is obtained subject to the minimization of the mean of the squares of this error over the data window. In another type, a polynomial fit (for example, a straight line fit over three points, a quadratic fit over five points or a cubic fit over seven points) is determined subject to the least square error criterion. Differentiating this polynomial, the necessary time derivatives can be found. In yet another type, a waveform containing a decaying d.c. offset, the fundamental and a desired number of harmonic components, is assumed, and the least square error criterion is applied to determine the unknown parameters of the fundamental component. All these filters are rather slow and their accuracy depends on the data window as well as number of samples per cycle.

Orthogonal transform filters. Of these, the Fourier transform filter is the most widely used one, and ultilizes sine and cosine functions as an orthogonal set. This filter suppresses all the unwanted components and, therefore, offers the best accuracy. But, it requires a data window of one full fundamental period. However, filters employing half-a-cycle and less than half-a-cycle data window with tolerable errors have been proposed. Filters using odd and even square waves, Walsh functions, sample values and their derivatives and the first and second derivatives of the samples as orthogonal functions have also been proposed.

Finite transform filter. The fundamental frequency impedance is determined by carrying out the filtering process in the frequency domain through the use of finite transform spectral analysis techniques. Acceptable accuracy limits could be achieved only with a speed of three-fourth of a cycle.

Kalman filters. The nonfundamental components such as harmonics and d.c. component in the voltage and current waveforms are considered as noise signals. The noise signal in the voltage waveform is considered as a white noise sequence with a decreasing variance while that in the current waveform as an exponential process plus a white noise sequence with a decreasing variance. Then, a two-state Kalman filter is used to extract the fundamental voltage phasor and three-state Kalman filter to extract the fundamental current phasor. The error in these filtering processes has been reported to be less than 1 per cent after half-a-cycle.

The filtering schemes, described so far suppress the harmonics as well as d.c. offset from the post-fault current and voltage waveforms. However, in the case of ultra high speed relays, based on the travelling wave techniques, the transient components, such as high frequency harmonics and d.c. offset present in the post-fault current and voltage waveforms are utilized for detecting the faults. As a consequence, these relays are faster and more reliable in operation. Hence, the filters described above will not be useful in the case of travelling wave relays. The cycle-to-cycle comparison scheme, proposed by Mann and Morrison, is adapted, in this case, as a digital filter for deriving the fault-generated components, which are used for forming suitable relay signals using the travelling wave techniques.

6.6 HARDWARE DESIGN

A simplified hardware configuration of the proposed microprocessor-based relaying scheme is shown in Fig. 6.5. This can be applied for the protection of EHV/UHV transmission lines. Here, data acquisition is done after filtering all the transients and other harmonics by an active band pass filter. And then by sample and hold

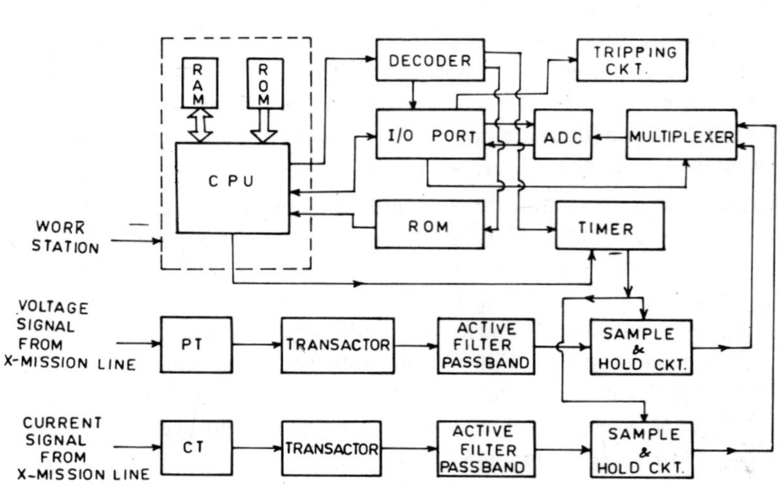

Fig. 6.5 Block diagram of the complete (hardware) system

circuits, these are converted into the digital form using an A/D converter and transmitted to the input ports of the microprocessor. The sampling interval is set by a timer which is also controlled by microprocessor. The work station (WS) which is used for this realization is an Intel 8086A-based system developed at IIT, Kanpur.

The hardware part of the relay which has been designed and developed can be subdivided into two main parts: (a) Data acquisition system and (b) Microprocessor based system.

6.6.1 Data Acquisition System (DAS)

Data acquisition system primarily includes analog input circuit, sample and holds circuit and a multiplexer.

Analog input circuit. The analog input circuit for a single channel is shown in Fig. 6.6. The second-order Butterworth active bandpass filter uses a general purpose operational amplifier µA741 and has been designed for a pass band of 48 to 52 Hz, thus eliminating the high harmonics and the dc offset. The circuit diagram of the

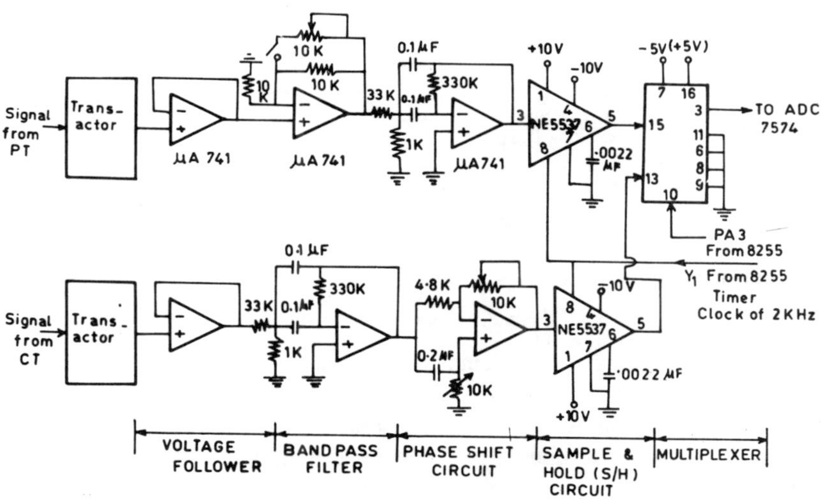

Fig. 6.6 Data acquisition system consists of band pass filter (S/H) circuit and multiplexer

variable gain amplifier is shown in Fig. 6.7, also uses µA741 operational amplifier. For channels with system voltage as input signals, the output of the amplifier is adjusted to V_{PK} under normal operating voltage ($V_{PK} = \pm 10$) V. For the channels with line current as input signals, the amplifier output is adjusted to $\pm 0.1\ V_{PK}$ under full load condition. Since during testing, the maximum fault current has been restricted to 10 times the full load current, the input to the ADC does not exceed its rated input of ± 10 V under any condition.

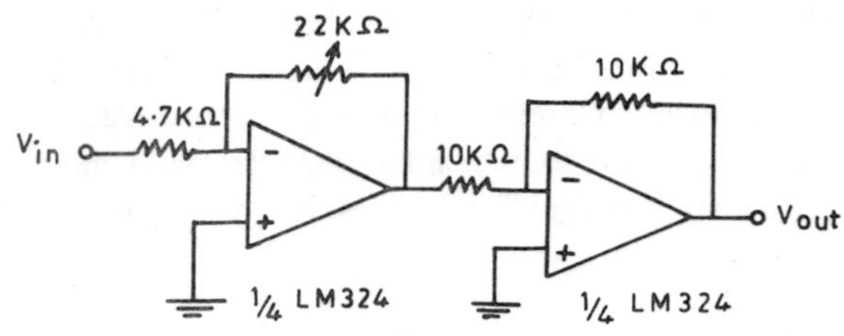

Fig. 6.7

Phase Shifter Circuit. For testing purpose, the signal is taken from a signal generator. To get the phase shift between voltage and current which are in phase when obtained from the signal generator, a phase shifter circuit is used. The μA741 operational amplifier with variable resistances and capacitors is used to get the desired phase differences as shown in Fig. 6.8.

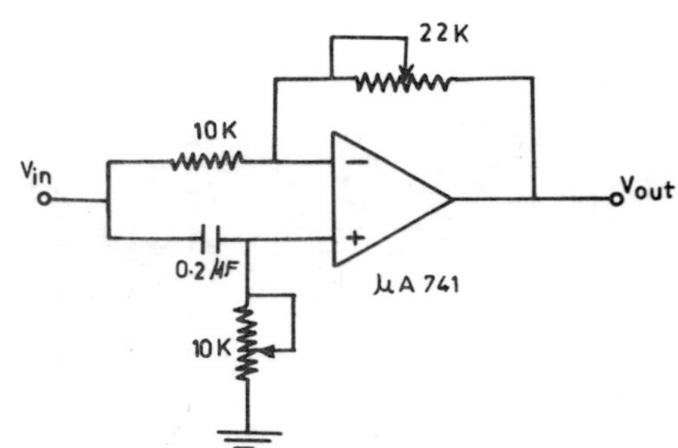

Fig. 6.8 Phase shifter circuit

S/H circuit. The samples are taken at an interval of 0.5 ms, to yield 40 samples per cycle. This is achieved by an 8253 programmable timer. The sample and hold is implemented using the NE5537 chip. It operates from ± 5 V to ± 18 V supplies. The acquisition time is less than 10 μs. It has a wide bandwidth with 0.5 mV typical hold step at $C_n = 0.01$ μF. The circuit diagram and pin connections of the S/H circuit are shown in Fig. 6.9.

Analog multiplexer circuit. In order to select the voltage or current samples, the output of the S/H are fed to the input of the ADC for digitization. For this purpose, the CMOS eight channel analog multiplexer (MUX) IC4051 is used. The enabling of the MUX IC is done by the INTEL 8255 PPI port as shown in Fig. 6.10. The output of the MUX IC is fed to the analog input pin of the ADC.

ADC circuit. The ADC chosen is AD7574 IC. This is a CMOS microprocessor compatible 8 bit ADC which uses the successive approximations technique to provide a conversion time of 15 μs. Designed to be operated as a memory-mapped input device, the AD7574 can be interfaced like static RAM, ROM or slow memory. Here it is operated in bipolar operation (–10 V to +10 V) in slow memory mode.

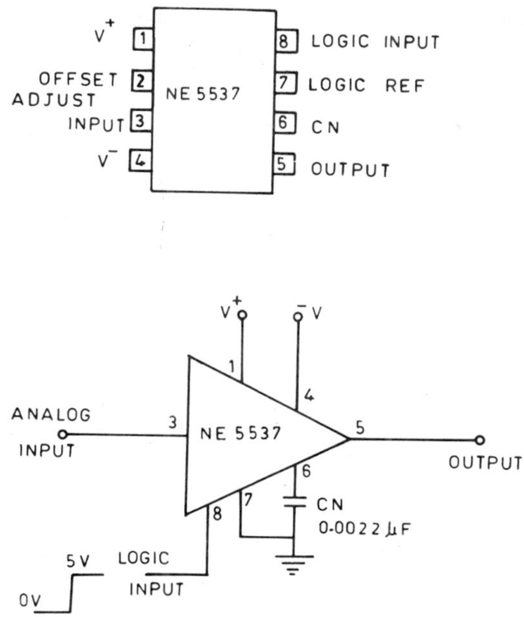

Fig. 6.9 Sample and hold circuit

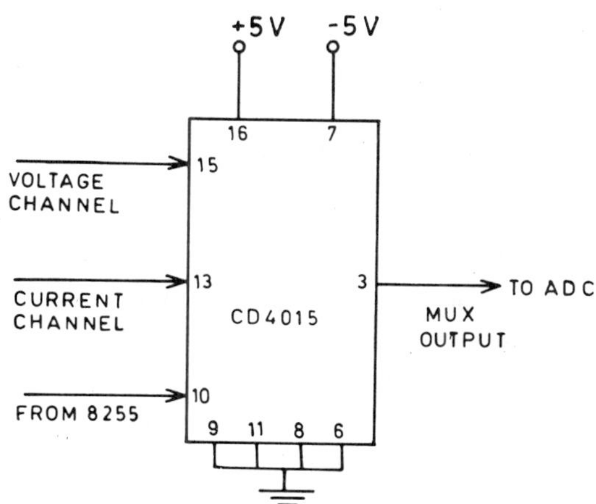

Fig. 6.10 Analog multiplexer circuit

Hence, an external clock of R_{CLK} (= 180 KΩ), C_{CLK} (= 100 pF) is used for applications requiring a conversion. Fig. 6.11 shows the circuit diagram of the ADC and its timing diagram.

In slow memory mode, $\overline{CS}$ and $\overline{RD}$ are tied together which is connected to the port A of 8255A. The Busy line is connected to port C of 8255 PPI; when the AD 7574 is NOT addressed, the $\overline{CS}$ and $\overline{RD}$ inputs are high. Conversion is initiated by

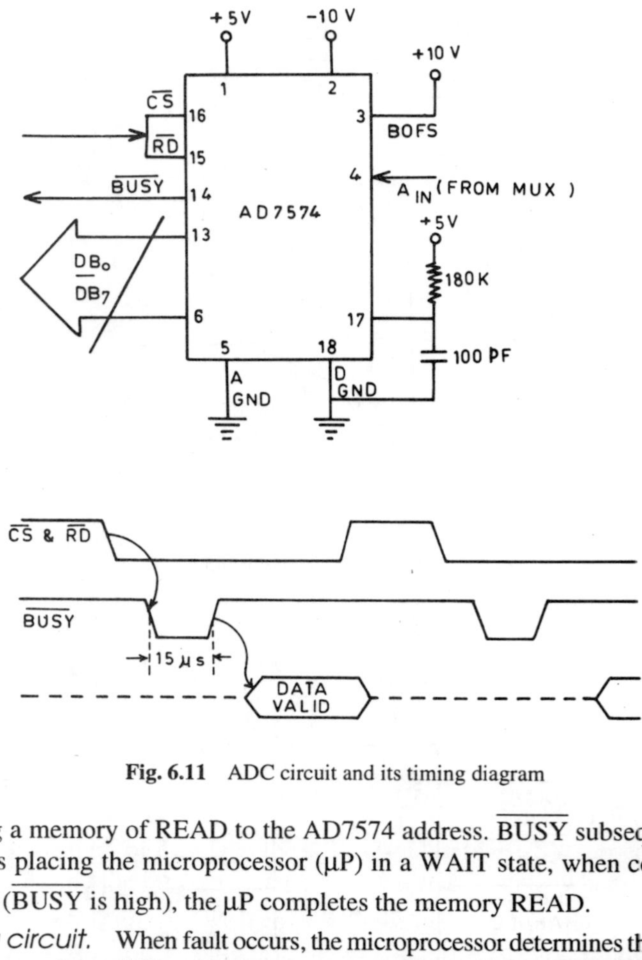

Fig. 6.11 ADC circuit and its timing diagram

executing a memory of READ to the AD7574 address. $\overline{\text{BUSY}}$ subsequently goes low. Thus placing the microprocessor (μP) in a WAIT state, when conversion is complete ($\overline{\text{BUSY}}$ is high), the μP completes the memory READ.

Tripping circuit. When fault occurs, the microprocessor determines the location of the fault zonewise and then gives proper command by glowing of the LED, which is connected to the output port A of 8255. The connection diagram is shown in Fig. 6.12.

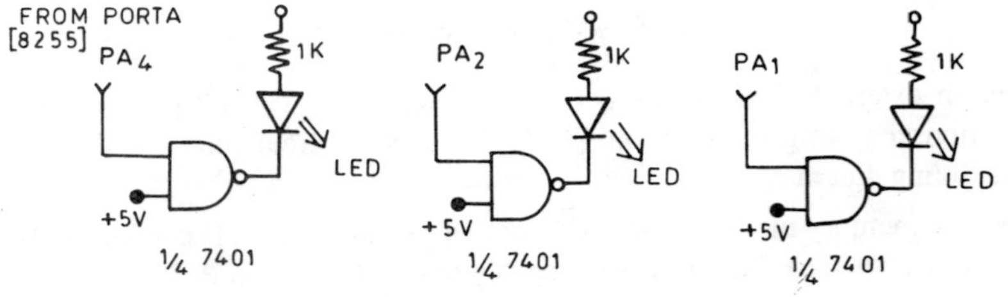

Fig. 6.12 Connection diagram of tripping circuit

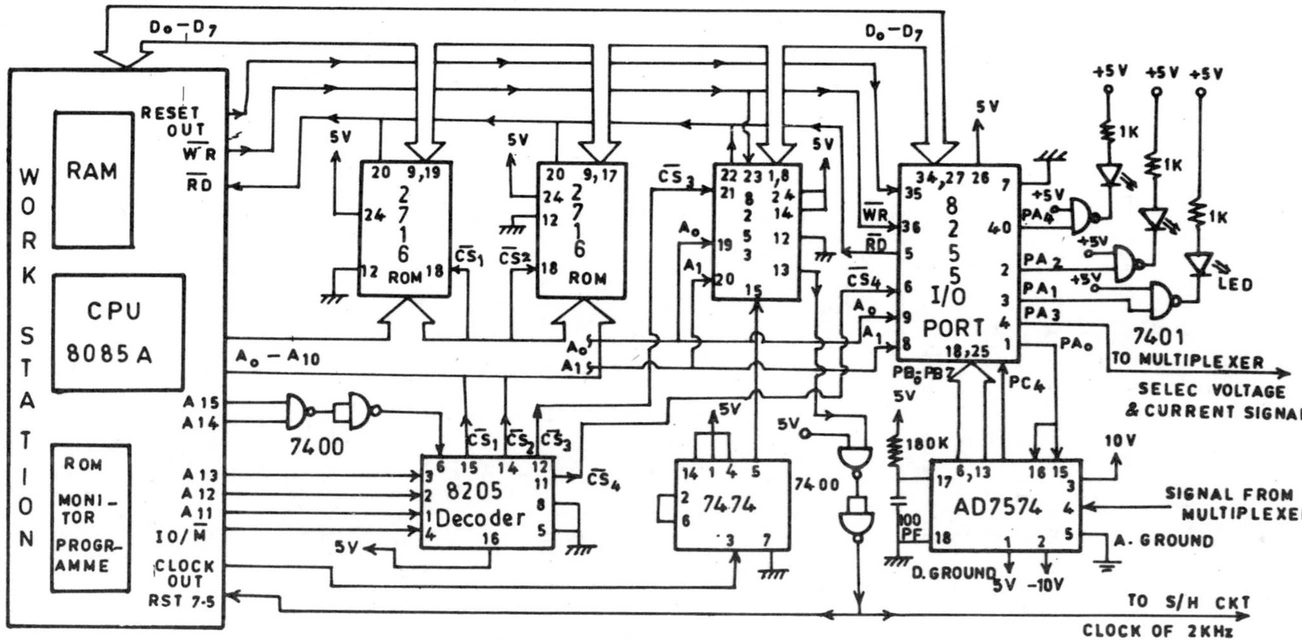

Fig. 6.13 Hardware interface circuit containing ADC, I/O port, timer, decoder, flip-flop and the work station edge connector

6.6.2 Microcomputer Based System

The circuit diagram of the work station interface is shown in Fig. 6.13. The work station contains an 8085A CPU, user RAM, monitor software on EPROM and other facilities. The interface contains an 8255A PPI providing programmable input/output ports, three 16-bit programmable timers obtained from 8253 timer/counter, an ADC 7574 and a decoder 8205. The circuit works in memory mapped mode.

The start of conversion pulse (SOC) is generated using port A of the 8255A and is given to the ADC via $\overline{CS}$ and $\overline{RD}$ pin, which is tied together. The ADC converts the sampled voltages and currents, one by one, through the multiplexer which is controlled by Port A of the 8255A. The conversion process is initiated by an interrupt signal from the 8253 timer which is fed to the RST 7.5 and to the CPU. This is also used to trigger the S/H for both the voltage and current measurements. By feeding an appropriate signal from the port A of 8255 to the multiplexer, one of the sampled voltage or current waveform is fed to the ADC, which starts converting this on receiving the associated pulse of duration 0.5 ms. The ADC outputs an end of conversion (EOC) i.e. $\overline{BUSY}$, equal to 1, after the conversion is complete. This is monitored by the CPU through port C of the 8255A. On finding EOC is 1, the CPU reads the 8-bit digitized data through port B of the 8255A and stores it in the RAM.

The RST 7.5 interrupt, therefore, allows the CPU to periodically sample and store digitized voltage and current levels once every 0.5 ms. It also initiates the programme for fault detection by comparing the voltage at each position of the present cycle with that of the corresponding position of the previous cycle stored in the memory of the microprocessor. When this signal exceeds threshold, the CPU starts its calculation of the apparent impedance and its angle and compares this with the relay characteristic to be implemented which are stored in an EPROM (2×2716). A flip flop (7474) is used to divide the clock generated by the work stations CPU by 2 to generate a clock signal with frequency 1.536 MHz for use by 8253. Figure 6.13 shows the circuit diagram of timer to generate the clock signal with the flip flop. The address decoding is done using the IC 8205 decoder to generator the different chip select (CS) signals required in the system. The address (i.e. system bus) lines are taken from the edge connector of the work station (WS). Thus the address of EPROM, Timer and PPI are expressed as follows for the purpose of the hardware system and are shown in Fig. 6.13.

EPROM	: Y_0 :	Cϕϕϕ – C7FF	2 K of memory
	Y_1 :	C8ϕϕ – CFFF	2 K of memory
8253 timer	: Y_3 :	D8ϕϕ – DFFF	2 K of memory
8255 PPI	Y_4 :	Eϕϕϕ – EFFF	2 K of memory

The tripping circuit which consists of LEDs and an open collector NAND gates is shown in Fig. 6.12. These gates are used to indicate the occurrence of faults in different zones. The unused lines of port A (8255A) are used to give the trip command. In an actual system, the trip command is expected to trigger a circuit breaker, possibly through an SCR or some other triggering device.

6.7 SOFTWARE DESIGN

The DAS simultaneously samples the filtered voltages and currents of the protected line, and by the interface system these sampled values are stored in the memory of the work-station. After a sample sweep, the voltage and current are compared with its corresponding samples in the previous power (50 Hz) cycle stored in the memory of the microprocessor. If any five consecutive voltage (current) samples are found to have lower (or higher), value than the threshold limit (i.e. $6.25\% = \frac{1}{16} = \frac{1}{2^4}$ shifting of the bit), a significant disturbance is deemed to have occurred. This cycle by cycle comparison is developed by Mann and Morrison. On detecting a significant disturbance, the microprocessor disables the interrupt, predicts the peak value of voltage and current and thereby calculates the apparent impedance (both the magnitude and phase angle) up to the fault point according to Eq. (6.52) and (6.53) in case (1) or calculates the values R and L to the point of fault according to Eq. (6.54) and (6.55).

This apparent fault impedance (magnitude and angle) or R and L are then compared with desired relay characteristics of 3-zones offset Mho with blinder (Fig. 6.14) or the quadrilateral characteristics with 3-zones (Fig. 6.15) which are stored

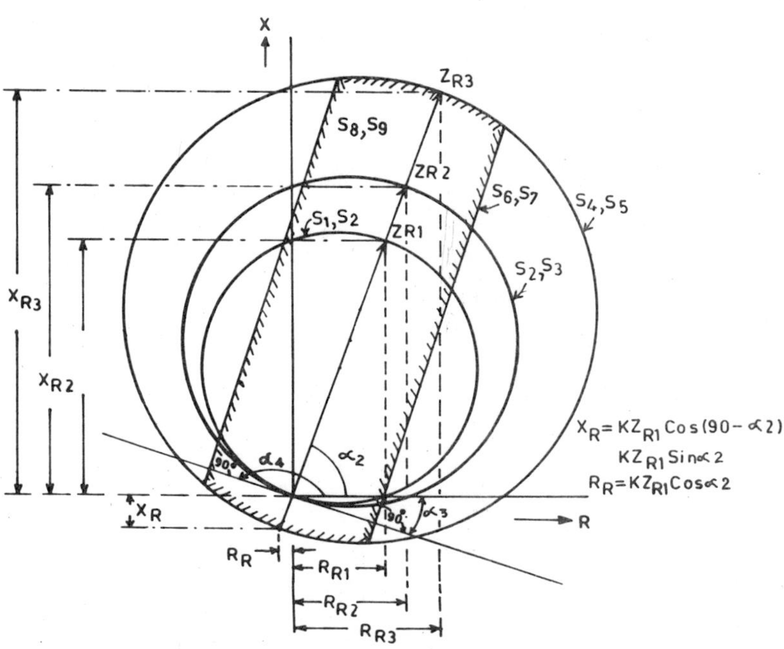

Fig. 6.14 Zone offset Mho characteristics with blinder

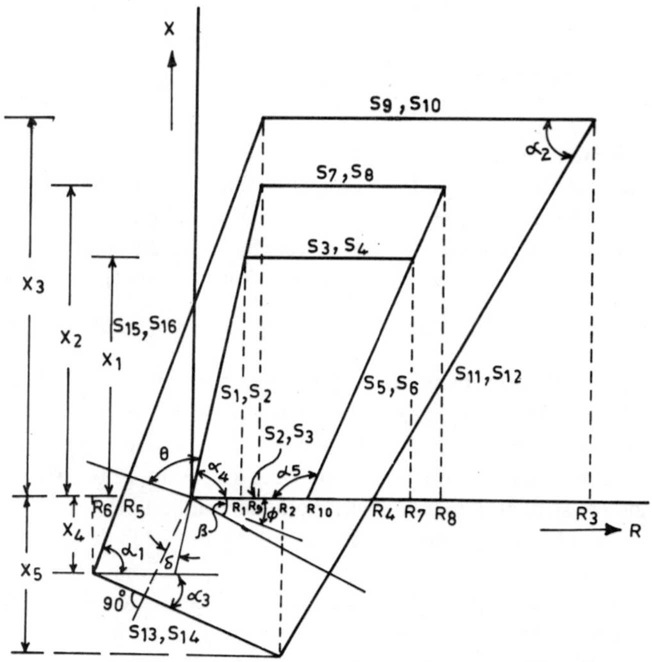

Fig. 6.15 3 zone offset quadrilateral characteristics

in the EPROM. The signals for 3-zone offset Mho with blinder are expressed as follows:

$$
\begin{aligned}
S_1 &= Z_{R1}\angle\alpha_2 - Z\angle\alpha & S_2 &= Z\angle\alpha \\
S_3 &= Z_{R2}\angle\alpha_2 - Z\angle\alpha & S_4 &= Z_{R3}\angle\alpha_2 - Z\angle\alpha \\
S_5 &= Z\angle\alpha - K_0 Z_{R3}\angle(\alpha_2 - 180°) & S_6 &= K R_{R1}\angle{-\alpha_3} \\
S_7 &= K R_{R1}\angle{-\alpha_3} - Z\angle\alpha & S_8 &= K R_{R1}\angle(-\alpha_3 + 180°) \\
S_9 &= K R_{R1}\angle(-\alpha_3 + 180°) - Z\angle\alpha
\end{aligned}
\tag{6.56}
$$

where K_1 and K_0 both are < 1.

Signals for 3-zone quadrilateral characteristics with offsets are expressed as follows,

$$
\begin{aligned}
S_1 &= Z_1\angle(\alpha_4 - 90°) & S_9 &= K_4 X_1 \\
S_2 &= Z\angle\alpha & S_{10} &= K_4 X_1 - Z\angle\alpha \\
S_3 &= X_1 & S_{11} &= K_5 R_1\angle{-\beta} \\
S_4 &= X_1 - Z\angle\alpha & S_{12} &= K_5 R_1\angle{-\beta} - Z\angle\alpha \\
S_5 &= K_1 R_1\angle{-\phi} & S_{13} &= K_6 Z_1\angle(\alpha_4 - 180° - \delta) \\
S_6 &= K_1 R_1\angle{-\phi} - Z\angle\alpha & S_{14} &= K_6 Z_1\angle(\alpha_4 - 180° - \delta) - Z\angle\alpha
\end{aligned}
$$

$$S_7 = K_3 X_1 \qquad S_{15} = K_7 Z_1 \angle(\alpha_4 + \theta)$$
$$S_8 = K_3 X_1 - Z\angle\alpha \qquad S_{16} = K_7 Z_1 \angle(\alpha_4 + \theta) - Z\angle\alpha \qquad (6.57)$$

where K_1, K_2, K_3, K_4, K_5 are greater than 1 and K_6, K_7 are less than 1. Tripping occurs in both the cases when $90° \geq \xi \geq -90°$, where ξ is the angle between the desired signals.

The reach of the first zone is set at 0.8 of the impedance of 456 km lines of 400 kV/110 VPT and 500 A/1A CT ratio. In this case, this result in a reactance reach of 16 ohm and a set angle of 71°. The reach of the second zone relay is set to 1.50 times that of 1st zone. In this case, this is 24 ohm. The third zone is set at twice that of the first zone with an offset of 32 ohm in both the Mho and the quadrilateral characteristics. The segment of the blinder is set at 4 ohm and the angle is set at 18° and 342° with the *R* axis of the Mho relay characteristics in a clockwise direction. Similarly, the relay characteristics of the 3-zone offset quadrilateral relay is also stored with the angle $\alpha_4 = 78°$, $\alpha_5 = 120°$, for the first two zones and for the third zone $\alpha_1 = 70°$, $\alpha_2 = 60°$, $\alpha_3 = 24°$. If the apparent impedance to the point of fault lies inside the characteristics zone, the proper trip signal is issued to the tripping circuit and a print message to the work station; otherwise, it gives print message for external fault and enables the interrupt signal.

6.8 DIGITAL PROTECTION OF EHV/UHV TRANSMISSION LINE BASED UPON TRAVELLING WAVE PHENOMENA

With the growth of power systems, u.h.s. fault clearance is recognized as an effective method of increasing power transfer and improving the transient stability. The EHV/UHV transmission line is a long heavily loaded line having distributed parameters. When a fault occurs on such lines, the subsequent voltage at the fault position is affected. As a result, travelling waves of voltage and accompanying current are initiated on overhead transmission lines in the network. The development of u.h.s protective relays has been possible with the utilization of the travelling wave phenomena. Important contributions in this area were made by Chima and Liberman, Dommel and Michels and Johns. All of them proposed communication links for the exchange of information between the ends of an individual line. McLaren and Crossly proposed a scheme which did not require a communication link; here, the position of fault is determined by a correlation technique. Improvements to this scheme were reported by Rajendra and McLaren. The accuracy of both these algorithms using the correlation technique is dependent on the voltage angle of fault inception. This is because there is no obvious travelling wave signal at relay point in the case of a fault inception at zero voltage.

6.8.1 Amplitude Comparison Relaying Scheme

A long line is characterized by distributed series and shunt parameters. If faults take place on such lines, travelling waves [both forward and backward] of voltages and currents are produced because of the redistribution of energy in the electric and magnetic fields. This may be illustrated by considering, for simplicity, a single-phase transmission line interconnecting two large power systems as shown in Fig. 6.16 (a).

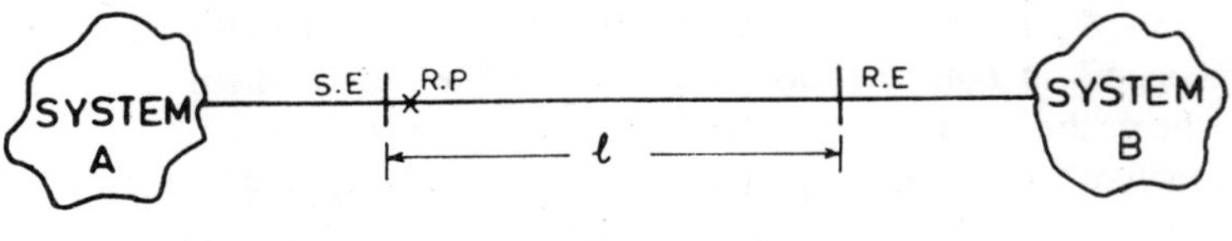

Fig. 6.16 (a) A transmission line interconnecting two power systems

Let v and i be the voltage and current at any point in the system after the occurrence of the fault. These can be regarded as the sum of the prefault and fault generated components, that is

$$v = v_{pf} + v_f \tag{6.58}$$

$$i = i_{pf} + i_f \tag{6.59}$$

where v_{pf} and i_{pf} are the prefault and v_f and i_f are the (transient) fault-generated components respectively. v_f and i_f can be determined using the well known telegraph (i.e. wave) equations as shown,

$$v_f = f_1\left[t - \frac{x}{u}\right] + f_2\left[t + \frac{x}{u}\right] \tag{6.60}$$

$$i_f = \frac{1}{Z_0}\left[f_1\left(t - \frac{x}{u}\right) - f_2\left(t + \frac{x}{u}\right)\right] \tag{6.61}$$

where f_1 and f_2 are functions determined by the boundary conditions.
t – travel time from the instant of fault occurrence
u – velocity of propagation of the travelling waves

$$= \sqrt{\frac{1}{LC}}$$

Z_0 – surge impedance of the line.

$= \sqrt{L/C}$ where L and C are in p.u.

In Eqs. (6.60) and (6.61), the first term, which is a function of f_1, is a forward wave and the second term, which is a function of f_2, is a backward wave. It is clear from the above, that the forward components of voltage and current are in the same direction while the backward components of voltage and current are in opposite directions.

Thus the travelling waves of the fault generated components of voltage and current originating at the fault point travel towards the ends of the line where they undergo reflection and refraction. If the voltage reflection coefficients at the sending and receiving ends are ρ_s and ρ_r respectively, these incidents can be shown by means of the lattice diagram as illustrated in Fig. 6.16 (b) where V_{f1} is the fault-generated component of the voltage at the fault point.

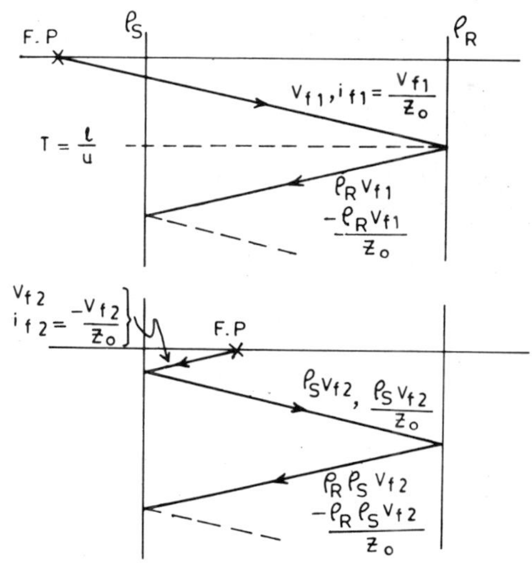

Fig. 6.16 (b) Lattice diagram of travelling waves of voltage and current

A very fast relaying scheme using the principle of amplitude comparison can be designed having the following signals,

$$S_1 = v_f - Z_0\, i_f \tag{6.62}$$

$$S_2 = v_f + Z_0\, i_f \tag{6.63}$$

where Z_0 is the resistance equal to $\sqrt{[L/C]}$ with L and C being respectively the inductance and capacitance per unit length of the line.

It can be easily verified that for a fault ahead of the relaying point (i.e. internal fault) $|S_1| > |S_2|$. For a fault behind the relay there would be, at the relay location, only forward travelling waves of voltage and current up to a least $2T$ seconds where $T = l/u$, and

l = length of the line

u = velocity of propagation.

However, for a fault at a distance x ahead of the relay, the current and voltage waves will be of opposite sign from x/u to $(x/u + 2T)$ seconds and hence only for internal fault $|S_1| > |S_2|$. Reflections beyond line terminals will appear as an external fault i.e. $|S_1| < |S_2|$.

6.8.2 Frequency Domain Model of Transmission Line

The fault analysis is done in the frequency domain and hence, the time domain values can then be obtained by digital computation through standard numerical inverse transformation method. The prefault components can be determined in the usual way by load flow analysis. The fault-generated components are used for designing the ultra high speed relays. Since the superposition principle is being used this method is only valid for linear systems.

Application of the superposition principles. The prefault three-phase power system network is shown in Fig. 6.17 (a) where only the faulted node has been shown in detail. The open three-pole switch represents the 'no fault' condition. It can be replaced by a three-phase transform voltage source $\overline{V}_{PF}^{a,b,c}$ having polarities as shown in Fig. 6.17 (b). $\overline{V}_{PF}^{a,b,c}$ are the transform of three-phase prefault voltage at the fault point. The fault can be simulated by connecting another three phase transform voltage source $\overline{V}_{FF}^{a,b,c}$, in series opposition to $\overline{V}_{PF}^{a,b,c}$ as shown in Fig. 6.17 (b). $\overline{V}_{FF}^{a,b,c}$ depends upon the type of fault to be simulated, i.e. $\overline{V}_{FF}^{a,b,c} = \overline{V}_{PF}^{a,b,c}$ for a symmetrical three-phase fault, for LG fault on phase a,

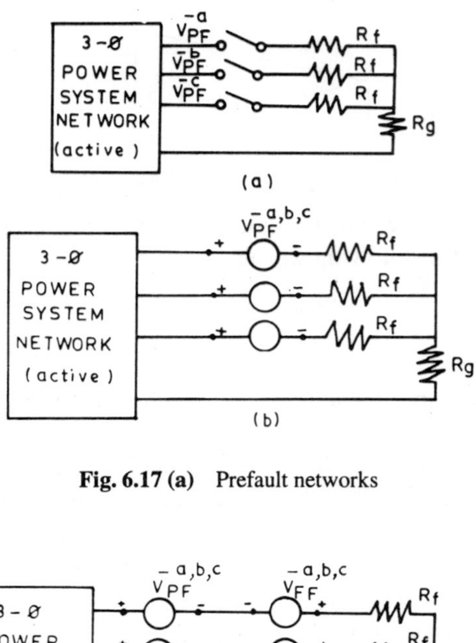

Fig. 6.17 (a) Prefault networks

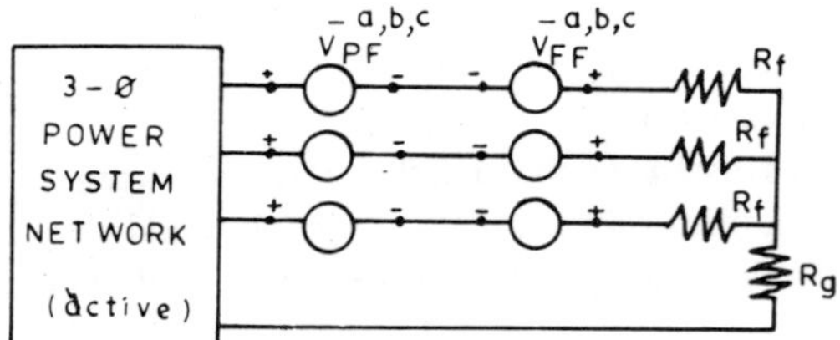

Fig. 6.17 (b) Postfault networks

$\overline{V}_{FF}^{a} = \overline{V}_{PF}^{a}$ and the values of $\overline{V}_{F}^{b}$ and $\overline{V}_{F}^{c}$ are such that the fault currents in phases *b* and *c*, i.e. $\overline{I}_{F}^{b}$ and $\overline{I}_{F}^{c}$ are zero. The fault resistance network as shown remains the same irrespective of the type of fault. We get the network of Fig. 6.17 (c) by applying the superposition principle. This is used for determining the fault-generated components.

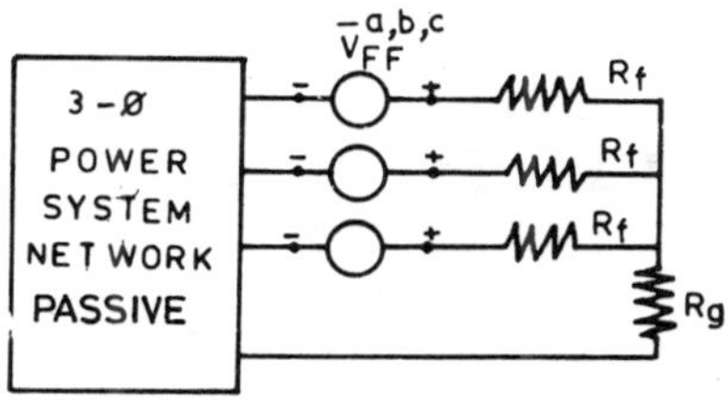

Fig. 6.17 (c) Network for evaluating only the fault-generated components

Nodal representation. To conduct the nodal analysis, the three-phase fault (arcing resistance) together with three phase voltage source at the fault node and three phase transmission lines are represented as explained below.

In order to apply the nodal analysis, a series branch having a three-phase voltage source $\overline{V}_{FF}^{a,b,c}$ and the three-phase fault resistance $R_F^{a,b,c}$ to ground is replaced by an equivalent three phase current source, $\overline{J}_F^{a,b,c}$ in parallel with three phase conductance $\overline{G}_F^{a,b,c}$ as shown in Fig. 6.17 (d), where

$$\overline{R}_F^{a,b,c} = \begin{bmatrix} R_f + R_g & R_g & R_g \\ R_g & R_f + R_g & R_g \\ R_g & R_g & R_f + R_g \end{bmatrix} \quad (6.64a)$$

therefore $G_F^{a,b,c} = [R_F^{a,b,c}]^{-1} = \overline{Y}_F^{a,b,c}$

and $\overline{J}_F^{a,b,c} = G_F^{a,b,c} \cdot \overline{V}_{FF}^{a,b,c} = \overline{Y}_F^{a,b,c}\ \overline{V}_F^{a,b,c}$ (6.64b)

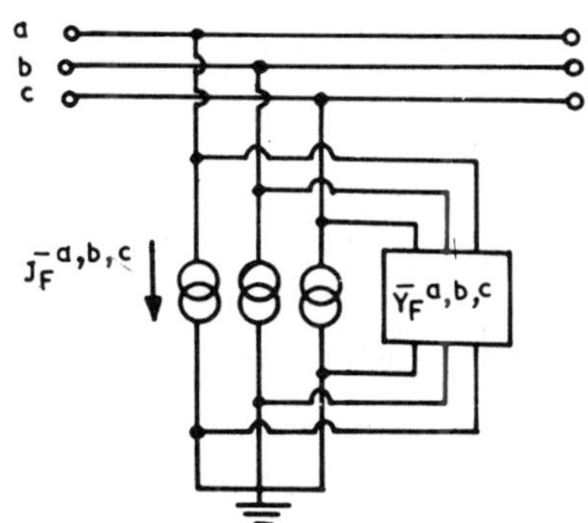

Fig. 6.17 (d) Equivalent current source at the faulted node

The equivalent circuit of the three phase transmission line is shown in Fig. 6.17 (e).

The frequency-domain nodal (matrix) equation can be developed by assuming $(N + 1)$ buses including the faulted bus F, with ground as the reference node.

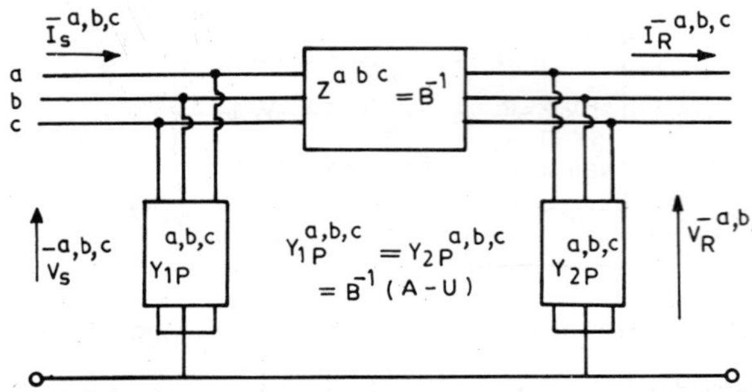

Fig. 6.17 (e) π-Equivalent circuit of a transmission line

$$\begin{bmatrix} \bar{Y}_{11}^{a,b,c} & \bar{Y}_{12}^{a,b,c} & \cdots & \bar{Y}_{1N}^{a,b,c} & \bar{Y}_{1F}^{a,b,c} \\ \bar{Y}_{21}^{a,b,c} & \bar{Y}_{22}^{a,b,c} & \cdots & \bar{Y}_{2N}^{a,b,c} & \bar{Y}_{2F}^{a,b,c} \\ \cdot & \cdot & & & \\ \cdot & \cdot & & & \\ \cdot & \cdot & & & \\ \cdot & \cdot & & & \\ \bar{Y}_{N1}^{a,b,c} & \bar{Y}_{N2}^{a,b,c} & \cdots & \bar{Y}_{NN}^{a,b,c} & \bar{Y}_{NF}^{a,b,c} \\ \hline \bar{Y}_{F1}^{a,b,c} & \bar{Y}_{F2}^{a,b,c} & \cdots & \bar{Y}_{FN}^{a,b,c} & \bar{Y}_{FF}^{a,b,c} \end{bmatrix} \begin{bmatrix} \bar{V}_1^{a,b,c} \\ \bar{V}_2^{a,b,c} \\ \\ \\ \\ \\ \bar{V}_N^{a,b,c} \\ \hline \bar{V}_F^{a,b,c} \end{bmatrix} = \begin{bmatrix} 0 \\ 0 \\ \cdot \\ \cdot \\ \cdot \\ \cdot \\ 0 \\ \hline -\bar{J}_F^{a,b,c} \end{bmatrix} \tag{6.65}$$

where, $\bar{V}_1^{a,b,c}$ – column vector of the transform of the voltages of phases a, b, c, at the *i*th bus for $i = 1, 2, \ldots N, F$. Equation (6.65) is partitioned as follows.

$$\begin{bmatrix} \bar{Y}_M^{a,b,c} & \bar{Y}_N^{a,b,c} \\ \bar{Y}_P^{a,b,c} & \bar{Y}_{FF}^{a,b,c} \end{bmatrix} \begin{bmatrix} \bar{V}_M^{a,b,c} \\ \bar{V}_F^{a,b,c} \end{bmatrix} = \begin{bmatrix} 0 \\ -\bar{J}_F^{a,b,c} \end{bmatrix}$$

i.e.
$$[\bar{Y}_{\text{bus}}^{a,b,c}]\, \bar{V}_{\text{bus}}^{a,b,c} = \bar{I}_{\text{bus}}^{a,b,c} \tag{6.66}$$

Equation (6.66) can be solved for determining any desired bus voltage transform. Knowing the bus voltage transform, the current transform in any element can be evaluated. From these transform values, the time domain values can be determined by any standard inverse transform technique, using numerical methods. For the solution of Eq. (6.66), $\bar{J}_F^{a,b,c}$ should be known *a priori*. However, in order to solve $\bar{J}_F^{a,b,c}$, $\bar{V}_{FF}^{a,b,c}$ has to be determined for different types of faults, as shown in what follows.

Determination of $\bar{V}_{FF}^{a,b,c}$

3-ϕ symmetrical fault

By examining the postfault networks in Fig. 6.17, it is clear that $\bar{V}_{FF}^{a,b,c} = \bar{V}_{PF}^{a,b,c}$.

1-ϕ to ground fault [L.G.] on any phase

If the fault is in phase 'a', then $\bar{V}_{FF}^{a} = \bar{V}_{PF}^{a}$ and $\bar{I}_F^b = \bar{I}_F^c = 0$. The values of $\bar{V}_{FF}^{b}$ and $\bar{V}_{FF}^{c}$ such that $\bar{I}_F^b = \bar{I}_F^c = 0$ can be determined as shown in the following.

From Eq. (6.66) we have

$$[\bar{Y}_P^{a,b,c}(\bar{Y}_M^{a,b,c})^{-1}\bar{Y}_N^{a,b,c} - \bar{Y}_{FF}^{a,b,c}]\,\bar{V}_F^{a,b,c} = \bar{J}_F^{a,b,c}$$

$$= \bar{Y}_F^{a,b,c}\,\bar{V}_{FF}^{a,b,c} \tag{6.67}$$

Also at the fault bus, the 3-ϕ fault current is given by

$$\bar{I}_F^{a,b,c} = \bar{J}_F^{a,b,c} + \bar{Y}_F^{a,b,c}\,\bar{V}_F^{a,b,c} \tag{6.68}$$

Solving Eqs. (6.67) and (6.68), we get

$$\bar{V}_{FF}^{a,b,c} = \bar{Z}^{a,b,c}\,\bar{I}_F^{a,b,c} \tag{6.69}$$

where

$$\bar{Z}^{a,b,c} = \bar{Z}_F^{a,b,c} - [\bar{Y}_F^{a,b,c} - \bar{Y}_{FF}^{a,b,c} + \bar{Y}_P^{a,b,c}(\bar{Y}_M^{a,b,c})^{-1}\,\bar{Y}_N^{a,b,c}]^{-1}$$

and

$$\bar{Z}_F^{a,b,c} = [\bar{Y}_F^{a,b,c}]^{-1}$$

Now let,

$$\bar{Z}^{a,b,c} = \begin{bmatrix} \bar{Z}_{aa} & \bar{Z}_{ab} & \bar{Z}_{ac} \\ \bar{Z}_{ba} & \bar{Z}_{bb} & \bar{Z}_{bc} \\ \bar{Z}_{ca} & \bar{Z}_{cb} & \bar{Z}_{cc} \end{bmatrix} \tag{6.70}$$

Solution of the Eq. (6.69) with the condition that $\bar{I}_F^b = \bar{I}_F^c = 0$, yields

$$\bar{V}_{FF}^{a,b,c} = \begin{bmatrix} \bar{Z}_{aa} \\ \bar{Z}_{ba} \\ \bar{Z}_{ca} \end{bmatrix} \frac{\bar{V}_{PF}^{a}}{\bar{Z}_{aa}} \tag{6.71}$$

Inverse of the time domain. The time domain values of voltage and current at the relaying point can be obtained from the frequency domain values by modified Fourier transform techniques. The inverse modified Fourier transform is used to determine the corresponding time variation of any voltage or current at discrete values of ω which has the wide spectrum,

$$f(t) = \frac{e^{at}}{2\pi}\int_{-\infty}^{\infty} f_+^-(a + j\omega)\,e^{j\omega t}\,d\omega \tag{6.72}$$

where ω – angular frequency as well as transform parameter

a – frequency shift constant which is used to reduce aliasing errors when the integral is evaluated digitally

and $f_+^-(a + j\omega)$ – modified Fourier transform of the function $f(t)$.

In order to carry out the numerical integration, it is necessary to truncate the infinite range of the integral in Eq. (6.72) to some finite value say $(-\Omega, \Omega)$. This introduces truncation error which is suppressed by using the Lancgos sigma factor, defined by,

$$\sigma = \frac{\sin(\pi\omega/\Omega)}{(\pi\omega/\Omega)} \tag{6.73}$$

Then Eq. (6.72) becomes

$$f(t) = \frac{2e^{at}}{\pi}\int_0^{\Omega} P\cos\omega t\, d\omega \tag{6.74}$$

where, $P = \text{Re}\,[f_+^-(a + j\omega)]$.

For the numerical computation of the above equation, the n-point trapezoidal rule is applied to yield

$$f(t) = \frac{2e^{at}}{\pi}\frac{\Delta\omega}{2}\,[\sigma_0 P_0 + 2\sigma_1 P_1 \cos(\Delta\omega) + \ldots$$

$$+ 2\sigma_{n-2}P_{n-2}\cos([n-2]\,\Delta\omega\cdot t) + \sigma_{n-1}P_{n-1}\cdot\cos([n-1]\,\Delta\omega\cdot t)] \tag{6.75}$$

where $\omega = \Omega/n$, the step size

$$\sigma_K = \frac{\sin(K\pi\Delta\omega/\Omega)}{(K\pi\Delta\omega/\Omega)};\quad K = 0, 1, \ldots, (n-1)$$

and, $$P_K = \text{Re}\,[f_+^-(a + jK\Delta\omega)];\ K = 0, 1, \ldots, (n-1) \tag{6.76}$$

Now let

$$0.5\,\sigma_0 P_0 = P_0'$$

$$\sigma_K P_K = P_K';\quad K = 1, 2, \ldots, (n-2) \tag{6.77}$$

$$0.5\,\sigma_{n-1} = P_{n-1}'$$

and,

$t = r\Delta t$ where Δt is the time step.

Then Eq. (6.75) can be written as follows.

$$f(r\cdot\Delta t) = \frac{2e^{at}}{\pi}\cdot\Delta\omega\sum_{K=0}^{n-1} P_K'\cos(Kr\cdot\Delta\omega\cdot\Delta t) \tag{6.78}$$

Normally, the value of the function is required at several instants of time. In such a case P_K's can be computed before-hand and stored.

6.8.3 Numerical Evaluation of the Voltage and Current Signals at the Relay Point (Fig. 6.18)

The 4-bus power system network given in the reference is reproduced. All the lines are 128 km in length and an earth resistivity of 100 ohm-m is assumed. The faults are assumed to occur in the line between the buses 1 and 2; at the extreme end of bus 1 and 2 separately and also in the line between buses 1 and 3 which is external to bus 1.

The equivalent circuit of the sample power system network is shown in Fig. 6.19 when the fault is between bus 1 and bus 2.

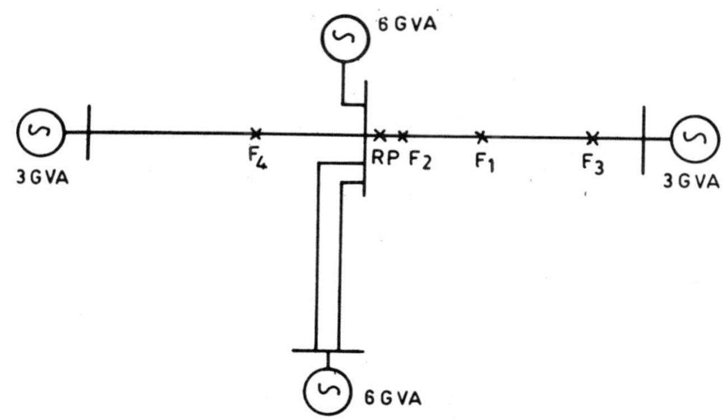

Fig. 6.18 A sample 4-bus power system

The nodal equation of the sample system is given by

$$\begin{bmatrix} 3B^{-1}A + B_1^{-1} + Y_{S2}^{a,b,c} & 0 & -B^{-1} & -2B^{-1} & -B^{-1} \\ 0 & B_2^{-1}A_2 + Y_{S1}^{a,b,c} & 0 & 0 & -B_2^{-1} \\ -B^{-1} & 0 & B^{-1}A + Y_{S1}^{a,b,c} & 0 & 0 \\ -2B^{-1} & 0 & 0 & 2B^{-1}A + Y_{S2}^{a,b,c} & 0 \\ -B_1^{-1} & -B_2^{-1} & 0 & 0 & B_1^{-1}A_1 + B_2^{-1}A_2 + Y_F^{a,b,c} \end{bmatrix} \begin{bmatrix} \overline{V}_1^{a,b,c} \\ \overline{V}_2^{a,b,c} \\ \overline{V}_3^{a,b,c} \\ \overline{V}_4^{a,b,c} \\ \overline{V}_F^{a,b,c} \end{bmatrix} = \begin{bmatrix} 0 \\ 0 \\ 0 \\ 0 \\ -\overline{J}_F^{a,b,c} \end{bmatrix} \quad (6.79)$$

Solving Eq. (6.79) yields the voltage and current trnasform at the relaying point which is considered to be at the bus 1 and on the line connecting buses 1 and 2. They are given by,

$$\overline{V}_1^{a,b,c} = [\beta]\,[B_1^{-1}]\,[\alpha]\,Y_F^{a,b,c}\,\overline{V}_{FF}^{a,b,c} \quad (6.80)$$

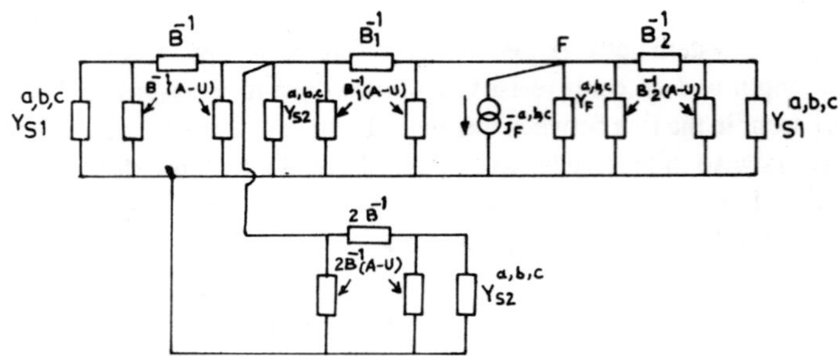

Fig. 6.19 Equivalent circuit of the given sample power system network

where

$$\beta = [B^{-1} K^{-1} B^{-1} + 4 B^{-1} T^{-1} B^{-1} - M]^{-1}$$

$$K = [B^{-1} A + Y_{S1}^{a,b,c}]; \; T = [2 B^{-1} A + Y_{S2}^{a,b,c}]$$

$$M = [3 B^{-1} A + B_1^{-1} A_1 + Y_{S2}^{a,b,c}]$$

$$\alpha = [B_2^{-1} R^{-1} B_2^{-1} - \omega - B_1^{-1} \beta B_1^{-1}]^{-1}$$

$$R = [B_2^{-1} A_2 + Y_{S1}^{a,b,c}]; \quad \omega = B_1^{-1} A_1 + B_2^{-1} A_2 + Y_F^{a,b,c}$$

$$\overline{I}_{1F}^{a,b,c} = -B_1^{-1} (\beta B^{-1} + U) \alpha Y_F^{a,b,c} \overline{V}_{FF}^{a,b,c} \tag{6.81}$$

$\overline{V}_{FF}^{a,b,c}$ required in the above equation are determined by 3ϕ and LG fault as detailed in the following:

3-ϕ Symmetrical fault

$$\overline{V}_{FF}^{a,b,c} = \overline{V}_{PF}^{a,b,c}$$

$$\begin{bmatrix} V_m [S \sin \phi_0 + \omega_0 \cos \phi_0]/(S^2 + \omega_0^2) \\ V_m [S \sin (\phi_0 - 120°) + \omega_0 \cos (\phi_0 - 120°)]/(S^2 + \omega_0^2) \\ V_m [S \sin (\phi_0 + 120°) + \omega_0 \cos (\phi_0 + 120°)]/(S^2 + \omega_0^2) \end{bmatrix}$$

where,

V_m — peak value of the prefault voltage at the faulted bus

ω_0 — nominal angular frequency of the system

ϕ_0 — fault initiation angle

and S — $(a + j\,\omega)$, the modified Fourier transform parameter.

LG fault in phase 'a'

For the sample system, the matrix $Z^{a,b,c}$ is given by

$$\bar{Z}^{a,b,c} = \bar{Z}_F^{a,b,c} + [B_1^{-1} A_1 + B_2^{-1} A_2 + B_1^{-1} \quad (B^{-1} K^{-1} B + 4 B^{-1} T^{-1} - M) B^{-1} - B_2^{-1} R^{-1} B_2^{-1}]^{-1} \tag{6.82}$$

We can solve $\bar{V}^{a,b,c}$ with the help of Eq. (6.69), in conjunction with above matrix $\bar{Z}^{a,b,c}$ [Eq. (6.82)].

For both faults V_{max} is assumed to be 1.0 p.u. and $R_f = 100$ ohms with the base-phase voltage chosen as $\frac{400\sqrt{2}}{\sqrt{3}}$ kV and line current = 600 kA. The time domin values are obtained by using values specified in the next section with the help of inverse modified Fourier Transform with different values of a, n, θ_0 with $t = 20$ μs.

6.8.4 Computer Programme and Digital Simulation

A computer programme is developed on the basis of the procedure outlined in the earlier sections to solve for the time domain values of the relaying point voltages and currents. A simplified procedure is outlined according to the following steps. The steps are given in sequence briefly.

1. Read the data of the transmission lines: sources, fault resistance, prefault voltages at the faulted bus, fault initiation angle and inverse modified Fourier transformation parameters.
2. Calculate the P_K's ($K = 0, 1, 2, \ldots, n-1$) as defined in Eqs. (6.76) and (6.77) for voltage and current transform separately, using the following steps.
   (i) Initialization, i.e. set $\omega = 0.0$
   (ii) Set the transform parameters, $S = (a + j\,\omega)$
   (iii) For $\omega = 0.0$, assign $\omega = 10.0$
   (iv) Calculate the transmission line frequency-dependent inductance (L) and resistance of the line from the above.
   (v) When $\omega = 10.0$, take $\omega = 0.0$
   (vi) Calculate the per unit length of series impedance $\bar{Z}_L^{a,b,c}$ and shunt admittance $\bar{Y}_L^{a,b,c}$ of the line as a function of S.
   (vii) Calculate the eigenvalues and eigenvectors of the matrix ($\bar{Z}^{a,b,c}\,\bar{Y}_L^{a,b,c}$ through a sub-routine.
   (viii) Calculate the voltage and current transformation matrices S and Q.
   (ix) Calculate the frequency domain A, B, C, D parameters of the line.
   (x) Calculate the source admittances as a function of S.
   (xi) Calculate the relaying-point voltage and current transform using appropriate equations.
   (xii) Calculate P_K's for the above, using Eqs. (6.76) and (6.77).
   (xiii) Increment ω by $\Delta\omega = \Omega/n$ and go to step 2(ii).
3. Using Eq. (6.78), compute the time domain values of the voltage and currents at all the desired instances of time.

The step 2 (iii) and 2 (v) are necessitated by the fact that the frequency-dependent series self and mutual impedances of the line cannot be evaluated at $\omega = 0.0$ by the formulae given in the reference. Hence, they are evaluated at an angular frequency close to zero. Sub-routines have been used also for complex matrix inversion as well as multiplication.

6.9 NEW RELAYING SCHEME USING AMPLITUDE COMPARISON

A fault detection algorithm based on amplitude comparison is proposed for the detection of faults. This is used to detect whether the fault lies ahead of the relay point (internal fault) or behind it (external fault). The proposed relaying scheme may be used for the protection of EHV/UHV transmission lines.

For the proposed algorithm, it is preferable for the elimination of the fundamental prefault component, i.e. 50/60 Hz in the monitored currents and voltages by means of appropriate band reject (notch) filters. This filtering scheme removes the prefault components of voltages and currents and leaves behind only the ones generated by the fault. These filtered components are used in subsequent calculations. Note that, in the absence of a fault, these (filtered) line currents will be almost zero.

The absolute magnitudes of the (filtered) line currents (complex waveforms) in each of the three phases are continuously compared against a fixed threshold by hardware comparators. A single line-to-ground, i.e. an L-G fault is assumed to occur if two of the three line currents remain below threshold whereas the third crosses above this threshold value. Similarly, a three-phase fault is indicated if the average (within a pre-set window) of the peak of (filtered, absolute magnitude) each of the individual line currents exceeds a pre-set minimum value. For this averaging process, a typical window length of about 400 μs is suggested.

From the voltage and current waveforms, one can also conclude that 3-ϕ (LLLG) fault may be indicated if there is any zero crossing of any of the line voltages and currents within a stipulated time-period (e.g. 400 μs). Since the (filtered) pre-fault values are almost zero, this method must include a sufficient noise-margin in order to be applicable.

6.9.1 Hardware and Software Design

The overall relay hardware includes a six-channel Data Acquisition System (DAS), a three-channel Fault Detection Circuit (FDC) and a microcomputer system. The block diagram is shown in Fig. 6.20 (a).

Data acquisition system (DAS). The DAS accepts six channels of analog input from the transmission line (V_a, V_b, V_c, i_a, i_b, i_c) through appropriate transducers. The input signals pass through 50 Hz (band reject) notch filters. Fig. 6.20 (b) shows the circuit diagram of notch filters using dual opamps, in a single chip (μA7474J).

The output signals from the band reject filters pass through a variable gain amplifier (VGA) so that the amplitude of its output can be adjusted to any desired value. The output signals of three line currents from the VGA pass through the FDC to indicate LG or 3-ϕ fault.

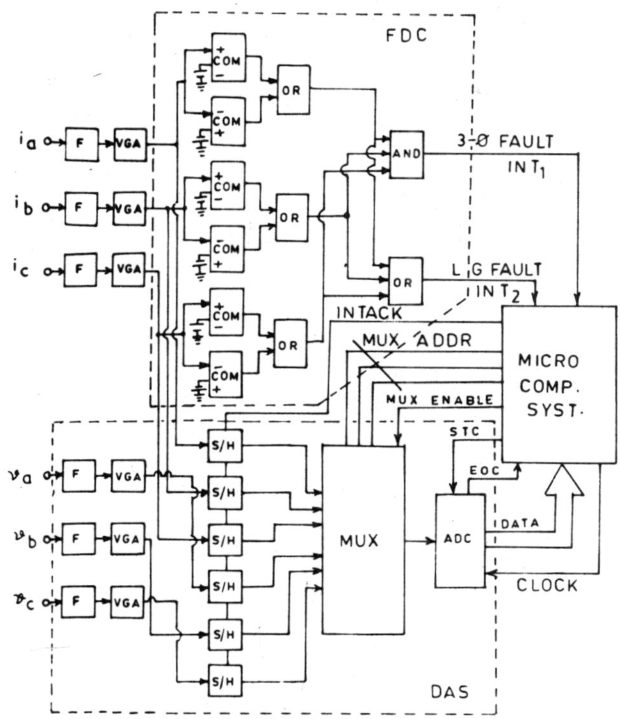

Fig. 6.20 (a) Relay hardware scheme (block diagram)

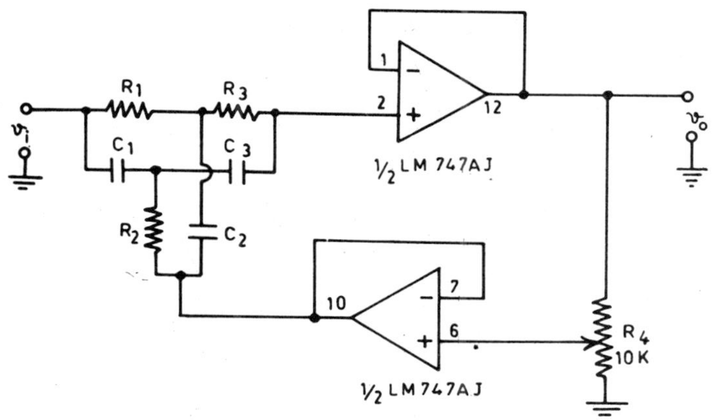

$R_1 = R_3 = 680\text{K}$ $\qquad C_1 = C_3 = 0.004\ \mu\text{F}$

$R_2 = R_1/2 = 340\text{K}$ $\qquad C_2 = 0.01\ \mu\text{F}$

Fig. 6.20 (b) 50 Hz notch (band reject) filter

Fault detector circuit (FDC). The FDC is shown in Fig. 6.20 (c). The first stage is an opamp circuitry with dual comparators, that compares the output of the amplifier with the threshold voltage V_T. The output of this stage is converted into TTL compatible levels using zener diodes. The second stage is a digital logic that compares the polarities of current. In this circuit, the currents in the three phases are compared against a pre-set threshold through hardware comparators to generate a logical 1 from the associated OR gate in case the absolute values of current exceeds the threshold. The output of the three OR gates are once again logically combined to detect the presence of either a L-G or 3-ϕ fault with the help of microcomputer.

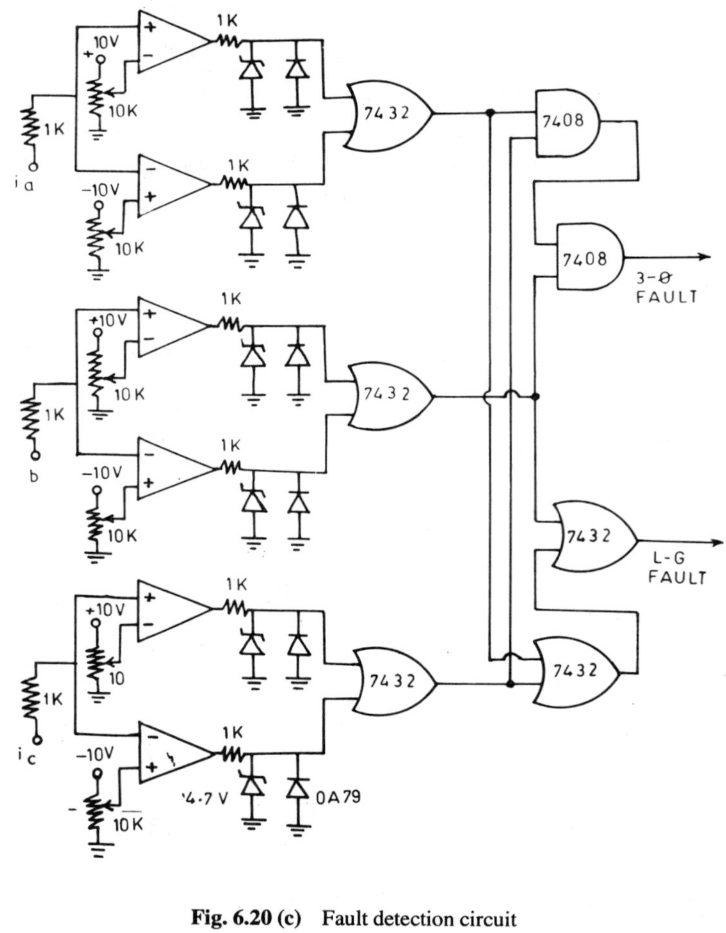

Fig. 6.20 (c) Fault detection circuit

On getting this 'fault-present' signal through its interrupt lines, the microcomputer acquires the three currents and voltages simultaneously by triggering all the S/Hs at the same instant of time. It then reads the values of these currents and voltages through the MUX-ADC combination. The digital output from the ADC is read by the microcomputer system. By proper software control, it is sufficient to get the data of only one channel and corresponding voltage for L-G (fault involved phase) or 3-ϕ fault. The control of the S/H circuit, enabling an address selection of the MUX, issuing the start of conversion pulse (SOC) to the ADC, checking for the end of conversion (EOC) from the ADC are done by the microcomputer system. Knowing the value of voltage and current in the microcomputer system, the value of S_1 and S_2 can be determined to ascertain whether the fault is external or internal.

Fault simulator. The fault simulator has been designed to enable simulation of various types of faults (L–G, LLLG fault) at various inception angles. The duration of fault can also be chosen.

The block diagram of the fault simulator is shown in Fig. 6.21 and the corresponding timing diagram in Fig. 6.22. The prefault voltage at the fault location

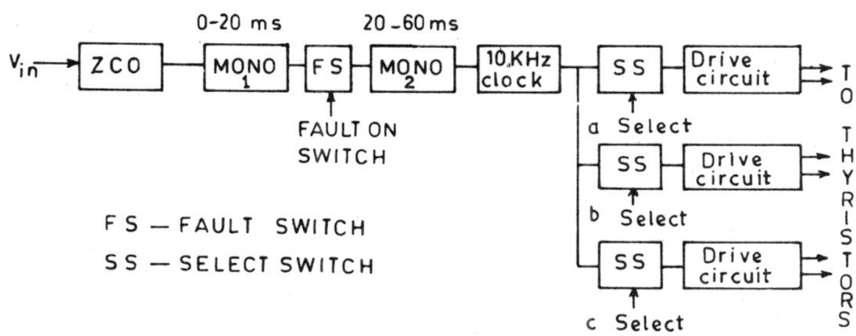

(a) BLOCK DIAGRAM OF FAULT SIMULATOR

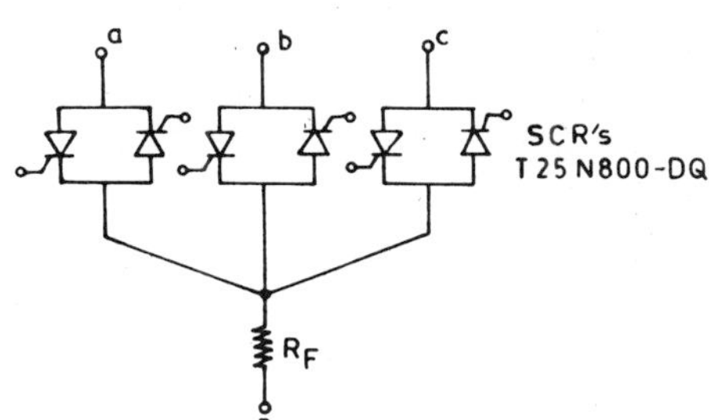

(b) POWER CIRCUIT OF THE FAULT SIMULATOR

Fig. 6.21 Fault simulator schematic

is stepped down and fed as the input to the zero-crossing detector circuit. The rising edge of the ZCD output pulse triggers a monostable pulse of adjustable width (0–20 ms). The falling edge of the monostable output pulse determines the instant of fault inception. The falling edge of the monostable triggers another monostable when the fault switch is enabled. This monostable also has an adjustable pulse width (20–60 ms) and determines the duration of fault. The output of this monostable enables a 10 kHz clock to be applied to the input of thyristor drive circuits in the phases selected for fault. The fault resistance is connected externally and is made equal to zero for solid faults. The circuit diagram of the control circuit of the fault

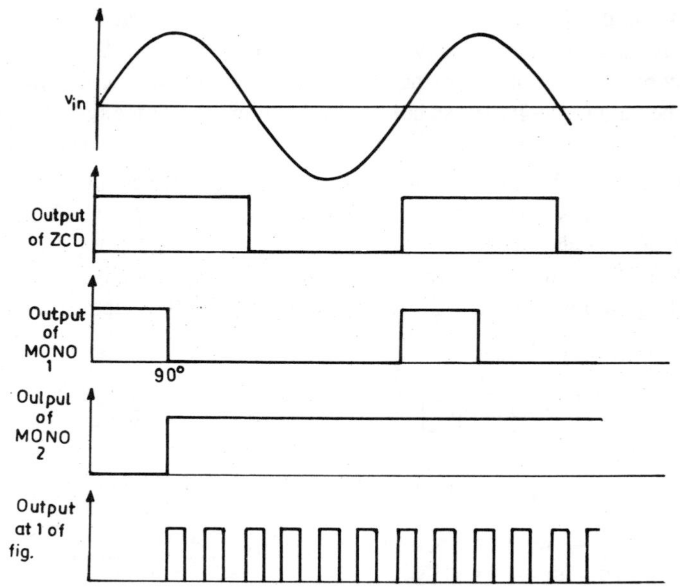

Fig. 6.22 Timing diagram for the fault simulator

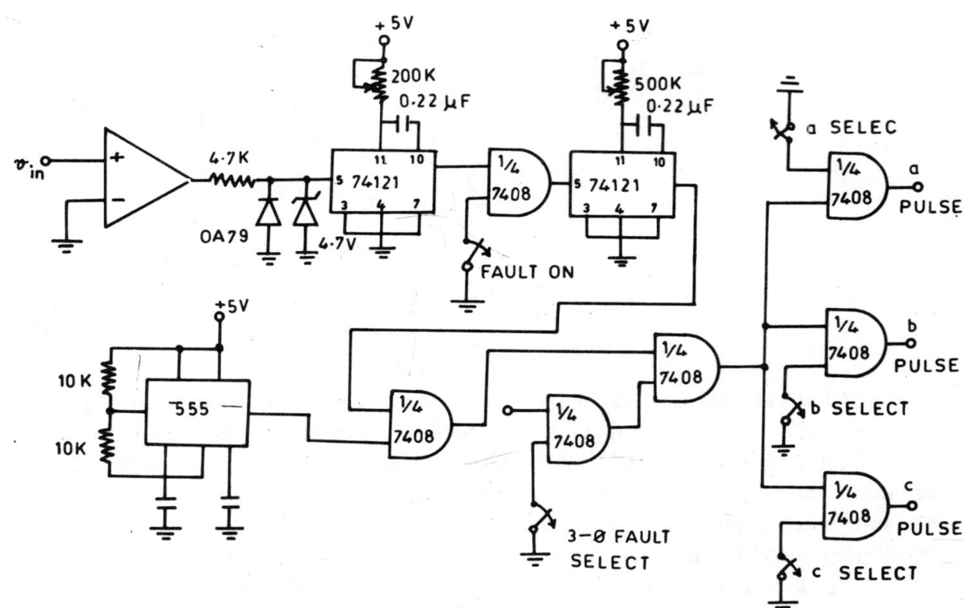

Fig. 6.23 Control circuit of the fault simulator

simulator is shown in Fig. 6.23. Figure 6.24 shows the pulse amplifier circuit for one phase.

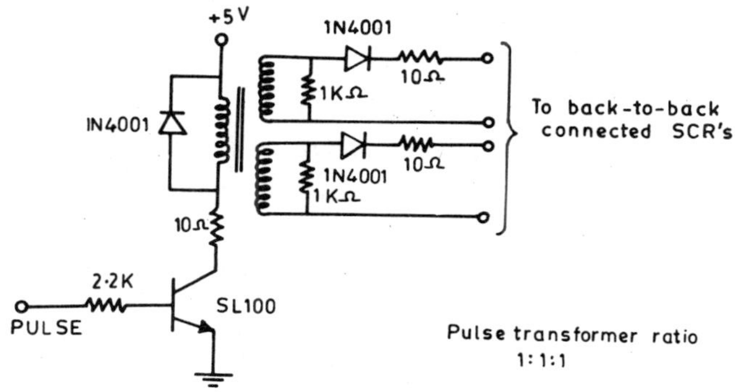

Fig. 6.24 Pulse amplifier circuit

6.9.2 Phase Comparison Relaying Scheme Based upon Correlation Technique

For the distance algorithms, correlation technique is used here. The correlation technique earlier reported by the authors is dependent on the voltage angle of fault inception, since there is no obvious travelling wave signal at relay point in the case of fault inception at zero voltage. Here the distance to fault can be identified under even zero voltage.

Relay signals. According to the superposition principle, the postfault voltage and current components can be separated according to Eqs. (6.58) and (6.59). Here, only the incremental signal ΔV and Δi are considered. The wave equations for ΔV and Δi at any instant of time and at any point of the line, which is taken as a lossless line (Fig. 6.25), can therefore be expressed as follows:

$$\frac{\delta(\Delta V)}{\delta x} = -L' \frac{(\delta \Delta i)}{\delta t} \tag{6.83}$$

$$\frac{\delta(\Delta i)}{\delta x} = -C' \frac{\delta(\Delta V)}{\delta t} \tag{6.84}$$

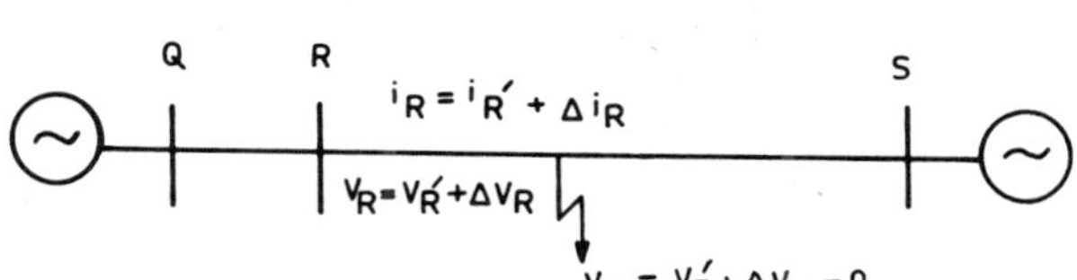

Fig. 6.25 Superposition principle on a sample power system network

The solution of the above wave equation can be rewritten directly from Eqs. (6.60) and (6.61) in the following form:

$$i(x, t) = F_1(x - ut) + F_2(x + ut) \quad (6.85)$$

$$V(x, t) = Z_0 F_1(x - ut) - Z_0 F_2(x + ut) \quad (6.86)$$

With the incremental signals, ΔV_R and Δi_R at the relay point R, two signals S_1 and S_2 can be obtained as,

$$S_1 = V_R(t) - Z_0 \Delta i_R(t) \quad (6.87)$$

$$S_2 = V_R(t) + Z_0 \Delta i_R(t) \quad (6.88)$$

S_1 represents forward travelling wave characteristics (fault to source) while S_2 represents backward travelling wave characteristics (source to fault). Let D_F and D_B define forward and backward travelling wave discriminant functions as shown, by Eqs. (6.89) and (6.90).

$$D_F = S_1^2 + \left[\frac{dS_1}{d\omega t}\right]^2 \quad (6.89)$$

$$D_B = S_2^2 + \left[\frac{dS_2}{d\omega t}\right]^2 \quad (6.90)$$

Under the fault condition: For a solid fault at F, $R_f = 0$ and hence, the reflection coefficients,

$$\rho_F = \frac{Z_0 - R_f}{Z_0 + R_f} = 1 \quad (6.91)$$

Assuming an infinite bus system behind the relay point ($Z_Q = 0$) the reflection coefficient at the discontinuity Q can be written as,

$$\rho_Q = \frac{Z_0 - Z_Q}{Z_0 + Z_Q} = 1 \quad (6.92)$$

Prefault voltage at the fault point

$$V_F' = -V\sqrt{2}\sin(\omega t + \phi) \quad (6.93)$$

where V is r.m.s. value of prefault voltage at the fault point F and ϕ is the inception angle of fault.

6.9.3 Forward Travelling Wave Discriminant Function

After fault inception at $t = 0$, the forward travelling wave cannot reach the relay point R before travel time τ_1, which is shown in Fig. 6.26 (a). Thus the relay signal $S_1^{(1)}$ can be written as,

$$S_1^{(1)} = \Delta V_R(t) - Z_0 \Delta i_R(t) = 0 \quad \text{for } t < \tau_1 \quad (6..94)$$

It is assumed that incremental voltage and current produced by the fault at the fault point F are ΔV_F and Δi_F. Considering Eq. (6.93), the incremental voltage and current at fault point can be deduced as

$$\Delta V_F(t) = 0 - V_F' = V\sqrt{2}\sin(\omega t + \phi) \quad (6.95)$$

$$\Delta\, i_F = \frac{\Delta\, V_F}{Z_0} \tag{6.96}$$

ΔV_F and Δi_F arrive at the relay point at time τ_1, the signal S_1^2 from τ_1 to τ_3 can be expressed by

$$S_1^{(2)} = \Delta V_R\,(t) - Z_0\,\Delta i_R\,(t) = \Delta V_F\,(t - \tau_1) + Z_0\,\Delta i_F\,(t - \tau_1) \tag{6.97}$$

Substitution from Eqs. (6.95) and (6.96) in Eq. (6.97), gives

$$S_1^{(2)} = 2\sqrt{2}\,V\,[\sin\omega\,(t - \tau_1) + \phi] \qquad \text{for } \tau_1 < t < \tau_3 \tag{6.98}$$

At time t_3, the wave arrives at the relay point again after being reflected at the fault point. Considering Eq. (6.92), the signal $S_1^{(3)}$ from τ_3 can be deduced as:

$$S_1^{(3)} = \Delta\, V_R\,(t) - Z_0\,\Delta\, i_R\,(t) = [\Delta V_F\,(t-\tau_1) - \Delta V_F\,(t-\tau_2)$$
$$+ \Delta V_F\,(t-\tau_3)] + Z_0\,[\Delta\, i_F\,(t-\tau_1) + \Delta\, i_F\,(t-\tau_2) + \Delta\, i_F\,(t-\tau_3)] \tag{6.99}$$

Substituting from Eqs. (6.95) and (6.96) into Eq. (6.99), the relay signal $S_1^{(3)}$, can be deduced as follows

$$S_1^{(3)} = 4\sqrt{2}\,V\sin\,(\omega\,[t - (\tau_1 + \tau_3)/2] + \phi) \times \cos\,(\omega\,(\tau_3 - \tau_1)/2)$$
$$\text{for } \tau_3 \le t$$

It is assumed that $(\tau_3 - \tau_1) \le T = \dfrac{1}{50\text{ Hz}}$

then, $\cos\,(\omega\,(\tau_3 - \tau_1)/\sqrt{2} \simeq 1$ and the relay signal $S_1^{(3)}$ from τ_3 can be expressed as follows

$$S_1^{(3)} = 4\sqrt{2}\,\sin\,(\omega\,(t - [\tau_1 + \tau_3]/2) + \phi) \text{ for } \tau_3 \le t \tag{6.100}$$

Summing Eqs. (6.94), (6.98) and (6.100), yields:

$$S_1 = 2\sqrt{2}\,V \begin{bmatrix} 0 & t < \tau_1 \\ \sin\,[\omega\,(t-\tau_1) + \phi] & \tau_1 \le t < \tau_3 \\ 2\sin\omega\,[(t - [\tau_1 + \tau_3]/2) + \phi] & \tau_3 \le t \end{bmatrix} \tag{6.101}$$

and hence the discriminant function D_F is given after substituting Eq. (6.101) in Eq. (6.89)

$$D_F = V^2 \begin{bmatrix} 0 & t < \tau_1 \\ 8 & \tau_1 \le t \le \tau_3 \\ 32 & \tau_3 \le t \end{bmatrix} \tag{6.102}$$

which is independent of the angle of fault inception.

6.9.4 Backward Travelling Wave Discriminant Function

The other relay signals S_2 can also be derived in a similar manner. As shown in Fig. 6.26, the backward travelling wave cannot arrive at the relay point R before the time τ_2; thus, the relay signals S_2 from 0 to τ_2 can be written as,

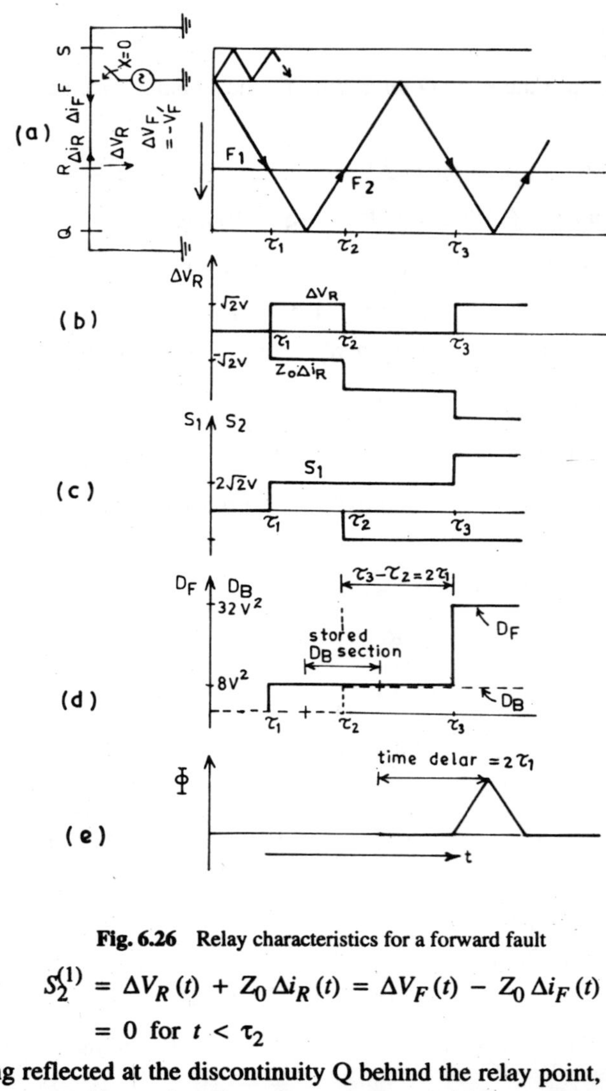

Fig. 6.26 Relay characteristics for a forward fault

$$S_2^{(1)} = \Delta V_R(t) + Z_0\,\Delta i_R(t) = \Delta V_F(t) - Z_0\,\Delta i_F(t)$$
$$= 0 \text{ for } t < \tau_2 \qquad (6.103)$$

After being reflected at the discontinuity Q behind the relay point, the backward travelling wave arrives at the relay point at time τ_2 and this causes a sudden change in relay signals S_2. The relay signal $S_2^{(2)}$ from τ_2 can be deduced as,

$$S_2^{(2)} = 2\sqrt{2}\,V\sin(\omega(t-\tau_2)+\phi) \quad \text{for } \tau_2 \le t \qquad (6.104)$$

Therefore summing Eqs. (6.103) and (6.104) yields:

$$S_2 = \sqrt{2}\,V\begin{bmatrix} 0 & t < \tau_2 \\ 2\sin\{\omega(t-\tau_2)+\varphi\} & \tau_2 \le t \end{bmatrix} \qquad (6.105)$$

Substituting from Eq. (6.105) the backward travelling discriminant function D_B [Eq. (6.90)] yields:

$$D_B = V^2 \begin{bmatrix} 0 & t < \tau_2 \\ 8 & \tau_2 \le t \end{bmatrix} \quad (6.106)$$

which is also independent of the fault inception. Figs. 6.26 (a, b, c and d) illustrate the incremental voltage and current, the relay signals S_1, S_2 and the discriminant functions D_F and D_B.

For a reverse fault also, as shown in Fig. 6.27, S_1 and S_2 and D_F and D_B can be derived using the same analytical method described earlier. In this case the discriminant functions D_B and D_F, can be expressed as follows:

$$D_B = V^2 \begin{bmatrix} 0 & t < \tau_1 \\ 8 & \tau_1 \le t \le \tau_3 \\ 32 & \tau_3 \le t \end{bmatrix} \quad (6.107)$$

$$D_F = V^2 \begin{bmatrix} 0 & t < \tau_2 \\ 8 & \tau_2 \le t \end{bmatrix} \quad (6.108)$$

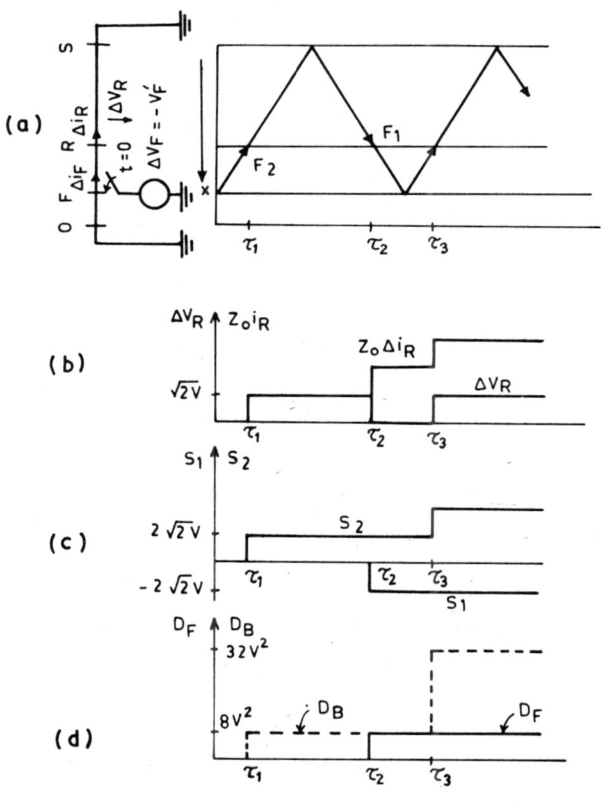

Fig. 6.27 Relay characteristics for a backward fault

Equations (6.107) and (6.108) are illustrated in Fig. 6.27 (d). During normal operating conditions, the two functions D_F and D_B are zero and become finite when a fault or disturbance occurs. The direction can be determined by detecting the sequence in which the two functions exceed a predetermined threshold.

6.9.5 Distance Measurement Using Correlation Technique

It can be seen from Eqs. (6.102) and (6.106) and Fig. 6.26 that D_F and D_B are step functions. The sudden change in steps of the two functions occurs at those instants of time when the incident wave and reflected wave arrive at the relay point and there is a sudden change of step at τ_1 from 0 to $8V^2$. The incident wave passes through the relay point and is reflected by the discontinuity behind the relay point. This reflected wave arrives at the relay point at time τ_2 and results in a sudden step function D_B from zero upto a very high value $8V^2$. The reflected wave propagates towards the fault point and is again reflected back at the fault point. This reflected wave causes the second high step of the function D_F from $8V^2$ to $32V^2$ at time τ_3. It can be seen from Fig. 6.26 that the time delay between the step at time τ_2 of the function D_B and the step at time τ_3 of the function D_F equals twice the wave travel time of fault distance. The correlation technique can be used here to.detect the time delay in order to determine the distance to fault.

The function D_B, as shown in Fig. 6.26, will be stored as one of the correlation signals, and the function D_F will be correlated against the stored section of the function D_B. The continuous correlation function between D_B and D_F can be expressed as follows;

$$\Phi(\tau) = \int_0^{\infty} D_F(t + \tau) \times D_B(t)\, dt \tag{6.109}$$

The discrete cross-correlation between the sections of D_B and D_F with zero mean, yields:

$$\Phi_{D_F \cdot D_B}(\tau) = \frac{1}{N} \sum_{K=1}^{N} \{D_B(K\Delta t) - \overline{D}_B\} \times \{D_F(K\Delta t + \tau) - \overline{D}_F(\tau)\} \tag{6.110}$$

where

$$\overline{D}_B = \frac{1}{N} \sum_{K=1}^{N} D_B(K\Delta t) \tag{6.111}$$

$$\overline{D}_F = \frac{1}{N} \sum_{K=1}^{N} D_F(K\Delta t + \tau) \tag{6.112}$$

$\overline{D}_B$ and $\overline{D}_F$ are the mean levels of their respective data group. As shown in Fig. 6.26 (e), the maximal output of the correlation function indicates the best match between the functions D_F and D_B. The time delay between the first correlation output and the maximal correlation output indicates twice the wave travelling time from the relay point to the fault point. The distance to fault can be calculated by multiplying the time delay with the corresponding wave velocity.

The performance of the distance algorithm based on travelling wave principle will be affected by a number of factors associated with system configuration and fault conditions such as reflection coefficient behind the relay point and discontinuity at the relay point.

The source impedance Z_Q behind the relay point is usually small in comparison to surge impedance Z_0. The reflection coefficient ρ_Q has no significant influence on relay performance. When there is a discontinuity at bus bar of the relay point, the wave, which arrives at the relay point from the fault point, will be immediately reflected at the discontinuity. So there will be no time delay between the first steps of the functions D_F and D_B. The cross-correlation will result in a very high output value at the beginning of the cross-correlation. In this case, the maximal output value at the first correlation output must be ignored. Using the travelling wave for distance measurement appears to be more difficult than for directional relaying using microcomputer.

6.10 SUMMARY

The continuous growth in the size and complexity of electric power system, has given rise to the need for extremely fast and highly reliable protection schemes. The utilization of travelling wave phenomenon has enabled the realization of ultra high speed relaying schemes for the protection of EHV/UHV transmission lines. And, the application of digital computer for the protective relaying purposes has several advantages, the chief amongst them being self checking feature and maximum flexibility. Therefore, the use of travelling wave phenomena along with digital computer for the protection of EHV/UHV transmission lines, has outstanding merits. In this chapter, the digital protection of transmission lines based upon fundamental sinusoidal component as also upon travelling wave phenomenon has been discussed in detail. The former is known as distance relaying scheme which has been discussed in the earlier chapter using static components. The transient fault analysis based upon a nodal formulation has been carried out and expressions for the voltage and current waves at different frequencies which are used in the u.h.s. protective relays employing travelling wave phenomena, have been obtained. Both the software as well as hardware aspects of digital relaying schemes have been discussed in detail. Digital protection is certainly reliable and efficient with very bright future prospects.

EXERCISES

1. (a) What are the different types of faults in an overhead transmission line? Write in the sequence of their severity.
   (b) How are the sequence networks connected to simulate (i) LLG fault (ii) LL fault and (iii) LG fault? Show with the help of neat diagrams.

2. What are the advantages of digital protection? Discuss briefly. Explain what do you understand by centralized and decentralized digital protection schemes.
3. (a) What is the function of filters in digital protection scheme? Discuss briefly analog and digital filters along with their merits and limitations.
   (b) Discuss briefly the different types of digital filters you are familiar with.
4. Discuss the theory and basic principle of digital protection of a transmission line. Also discuss, with the help of neat diagrams, the hardware and software of the digital protection scheme using distance (i.e. impedance) relays.
5. What do you understand by travelling wave based relaying scheme of a long transmission line? Discuss briefly. Discuss the digital protection of a long transmission line based upon travelling wave phenomena with the help of neat diagrams showing hardware and software details. Discuss also the merits and limitations of this relaying scheme.

REFERENCES

1. Basu, S.K., S. Chaudhuri, R. Chakrabarti, "Polyphase Distance Relaying by Phase Sequence Detection", *J. Instn. Engrs. (India)*, Vol. 54, Part EL-4, 1974, pp. 135–141.
2. Bernard, P., and J.C. Bastide, "A Prototype of Multi-processor Based Distance Relay", *IEEE Trans. Pwr. Apparat. & Syst.*, Vol. PAS-101, Feb. 1982, pp. 491–498.
3. Carr, J., and R.V. Jackson, "Frequency Domain Analysis Applied to Digital Transmission Line Protection", *IEEE Trans. Pwr. Apparat. & Syst.*, Vol. PAS-94, July/Oct. 1975, pp. 1157–1166.
4. Chamia, M., and S. Liberman, "Ultra High Speed Relay for EHV/UHV Transmission Lines —Development, Design and Application", *IEEE Trans. Pwr. Apparat. & Syst.*, Vol. PAS-97, Nov./Dec. 1978, pp. 2104–2116.
5. Chandra, A., Sachchidanand and L.P. Singh, "Proposed Ultra High Speed Distance Relaying Scheme for High Phase Order (HPOT) System", Proc. of the 16th Ann. Conf. IEEE *Industr. Electron. Soci.* (IECON 90), Pacific Grove (California), U.S.A.
6. Choudhury, S., S.K. Basu and S.P. Patra, "Polyphase Ground Distance Relaying by Phase Coincidence Principle", Transaction Paper No. T-72, 4281, Presented at IEEE, Summer Power Meeting, 1972, *IEEE Trans. Pwr. Apparat. & Syst.*, PAS-92, 1972, pp. 626–634.
7. Dasgupta, K.S., O.P. Malik and G.S. Hope, "Kalman Filtering Approach to Impedance Protection", *Trans. Engng. & Operating Div., Can. Elect. Assoc.*, March 1983, Paper, No. 83-SP-171, pp. 1–14.
8. Desikachar, K.V., Y. Asthana and L.P. Singh, "New Relay Scheme for EHV/UHV Transmission Lines", *J. Instn. Engrs.* (*India*), Vol. 63, Pt: EL3, Dec. 1982, pp. 159–164
9. Desikachar, K.V., and L.P. Singh, "Fault Analysis of Multinode Power System for Designing Ultra Speed Protective Relays along with Proposed Relaying Scheme", *Elect. Pwr. Syst. Res.*, Vol. 6, 1983, pp. 13–25.
10. Desikachar, K.V., "Ultra High Speed Protective Relaying Scheme for EHV/UHV Transmission Line Based Upon Travelling Wave Phenomena", *Ph. D. thesis* submitted to IIT Kanpur, May 1983.
11. Desikachar, K.V. and L.P. Singh, "Digital Travelling Wave Protection of Transmission Lines", *Elect. Pwr. Syst. Res.*, Vol. 7, 1984, pp. 19–28.
12. Dommel, H.W., and J.M. Michels, "High Speed Relaying Using Travelling Wave Transient Analysis", Paper presented at the IEEE PES Winter Meeting, Jan. 1978, *IEEE Publ.* No. 78CH1295-PWR, Paper No. A78, pp. 214–219.

13. Esztergaloys, J., M.T. Yee, M. Chamia and S. Liberman, "The Development and Operation of an Ultra High Speed Relaying System for EHV Transmission Lines", CIGRE, Paris, 1978, Paper No. 34–04.
14. Gilbert, J.G., and R.J. Shovlin, "High Speed Transmission Line Fault Impedance Calculation Using a Dedicated Minicomputer", *IEEE Trans. Pwr. Apparat. & Syst.*, Vol. PAS-94, May/June, 1975, pp. 872–883.
15. Gilbert, J.G. E.A. Udren and H. Sackin, "The Development and Selection of Algorithms for Relaying of Transmission lines, by Digital Computers", *Power System Control and Protection,* edited by B.D. Russel and M.E. Council, Academic Press, New York, 1978, pp. 83–127.
16. Gilcrest, G.B., G.D. Rockefeller and E.A. Udren, "High-Speed Distance Relaying Using a Digital Computer: Part I — System Description", *IEEE Trans. Pwr. Apparat. & Syst.*, Vol, PAS-91, May/June 1972, pp. 1235–1242.
17. Girgis, A.A., and R.G. Brown, "Application of Kalman Filtering in Computer Relaying", *IEEE Trans. Pwr. Apparat. & Syst.*, Vol. PAS-100, July 1981, pp. 3387–3395.
18. Girgis, A.A., "A New Kalman Filtering Based Digital Distance Relay", *IEEE Trans. Pwr. Apparat. & Syst.*, Vol. APS-101, Sept. 1982, pp. 3471–3480.
19. Gokul, P., V.P. Sunak and L.P. Singh, "Digital Protection of EHV Transmission Line", *Proceeding 51st, R&D Session of CBIP* at Vadodara (India), Jan. 1984, pp. 75–88.
20. Hope, G.S., and V.S. Umamaheswaran, "Sampling for Computer protection of Transmission Lines", *IEEE Trans. Pwr. Apparat. & Syst.*, Vol. PAS-93, Sept./Oct. 1974, pp. 1522–1534.
21. Hope, G.S., O.P. Malik and M.E. Rasmy, "Digital Transmission Line Protection in Real Time", *Proc. IEE,* Vol. 123, December 1976, pp. 1349–1354.
22. Horton, J.W., "Walsh Functions for Digital Impedance Relaying for Power Lines", *IBM J. Res. & Devlp.,* Vol. No. 10, 1976, pp. 530–541.
23. Islam, K.K., and L.P., Singh, "Microprocessor: Application to Power System Protection", *52nd R&D Session of CBIP*, held at Anurangabad, Feb. 1985, Vol. III, pp. 7–12.
24. Islam, K.K., S.K. Bose and L.P. Singh, "On Line Microprocessor Based Relaying Scheme", *Proc. Platinum Jubilee Conf. Systems and Signal Processing*, held at I.I.Sc., Bangalore, Dec. 1986, pp. 241–244.
25. Islam, K.K., S.K. Bose and L.P. Singh, "On Line Microprocessor Based Relaying Scheme for EHV/UHV Transmission Line : An Existing 400 kV Transmission Line", *Electr. Machines and Pwr. System,* Vol. 5, No. 12, 1987, pp. 313–324.
26. Islam, K.K., S.K. Bose and L.P. Singh, "Digital Protection of EHV/UHV Transmission Line Based Upon Travelling Wave Phenomena", *Electr. Machines and Pwr. Syst.*, No. 14, 1988, pp. 413–431.
27. Islam, K.K. "Digital Protection of EHV/UHV Transmission Line", *Ph. D. thesis* submitted to IIT Kanpur, Sept. 1988.
28. Jackson, L., J.B. Patrickson and L.M. Wedepohl, "Distance Protection: Optimum Dynamic Design of Static Relay Comparators", *Proc. IEE,* Vol. 113, Feb. 1968, pp. 280–287.
29. Jeyasura, B.J., W.J. Smolinski, "Design and Testing of a Microprocessor Based Distance Relay", *IEEE Trans.,* Vol. PAS-103, No. 5, May, 1984, pp. 1104–1110.
30. Johns, A.T. "Generalised Phase Comparator Techniques for Distance Protection, Theory and Operation of Multi-Input Devices", *Proc. IEEE,* Vol. 119, Nov. 1972, pp. 1595–1603.
31. Johns, A.T., and M.A. Martin, "Fundamental Digital Approach to the Distance Protection of EHV Transmission Lines", *Proc. IEE,* Vol. 125, May 1978, pp. 377–384.
32. Johns, A.T. "New Discriminative Distance—Protective Relays for Selective Pole Autoreclosure Applications", *Proc. IEE,* Vol. 126, Feb. 1979, pp. 159–161.
33. Johns, A.T., M.A. Martin, *et. al.*, "A New Approach to EHV Direction Comparison Protection Using Digital Signal Processing Techniques", *IEEE Trans. Pwr. Delivery, (USA),* Vol. PWRD-1, 1986, pp. 24–43.
34. Kellog, A.J., L.P. Singh and G.K. Dubey, "General Purpose Static Relay Using Digital Techniques", *J. Instn. Engrs. (India)*, Vol. 63, Part EL2, August 1982, pp. 5–11.
35. Kellong, A.J., L.P. Singh and G.K. Dubey, " High Speed 3-zone Distance Relay Using Digital Circuit", *Electr. Pwr. Syst. Res.*, Vol. 9, 1984/85, pp. 187–195.

36. Khincha, H.P., K. Parthasarathy and B.S. Ashok Kumar, "Developments in Amplitude-Comparator Techniques for Distance Relays", *Proc. IEE,* Vol. 117, June 1970, pp. 1118–1124.
37. Luckett, R.G., P.J. Munday and B.E. Murray, "A Substation Based Computer for Control and Protection", Conference on Modern Developments in Protection, *IEE* (London) *Publ.* No. 125, 1975, pp. 252–260.
38. Mann, B.J. and I.F. Morrison, "Digital Calculation of Impedance for Transmission Line Protection", *IEEE Trans. Pwr. Apparat. & Syst.,* Vol. PAS-90, Jan./Feb. 1971, pp. 270–279.
39. Mann, B.J., and I.F. Morrison, "Relaying a Three-Phase Transmission Line with a Digital Computer", *IEEE Trans. Pwr. Apparat. & Syst.,* Vol. PAS-90, March/April 1971, pp. 742–750.
40. Mansour, M.M., G.W. Swift, "A Multiprocessor Based Travelling Wave Relay", *IEEE Trans. Pwr. Delivery (USA),* Vol. PWRD-1, 1986, pp. 272–279.
41. McLaren, P.G. and S. Rajendra, "Ultra High Speed Distance Protection Based on Travelling Waves", Third International Conference on Developments in Power System Protection, *IEE Conf. Publ.* No. 249, 1985, pp. 106–110.
42. Miki, Y., Y. Sano and J.I. Makino, "Study on High-Speed Distance Relay Using Microcomputer", *IEEE Trans. Pwr. Apparat. & Syst.,* Vol. PAS-96, No. 2, March/April 1977, pp. 602–613.
43. Paithankar, Y.G., and M.V. Deshpande, "Polyphase Distance Relay", *Proc. IEE,* Vol. 120(9), 1973, pp. 1013–1015.
44. Paithankar, Y.G., and V.T. Ingole, "New Techniques in Multi-Input Amplitude Comparators to Generate Quadrilateral Distance Relay", *J. Inst. Engrs. (India),* Vol. 54, Part EL3, Feb. 1974, pp. 79–85.
45. Paithankar, Y.G., and M.T. Sant, "A New Algorithm for Relaying Fault Location Based on Travelling Waves", *Electr. Pwr. Syst. Res.* (Switzerland), Vol. 8, 1985, pp. 179–185.
46. Parthasarathy, K., "New Static 3-Step Distance Relay", *Proc. IEEE,* Vol. 113, April 1966, pp. 633–640.
47. Parthasarathy, K., "Three-System and Single-System Static Distance Relay", *Proc. IEEE,* Vol. 113, April 1966, pp. 641–651.
48. Parthasarathy, K., H.P. Khincha and B.L. Mathur, "An, Adaptive Distance Relay for the Protection of Transmission Lines", *Conference Papers,* Vol. 1 : *Conference on Power System Protection,* Madras (India), April 16–19, 1980, Paper No. A3.
49. Phadke, A.G., T. Hlibka and M. Ibrahim, "A Digital Computer System for EHV Substations : Analysis and Field Tests", *IEEE Trans. Pwr. Apparat. & Syst.,* Vol. PAS-95, Jan./Feb. 1976, pp. 291–301.
50. Poncelet, R., "The Use of Digital Computers for Network Protection", CIGRE, Paris, 1972, Paper No. 32–08.
51. Rajendra, S., and P.G. McLaren, "Travelling Wave Techniques Applied to Protection of Teed Circuits: Principles of Travelling Wave Techniques", *IEEE Trans. Pwr. Apparat. & Syst.,* Vol. 104, 1984, pp. 3544–50.
52. Rajendra, S., and P.G. McLaren, "Travelling Wave Techniques Applied to Protection of Teed Circuits : Multiphase/Multiconductor System", *IEEE Trans. Pwr. Apparat. & Syst.,* Vol. PAS-104, 1985, pp. 3551–3557.
53. Ramamoorthy, M., "A Note on Impedance Measurement Using Digital Computers", *IEE-IERE Proc. (India),* Vol. 9, Nov./Dec. 1971, pp. 243–247.
54. Ramamoorthy, M., and S.N. Lall, "A Versatile Phase Comparator Relay Using Digital Circuits", *J. Instn. Engrs. (India),* Vol. 59, Part EL6, June 1979, pp. 309–314.
55. Ramamoorthy, and S.N. Lall, "Digital Multi-Input Phase Comparator", *Conference Papers,* Vol. 1, *Conference on Power System Protection,* Madras (India), April 16–19, 1980, Paper No. A5.
56. Rajbar, A.M., and B.J. Cory, "An Improved Method for the Digital Protection of Transmission Lines", *IEEE Trans. Pwr. Apparat. & Syst.,* Vol. PAS-94, March/April 1975, pp. 544–550.
57. Rockefeller, G.D., "Fault Protection with a Digital Computer", *IEEE Trans. Pwr. Apparat. & Syst.,* Vol. PAS-98, April 1969, pp. 438–464.

58. Sachdev, M.S. and M.A. Baribeau, "A New Algorithm for Digital Impedance Relay", *IEEE Trans. Pwr. Apparat. & Syst.*, Vol. PAS-98, May/June 1979, pp. 2232–2240.
59. Singh, L.P., "Advanced Power System Analysis and Dynamics", 3rd Edition, Wiley Eastern Ltd., New Delhi, 1993
60. Siyaram, and L.P. Singh, "Digital Protection of Transmission Line", *53rd R&D Conference of CBIP*, held at Bhubaneswar, May 1986, Vol. VII, pp. 85–98.
61. Slemon, G.R., S.D.T. Robertson and M. Ramamoorty, "High Speed Protection of Power Systems Based on Improved System Models", CIGRE, Paris, 1968, Paper No. 31–09.
62. Smolinski, W.J., "An Algorithm for Digital Impedance Calculation Using a Single Pi Selection Transmission Line", *IEEE Trans. Pwr. Apparat. & Syst.*, Vol. PAS-98, Sept./Oct. 1979, pp. 1546–1551.
63. Sunak, V.P., and L.P. Singh, "Microprocessor Based Protection Scheme for EHV/UHV Transmission Line", *J. Instn. Engrs.* (India), Vol. 65, Pt. EL2 and 3, Oct.-Dec. 1984, pp. 89–96.
64. Sunak, V.P., and L.P. Singh, "On Line Protection of EHV/UHV Transmission Line Using Microprocessor", *Proc. Int. Conf. Microprocessor for Power System Applications,* held at Madras (India).
65. Thirupathaiah, G., A. Varshney and L.P. Singh, "On-Line Digital Protection Using a Microcomputer — A decentralized Approach", *Tech. Proc., Natl. Conf. Planning, Operation and Control of Large Scale Power Systems,* Annamalai University, India, June 24–25, 1982, Paper No. S5.3.
66. Vitins, M., "A Correlation Method for Transmission Line Protection", *IEEE Trans. Pwr. Apparat. & Syst.*, Vol. PAS-97, Sept./Oct. 1978, pp. 1607–1616.
67. Vitins, M., "A Fundamental Concept for High Speed Relaying", *IEEE Trans. Pwr. Apparat. & Syst.*, Vol. PAS-100, Jan. 1981, pp. 163–173.
68. Walker, L.N., *et al.,* "Special Purpose Digital Computer Requirements for Power System Substation Needs", *IEEE Winter Meeting,* Paper No. 70CP142-PWR, 1970.

7

DIGITAL PROTECTION OF SYNCHRONOUS GENERATOR

7.1 INTRODUCTION

One of the major and vital components in a power system is the synchronous generator. Any fault in the very source of power, i.e. synchronous generator may hamper the available power to a great extent. Hence, the problem of protecting this vital unit against all abnormal conditions including fault and at the same time, keeping the protection scheme simple, reliable and fast in operation, has always posed a challenge to the power system engineers.

For the protection of a synchronous generator, high speed protective relay and associated switch gear is necessary. It is shown earlier that electromechanical, electronic and static relays have not been able to provide the required high speed, simplicity, flexibility, sensitivity and reliability. These features can be achieved very easily in the digital protection schemes, especially in the microprocessor (i.e. mini computer or PC-based) relaying schemes, with an additional self checking feature. It is possible to change the threshold characteristics of the relay just by modifying the software only or by minor changes in the hardware. This is not possible in the case of electromechanical, electronic or static relays. Therefore, we can state that the microprocessor-based relaying scheme is probably the best relaying scheme for a synchronous machine.

The concept of percentage differential relay to protect synchronous generator against stator faults has been used since the early 40s. The problem with percentage differential relay in the case of interturn faults was looked into by Kinitsky. The existence of negative sequence current in the case of all unbalanced faults was first recognized by Morris. He used the negative sequence current as a signal to indicate external fault and therefore to provide backup protection. As a matter of fact, the area of protective relaying became more attractive with the introduction of digital protection. The possibility of using digital computer for protection against various faults in different components was first investigated in a detailed manner by Rockfeller. The advantages of using digital techniques were quite evident, and since then almost all subsequent efforts have been on digital relaying. The detailed studies regarding different types of faults that are likely to occur in a synchronous generator along with the three modern schemes of digital protection of synchronous machines are discussed in this chapter.

7.2 FAULTS IN SYNCHRONOUS GENERATOR

Generators are subjected to varieties of possible hazards for which protection should be considered and careful attention be given. This section attempts to discuss these faults and/or abnormal operating conditions, which are likely to occur in any synchronous generator connected to a large power system. The causes of these faults and their possible effects on generator are also discussed.

The possible hazards or faults which may occur in a synchronous generator can broadly be classified into two categories: (a) Internal faults within generator protection zone, and (b) Abnormal operating and/or abnormal system conditions.

Internal faults can further be classified into two sub-categories, *viz.* (i) Stator faults, and (ii) Rotor faults.

7.2.1 Stator Faults

Within the stator winding, faults can occur due to failure of insulation (i.e. dielectric) and open circuit of conductor. Failure of insulation can lead to the short circuit between; (a) two or more phases, (b) phase and core, and (c) two or more turns of the same phase (i.e. interturn fault).

Failure of insulation can occur due to overvoltage, overheating caused by unbalanced loading, by overloading, by ventilation trouble, by improper cooling of lubrication oil. It may also be caused by conductor movement due to forces exerted by short circuit currents or out-of-step operation. The most common fault in the stator winding is ground fault; about 85% of the faults are phase to ground faults in any generator winding. Phase to ground fault if persists may lead to phase to phase fault and even to phase-phase-phase fault (three-phase short circuit), which is the most severe fault though least common. The cause of overvoltage which ultimately results into failure of insulation can be due to overspeed of the prime mover, or due to defective voltage regulator; however, these days governers and voltage regulators act very fast and prevent any damage to the winding insulation.

7.2.2 Rotor Faults

In the rotor winding also failure of insulation between field winding and core or two or more turns can occur. These faults may ultimately result in unbalanced currents and heating of the rotor. If the rotor is ungrounded, first earth fault does not show any effect but a second earth fault increases the current in the affected portion of winding which may cause distortion and permanent damage. It is advisable to open the field circuit breaker even with single earth fault to avoid second earth fault so as to prevent local heating.

7.2.3 Abnormal Operating Conditions/Miscellaneous Faults

There are a number of abnormal conditions which do not occur in the stator or rotor winding, but are undesirable since they can damage the generator. Each of these conditions are discussed in the following.

(a) *Loss of synchronism (Figs. 7.1 and 7.2).* This condition can occur either due to loss of field excitation or governer becoming defective. Loss of synchronism is discussed in two parts, viz. characteristics and its effects on the generator.

Characteristics

During the power swing, the angle of separation between voltages E_A and E_B (Fig. 7.1) is δ. Due to disturbance, the angle of separation δ will increase and becomes 180° when it bisects line AB. Further increase of δ will move the operating point form P to Q (Fig. 7.2) and on completion of one slip cycle they will be in phase again.

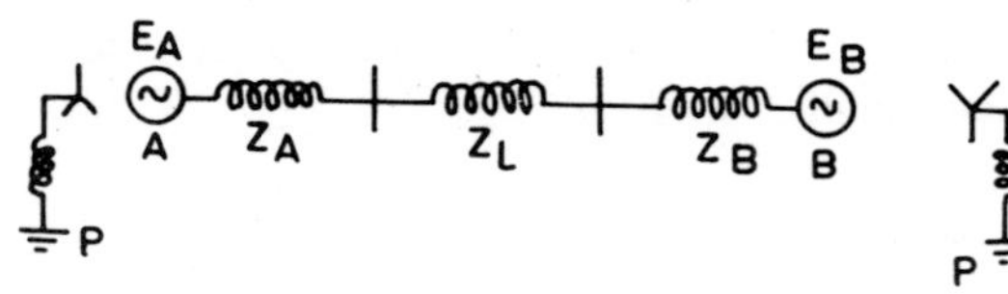

Fig. 7.1

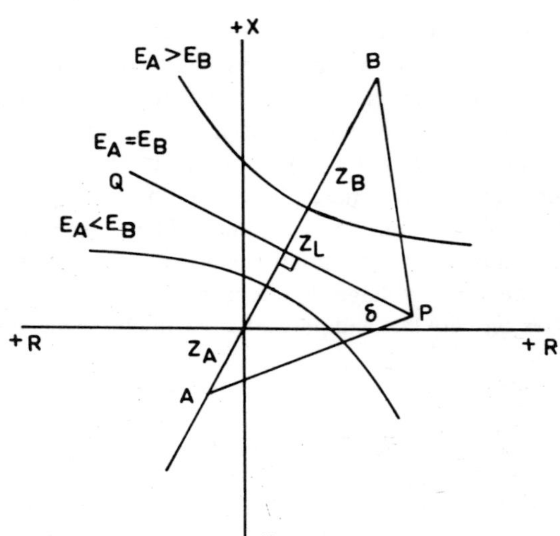

Fig. 7.2 Loss of synchronism characteristics

Effect on generator

During out of step condition as the swing angle between generated voltage of the machine changes with respect to that of other units in the system, the current in any such unit varies in magnitude. The current surges that result are cyclical in nature, their frequency being a function of reactive rate of slip of the poles in the machine. The resulting high peak currents and off-frequency operation can cause winding stresses, and pulsating torques which can excite mechanical resonances that can be potentially damaging to the generator and to the shafts. Thus generator should be tripped without any delay within the first slip cycle to avoid any major damage.

(b) *Overspeed.* The cause of overspeed is sudden loss of a very large load; sometimes this happens due to tripping of circuit breaker near the generator end. In the case of steam turbine, the steam can be shut off immediately but in case of hydro turbine, the water flow cannot be stopped quickly, due to mechanical and hydraulic inertia. The governer controls the over speeding so as to avoid any high voltage, high frequency and mechanical damage to the generators. The setting of an overspeed rating may be 115% for steam turbines and 140% for hydro turbines.

(c) *Motoring.* In the multi-generator system, when prime mover fails to provide required speed, the generator may act as a motor, drawing power from the system, instead of supplying power. Generally motoring is prevented by sensitive reverse power relay which operates on about 0.5% reverse power.

(d) *Underspeed.* Due to failure of steam or water supply to the prime mover, the speed of the generator will reduce and if the reverse power relay fails, then underspeed and/or underfrequency relay comes into picture and trips the circuit breaker.

(e) *Loss of excitation.* Excitation failure may be caused by a faulty field circuit breaker or failure of the exciter. It can be detected by an undercurrent d.c. relay. Due to failure of excitation, the synchronous generator may act as an induction generator thereby absorbing reactive power (i.e. sink of reactive power). Turbo generator tends to overheat the rotor and the slot wedges under these conditions because of heavy currents induced in these parts and sometimes arcing occurs at metal wedges in the slots. The most reliable relay to correct field failure is a MHO relay with the characteristics as shown in Fig. 7.3.

(f) *Overvoltage.* This may be caused due to overspeed or overexcitation when speed governer or voltage regulator fails to act as desired. To avoid damage to the insulation, an overvoltage relay is incorporated.

(g) *Stator overheating.* Overheating may occur due to bearing failure, overloading, inadequate lubrication, or improper cooling of lubricating oil, etc. Overheating affects the dielectric strength of insulation.

(h) *External faults.* Whenever abnormal conditions occur beyond the generator protection zone, the generator is also affected since the very source of power to the external fault is the generator itself. These conditions can be detected by the magnitude of negative sequence current, second harmonic current in field current and line overcurrent relay.

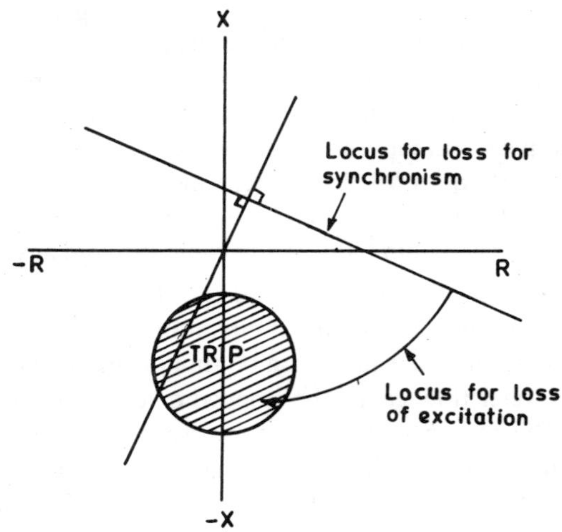

Fig. 7.3 MHO relay characteristics to correct loss of excitation

(i) *Auxiliary failure.* Abnormal functioning of auxiliary systems like loss of vacuum, loss of boiler pressure, inadequate circulation of lubricating oil, etc. will also affect healthy running of the generator.

7.3 PROTECTION SCHEMES FOR SYNCHRONOUS GENERATOR

With the growth in the size and complexity of the power system network day by day, the size and rating of synchronous generator are also increasing. With this increase in size and cost, the protection of modern synchronous machines has also become more and more complex. The synchronous generators are susceptible to a number of faults and abnormal conditions, and the types of protection schemes to be provided, depend greatly upon the size of the synchronous machine, for which a rough guide is provided in Table 7.1. The existing protection schemes of synchronous generators are discussed briefly in the in the following sub-sections.

7.3.1 Unit Protection Scheme

The differential (i.e. unit) protection scheme is that which responds to the vector difference between two or more similar electrical quantities. In the case of synchronous generator differential protection scheme, the CTs are provided at each end of the armature winding of the synchronous generator. If there is no internal fault in the winding or there is a through (i.e. external) fault, the CT secondary currents are equal and the vector difference of the currents, $I_2 - I_1$ which flows in the operating coil of the relay is zero. However, during internal fault in the armature winding, the CT secondary currents are not equal, i.e. $I_2 - I_1$ is finite. This differential current $I_2 - I_1$ flows in the operating coil of the protective relay thus giving trip signal to the associated circuit breaker (Fig. 7.4). The serious drawback

Table 7.1 Generator Protection

Type of protection		*Generator capacity*			
		below 1 MW	*above 1 MW*	*above 10 MW*	*above 100 MW*
1.	Differential	–	–	*	*
2.	Restricted earth fault	–	*	*	*
3.	Stator turn to turn fault	–	–	–	*
4.	Line overcurrent	*	*	–	–
5.	Thermo-detector	–	*	*	*
6.	Negative sequence relay	–	–	*	*
7.	Loss of load	–	–	*	*
8.	Loss of input-anti-motoring	*	*	*	*
9.	Loss of field	–	–	*	*
10.	Loss of synchronism	–	–	*	*
11.	Overspeed and overvoltage	ONLY FOR HYDRO GENERATORS			
12.	Rotor earth fault	–	–	*	*
13.	Bearing temperature	–	–	*	*
14.	Bearing insulation	–	–	–	*
15.	Backup overcurrent	–	*	*	*

* **Relaying scheme is used**
– **Relaying scheme is not used**

of the differential relay is that if a short circuit occurs external to the winding being protected by the differential relay and if this short circuit is close by, then a very high through current flows in the primary of both the CTs. At such very high currents, the CTs at the two ends of the winding being protected may have different levels of saturation and hence the CTs secondary currents may not be equal, i.e. the vector difference $I_2 - I_1$ may be finite and since this current difference flows in the operating coil of the relay, the relay may give trip command even though there is no internal fault in the winding.

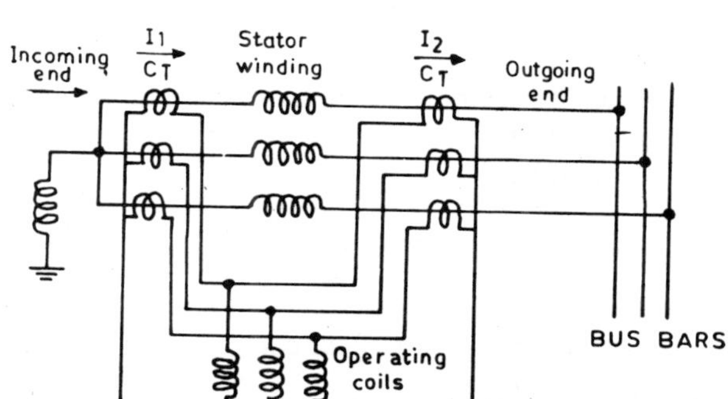

Fig. 7.4 Differential protection

In case CTs were ideal (i.e. exactly similar) and leads from the relay to the CTs were equal in length, very sensitive relay setting could be realized. But, unfortunately, this being not the case and since differential current increases with the increased current through the winding, as stated earlier, on a heavy close by external fault, the sensitivity of the relay is reduced by bias factor which is made proportional to the mean through current which makes the relay stable with negligible loss of sensitivity on high faults or momentary overloads. This improved differential relay is known as a percentage differential relay (Fig. 7.5).

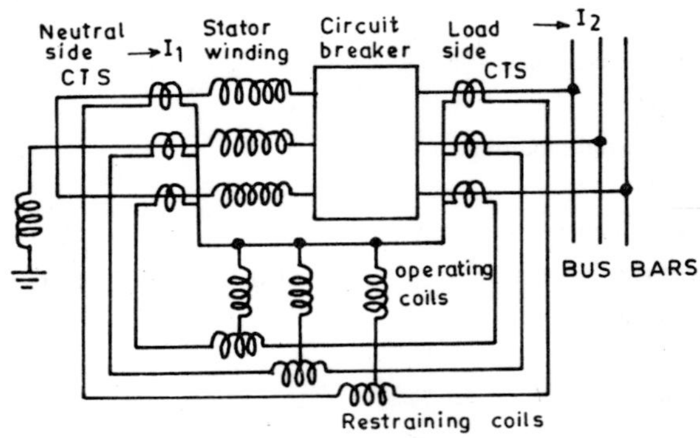

Fig. 7.5 Percentage differential relay

The tripping criterion for percentage differential relay is as shown,

$$|I_1 - I_2| \geq S \left| \frac{I_1 + I_2}{2} \right|$$

Here S is a bias factor which lies in the range of 0.05 to 0.15. In other words, if operating signal $I_1 - I_2$ exceeds S times the restraining signal, the relay gives trip command to the circuit breaker. The operating signal is the vector difference of CTs secondary currents (i.e. $I_1 - I_2$) and restraining signal is the mean through current, i.e. $(I_1 + I_2)/2$. Even though the percentage differential relaying scheme provides very fast primary protection, this needs two similar current transformers at both the ends of the stator (i.e. primary) winding. This is quite difficult because normally the ends of the winding towards the neutral side are not accessible.

It is possible to protect complete alternator winding against phase to ground faults, but since generally neutral is grounded through impedance, portion of the winding near the generator neutral is likely to remain unprotected. This unprotected portion can be determined as

$$\% \text{ of winding unprotected} = \frac{Z \times I_0 \times 100}{V}$$

where Z = neutral impedance in ohms
I_0 = minimum pickup value of current
V = line to neutral voltage

Normally, this percentage is about 15% to 20%, hence there is a requirement of having 100% protection of stator winding against ground fault. Such a protection scheme will be discussed later.

Protection against turn to turn fault on stator winding. The incidence of turn to turn (i.e. interturn) fault in the synchronous generator is rare and such protection is rarely provided in modern turbo generators. One method of detecting interturn faults is by employing a voltage transformer with the tertiary connected to a watt hour meter type induction relay. The inter turn faults are detected by measuring the residual voltage of generator terminals. This voltage appears across the tertiary winding which is connected to operating winding of a three-element directional relay. The quadratic winding is operated from secondary side of the voltage transformer (Fig. 7.6).

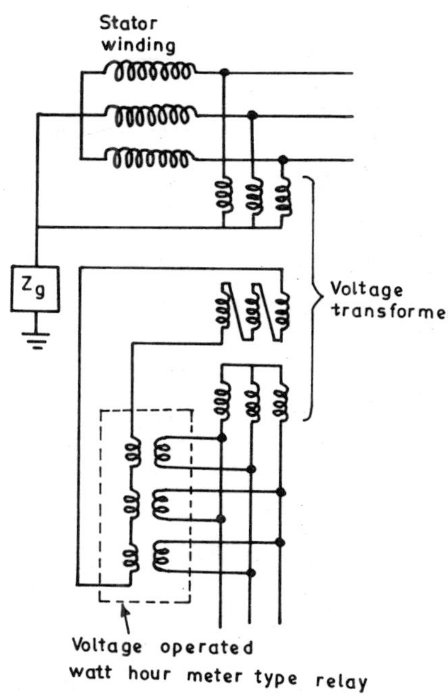

Fig. 7.6 Interturn protection

Short circuit protection of stator winding by overcurrent relay. If generator neutral is not grounded, sensitive fast overcurrent protection can be provided. If neutral is grounded, which is normally true, directional overcurrent relay should be used. If non-directional voltage restrained over current relays are used for external faults to provide backup protection, they can also provide protection against generator phase faults. The arrangement is shown in Fig. 7.7 (a).

Stator overheating protection. The temperature detector-operated devices are used for the protection against stator overheating as they respond more to the actual temperature of the stator. As a matter of fact stator upper temperature is 25°C higher than the temperature at detector; this should be taken into account in the adjustment of the temperature relay. Wheatstone bridge is used to actuate the relay operating coil as shown in Fig. 7.7 (b).

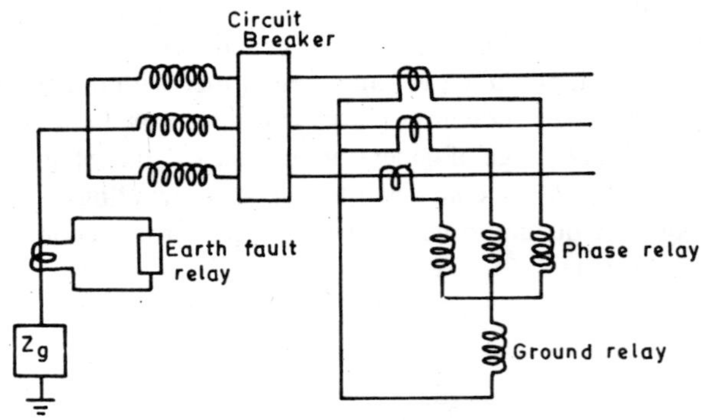

Fig. 7.7 (a) Overcurrent protection

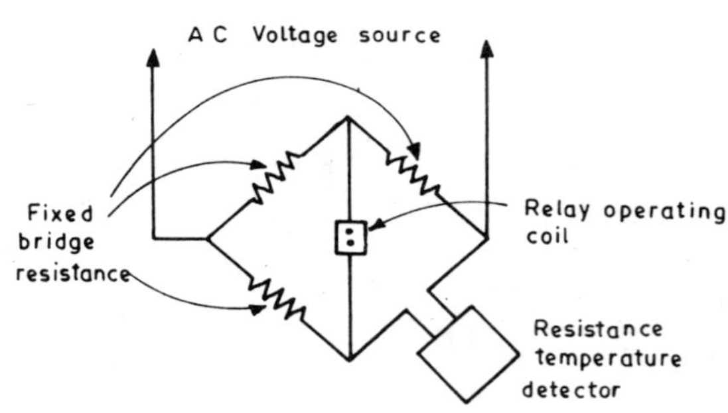

Fig. 7.7 (b) Stator overheating protection

Overvoltage protection. This protection is often provided by the voltage regulating equipment. An a.c. overvoltage relay can also be provided and should have a time-delay unit with pick up at about 110% of the rated voltage, and an instantaneous unit with pick up at about 150% of the rated voltage. Both the units should be compensated against the effect of varying frequency.

Loss of synchronism protection. The characteristics of loss of synchronism are described earlier. MHO relay can be used for the protection against loss of synchronism. Two blinders are arranged to operate two auxiliary relays. If the impedance crosses the characteristic of the one of them before the other, in either direction, this auxiliary relay can be arranged to operate an alarm, trip a circuit breaker or initiate a firm control. The advantages of this type of out of step relay are:

(a) Its operation is not affected by variation in the location of the electrical centre of the system.

(b) It will not trip under any other fault conditions.

(c) It trips instantly after the first half cycle of the system oscillation.
(d) Distinction can be made between speeding up and slowing down of the local generator.

Rotor earth fault protection. Either an a.c. or d.c. voltage may be impressed between the field circuit and ground, through an overvoltage relay. A ground fault anywhere in the field circuit will be picked up by the relay as shown in Fig. 7.8.

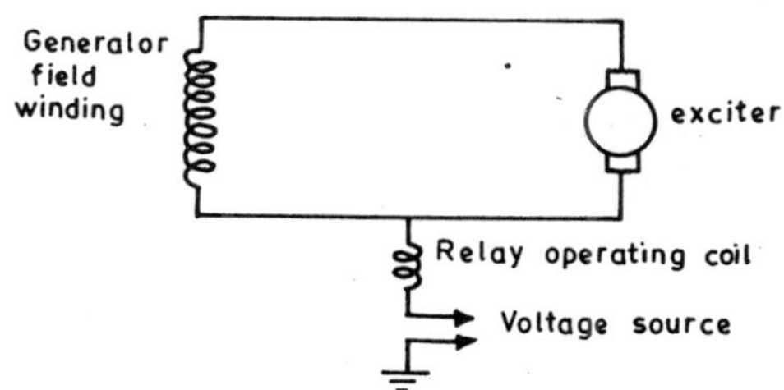

Fig. 7.8 Rotor earth fault relay

Reverse power protection. Protection against motoring is mainly for the benefit of the prime mover, and load coming on generator bus while motoring. Reverse power protection measures the power flow from busbars to the generator running as a synchronous motor. Normally, the power taken in most of the cases is low, of the order of 0.5 to 10% of the rated power.

Other protections. Failure of excitation can be detected by undervoltage relay. Overspeed and underspeed can also be detected by measuring frequency of generator voltage. Unbalanced loading can be detected by negative sequence relay. Bearing insulation failure and other auxiliary system faults can be detected by simple appropriate relays.

7.3.2 Filtering Circuit Design

For this purpose, we require to obtain the fundamental components of currents entering and leaving the generator winding; call this filter as '50 Hz filter'. We also require to obtain second harmonic components present in field current; call it as '100 Hz filter', and call the filter to be used for 12.5 Hz frequency as 'subharmonic filter'. We have two options, to use either analog or digital filters. Analog filters will increase the complexity of hardware and will require a separate filter for each input signal, thus defeating the very basic objective 'SIMPLICITY'. The advantages of using digital filters are high accuracy, high reliability and no effect of aging of components. Computational data, as shown in Table 7.2, indicate that Haar transform achieves such a drastic reduction in computational efforts, which will reduce overall processing time.

Besides this, the Haar function has got several important properties such as;

(a) Ability to represent a given function with a few consistent terms to a high degree of accuracy.

(b) Convergence features of expansion in Haar function are superior to those of the Walsh function.

(c) Computational efficiency can be improved using a factorization algorithm similar to that used for fast Fourier and Walsh transforms.

(d) Total number of additions and subtractions is 2 $(N-1)$. Hence, transformation time is linearly proportional to the number of terms N in contrast to Walsh and Fourier algorithm.

Table 7.2 Computational Data

	Transform name	*Order of computation*
1.	Singular value decomposition	$4N^3$
2.	Karhunen, Leave, Hotelling, principal component factor analysis	$2N^3$
3.	Cosine	$2N^2 \log_2 N$
4.	Fourier	$2N^2 \log_2 N$ (complex)
5.	Slant	$2N^2 \log_2 N$
6.	DLB	$2N^2 \log_2 N$ (integer)
7.	Walsh	$2N^2 \log_2 N$ (additions)
8.	Haar	$2(N-1)$ (additions)
9.	Hybrid	$N^2 \log n + nN^{2*}$
10.	DPCM	$2NN^{2*}$

Note: The entry marked with *, is proportional to the order of predictor used, N is number of samples. For instance; Walsh, Haar; $N = 2^k$ where k is an integer. For Cosine, Fourier, DBL, order of computation is more than the estimate given, if $N \neq 2^k$ with k being an integer.

In Haar functions, the sine and cosine Fourier coefficients are expressed in terms of Haar coefficients which, in turn, are obtained by merely additions and subtractions of data samples, with lesser number of multiplications as compared to other algorithms. This functions set forms a complete set of orthogonal and rectangular functions with three possible states, 0, + A and − A, where A is a functions of $\sqrt{2}$. For the time base defined as $0 \le t \le 1$, the functions are given as;

$$\text{Haar}(0, t) = 1 \qquad 0 \le t \le 1$$

$$\text{Haar}(1, t) = 1 \qquad 0 \le t \le 1/2$$

$$-1 \qquad 1/2 \le t \le 1$$

$$\text{Haar}(2^p + n, t) = \sqrt{2}p \qquad \text{For } n/2^p \le t \le (n + 1/2)/2^p$$

$$-\sqrt{2}p \qquad \text{For } (n + 1/2)/2^p \le t \le (n + 1)/2^p$$

A given continuous function, $f(t)$ within interval $0 \le t \le 1$ and repeated periodically outside this interval, can be synthesized from a Haar series by,

$$f(t) = \sum_{n=0}^{\infty} C_n \ \text{Haar}(n, t) \tag{7.1}$$

$$C_n = \int_{t=0}^{1} f(t) \quad \text{Haar}\,(n, t)\; dt \qquad (7.2)$$

For a function $f(t)$ specified by N samples $(X_1, X_2, \ldots. S_n)$ during the given time period, we cannot use a Haar series for it. However, we can define the discrete Haar transform and its inverse from Eqs. (7.1) and (7.2) as,

$$X_n = \frac{1}{N} \sum_{i=1}^{N-1} C_i \;\text{Haar}\;(n, i/N) \qquad (7.3)$$

$$C_i = \sum_{n=1}^{N-1} X_n \;\text{Haar}\;(n, i/N) \qquad (7.4)$$

The Haar coefficients can be calculated by making use of fast Haar transform technique which is represented in Fig. 7.9 (a).

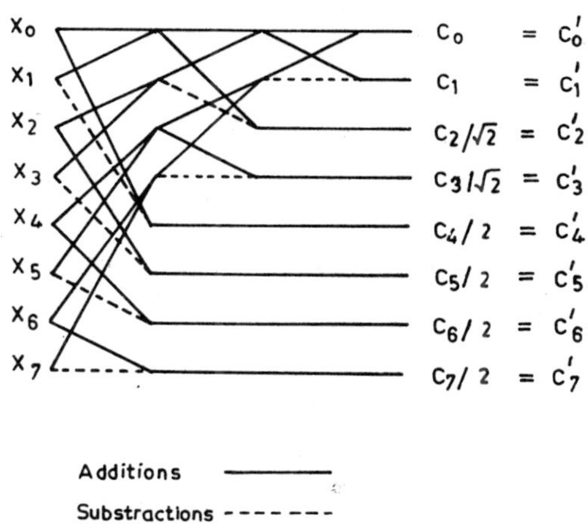

Fig. 7.9 (a) Technique to get Haar coefficients

Extraction of fundamental and second harmonic components. For Haar coefficient, since and cosine components of fundamental and second harmonic contents can be calculated.

A given function $f(t)$ can be expressed as;

$$f(t) = F_0 + \sqrt{2}\; F_1 \;\sin\,(2\,\pi/T)\,t + \sqrt{2}\; F_2 \;\cos\,(2\,\pi/T)\,t + \ldots \text{ and so on} \qquad (7.5)$$

where t is a time period.

Assuming, without any loss of generality, that for the fundamental component time period $T = 1$, the coefficients F_1 and F_2 can be given by,

$$F_1 = \sqrt{2} \int_{0}^{1} f(t) \;\sin 2\,\pi\,t \;\; dt$$

$$F_2 = \sqrt{2} \int_0^1 f(t) \cos 2\pi t \, dt \tag{7.6}$$

but since, $f(t) = \sum_{n=0}^{\infty} C_n \text{ Haar } (n, t)$

we get,

$$F_1 = \sqrt{2} \int_0^1 \sum_{n=0}^{\infty} C_n \text{ Haar } (n, t) \sin 2\pi t \, dt$$

$$= 0.9\, C_1 + 0.1865\, (-C_4 + C_5 + C_6 + C_7)\ldots \tag{7.7}$$

Similarly,

$$F_2 = 0.6366\, (C_2 - C_3) + 0.1865\, (C_4 + C_5 - C_6 - C_7)\ldots \tag{7.8}$$

Similarly coefficients for the second harmonic are,

$$F_3 = 0.6366\, (C_2 + C_3) \tag{7.9}$$

$$F_4 = 0.6366\, (C_4 - C_5 + C_6 + C_7) \tag{7.10}$$

If we define modified Haar coefficients (primed Cs) as indicated in Fig. 7.9 (a), these expression become,

$$F_1 = 0.9\, C_1' + 0.373\, (C_5' + C_6' - C_4' - C_7')$$

$$F_2 = 0.9\, (C_2' - C_3') + 0.373\, (C_4' + C_5' - C_6' - C_7')$$

$$F_3 = 0.9\, (C_2' - C_3')$$

$$F_4 = 0.9\, (C_4' - C_5' + C_6' - C_7') \tag{7.11}$$

RMS values of the first and second harmonic components are given by,

$$A_1 = \sqrt{(F_1^2 + F_2^2}\,; \quad A_2 = \sqrt{(F_3^2 + F_4^2)} \tag{7.12}$$

The frequency response of the Haar filter is plotted in Figs. 7.9 (b) and 7.9 (c).

Actual filtering. At an interval of 2.5 ms, eight samples are taken over a full power cycle (i.e. $8 \times 2.5 = 20$ ms). Thereafter, Haar coefficients are calculated as shown in Fig. 7.9 (a). The modified Haar-Fourier coefficients can be calculated as under;

$$F_1 = 0.90625\, C_1' + 0.375\, (C_5' + C_6' - C_4' - C_7')$$

$$F_2 = 0.90625\, (C_2' - C_3')\; 0.375\, (C_4' + C_5' - C_6' - C_7')$$

$$F_3 = 0.90625\, (C_2' + C_3')$$

$$F_4 = 0.90625\, (C_4' + C_5' - C_6' - C_7') \tag{7.13}$$

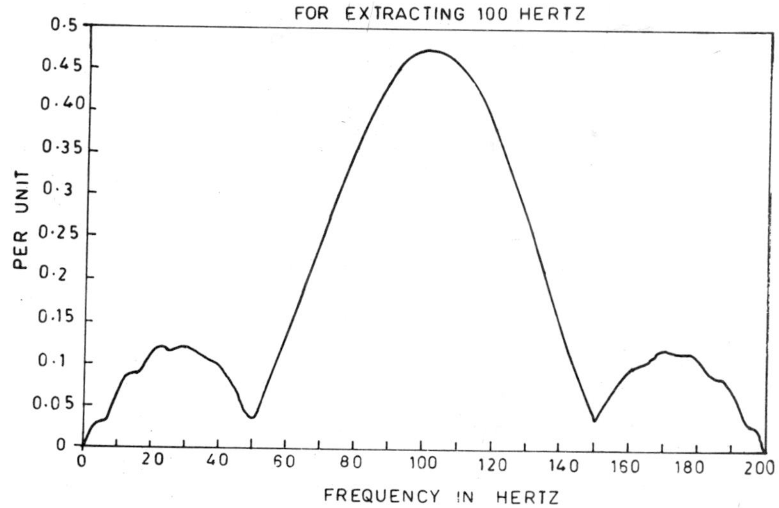

Fig. 7.9 (b) Frequency response of the Haar filter

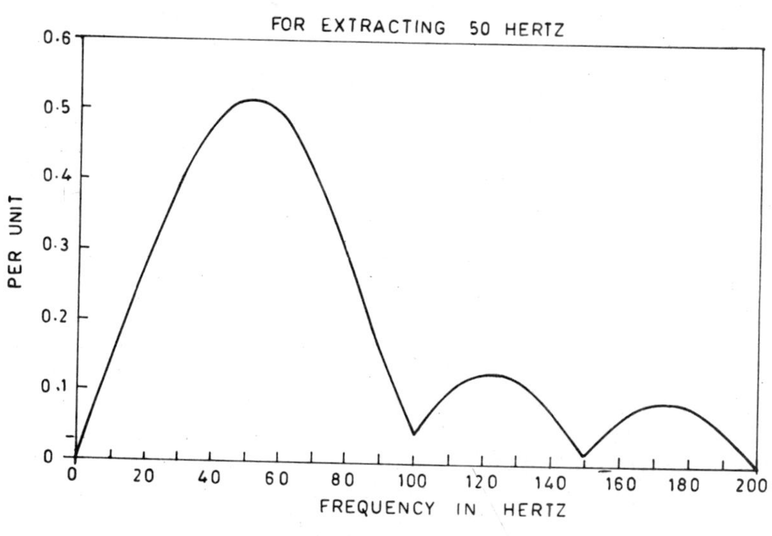

Fig. 7.9 (c) Frequency response of the Haar filter

The above modifications (i.e. 0.90625 instead of 0.9 and 0.375 instead of 0.373) is done to perform multiplication faster, just by shifting bits and adding them to economize on computation time instead of performing floating point multiplication. One bit right shift gives multiplication by 0.5 (1/2). During this type of multiplication, there will be rounding off error because last bit is lost due to bit shift.

The fraction can be represented in various ways. For example, 0.375 can be expressed as $(2^{-1} - 2^{-3})$. Multiplication factors required for our use are 0.373 and 0.9, and these can be programmed as;

$$0.373 \quad 2^{-1} - 2^{-3} = 0.375$$

$$0.9 \quad 2^{-1} + 2^{-3} + 2^{-3} + 2^{-5} = 0.90625$$

The accurate rms values can be calculated as per Eq. (7.12) but this type of operations cannot be performed by microprocessor 8085. So, with given components, rms values can be found as;

where $u = \text{Max}\ (|F_1|, |F_2|)$

$v = \text{Min}\ (|F_3|, |F_4|)$

R = constant chosen, whose value is assumed as 0.5.

This error can be observed in the safety margin of tipping criteria. Therefore,

$$A_1 = \text{Max}\ (|F_1|, |F_2|) + \frac{1}{2}\ \text{Min}\ (|F_1|, |F_2|)$$

$$A_2 = \text{Max}\ (|F_3|, |F_4|) + \frac{1}{2}\ \text{Min}\ (|F_3|, |F_4|) \tag{7.14}$$

7.4 DIGITAL PROTECTION OF SYNCHRONOUS GENERATOR

Digital protection of synchronous generator has been an area of active research for the last several years. It has been a challenging job because of conflicting requirements of high reliability on one hand and fast operation of protective equipment on the other hand. These conflicting requirements can easily be met by having microprocessor-based digital relaying scheme which has also the additional merits of flexibility and self checking features.

7.4.1 Microprocessor-based Unit Protection Scheme

This scheme is also known as percentage differential scheme, and is shown in Fig. 7.5. Here the current I_1 entering the element (i.e. stator winding) and current I_2 leaving the element is monitored through CTs connected at each end of the winding. The CTs are similar in all respects. The criterion for tripping is that,

$$|I_1 - I_2| > s \left| \frac{I_1 + I_2}{2} \right| \tag{7.15}$$

Here S is a bias factor and its value lies in the range of 0.05 to 0.15. $|I_1 - I_2|$ is the operating signal and $\left| \frac{I_1 + I_2}{2} \right|$ is the restraining signal. It is obvious that during normal load condition or during external fault, the operating signal which is the vector difference of currents at the two ends of the winding, is negligible, while during internal fault in the winding, the currents at the two ends of the winding change considerably in magnitude and in phase relation and hence, the operating signal $I_1 - I_2$ is quite high and may exceed S times the mean through current $\left|\frac{I_1 + I_2}{2}\right|$, i.e. restraining signal, thus giving trip command to the circuit breaker.

The currents I_1 and I_2 obtained from the current transformers are first converted into voltages by passing these currents through transactors, i.e. air core transformers. After this, they are selected one by one by multiplexer and sampled. Then these are converted into the digital form by A/D converter. With the help of digital filter, the harmonics and d.c. components are filtered out and only rms values of digital samples $I_1 - I_2$ and $(I_1 + I_2)/2$ are stored in the memory of microprocessor. Trip signal is given if the rms value of $(I_1 - I_2)$ exceeds S times the rms value of $(I_1 + I_2)/2$. Usually, since the ends of the winding on the neutral side of the synchronous generator are not accessible, it is difficult to use unit protection scheme in th case of synchronous generator.

The differential protection scheme though very fast, cannot detect two types of fault, viz. (a) interturn fault in the same phase and (b) fault near generator neutral, as the short circuit current in this case is very small. Both the hardware as well as the software details of unit protection scheme, which is very common for transformer protection, are given in detail in the next chapter.

7.4.2 Digital Protection Scheme Based upon 2nd Harmonic Current Induced in the Rotor Field Circuit

Concepts of power system studies indicate the appearance of negative sequence current and voltage in the event of an unbalance in the system. This unbalance may be internal or external to the generator. An internal unbalance to the generator is an indication of fault or abnormality in the generator. Stator field (i.e. resultant field due to 3-ϕ armature winding) due to the positive sequence current rotates with the synchronous speed in the same direction as that of the rotation of the rotor of the synchronous generator. In other words, the stator field due to the positive sequence stator current rotates in the same direction and with the same speed as that of the rotor. The stator field, thus, remains decoupled with respect to the rotor and no induced emf due to this field is generated in the rotor circuit. However, stator field caused by negative sequence currents in the stator winding rotates at the synchronous speed in a direction opposite to that of the direction of rotation of the rotor and, therefore, induces emf of twice the synchronous frequency in the rotor circuit. Hence, the negative sequence current in the stator winding produces second harmonics in the generator rotor (i.e. field) circuit.

The proposed scheme uses second harmonic component in the field curient as the primary source to detect the presence of abnormality or fault in the stator winding and the direction of positive sequence current flow at the terminals of synchronous generator to discriminate between external fault and internal fault. The type of fault is also sensed by detecting the proper magnitude and phase relations between different sequence currents being sampled. Since we are sampling field current, loss of excitation can also be monitored simultaneously after taking care of a.c. induced in the field.

It may be noted that in the case of interturn fault, even though the difference between synchronous (i.e. steady state) and transient reactance of a single turn is very small, the current in a short circuited turn can be few orders of magnitude greater than rated current and therefore second harmonic current in the field circuit is easily measurable.

The relay has been realized using 8085 or 8086 microprocessor. 8 Samples per cycle can be taken to make the relay fairly fast. Data acquisition is done by simultaneously sampling positive and negative sequence currents in the armature circuit as well as the field current, which are then converted into the digital form using an A/D converter and transmitted to the input port of the microprocessor. The sampling interval is set by the timer which is also controlled by the microprocessor.

The entire hardware can be subdivided into Data Acquisition system (DAS) and interface with work station. The DAS consists of an analog multiplexer and analog to digital converter. As stated, the samples are taken at an interval of 2.5 ms. This is achieved by a 8253 programmable timer, the output of which is connected to the interrupt RST 7.5. Selection of sequence currents in the stator (i.e. armature) circuit or field current for the input to ADC is done through an analog multiplexer CD4052BM. The select input of this multiplexer is driven by two lower bits of upper half of output port C of 8255 A device. The start of conversion (SOC) is generated using the most significant bit of port C is 8255 A and is driven to ADC570. The ADC converts the currents one by one. The trip signal is the output from port B of 8255 A which has been programmed in mode D. Also the information regarding the type of fault is indicated on the screen.

In this scheme, by the appropriate software stored in the memory of microprocessor, the sequence currents using standard transformation, viz. symmetrical component transformation, are obtained. Sequence currents thus obtained (Fig, 7.10) are utilized for detecting various types of faults with the help of the following logical possibilities:

(a) if all the sequence currents are equal in magnitude, the fault is LG fault.
(b) if positive and negative sequence currents are equal in magnitude and zero sequence current is absent , it is LL fault.
(c) if there is only positive sequence current present, i.e. negative sequence and zero sequence currents are absent, it is LLL or LLLG fault.

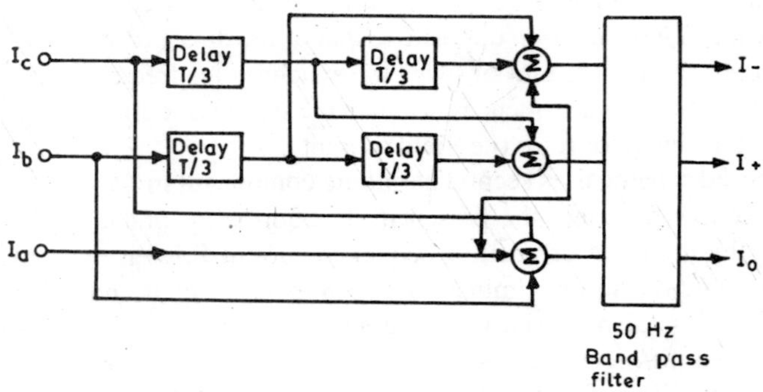

Fig. 7.10 Phasecurrents to sequence currents

If the field current is less than 0.2 p.u., the failure of excitation is indicated.

In this scheme, the field current is monitored and also, with appropriate filter circuit, the second harmonic content of the field current is obtained. The presence of second harmonic component in the field circuit more than 0.2 p.u. is an indication of abnormality or fault in the stator circuit or external to the stator circuit. To ensure that the fault is internal for which the relay gives trip command, a reverse power relay is needed which shows the direction of current or power flow at the stator terminals. If, in addition to the presence of second harmonic component in the rotor field, there is also power flow towards the synchronous generator at its terminals, it indicates fault in the stator winding of synchronous generator for which the relay gives trip command to the associated circuit breaker.

7.4.3 Digital Protection Scheme Based upon Injection of Subsynchronous Component in the Rotor Circuit

Single phase to ground fault in the synchronous generator is very common but when the neutral of the generator is grounded through a transformer, the maximum ground fault current is too small for the relay to pickup. With the high resistance grounding, the possibility of fault damage is greatly reduced; but still the generator should be isolated immediately on the occurrence of ground fault. The detection of stator-ground fault in 100% winding is based on the fact that when the ground fault occurs the generator capacitance gets short circuited and this change in capacitive reactance is detectable at sub-harmonic frequency. The neutral voltage sub-harmonic injection scheme detects ground faults by injecting a 12.5 Hz voltage between the neutral and the ground and monitoring the reultant 12.5 Hz current. When the ground fault occurs, the 12.5 Hz current increases due to shorting of generator capacitance and causes the relay to operate. The use of a sub-harmonic injection frequency will improve the sensitivity due to high impedance path of the generator and connected equipment capacitance at low frequency. The scheme recommended is shown in the schematic diagram (Fig. 7.11 a) and 12.5 Hz current path is shown in Fig. 7.11 (b).

Symbols used are as follows

$$R = R_S + R_{GT} + R_{GW}$$

R_S = Secondary resistance when referred to primary

R_{GT} = Resistance of grounding transformer

R_W = Resistance of i[illegible]ion transformer

X_T = Three-phase capacitive reactance to ground of protected zone

$$X = X_{GT} + X_W$$

X_{GT} = Leakage reactance of generator grounding transformer

X_W = Leakage reactance of injection transformer

V = 12.5 Hz generated voltage

Now from the above we can calculate maximum and minimum theoretical setting current as:

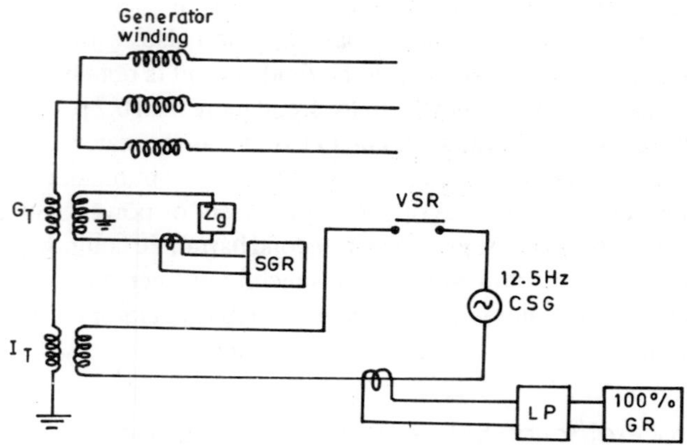

GT = Generating transformer, CSG = Coded signal generator 12.5 Hz
IT = Injection transformer, LP = Low pass filter
Zg = Impedance, 100% GR = 100% Ground relay
SGR = Standard ground relay, VSR = Voltage supervision relay

Fig. 7.11 (a) 100% stator-ground fault protection

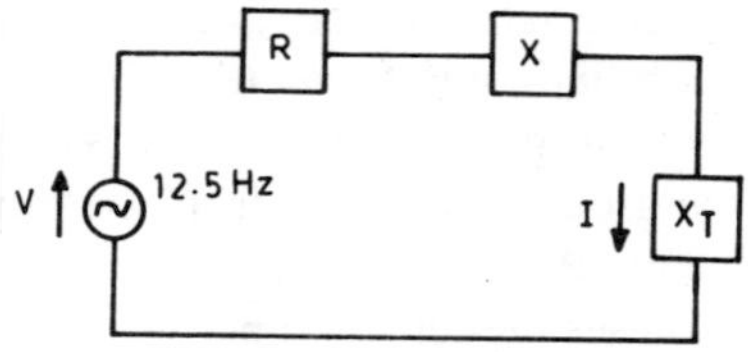

Fig. 7.11 (b) 12.5 Hz current path

$$\text{Minimum theoretical setting current } I_{min} = \frac{V}{R + j(X + X_T)}$$

$$\text{Maximum theoretical setting current } I_{max} = \frac{V}{R + jX} \quad (7.16)$$

From safety point of view, when the generator is on turning gear and not excited, the injection voltage must be turned off. A voltage supervision relay is used to deactivate the injection scheme when generated voltage is below 0.4 p.u.

Hardware used. Hardware is developed based on Intel 8086A system. Work-station available has built-in CPU, RAM, ROM, MONITOR, keyboard, etc. and 44 buses (22 upper and 22 lower) for external connections. The simplified schematic diagram of the hardware is shown in Fig. 7.12.

Data acquisition system consists of 4-channel analog multiplexer (CD4052BM) and analog to digital converter (AD570). We are required to take samples of three waveforms I_1, I_2 and field current. Analog multiplexer enables to connect the channels one by one and ADC feeds converted digital values to input ports of

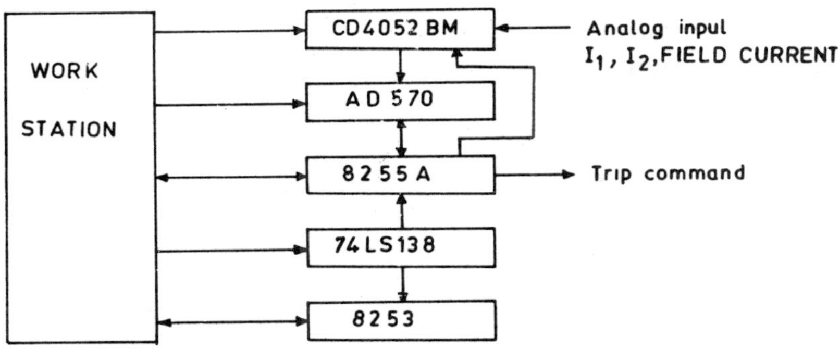

Fig. 7.12 Schematic diagram of hardware

8255A. Chip select for 8255 and 8253 (timer) is generated with the help of 74LS138. We need eight samples (X_0 to X_7) each of the three currents (I_1, I_2 and field current) at an interval of 2.5 ms over a full wave form (8×2.5 ms = 20 ms for 50 Hz). Sampling at 2.5 ms is obtained by timer 8253 which initiates interrupts (RST 7.5), CPU stops main processing, ADC 570 starts conversion as blank and convert pin goes low, it takes 25 to 40 μs to complete conversion which is indicated by 'data ready' pin. CPU takes processing time of about 4.6 ms. With above arrangements, every 5 ms, we can do the complete analysis and give appropriate trip command or repeat the analysis with two samples renewed (upgraded). Interconnection of the chips is shown in Fig. 7.13.

Software developed. The software is developed with the help of 8080 micro-assembler and simulator available in DEC-10. Initial testing of software can be done by storing different waveforms with various harmonics and DC contents. Several such combinations can be tried for obtaining satisfactory results. The execution time is 4.478 ms excluding sampling and conversion time.

7.5 CONCLUSION

The digital protection of a synchronous generator based upon three criteria are discussed in this chapter. The complete protection scheme of a synchronous generator showing its connection to the infinite bus is shown in the Fig. 7.14. In the event of fault as sensed by the protective relay, the circuit breaker which connects the synchronous generator to the infinite bus opens, thus disconnecting the generator from the infinite bus. There is also a circuit breaker in the field circuit which also opens so as to stop the generator from generating and supplying power to the earth fault. One more circuit breaker in the neutral circuit may also be connected which opens last. This circuit breaker is needed because even though the circuit breaker in the field circuit opens, the generator may generate power due to residual magnetism and supply it to its own fault. Thus by opening the circuit breaker in the neutral circuit there is complete stoppage of power even due to residual magnetism.

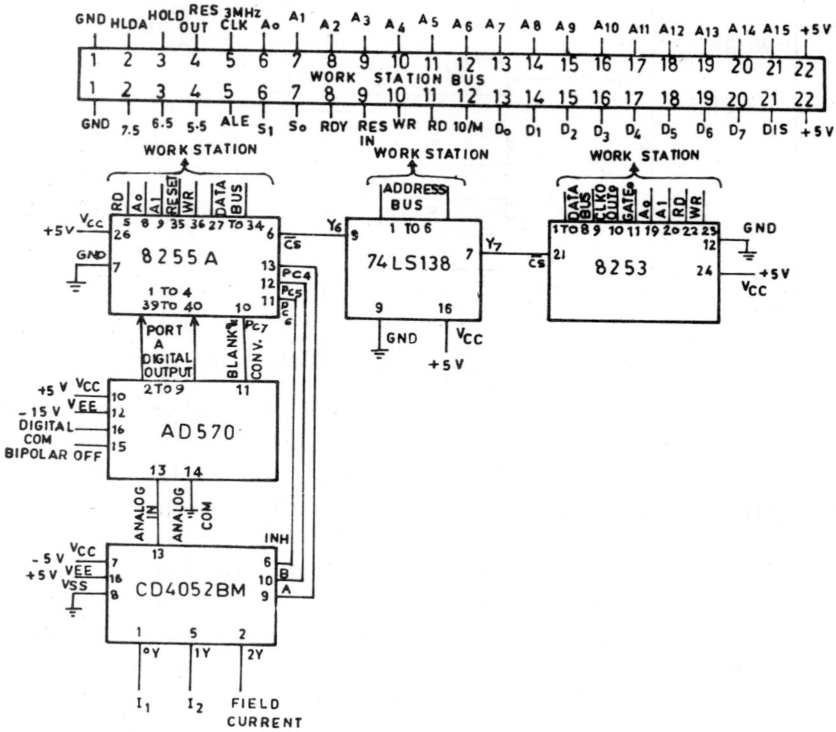

Fig. 7.13 Detailed diagram of hardware

EXERCISES

1. Name different types of faults in synchronous machines. Discuss briefly the protection schemes to protect the synchronous machines against these faults.
2. Why differential relaying scheme of protection is not very reliable for the protection of the device? Discuss with the help of neat diagram. What additional signal is added to the percentage differential relaying scheme to make it reliable? With the help of neat diagram, discuss the theory and principle of operation of the percentage differential relaying (i.e. unit protection) scheme for the protection of a synchronous generator.
3. What are the merits of microprocessor-based relaying scheme? Discuss briefly. Explain the theory and working principle of microprocessor-based unit protection scheme of a synchronous generator.
4. Discuss, with the help of neat diagram, the microprocessor based relaying scheme for the protection of synchronous generator by monitoring the field current of the synchronous generator. When an unbalanced current is produced in the stator caused by fault or external disturbances, which har-

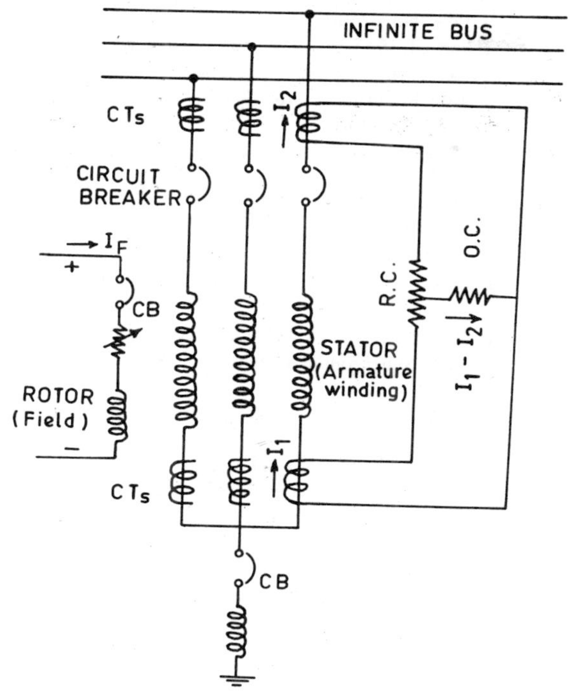

Fig. 7.14 Protection scheme of synchronous generator

monic component is induced in the field circuit? How do you distinguish between internal fault and external disturbances in this scheme? Write the algorithms in this scheme to determine the type of fault.

5. What do you understand by interturn fault in the synchronous machine? Why unit protection scheme fails during interturn fault? Discuss the microprocessor-based relaying scheme which will also operate during interturn fault. Discuss also the hardware and software schemes of the relay.
6. What is the effect of a ground (i.e. LG) fault near the neutral of the neutral grounded synchronous generator on the performance of the protection scheme? Discuss, with the help of neat diagram, the digital protection scheme based upon the injection of sub-synchronous component in the rotor circuit.
7. Sketch the detailed diagram of a synchronous generator and mark the placement of circuit breakers. In the event of stator fault, in what sequence these circuit breakers operate?

REFERENCES

1. Agrawal, Ravi and L.P Singh, "On-Line Protection of Synchronous Generators Using Microprocessor", *Proc. Natl. Pwr. Syst. Conf.*, Bangalore, Sept. 1988, pp. 157–161.

2. Barkle, J.E. and Frankvon Roeschaub, "Application of Relays for Unbalanced Faults on Generators", *Trans. AIEE*, Vol. 72, Part III, 1953, pp. 277–282.
3. Barkle, J.E. and W.E. Glassburn, "Protection of Generators against Unbalanced Currents". *Trans. AIEE*, Vol. 72, Part III, 1953, pp. 282–286.
4. Berdy, John, "Loss of Excitation Relaying", *IEEE Trans.*, Vol. PAS 94, 1975, pp. 1457–1463.
5. Brown, P.G., "Generating Requirement for System Faults", *IEEE Trans.*, Vol. Pas 72, Jul/Aug. 1973, pp. 1247–1251.
6. Danniel, J., "Generator Protection with New Static Negative Sequence Relay", *IEEE Trans.*, Vol. PAS 94, 1975, pp. 1205–1213.
7. Degan, A.J., "Microprocessor-implemented Digital Filter for the Calculation of Symmetrical Components", *Proc. IEE*, Vol. 129, May 1982, pp. 111–118.
8. Desikachar, K.V., and L.P. Singh, "Application of FFT to the Computation of Electrical Transients", *Proc. Natl. Pwr. Syst. Conf.*, Annamalai University, Chidambaram, Aug. 1986, pp.
9. Fakhruddin, D.R., K. Parthsarthy and D. Tukaram, "An Integrated Scheme Based on Haar-Functions for Protection of Synchronous Generators", *Proc. Third. Natl. Pwr. Syst. Conf.*, 1984.
10. Hope G.S., P.K. Dash and O.P. Malik, "Digital Differential Protections of a Generation Unit". *IEEE Trans.*, PAS 75, 1976.
11. Lee, D.C., "Loss of Excitation Protection Scheme to Prevent Coupling of Sensitive Load Adjacent to Station with Only One Unit Operation", *IEEE Trans.*, Vol. PAS 98, 1979, pp. 1895–1897.
12. Mason, C.R., "A New Loss of Excitation Relay for synchronous Generators", *Trans. AIEE*, Vol. 68, 1949, pp. 1240–1245.
13. McConnell, A.J., "A Generator Differential Relay", *Trans. AIEE*, vol. 62, Jan. 1943, pp. 11–13.
14. Moris, W.C., and L.E. Goff, "A Negative Sequence Overcurrent Relay for Generator Protection", *Trans. AIEE*, Vol. 72, Part III, 1953, pp. 615–621.
15. Rockefeller, G.D., "Fault Protection with Digital Computer", *IEEE Trans.*, PAS-88, April 1969, pp. 438–464.
16. Singh, L.P., *Advanced Power System Analysis and Dynamics*, 3rd Edition, Wiley Eastern Ltd., New Delhi, 1992.
17. Singhal, Arun, and L.P. Singh, "On-line Protection of Power Transformer Using Microprocessor", *J. Instn. Engrs.*, Vol. 69, Pt El-2, Oct. 1988, pp. 52–58.
18. Sonnemann, W.K., "A High Speed Differential Relay for Generator Protection:", *Trans., AIEE*, Vol. 59, Nov. 1940, pp. 608–612.
19. Trivedi, Maj. V.I., "Digital Protection of a Synchronous Generator", *M. Tech. thesis*, submitted to IIT Kanpur, March 1989.
20. Warrington, A.R. Van C., *Protective Relays, Theory and Practice*, Vol. 1, Chapman and Hall Ltd, London, 1976.
21. Trivedi, V.I., Ravi Agarwal and L.P. Singh, "Integrated Digital Protection of a Synchronous Generator", Proceeding Power System Conference, Calcutta Feb. 1993, pp. 130–134.

8

DIGITAL PROTECTION OF POWER TRANSFORMER

8.1 INTRODUCTION

The problem of protection of power transformer against abnormal conditions such as faults etc. has been of great concern to power system engineers. Traditionally, percentage differential relays have been used to protect the transformer against all kinds of internal faults. However, such relaying scheme may fail in the case of magnetizing inrush current and also overvoltage inrush current caused by switching, interturn faults, etc. There may be other phenomena associated with the transformer protection such as the use of current transformers of different turn ratios and different ratings of the two sides of the main transformer and also tap changing provision in the main transformer. Digital protection of the transformer is an answer to all such problems. This is why digital protection of power transformer has been an area of active research for the last twenty years.

The transformer is a simple yet a very important link in the power system network. Faults both internal and external to the transformer can cause considerable damage to this unit. Faults external to the transformer are taken care of by the protection schemes used in the line. However, for protection against internal faults in the transformer, various schemes such as overcurrent relays, gas-actuated, i.e. Buchholz relay, restricted earth fault relay and percentage differential relay, have been adopted. The protection scheme selected depends upon the type of faults and also upon the type, rating, size and the importance of the transformer being protected. For example, a small distribution transformer is normally protected by H.V. fuses and overcurrent relays, whereas a large rating transformer needs a reliable and fast operating protective relay such as unit protection scheme. This chapter discusses various types of faults that may occur in a transformer along with digital-based unit protection scheme and other related problems.

8.2 FAULTS IN A TRANSFORMER

All cases of abnormal operations such as faults in a transformer can be broadly divided into two categories: (i) external, i.e. through faults, and (ii) internal faults. External faults include problems like short duration overloading, short circuits external to the transformer, etc. The primary protection schemes must not operate in such cases. It has been stated earlier that the external faults are taken care of by line relays. However, through faults are still of concern for the unit protection schemes. It is desirable that for external faults unit protection schemes should not operate.

Internal faults may be grouped into 3 categories: (a) Incipient faults, (b) Terminal faults, and (c) Winding faults.

Incipient faults

Incipient faults are those faults, which are initially minor in nature and of no immediate hazard but which could grow slowly into major faults if left unattended, thus causing damage to the transformer. Examples of such faults are:

(1) Core faults due to breakdown of insulation of lamination, of bolts or of clamping rings causing limited arcing inside oil.
(2) Poor electrical connection of conductors.
(3) Coolant failure i.e. failure of cooling arrangement.
(4) Improper oil flow, loss or blockage of oil causing development of local hot spots.
(5) Regulator failure and improper load sharing between transformers operating in parallel, causing circulating current.

All these faults cause overheating and pose consequent hazard. Earth fault very near the neutral point of the star connected transformer is sometimes classified as an incipient fault.

Terminal Faults

These faults include the following:

(i) Phase to phase fault on H.V. or L.V. terminals.
(ii) Phase to earth fault on H.V. or L.V. terminals.
(iii) Three-phase faults on H.V. or L.V. terminals.

Winding faults

These faults are as follows:

(i) Phase to phase fault in H.V. or L.V. windings.
(ii) Phase to earth fault in H.V. or L.V. windings.
(iii) Short circuit between turns of H.V. or L.V. windings.
(iv) Short circuit between turns of tertiary windings.
(v) Earth fault on tertiary windings.

Both the terminals as well as the winding faults are serious in nature. These can be detected by unbalance of voltage or current at the terminals of a transformer. They can cause immediate damage to the transformer. These faults are symbolically represented in Fig. 8.1.

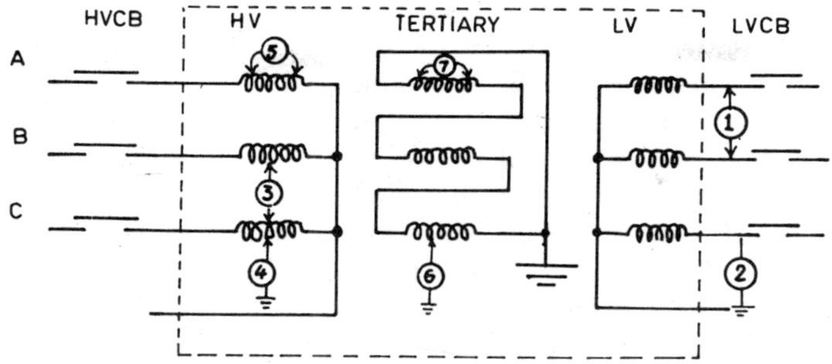

Fig. 8.1 Faults in a transformer

8.3 SCHEMES USED FOR TRANSFORMER PROTECTION

For the protection of transformer against external faults, slow blowing fuses and thermal relays or overcurrent relays (backup protection) have been used. The primary protection schemes of the transformer should not operate under such events. The overload (O/L) fuses shown in Fig. 8.2 also provide the backup protection against through fault, which when sustained can cause damage to the transformer. The protection against incipient faults is generally provided by gas-actuated relay whereas protection against serious internal faults is provided by reliable and fast operating relays such as unit protection schemes.

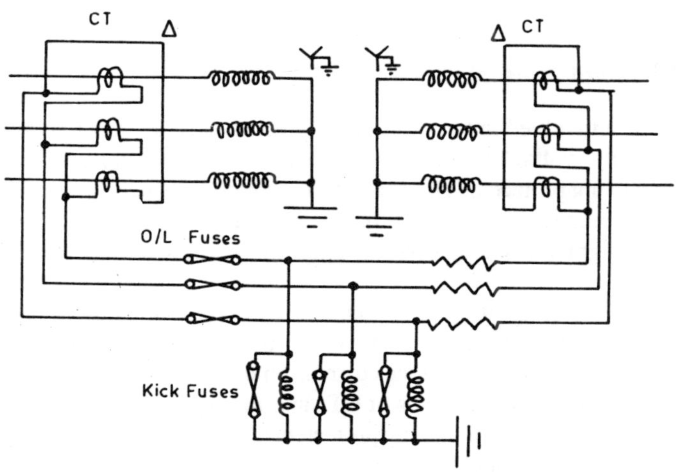

Fig. 8.2 Differential protection of transformer

8.3.1 Gas-actuated (i.e. Buchholz) Relay

A gas-actuated relay, also known as Buchholz relay, has been in use for several decades now. This relay also responds to the oil level fall due to blockage from the tank.

The Buchholz relay provides protection to the transformer against internal faults. The main principle of operation of such relay is that a fault in an oil filled transformer causes enough heat in the transformer oil which decomposes the oil and liberates dissolved gases in the transformer tank. The liberation of gas in the transformer tank is an indication of fault in the transformer. The incipient fault generates a very small quantity of gas where as serious faults generate a large quantity of gas thus increasing gas pressure. Buchholz relay normally has two elements, viz. (a) sensitive element which senses only slow accumulation of gas caused by incipient fault and sounds an alarm and (b) the quick acting element which responds to gas pressure caused by a serious fault, giving trip command to the associate circuit breaker, thus disconnecting the transformer with the rest of system by tripping the circuit breaker at both the ends of the transformer.

The gas-actuated relay can be used only in the case of an oil-cooled transformer having conservator. There are two arrangements of installing gas actuated relay; in one scheme, the relay is installed in the pipeline connecting the transformer tank with the conservator and in the other scheme, the relay is installed at the top (inside) cover of the transformer tank.

8.3.2 Overcurrent Protection Scheme

This is the simplest and cheapest protection scheme and is generally used for small size and rating transformer. For the protection of transformer, overcurrent (O.C.) relays are employed on both the sides of the transformer. However, where infeed to the transformer is only from one end, the over current relays are located only on the infeed side. In these schemes, Inverse Definite Minimum Time (IDMT) type O.C. relays are used.

8.3.3 Differential Protection Scheme

The general idea involved in the differential protection scheme is to compare the operating quantity (voltage or current) at the input and output ends, i.e. terminal of the equipment being protected. This is a vector comparison since the quantity being compared has the magnitude and the phase angle associated with it. Tripping is initiated if the magnitude of the difference exceeds a pre-determined constant value (i.e. base value).

For a transformer, the differential protection scheme is shown in Fig. 8.3. The CTs have been connected at the two sides (i.e. primary and secondary sides) of the transformer and I_1 and I_2 represent the currents on the primary and secondary side. By properly choosing the turn ratios of CTs and reversing its connections to that of the main transformer which is being protected, CTs secondary currents are made nearly the same during normal load conditions or external faults. However, during internal fault in the transformer, the current I_1 on the primary side of the transformer will differ from the current I_2 on the secondary in magnitude and/or in phase. The trip signal is given if the vector difference of these currents which flow in the operating coil exceeds in the base value. Hence for tripping

$$|I_1 - I_2| \geq k \tag{8.1}$$

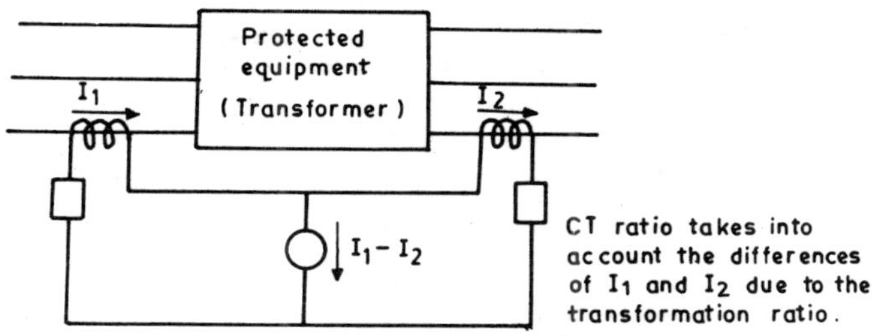

Fig. 8.3 The basic unbiased differential connection (only one phase connection are shown)

where k is a constant (i.e. base value).

The main problem with the differential relaying scheme is that at a large current due to close by external faults even though the CTs primary currents are equal, CTs secondary current $I_1$and I_2 may be significantly different due to different levels of saturation of CTs at that very high current on its primary side. Hence even though there is no internal fault, still $|I_1 - I_2|$ is quite large to operate the relay. To avoid such problem, percentage differential relay has been developed.

8.3.6 Percentage Differential Relaying Scheme

This scheme is also known as biased protection (BP) scheme. Here in addition to the operating signal, there is also a restraining signal. The operating signal is proportional to the vector difference of currents I_1 and I_2 and the restraining signal is proportional to the mean through current. For tripping, the vector difference of currents I_1 and I_2 exceeds S times the mean through current, i.e.

$$|I_1 - I_2| \geq S \left| \frac{I_1 + I_2}{2} \right| \tag{8.2}$$

where S is a bias factor which is in the range of 0.15 to 0.6; the higher value is used when tapping is included in the transformer.

CTs here do not compare the currents on the two ends of the same winding which is the same if there is no internal fault as in the case of synchronous generator, but compare the currents on the primary side of the transformer with the current on the secondary side of the transformer which is different even during normal operating condition because of the transformer turns ratio. Due to this reason, the CTs connected on the primary side of the main transformer have a turns ratio different from that of CTs connected on the secondary side of the main transformer, so as to make CTs secondary currents on the two sides of the transformer the same. Further, phase shift caused by Y-Δ connection of the main transformer is compensated by connecting CTs on the two sides of the main transformer in reverse manner, i.e. CTs are connected in Y on Δ-connected side of the main transformer and in Δ on the Y-connected side of the main transformer. The percentage differential relay for the transformer protection is illustrated in Fig. 8.4 and 8.5.

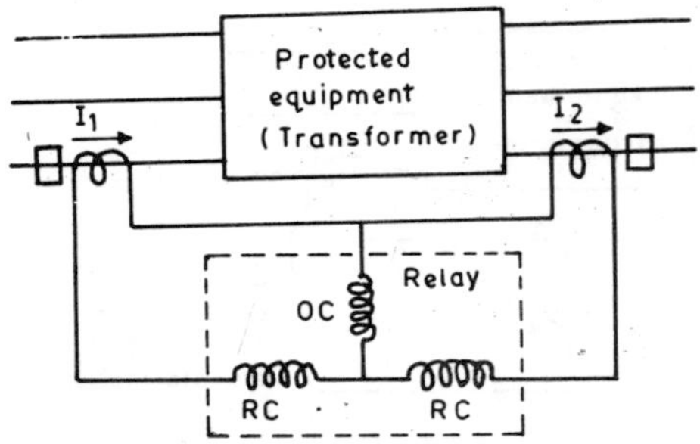

Fig. 8.4 Percentage differential type of relay connection (only one phase connections are shown)

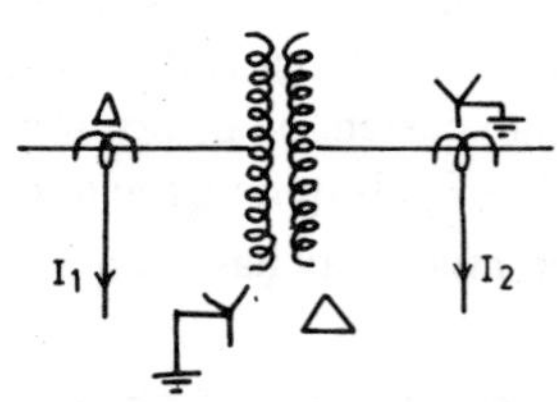

Fig. 8.5 CT connections for Y-Δ transformer

Reasons for taking High bias factor. The bias factor in the case of transformer protection by percentage differential relay is very large, in the range of 0.15 to 0.6. This is because of the following reasons.

(a) CTs on the two sides of the main transformer have different voltage and current ratings and also different turns ratio. Hence, during external close by fault, when the line currents are very high, CTs on the two sides of the main transformer will have very different levels of saturation making vector difference $I_1 – I_2$ quite large.

(b) While tappings are provided on the main transformer there is no such provision in CTs. And hence CTs turns ratios cannot match with the turns ratio of the main transformer when tappings of the main transformer are changed.

(c) CTs which are available in the market are of standard size which may not match with that of the main transformer turns ratio.

(d) Presence of no-load (i.e. exciting) current in the primary winding of the main transformer because of which the turn ratio of current transformer and the ratio of turns of the main transformer do not match.

Relay characteristics. The threshold characteristic of the percentage differential (BDP) relay is a circle along the real axis in the complex β- (i.e. *Z*-) plane as shown in the following.

Let I_1 be the reference current i.e. $|I_1| \angle 0$ and I_2 is then $|I_2| \angle \phi$. Thus the operating signal is

$$I_1 - I_2 = |I_1| \angle 0 - |I_2| \angle \phi = |I_1| - |I_2| (\cos \phi + j \sin \phi) \quad (8.3)$$

and restraining signal

$$\frac{1}{2} |I_1 + I_2| = \frac{1}{2} |I_1 + I_2| \quad (8.4)$$

The threshold condition is

$$|I_1 - I_2| = S \frac{1}{2} |I_1 + I_2| \quad (8.5)$$

i.e.

$$|I_1 - I_2|^2 = \frac{1}{4} S^2 |I_1 + I_2|^2 \quad (8.6)$$

Substituting Eqs. (8.3) and (8.4) in Eq. 8.6, we get

$$(I_1 - I_2 \cos \phi)^2 + (I_2 \sin \phi)^2$$

$$= \frac{S^2}{4} [(I_1 + I_2 \cos \phi)^2 + (I_2 \sin \phi)^2] \quad (8.7)$$

Dividing the above equation by I_1^2 and simplifying, we obtain

$$\left(1 - \frac{S^2}{4}\right)\left(\frac{I_2}{I_1}\right) + 2\left(1 + \frac{S^2}{4}\right)\left(\frac{I_2}{I_1}\right) \cos \phi = \frac{S^2}{4} - 1 \quad (8.8)$$

Dividing the above equation by $(1 - S^2/4)$ and then adding $\frac{4 - S^2}{2}$ to both sides, we get,

$$\frac{I_2^2}{I_1^2} + 2\left(\frac{I_2}{I_1}\right)\left(\frac{4+S^2}{4-S^2}\right)\cos \phi + \left(\frac{4+S^2}{4-S^2}\right)^2 = \left(\frac{4+S^2}{4-S^2}\right)^2 - 1 = \left(\frac{4\ S}{4-S^2}\right)^2 \quad (8.9)$$

Let us assume

$$C' = \frac{4+S^2}{4-S^2}, \quad r' = \frac{4\,S}{4-S^2} \quad \text{and } \alpha = \frac{I_2}{I_1} \quad (8.10)$$

Substituting these values in the Eq. (8.9), we get

$$\alpha^2 - 2\,\alpha\, C' \cos \phi + C'^2 = r'^2 \quad (8.11)$$

Eq. (8.11) is the equation of a circle.

8.3.5 Earth Fault Protection

The magnitude of the earth fault current in a faulted winding in the case of resistance grounded transformer depends directly on the voltage between neutral and the point of fault of the winding and inversely proportional to the neutral resistance.

In a solidly grounded transformer, the relation between the fault current and the position of fault along the winding is more complicated because the current is limited by the impedance of the winding, which increases as the square of the number of turns involved. Furthermore, the voltage is not proportional to turns involved by fault near the neutral, because of increased magnetic leakage. Due to above reasons, earth faults may involve light currents and cannot be cleared by ovecurrent relay alone. However, the negative sequence property of the unbalanced three phase currents can be employed to overcome this difficulty.

8.4 DIGITAL PROTECTION OF TRANSFORMER

The main objective before a protection engineer is to develop a relaying scheme which is reliable and fast in operation. Percentage differential relaying scheme is a step in this direction. The digital-based unit protection scheme which is reliable and very fast in operation, possesses several additional features such as high flexibility and self checking provision.

There are certain phenomena associated with the transformer protection which affect the reliable operation of protection scheme. These phenomena along with remedies will be discussed now.

8.4.1 Magnetizing Inrush Current

The magnetizing inrush current (MIC) is the current that flows in the primary winding of the transformer with its secondary winding open circuited just after closing the switch on the primary side. This current is as large as 10–15 times the normal load current and may last for 1–2 s as its time constant depends upon the magnetizing inductance which is very large.

To understand the phenomenon of MIC, let us take a 1-ϕ transformer. Under steady state conditions, with secondary winding open circuited, the flux ϕ lags the supply voltage V by 90°. When the supply voltage is switched on, the transformer core flux and the corresponding exciting current undergo a transient before reaching the steady state value. The severity of switching transient is dependent on the instant when the voltage is switched on, the worst case being switching on at zero of applied voltage. The resultant flux will have two components, one is the steady state sinusoidal flux component and the other a transient component starting at an initial value of $\phi_r + \phi_m$. As the transient decaying component (whose time constant depends upon magnetizing inductance) has a large decaying constant, the maximum flux level attained would be now $\phi_r + 2\,\phi_m$ as shown in Fig. 8.6.

Since most power transformers operate fairly close to saturation level, the asymmetrical flux required initially forces core deep into saturation, which leads to an abnormally high magnetizing current. Its exact shape is determined by the magnetization characteristic and may reach up to 10–15 times the rated value. In many cases, this current takes nearly 1–2 seconds to decay owing to a large magnetizing inductance. The phenomenon of MIC is more severe in a 3-phase transformer as the current flowing in a winding is dependent upon currents of remaining windings as well.

The magnitude of MIC depends upon several factors such as steel used for core construction, magnitude and polarity of residual magnetism, instant of switching and so on.

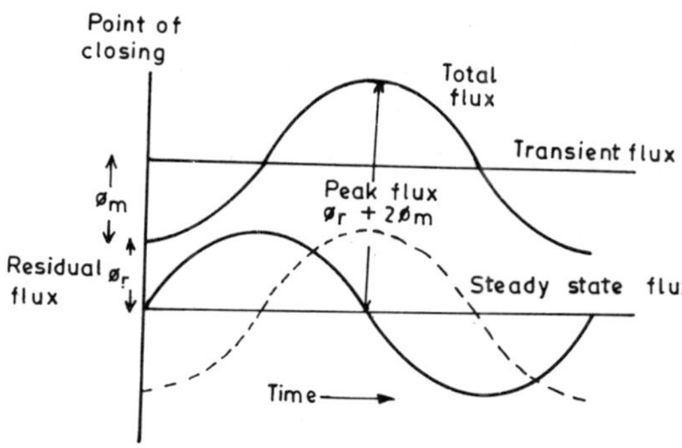

Fig. 8.6 Flux waveform for closing at zero of applied voltage

The (MIC) may cause false tripping of relays. This current is rich in second harmonics. It has been found that the second harmonic content of the (MIC) is never expected to be less than 16% of the fundamental both for 1-ϕ and 3-ϕ transformers . This observation has been used to distinguish between the (MIC) and fault current for the relaying purposes.

8.4.2 Overvoltage Inrush Current

Occasional, short duration voltage increase may arise during abnormal system conditions. Overvoltage may cause saturation of transformer resulting in high differential currents. Increased current may resemble internal fault current causing erroneous operation of protective relay. A 20 to 50% overvoltage in grain-steel may cause as high as 10 to 100% increase in excitation currents. The magnitude of such overvoltage is determined by several factors such as generator excitation system response, the line length remaining connected to a generating station after the loss of a load, existence of faults preceding load rejection, system shunt reactances, total generating capacity, etc.

An increase in magnetizing current due to overvoltage means a large increase in the odd harmonics components, especially increase in the third and the fifth harmonic components. Because of delta-connection, it is not possible to monitor the third harmonic component as it gets trapped inside a delta-connection, and hence the only option left is to monitor the fifth harmonic component. It has been found that for more than 140% overvoltage, the fifth harmonic content of the magnetizing current is not less than 8%. Thus the existence of fifth harmonic is an indication of overvoltage inrush current for which the relay must not trip.

8.4.3 Filtering Schemes

There are basically two types of filtering scheme, viz. analog filtering and digital filtering. However, using analog filter would increase hardware complexity and therefore decrease reliability, because separate filters would have to be provided for each input signal. The advantages associated with digital filters such as high accuracy, high reliability, non-critical component tolerance, performance unaffected by component aging and greater flexibility, are the reasons to go in for digital filters.

Two classes of digital filters are in use, viz. non-recursive filters, whose output is a function of previous and present inputs, and recursive filters, where by using feedback, the output becomes a function of past and present inputs and outputs. The non-recursive filter generates a finite impulse response and therefore, it is called '*Finite impulse response filter*'. Recursive filters, because of the feedback, have infinite impulse response and are referred to as '*Infinite impulse response filters*'.

The traditional approach to the design of Infinite impulse response (IIR) digital filter involves transferring an analog filter to digital filter that meets the prescribed requirements. This transformation can be achieved in a number of ways, viz. impulse invariance, direct transformation using S to Z-plane transforms, conversion of differential equations to difference equations and direct synthesis. For these filters, we observe that Legendre filter of the fourth order gives minimum settling time for a step input (tripping decision can be reliably taken only when filter outputs have settled down). This minimum settling time is 56.2 ms, i.e. of the order of three cycles. If we desire tripping within a cycle after the occurrence of fault, IIR filter will obviously not perform satisfactorily. Hence, attention is focused on FIR filters.

FIR filters are digital equivalent of a tapped delay line analog filter or transversal filters. Besides requiring a large number of delay elements (memory locations), they require a numerous operations, like multiplication etc. Hence a simple hardware realization of such filters becomes difficult.

The next option open is to use any one of the transforms, as indicated in the earlier chapter (see Table 7.2). The table shows that the Haar transform requires the least amount of computation; however, its frequency response is not very good, as its performance deteriorates heavily with slight frequency variations. Filters based on Walsh transform, besides being simple, are definitely better in this situation.

Walsh Transform Based Filter. Walsh functions form a complete set of orthonormal functions. These functions, which are denoted by Wal (k,t), bear a number of resemblances to the foregoing sines and cosines, appearing as the square version of them. They take only the values $\pm$ 1 and change sign only when t is a multiple of a power of 1/2. The first sixteen of these functions are shown in Fig. 8.8.

Any given continuous function, periodic with a time period T = 1, can be synthesized from a Walsh series given by

$$f(t) = \sum_{n=0}^{\infty} W_n \text{ Wal } (n, t) \tag{8.12}$$

where

$$W_n = \int_0^1 f(t) \text{ Wal } (n, t) \tag{8.13}$$

If a function $f(t)$ is specified by N samples (X_1, X_2, ..., X_N) during a time period, we cannot use a Walsh series for it. However, we can define the discrete Walsh transform and its inverse from Eq. (8.12) and (8.13) as,

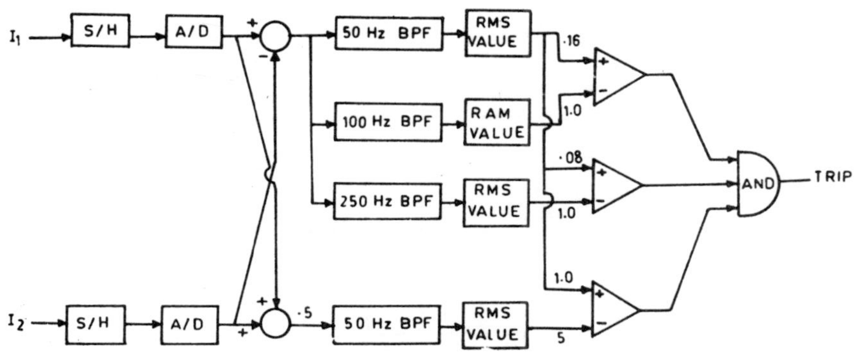

Fig. 8.9 % Differential Relay

$$X_n = \frac{1}{N} \sum_{K=0}^{N-1} W_k \text{ Wal } (n, k/N) \tag{8.14}$$

$$W_k = \sum_{k=0}^{N-1} X_n \text{ Wal } (n, k/N) \tag{8.15}$$

for $k, n = 0, 1, 2, ... N - 1$.

The settling time of this filter is less than 20 ms. The first 16 Haar functions are shown in Fig. 8.7.

8.4.4 Basic Theory of Relay

The currents I_1 and I_2 obtained from the current transformer, are fist converted into voltages by passing them through transactors. After this, they are selected one by one with the help of multiplexer and sampled.

From Nyquist theorem it follows that sampling frequency must be at least equal to twice the highest frequency that is to be detected by sampling process. One constraint may be the type of microprocessor used. In the present scheme, 16 samples per cycle is chosen in order that fifth harmonic component is also evaluated without causing more attenuation and distortion.

The tripping condition of the percentage differential relay is

$$|I_1 - I_2| \geq S \left| \frac{I_1 + I_2}{2} \right| \tag{8.16}$$

Here it is implicit that I_1 and I_2 are the fundamental components of the pure sinusoidal waveforms. However, this is not true in practice where, after the fault, the current waveform consists of fundamental as well as several harmonic components. Hence to implement the above criterion, we must filter out the harmonics, so as to obtain the fundamental component of $I_1 - I_2$ and $I_1 + I_2$. Thus with the help of a filter circuit, the following signal is obtained for tripping

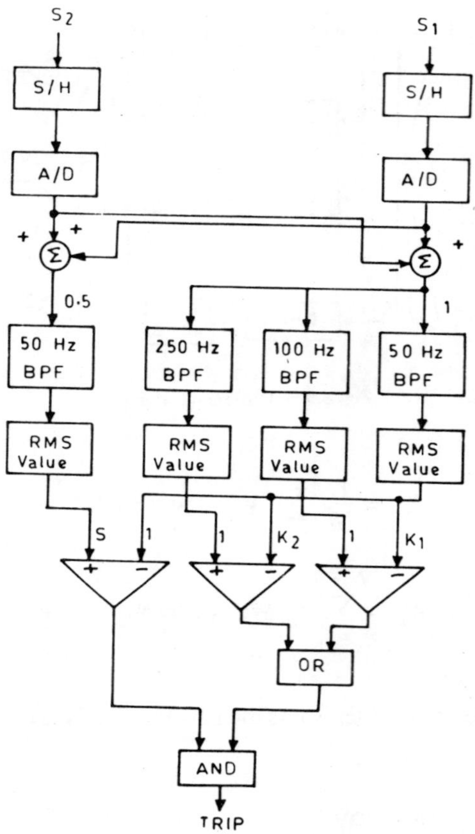

Fig. 8.10 % Differential Relay

$$|I_1 - I_2|_1 \geq S \left|\frac{I_1 + I_2}{2}\right|_1 \tag{8.17}$$

where 1 refers to the fundamental component. On the basis of earlier results, magnetizing inrush condition exists when,

$$|I_1 - I_2|_2 \geq 0.16\ |I_1 - I_2|_1 \tag{8.18}$$

and over voltage inrush condition exists when

$$|I_1 - I_2|_5 \geq 0.08\ |I_1 - I_2|_1 \tag{8.19}$$

Here 2 refers to second harmonic component and 5 refers to fifth harmonic component. Combining the Eqs. (8–17) - (8–19), we get the final tripping criterion as,

$$|I_1 - I_2|_1 \geq S \left|\frac{I_1 + I_2}{2}\right|_1 \tag{8.20}$$

and the final blocking criterion as,

$$|I_1 - I_2|_2 \geq 0.16\ |I_1 - I_2|_1$$
$$|I_1 - I_2|_5 \geq 0.08\ |I_1 - I_2|_1 \qquad (8.21)$$

Here S is a bias factor which is in the range of 0.15 to 0.6. The above tripping criterion makes the relay inrush proof. The task to be performed can be visualized as,

(i) Obtain samples of I_1 and I_2, convert them to digital form and construct $|I_1 - I_2|$ and $\left|\frac{I_1 + I_2}{2}\right|$

(ii) Extract the rms. values of

$$|I_1 - I_2|_1,\ |I_1 - I_2|_2,\ |I_1 - I_2|_5 \quad \text{and} \quad \left|\frac{I_1 + I_2}{2}\right|_1$$

(iii) Give tripping command if the criterion given by Eq. 8.21 is satisfied. The relaying scheme is shown in Figs. 8.9 and 8.10.

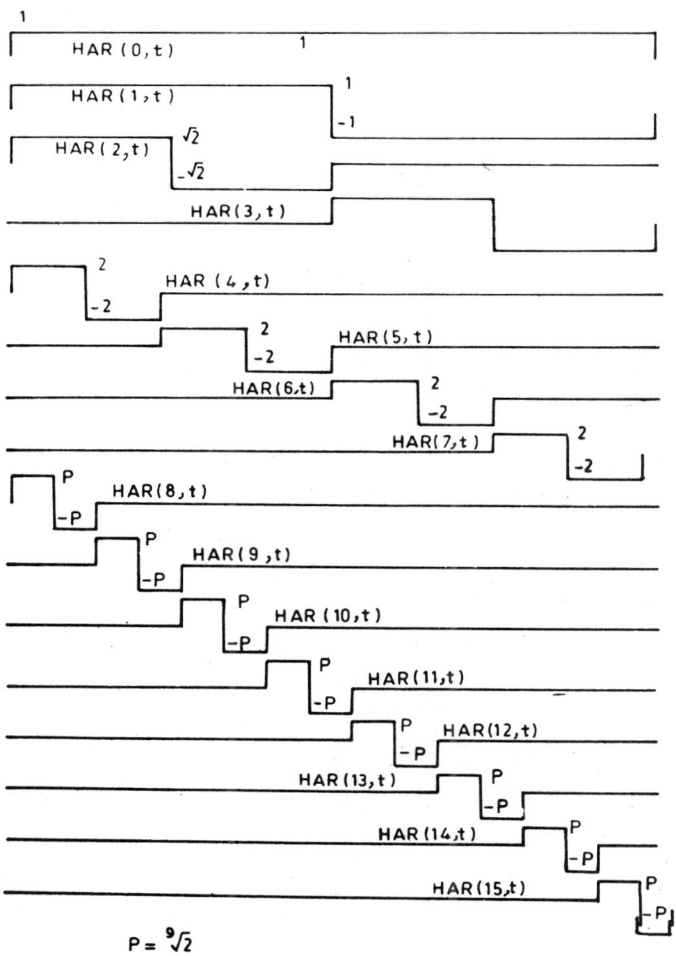

Fig. 8.7 First 16 Haar Function

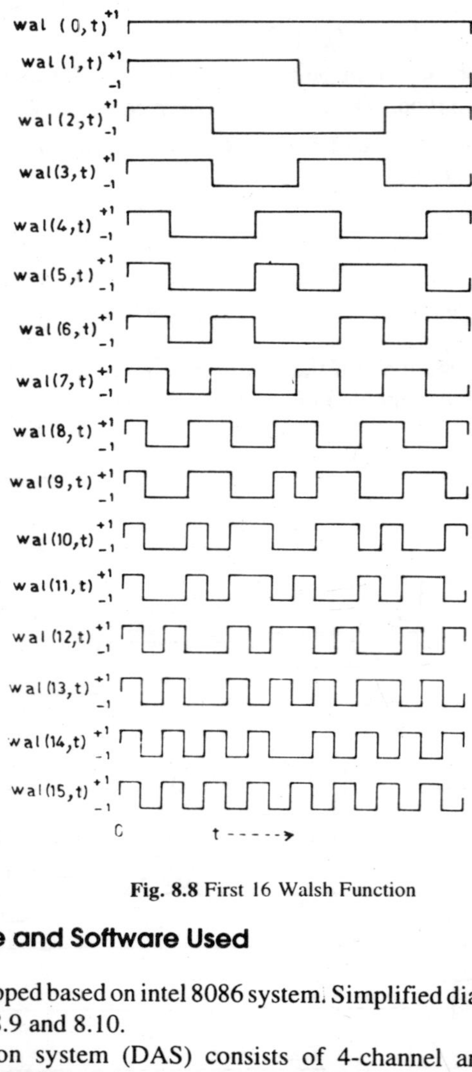

Fig. 8.8 First 16 Walsh Function

8.4.5 Hardware and Software Used

Hardware is developed based on intel 8086 system. Simplified diagram of hardware is shown in Figs. 8.9 and 8.10.

Data acquisition system (DAS) consists of 4-channel analog multiplexer (CD4052BM) and analog to digital converter (AD570).

In the actual scheme, the three primary and three secondary currents are obtained by CTs. These current signals are converted into voltage signals with the help of transactor. The six voltage signals are the input to the multiplexer. The analog signals from the multiplexer reach the ADC which converts analog signals into an equivalent 12-bit digital signal. The ADC has been connected in bipolar mode (± 5 V) to read both positive and negative values of the analog signals and gives minimum conversion time of aprpox. 3 μs. A 'convert start' pulse generated by timer (8253) starts the conversion at its falling edge. The 12-bit output is read by software through port *B* and *C* (lower) of PPI-8255 and is stored in the memory buffer for processing. The I/O interface, a link between external circuit and microprocessor comprises programmable interrupt controller (PIC8259), a programmable peripheral interface (PPI8255) and a programmable interval timer (PIT8253).'

16-bit intel-8086, Vinytics kit is used as microcomputer. This is connected to PC-XT through a serial interface using RS-232 connector. The kit and PC are interfaced by a software package named as PC-KIT. The software enables easy development of assembly language program on the PC using Microsoft Assembler and executing the code after down-loading it into the kit, i.e. it provides an interactive environment for the kit through PC-XT.

The relaying scheme is shown in Fig. 8.10.

8.5 SUMMARY

The chapter discusses the design and fabrication of a microprocessor based digital percentage differential relaying scheme for transformer protection using harmonic restraint to avoid tripping due to magnetizing inrush current and also overvoltage inrush current. The system has been configured around Intel-8086 microprocessor to realize the digital relay which is fast, reliable, flexible and also possesses self checking feature.

EXERCISE

1. What are the different types of faults in a transformer? Discuss briefly. Name protection schemes to protect transformer against these faults.
2. What do you understand by gas-actuated (i.e. Buchholz) relay? For which type of transformer and at which part of the transformer, it is used? Discuss the theory of operation of a gas-actuated relay. Discuss what do you understand by quick acting element and sensitive element of the relay.
3. Discuss, with the help of a neat diagram, the theory and principle of operation of a unit protection scheme (i.e. percentage differential relaying scheme) using static components for the protection of a $\Delta - Y$ connected transformer showing correctly CTs connection. What is the range of bias factor S in this case and why S in this case is so high?
4. (a) What do you understand by inrush magnetizing current in a transformer? Discuss the factors upon which the inrush magnetizing current depends. At what instant of voltage cycle is the inrush magnetizing current the most severe?

   (b) What do you understand by inrush magnetizing phenomena caused by switching due to overvoltage? Discuss briefly.
5. Discuss the theory and principle of operation of a microprocessor-based percentage differential relay scheme for the protection of a transformer. Also, discuss, with the help of neat diagram, the hardware and software schemes of the relay.
6. How is a unit protection scheme prevented to operate during inrush magnetizing current and also during inrush magnetizing current due to overvoltage

caused by switching. The inrush magnetizing current and overvoltage inrush current are rich in which harmonics? Write only tripping signals and also blocking signals for preventing relay operation during inrush phenomena for a unit protection scheme of a transformer.

7. (a) Why a digital filtering scheme is preferred? Discuss briefly. Discuss what you understand by recursive filter and non-recursive filter.
   (b) What are the main advantages of using Haar transform and Walsh transform? Discuss briefly.

8. What are the ranges of bias factor S in the case of unit protection of a synchronous generator and in the case of unit protection of a transformer? Why for a transformer S is very high? Discuss the method to obtain variable bias factor S of the transformer being protected by on-line microprocessor.

REFERENCES

1. Barnnwal, Rajiv Kumar, P.K. Kalra and L.P. Singh, "Walsh Transform Based Digital Protection of Power Transformer", *Proceedings of IEEE Annual Convention and Exhibition*, Bangalore, Jan. 1991, pp. 62–66.
2. Chandra, Amulya and L.P. Singh, "Fault Studies on 6-phase Systems and Proposed Ultra High Speed Relaying Scheme", *Proc. Nat. Seminar High Phase Order System*, Kanpur, March 1989, pp. 124–134.
3. Fakruddin, D.B., K. Parthasarathy, L. Jenkins and B.W. Hogg, "Application of Haar Functions for Transmission Line and Transformer Differential Protection", *Electr. Pwr. & Energy Syst.*, Vol. 6, No. 3, July 1984, pp. 169–180.
4. Jeyasurya, B., and M.A. Rohma, "Application of Walsh Functions for Microprocessor Based Transformer", Digital Protection of Power Transformer Vol. EMC-27, No. 4, Nov. 1985, pp. 221–225.
5. Jain, Rajeev and L.P. Singh, "Digital Protection of Transformer", *Proc. Sixth Nat. Pwr. Syst. Conf.*, Bombay, June 1990, pp. 564–569.
6. Rehman, M.A., and P.K. Dash, "Fast Algorithm for Digital Protection of Power Transformer", *Proc. IEE*, Vol. 129, Part C, March 1982, pp. 79–85.
7. Singh, L.P., *Advanced Power System Analysis and Dynamics*, 3rd Edition, Wiley Eastern Ltd., New Delhi, 1992.
8. Singhal, Arun and L.P. Singh, "Microprocessor Based Relaying Scheme for the Protection of Power Transformer", *Proc. Nat. Conf. Power System Protection*, Bangalore, Jan. 11–13, 1988, pp. B:2.1.
9. Singhal, Arun and L.P. Singh, "On line Protection of Power Transformer Using Microprocessor", *J. Instn. Engrs.*, Vol. 69, EL-2, Oct. 1988, pp. 52–58.
10. Thorp, J.S., and A.G. Phadke, "A Microprocessor Based 3-Phase Transformer Differential Relay", *IEEE Trans.*, Vol. PAS-101, Feb. 1982, pp. 426–432.
11. Warrington, A.R. Van C., *Protective Relays, Their Theory and Practice*, Vol. 1, Chapman & Hall Ltd., London, 1976.

9

DESIGN, FABRICATION AND APPLICATION OF DYNAMIC TEST BENCH

9.1 INTRODUCTION

The performance of the distance relay, once designed and developed can be checked, either by appropriate static signals or dynamic signals. The dynamic signals represent the actual system conditions and, also take into account the transients and d.c. offset component present in the fault current. The complete power system can be simulated by the dynamic test bench, to a scale down model (low power level); hence, it becomes an invaluable device for testing the performance of distance relays. Dynamic test bench proposed by Hamilton *et al.*, M/s General Electric (India) and M/s Robinson and Partners Ltd. is not very suitable for testing of the proposed relays, as a novel way of zone changing is incorporated in the present relaying scheme. Hence a special type of dynamic test bench is designed and developed at the IIT, Kanpur which provides the required signals for automatic zone changing and, also, for the testing of the polyphase relay. It can simulate all the fault conditions, and predict the performance of the static relay during transient conditions also, i.e. to verify the accuracy of the relay with respect to its reach and range and the operating time with respect to switching angle of the fault current.

9.2 DYNAMIC TEST BENCH

The dynamic test bench, as shown by Fig. 9.1, consists of the following units:

1. Point-on-wave selector and fault simulator
2. Voltage and circuit simulator
3. Phase angle measurement

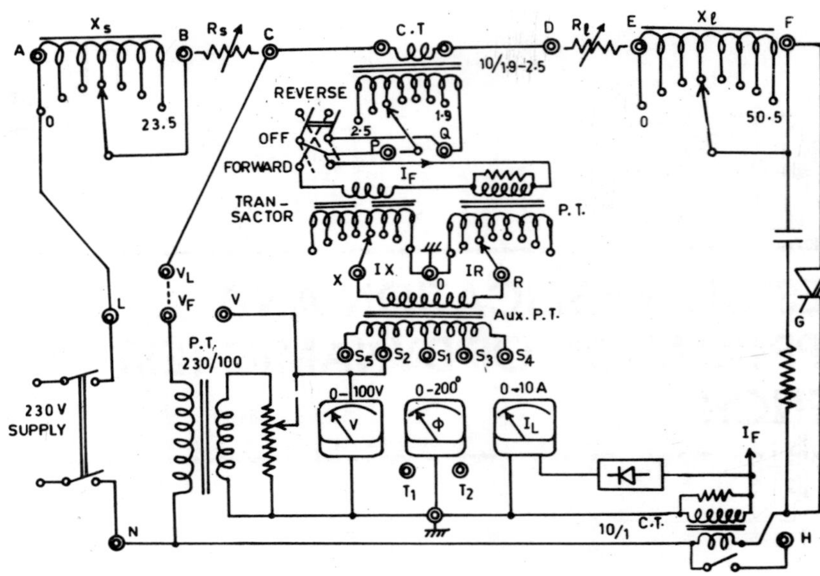

Fig. 9.1 Power and measuring circuit of dynamic test bench

4. Digital time measurement and display
5. Source and line impedance
6. Replica impedance with 3-zones
7. Power supply

In order to understand the design, development and operation of the dynamic test bench, a detailed description of each unit is necessary which is given in the following sub-sections.

9.2.1 Point-on-wave Selector and Fault Simulator

The heart of the dynamic test bench is the point-on-wave selector. The control circuit of point-on-wave selector is shown by the upper portion of Fig. 9.2, the operation of which is as follows.

A step-down P.T. is used as a reference line voltage, the secondary of which is connected to Op. Amp. via RC filter and diode limiters. The Op. Amp. is being used as inverter in open loop mode and hence it converts input sine wave into square wave, the negative cycle of which is clipped by another diode. Positive (0–180°) and negative (180–360°) cycle control is achieved by a SPDT toggle switch with logic 0/1, through 4-NAND gates using IC 74C00. A Triac is fired to simulate the fault condition, in which, the triggering can be delayed (phase angle control) by a monomulti (M–1) using a potentiometer (P–1) calibrated in degrees. Hence, the maximum time delay is 10 ms. which corresponds to an angle (α) equal to 180° during each half of the cycle. The triggering of triac is initiated by a push-button switch (START) which enables the monomulti, giving firing pulses through NOR

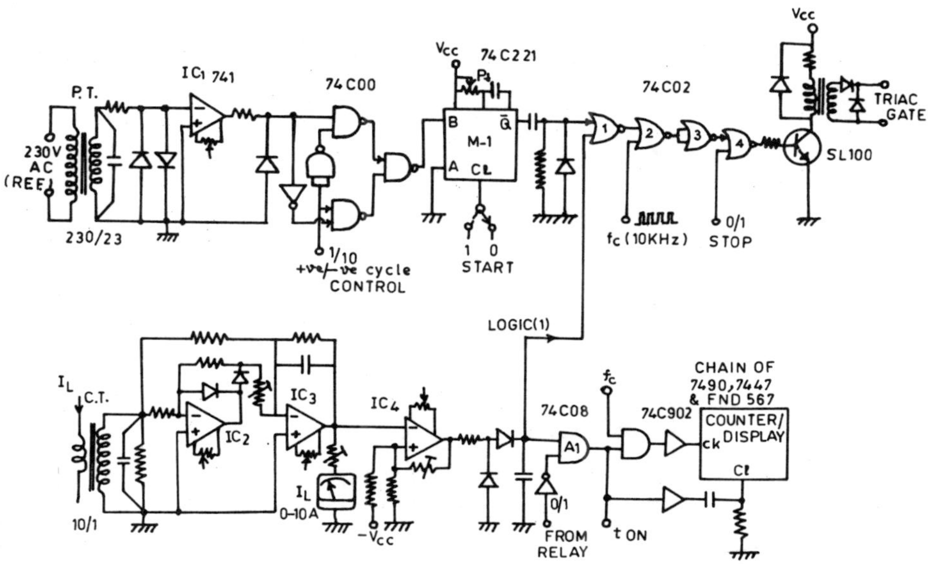

Fig. 9.2 Control & measuring circuit of dynamic test bench

gates using IC 74C02. Carrier frequency (10 kHz) gating control is used for firing the triac through pulse transformer. As soon as the triac fires, a logic (1) is established at the input of the first NOR gate; hence the firing pulses are maintained (continued). The power circuit can be turned off (short circuit or fault removed) by a push-button switch which stops the passage of 10 kHz pulses, at the base of the transistor, through the last NOR gate having logic (1) momentarily. Thus, the triac turns off at natural current zero. The presence of short circuit (fault simulation) is sensed by logic (1) using a precision detector, Schmit-trigger and peak detector. The operation of the point-on-wave selector can be understood by referring to Fig. 9.3.

9.2.2 Relay Voltage and Current Simulator and Measurement

A potential transformer of nominal turns ratio 230/100 and a current transformer of turns ratio 10/5 are designed and fabricated to supply the voltage and current to the relay unit. The CT turns ratio can be varied in the range 1.9–2.5, in steps of 0.1, i.e. the ratios available are 1.9, 2.0, 2.1. 2.2, 2.3, 2.4 and 2.5. Thus, the change of ratio between two consecutive steps is approximately 4 to 5%, by which over-and under-reach of the relay can be checked in the dynamic condition. The PT secondary is connected to a potentiometer (P–2) which is calibrated in percentage of voltage. Hence, the variation of PT ratio, together with CT ratio, can give fine control over the reach of the relay under test.

The measurement of a.c. voltage is done by a rectifier bridge and a d.c. voltmeter for higher accuracy. The precision detector, as shown by lower circuit of Fig. 9.2, is also used to measure line currents. A DPDT switch, with centre off position, is

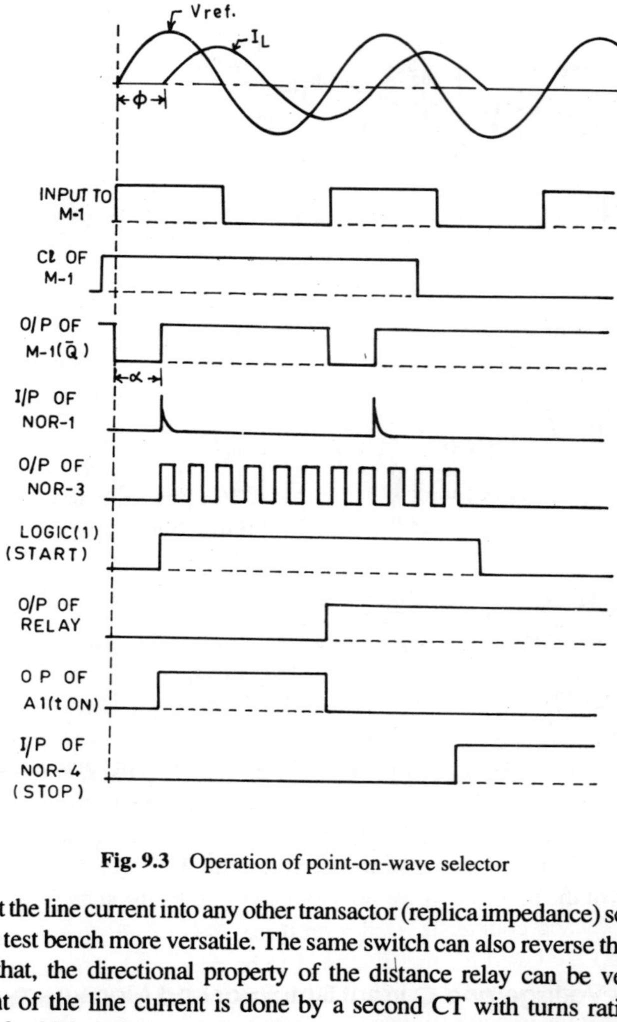

Fig. 9.3 Operation of point-on-wave selector

used to inject the line current into any other transactor (replica impedance) so as to make the dynamic test bench more versatile. The same switch can also reverse the transactor current, so that, the directional property of the distance relay can be verified. The measurement of the line current is done by a second CT with turns ratio 10/1, the secondary of which induces a voltage, proportional to line current across a low resistance, and provides IR reference vector for phase angle measurement etc.

9.2.3 Phase Angle Measurement

The Electronic Phase Angle Meter is shown by Fig. 9.4. The phase angle between any two sine waves can be measured by 'plug-in' and the display is shown by analog d.c. microammeter calibrated directly in degrees. An EX/OR gate is used to measure the phase difference of the standardized sine wave. Two Op. Amps. are used to convert sine wave into square wave which can be made to pass to 'inverter' through switches SW_1 and SW_2. Thus, the polarity of any one input signal can be reversed at will which may be desirable in certain cases. The resolution of the phase

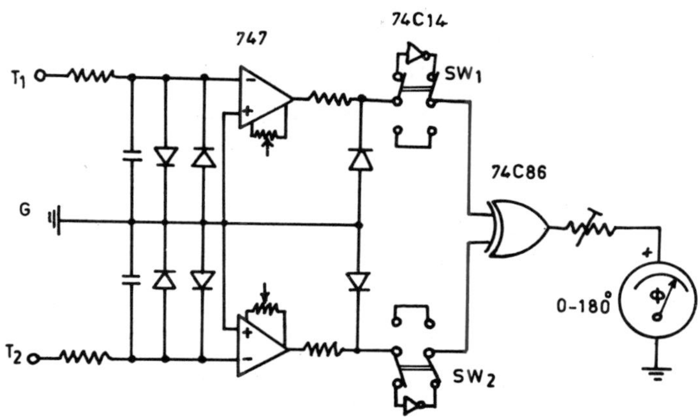

Fig. 9.4 Electronic phase angle meter

angle meter is 2° and the accuracy is better than ± 1%. Thus, the present phase angle meter, greatly, simplifies the measurement of phase difference with high degree of accuracy. The voltage sensitivity of the meter is from 100 mV to 100.

9.2.4 Digital Time Measurement and Display

The digital time interval meter can measure upto 999 ms which could be the maximum operating time of zone-3 for high speed relaying. The basic principle of operation of this unit is as follows.

A certain number of pulses (n) of known frequency (f_c) are counted during relay operating time (t_{on}), which gives the measure of time, thus,

$$t_{on} = \frac{n}{f_c} \; \alpha \, n \tag{9.1}$$

where f_c = constant.

A 4-stage decade counter is used with three, 7-segment display only. Input pulses (10 kHz) are gated for the time (t_{on}) to be measured. The fault initiation, with logic (1), start the counter and the relay operation, logic (1), stops the counter. It can be seen that the transient time is also included in relay operating time. As the line impedance is generally matched to replica impedance and the transactors themselves act as filter, the transient time could be 10 to 20 ms. which could be subtracted from the total operating time to get relay operating time. Four miniature sockets are provided on the control panel of the dynamic test bench so that, t_{on}, f_c, I_L can be displayed on C.R.O. and the relay output (trip signal) can be injected to stop the counter. The same I_L signal is used as reference for phase angle measurements. The lower half of Fig. 9.2 shows the time measurement and display device.

9.2.5 Source and Line Impedance (Table 9.1)

Two iron-cored tapped inductors, having air gaps, are used to simulate source and line reactance with continuous rating of 4A. Provision is also made to insert line and source resistance, externally, so as to vary the source and line phase angles. The tappings of inductor are brought out to a rotary switch by which a desired source and line reactance can be inserted into the main circuit. The phase angles of the source and line reactances vary between 83° to 87° and 85° to 88° respectively.

Table 9.1 Source and Line Impedances

ITEM	*STEPS*						
	1	2	3	4	5	6	7
X_S	3.0	4.8	9.5	15.5	19.5	23.5	–
r_S	0.40	0.52	0.73	0.95	1.07	1.20	–
X_L	5.0	10.8	15.8	20.5	30.5	40.5	50.5
r_L	0.41	0.58	0.75	0.87	1.11	1.32	1.52

These iron-cored inductors are designed and fabricated with shell type arrangement from grain-oriented silicon steel laminations. An air gap of about 3 mm is found adequate to give linearity over a wide range of reactance. The following expression can be used to calculate the number of turns to provide the required reactance:

as $$IT = \frac{796}{\sqrt{2}} B_g l_g$$

Hence, $$T = \frac{565\ B_g l_g}{I} \tag{9.2}$$

and $$T_1 = T \frac{\sqrt{X_1}}{X} \tag{9.3}$$

where,

I = maximum RMS current

T = number of turns

T_1 = number of turns at reactance X_1

B_g = flux density in air gap, in Wb/m^2

l_g = length of air gap, in mm

X = V/I = reactance

V = RMS supply voltage

Hence, turns for any other reactance (X_1) can be found out.

9.2.6 Replica Impedance with 3-Zones (Table 9.2)

An iron cored transactor, with air gap, is used to simulate replica reactance, the secondary of which has tappings to vary the reactance through a rotary switch. The replica resistance is simulated by passing the primary current of the transactor through a low resistance and then, stepping up this voltage drop by a PT. Tappings are provided on the PT secondary so as to vary the replica resistance through a rotary switch. This simulated impedance ($R_R + J\,X_R$) is isolated from the voltage circuit by an auxiliary PT, the secondary of which has 5-tappings to give a voltage proportional to kZ_{R1}, Z_{R1}, Z_{R2} and Z_{R3}. Hence, a 3-zone replica impedance is simulated in a novel way, without passing the line current directly through the inductor, as is normally done. The 1st zone replica impedance is kZ_{R1}, kZ_{R1} is about 20% of Z_{R1}, Z_{R2} is 150% of Z_{R1} and Z_{R3} is 200% of Z_{R1}. The zone-1 impedance (Z_{R1}) can be further reduced by a factor of k which varies in steps from 0.2 to 1.0 by a rotary switch. The voltage IR_R, IX_R, kIZ_{R1}, IZ_{R1}, IZ_{R2} and, IZ_{R3} are brought out on the control panel, through banana sockets.

Table 9.2 Replica Impedances

ITEM	*STEPS*						
	1	2	3	4	5	6	7
X_R r_R	5.0 23	10.0 43	15.0 60	20.5 75	25.5 96	29.5 105	35.0 140
X_R r_R	1.0 9	2.5 22	3.8 32	5.0 42	7.5 60	9.5 77	13.5 115

It can be observed from the above description that the replica reactance is produced fictitiously. The basic principle of the design of these reactances is, that if one ampere of primary current induces a voltage of one volt in secondary circuit, then the reactance of transactor is one ohm. The maximum value of replica impedance will deperd upon line impedance, i.e. the set impedance of the line to the balance point, and CT and PT turns ratio, hence,

$$Z_R = \frac{Z_L \cdot k N_1}{N_2} \tag{9.4}$$

where,

Z_R = Replica impedance

Z_L = Line impedance up to the balance point

N_1 = C.T. turns ratio of dynamic test bench = I_L/I

N_2 = P.T. turns ratio of dynamic test bench = V_L/V

k = Per unit setting step unit of voltage control.

9.2.7 Power Supply

A well regulated, built-in power supply is made so as to provide ± 12 V d.c. and + 5 V d.c. for the electronic control, measurement and instrumentation purpose. The circuit diagram is shown by Fig. 9.5. The IC-723 is used to provide + 12 V d.c. regulated supply whose current rating is boosted by a 'pass element' (power transistor). IC-320-12T is used to provide – 12 V d.c. regulated supply. A well regulated + 5 V d.c. supply, to drive the 7-segment LED display, is provided by using IC-LM323 voltage regulator. All these power supplies have built-in short circuit protection.

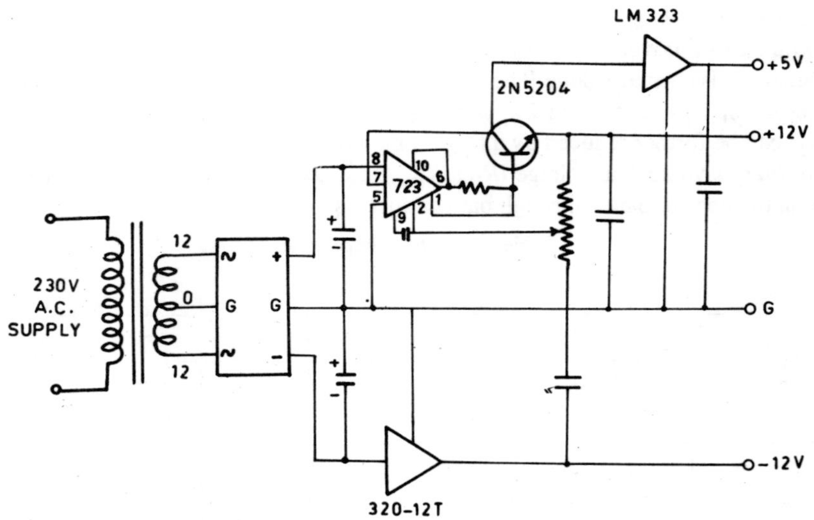

Fig. 9.5 Circuit diagram of power supply

9.3 APPLICATION OF DYNAMIC TEST BENCH

The front panel layout of the dynamic test bench is shown in Fig. 9.6 and its power and measuring circuit diagram is shown in Fig. 9.1. A multi-tapping source inductor

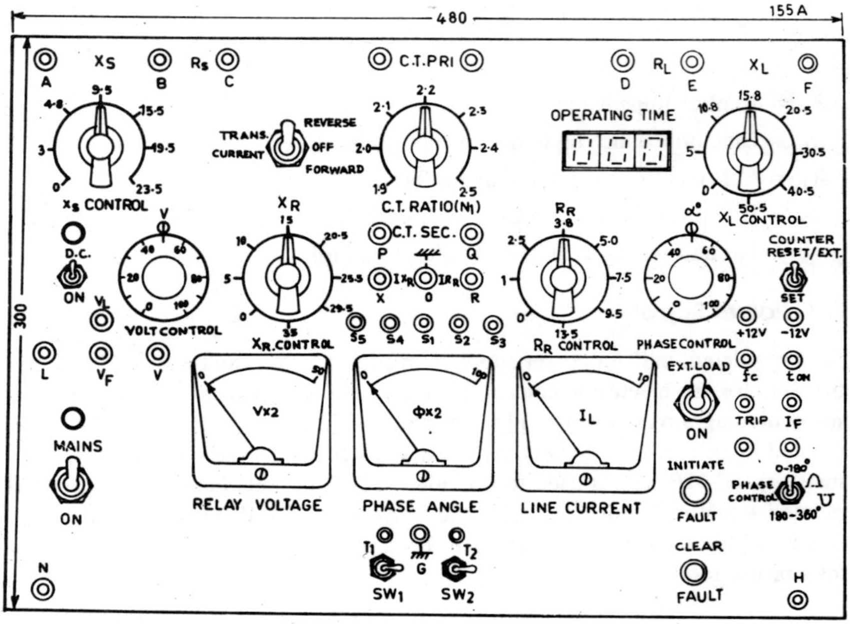

Fig. 9.6 Front panel layout of dynamic test bench

(X_S) and line inductor (X_L) are connected to terminals A–B and E–F respectively. Their magnitude can be controlled by rotary switches, 'X_S control' and 'X_L control' respectively. The source and line resistances R_S and R_L can be connected externally between terminals B–C and E–F respectively. The external load can be connected to terminals F–H via a switch 'Ext. Load'. The 230 V a.c. supply is connected to terminals L–N via a switch "Mains ON". The primary of main PT can be connected across line impedance ($R_L + jX_L$) via jumper between terminals V_L and V_F or it can be connected to the secondary of phase shifter. The secondary voltage of the main P.T. is measured by a voltmeter (*V*) and can also be connected to a relay through terminal (*V*). An ammeter (I_L) measures the fault current whereas the phase angle measurement is done by a 'phase meter' (ϕ) via switches SW_1, SW_2 and terminals T_1–T_2. The transactor current (I_F) can be controlled by a rotary switch. 'C.T. ratio' and the source current can be injected into an external transactor unit by a 3-position switch (Reverse-OFF-Forward) in OFF position through terminals P-Q. The secondary of transactor is connected to terminals X–R and hence, the replica reactance (X_R) and resistance (R_R) can be controlled by rotary switches 'X_R control' and R_R control' respectively. An auxiliary transformer (Aux. P.T.) is connected to terminals X–R, the secondary of which provides the required signals (S_1, S_2, S_3, S_4, S_5) for 3-zone operation of the relaying schemes.

The fault can be initiated by firing a Triac through 'Fault-Initiate' push button switch and is cleared by 'Fault Clear' switch. The 'Phase Control' is the 'Point-on-Wave Selector' which can control the switching angle of fault current (I_L). Positive and negative cycle control is affected by a 'Phase Control Switch'. Four miniature sockets are provided so that clock frequency (f_c), operation time (t_{on}) and line current (I_L) can be observed and recorded. The fourth socket is used to inject the 'Relay Trip' signal, to stop the digital time interval meter, so that, the operating time can be measured. A switch 'Counter Set/Reset' is provided to reset the counter.

9.3.1 Distance Relay Setting

The impedance of transmission line on H.T. side depends upon the length of the line and also on the transmission voltage. If the line to be protected has an impedance of,

$$Z'_{L1} = (R' + jX') \tag{9.5}$$

then, the impedance setting on dynamic test bench will be

$$Z_L \frac{0.8\ Z'_{L1} \times \text{CT ratio}}{\text{PT ratio}} = 0.8\ Z'_{L1} \frac{C_T}{P_T} \tag{9.6}$$

If the replica impedance angle (θ) and line phase angle (ϕ) are not equal then the value of replica impedance required will be

$$Z_R = \frac{Z_L}{\cos(\phi - \theta)} \times \frac{N_1 k}{N_2} \tag{9.7}$$

It should also be noted that, for line to ground fault, the relay voltage should be $V/\sqrt{3}$ and the value of line impedance setting is,

$$Z_L = \left(1 + \frac{k}{3}\right) \frac{Z_R N_2}{k N_1} \tag{9.8}$$

Similarly, the value of relay voltage, for all types of phase faults, should be V and the line impedance setting is,

$$Z_L = \frac{2\, Z_R\, N_2}{k\, N_1} \tag{9.9}$$

where V is the line to line (i.e. delta) voltage on the secondary side of the PT.

9.3.2 Relay Accuracy, Transient Over-reach and Range

The accuracy is defined as the ratio of impedance just causing operation of the relay to the set impedance when the fault takes place near the balance point. Thus

(a) Accuracy
$$x = \frac{Z}{Z_R} = \frac{V}{I\, Z_R} = \frac{N_1\, V}{I_L\, Z_R} = \frac{Z_L}{Z_R} \cdot \frac{N_1}{N_2} \tag{9.10}$$

If the relay trips by reducing the voltage, then

$$x = \frac{k\, V}{I\, Z_R} = \frac{k\, N_1\, V}{I_L^2\, Z_R} = \frac{Z_L}{Z_R} \cdot \frac{k\, N_1}{N_2} \tag{9.11}$$

Accuracy at any phase angle (ϕ),

$$x = \frac{k\, V}{I\, Z_R \cos(\phi - \theta)} = \frac{Z_L}{Z_R \cos(\phi - \theta)} \frac{k\, N_1}{N_2}$$

9.4 SUMMARY

The Dynamic Test Bench, designed, developed and fabricated is simple, compact, accurate and self-contained and does not require any other auxiliary unit for its operation. All the proposed or existing relaying schemes can be tested on it.

REFERENCES

1. Hamilton, F.L. and N.S. Ellis, "Development in Bench Testing Facilities for Protection Gears", *Op. Cit.*, June 1966 (166).
2. Kellog, A.J., "Novel Distance Relaying Schemes for the Protection of EHV/UHV Transmission Lines Using Digital Techniques, *Ph. D. thesis,* IIT Kanpur, July 1984.
3. Kellog, A.J., L.P. Singh and G.K. Dubey, "Protection of EHV Transmission Line by Using Static Relays", *Paper presented at the International Conference on Power System Protection,* Madras, April 1980, Paper B5.
4. Kellog, A.J., L.P. Singh and G.K. Dubey, "General Purpose Static Relay Using Digital Techniques" *J. Instn. Engrs.*, Vol. 63, pt. EL-1, Aug. 1982, pp. 5–11.
5. Kellog A.J., L.P. Singh and G.K. Dubey, "3-Phase (Polyphase) Distance Relay Using Digital Circuits", *Proc. 2nd Nat. Pwr. Syst., Conf.,* Hyderabad, Sept. 1983.
6. Kellog, A.J., L.P. Singh and G.K. Dubey, "A High Speed 3-zone Distance Relay Using Digital Circuit", *Electr Pwr Syst Res,* Vol. 8, 1984-85, pp. 187–195.
7. Kellog, A.J., L.P. Singh and G.K. Dubey, "A High Speed 3-zone Distance Relay Using Digital Circuits", *Proc. Int. IEEE. Conf.,* Bangalore, Dec. 1984, pp. 1349–1353.
8. Singh, L.P., *Advanced Power System Analysis and Dynamics*, 3rd Edition, Wiley Eastern Ltd., New Delhi, 1992.
9. Gupta, A.K., L.P. Singh and G.K. Dubey, "Design, fabrication and testing of a New Dynamic Test Bench", JIE (I) Nov. 1993, pp. 100–103.

10

DISTANCE (IMPEDANCE) AND OVER-CURRENT RELAY SETTING AND COORDINATION USING COMPUTER GRAPHICS

10.1 INTRODUCTION

The basic role of the protection scheme is to sense faults and isolate these faults by opening all incoming current paths. This sensing and switching operations must occur as fast as possible to minimize damages. However, the protection scheme must be selective so that only faulted element is removed i.e. isolated. This has led to the practice of providing primary protection with backup which functions only when primary fails. Primary protection is designed for high speed and minimum network disruption while backup system operates slowly and generally affects larger portion of the network. The proper coordination of primary and backup relays for all possible faults is the main criteria to be satisfied to avoid false tripping and malopertion of the relay.

Coordination amongst relays require the knowledge of type of protection schemes used and also their operating time. The relaying scheme may use over-current relays or distance relays. The overcurrent relay usually consists of an instantaneous unit and a time delay unit, in which the time delay depends upon the magnitude of current which is inversely proportional to the distance to fault. The distance relay usually consists of an instantaneous unit (Zone-1) and usually two time delay units (Zone-2, Zone-3).

One of the main topics of concern to the protection engineers is the proper coordination behaviour of different relay units so as to avoid relay maloperation. This problem is quite complex and needs careful thinking. Before arriving at proper relay coordination and relay settings, several factors have to be taken into account and several consequences are to be considered.

For the coordination of distance relays, first zone (*i.e.* Zone-1)is set to act instantaneoulsy for faults on the protected line and the other two zones (*i.e.* Zone-2 and Zone-3) protect the main and the adjacent lines with time delay increasing in discrete steps. A fully coordinated result should indicate the impedance setting values for all the zones in terms of various impedance taps available on the relays and also the timer settings associated with the second zone and the third zone relays. For coordinating overcurrent relays, we normally require three parameters associative with any kind of overcurrent relays, viz.the instantaneous tap values, the time-delay pickup tap values and the time-dial setting value for all the relays in the system to satisfy the coordination criterion.

The relay performs both primary and backup protection roles. Hence, one is concerned about the relative speed of operation of all primary/backup pairs of relays; for proper coordination, the primary relay ,must operate faster than the backup relay for the given fault current. Coordination of relay pair must be achieved through detailed fault analysis under different situations. Coordination also takes into account the different contingencies such as single line and double line out contingencies for all faults.

A large number of computations are involved as the performance of such primary and backup pairs must be checked for proper coordination involving each pair. Input data required for setting the relays and coordinating them is generated by conducting short circuit studies and load flow studies for all contingencies. Using data so generated, operating time of different relays and their settings are calculated and checked for coordination. Iterative procedure is followed for proper coordination of relays.

The present chapter discusses the desired design coordination criterion, minimum coordination criterion and enhanced criterion for both overcurrent relays and distance relays. For overcurrent relays, the procedure to determine instantaneous setting, pickup tap setting and time dial setting for two-terminal and multi- terminal lines are given. For distance relays, the Zone-1, Zone-2 and Zone-3 timer settings taking into account both, infeeds and outfeeds are discussed. To provide the desired flexibility and visual display, computer graphics have been made use of.

10.2 CLASSIFICATION OF CRITERIA

Three broad categories for coordination criteria are defined as follows,

Desired design criteria : These are the the existing criteria which will result in desired operation of the relay system.

Minimum criteria: These are the criteria adopted when the desired criteria can not be achieved. This is achieved through back-up relay operating time being relaxed *i.e.* allow back-up relay not to operate for some low fault currents.

Enhanced criteria: These are the criteria designed to produce optimum results. It might include consideration of additional fault at mid-line for the purpose of relay coordination.

10.3 DIRECTIONAL INSTANTANEOUS/IDMT OVER CURRENT RELAYS

10.3.1 Characteristics

a *Instantaneous over current relays* : If relay operates instantaneously without any internal time delay; this characteristic can generally be satisfied by a relay of non- polarized attracted armature type. Instantaneous relay is effective only when impedance between the relay and source (Zs) is small compared to the protected section impedance Ze.

In the case of instantaneous relays, there is a tendency for oversensitivity under transient fault currents with D.C.component. At the time of fault occurrence, the current wave is not symmetrical but offset as shown in Fig.10.1.The relay is set for symmetrical currents but responds to both symmetrical as well as

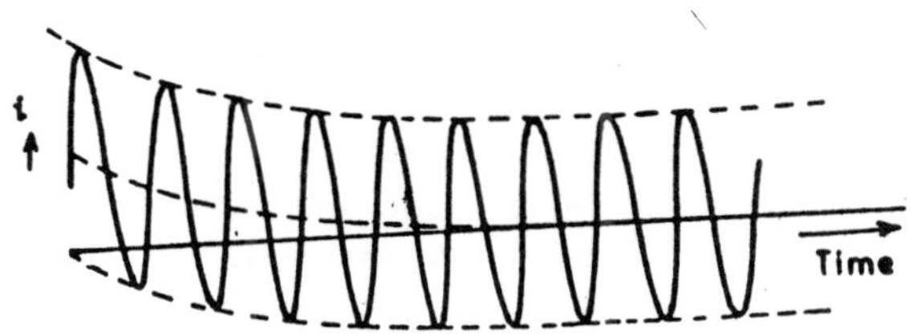

Fig 10.1 Offset current wave

offset current waves which persist for a few cycles. The overreach depends on the design of the relay as well as on the parameters of the power system on which it is used. The X/R ratio from the source to the fault of the system, controls the degree of offset and rate of decrement of current wave, and the ratio Zs/Ze determines the degree of overreach, which will occur.

The current setting is proportional to $\frac{1}{(z_s+z_e)}$ so that with 100% offset,the pick-up will occur with half the symmetrical value of current *i.e.*

$$\text{Operating current} \quad \alpha \quad \frac{1}{2(z_s+z_e)} \tag{10.1}$$

Since Z_S is fixed, the effective length of the line protected is increased, consequently there is overreach, if K be the overreach, then

$$Zs + KZe = 2(Zs + Ze) -> K = 2 + \frac{Z_S}{Z_e} \tag{10.2}$$

i.e. with 100% offset current wave, the instantaneous overcurrent relay will overreach to more than twice the length of the protected section.

Actually, the overreach will be reduced by the operating time of the relay because the d.c.component of the fault current will be decaying exponentially, so that,

$$\mathbf{i} = \frac{E_{max} \sin(\omega t + \varphi - \Phi)}{R^2 + (\omega L)^2} + \frac{E_{max}\, e^{kt/L} \sin(\varphi - \Phi)}{R^2 + (\omega L)^2} \tag{10.3}$$

$$\rightarrow \mathrm{i} = I_{max}\left[\sin(\omega t + \varphi - \Phi) + A\, e^{-kt/L}\right] \tag{10.4}$$

where,

ϕ : phase angle of the circuit.

φ : time in radians after time zero at which fault occurs and

t : time after inception of fault.

D.C.filters are used to overcome the overreach due to transients. Sometimes, induction cup instantaneous units are used as they are less sensitive to d.c. offset components. This way transient overreach is reduced to approximately 5%.

b. *Overcurrent relays:* The operating time of all overcurrent relays tends to become asymptotic to a definite minimum value with increase in the value of current. This is due to the saturation of magnetic circuit of eletromagnetic relays. So, by varying the degree of saturation, different characteristics are obtained. These relays are usually built using static components. In both cases, their characteristics remain the same. These characteristics are as shown below:

		Approximate equations
(a)	Definite Time	$I^0\, t = k$
(b)	Inverse definite minimum time (IDMT)	$I\, t = k$
(c)	Very inverse	$I^2 t = k$
(d)	Extremely inverse	$I^3 t = k$

(in general $I^n\, t = k$).

Definite time relay is employed in cases of wide variations of system generating conditions. Another possible application is the differential protection of transformers to prevent maloperation during magnetisation due to inrush currents. Definite time feature when used with inverse characteristic is more useful-gives inverse with definite time characteristic as used in the protection of induction motor against overloads. Definite time is preferred to instantaneous to serve as check against short-time asymmetrical currents.

Very inverse characteristic is employed where the source impedance is much smaller than the line impedance. These are more suitable for earth fault protection as there is a greater variation of zero sequence currents with distance than with phase faults.

Fuse coordination and thermal protection of transformers and induction motors require such characteristics. They are useful,in conjunction with negative sequence filters to protect against unbalanced operation of the generators.

The operating time of overcurrent relays is a function of:

i) Current through the relay

ii) pick-up current tap setting,and

iii) Time-dial setting.

10.3.2. Coordination Criteria

Two terminal lines

a. Instantaneous setting: It is specified in terms of threshold current above which the relay trips. The relay should be set to protect the fault on the primary line and should include a factor of safety to prevent against false trips for faults on the remote bus. Thus the setting will be given by,

Setting of instantaneous relay=MF IAxMax.current for a fault on the remote bus

This maximum fault current is maximized over all fault types and all single line out contingencies,namely,one line out at a time.

Generally, MFIA(multiplying factor for instantaneous action) is taken to be 1.2to1.3. The reason being to avoid overreaching causing false trip. As shown in Fig.10.2,faults F1,F2and F3 will produce almost same current through relay 4 but it is not desirable to trip relay 4 for faults at F2 and F3 as 4 is back-up to them. Hence,for instantaneous setting, fault is created at F1 and the quantity obtained is multiplied by a factor (1.2 - 1.3) to avoid overreaching. Instantaneous setting is specified in terms of maximum possible fault current times a factor of 1.2 to 1.3. This maximum fault current is maximised over worst possible situation arising in network for the relay to be set.

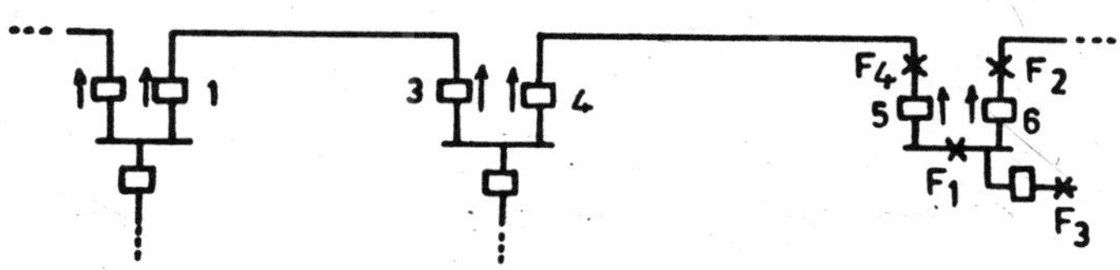

Fig 10.2 Two terminal line

Time-Delay operating setting

b. *Pick-up tap setting:* To set the pick-up tap of overcurrent relay,allowable range of tap values is determined by computing the following upper and lower limits. The lower limit is determined by maximum possible load current taking in to account the overload and power swing conditions for phase protection and tolerable unbalance factor for ground protection.

∴ Lower limit of pick-up tap = LCF x Max. load current (phase protection)

Lower limit of pick-up tap = CTU x Max. load current (ground protection)

Typically LCF (Load carrying factor) = 1.25 – 1.5

CTU (Tolerable unbalance factor) = 0.05 – 0.1

It should be ensured that the minimum remote bus fault current (*i.e.* determined by conducting LL fault during minimum generation) is picked by this relay, other wise it had to be replaced.

The upper limit is the smaller of:

b1: Normal remote bus fault current (all lines intact)x factor (NRBFF).This factor (may be 0.1 to 0.2) should be so chosen that normal remote bus fault current is 5 to 10 times that of normal load current (all lines in service, 3-phase fault for phase protection,1-phase to ground fault for ground protection).

b2: Minimum remote fault current through the relay x factor (MFCF). This factor (MFCF) accounts for condition generally prevailing in power system that minimum fault current (Phase-to- phase fault with minimum generation gives minimum fault current of all)is one and half or two times greater than the normal load current.

Hence,

MFCF(Minimum Fault Current Factor) : 0.5 to 0.6

The upper limit ensures that relay is set sensitive enough for all the fault current levels. One is free to select any value within this range, value near the lower end results in most senstive back - up relaying.

c. *Time-Dial Setting:* Time-dial settings are determined from the following criteria:

1. *Desired design criteria:* The operating time of the back-up relay should exceed that of its corresponding primary relay for all the faults considered (all fault types, normal and single-contingency conditions)by a coordination time -interval MCI.

   The actual value of coordination time is arrived at as follows:

   MCI = TIB(P) + TOT(B) + COFS

   TIB (P) : Short circuit interrupting time of primary breaker

   TOT(B) : Overtravel time of back-up relay

   COFS : Factor of safety

   Typical values of the above factors are:

   TIB(P) : 0.050 secs (3 cycles)

TOT(B) : 0.1667 secs (10 cycles)
COFS : 0.0833 secs (5 cycles)
∴ MCI= 0.3 secs.

When local breaker failure protection is used then MCI should consider the delay involved with local back-up schemes.

It is desirable to maintain the desired coordination time interval of 0.3 secs between primary and back-up operating times for a class of faults like remote bus fault,close in fault, line end fault and fault at the reach of instantaneous trip. If verified for remote bus fault, then it satisfies with others as well.

2. *Minium criteria:* Under those circumstances that demand a relaxation of the above specified crriteria, the actual setting must minimize the impact on power supply. This is, the number of customer or the amount of load affected by compromise of relay settings should be kept at minimum. Of the fault currents indicated under desired criteria, a relaxed minimum criterion will be to allow the back-up relay not to operate for some low fault currents.
3. *Enhance criteria:* This criteria might include the consideration of faults at mid of the lines and checking for coordination of the relays.

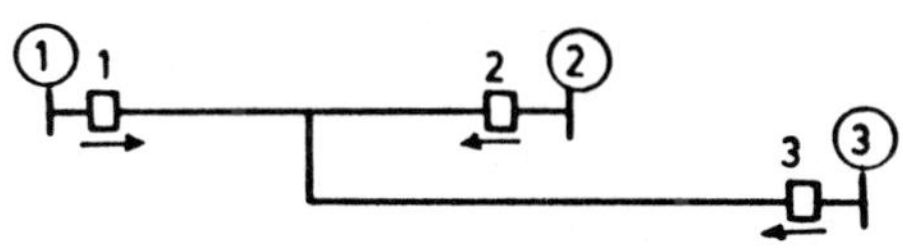

Fig 10.3 Multi terminal line

Multi-Terminal Lines

As shown in Fig.10.3, a single line terminates at two different buses. To take into account the existence of more than one remote bus, the coordination criteria is altered as follows. The instantaneous unit is to be set at MF_{IA} × Max. of all fault current at all the remote buses.

Additional Considerations: Overcurrent relays can not be used in case where the fault current levels are below the maximum load current value. However, voltage restrained directional overcurrent relays may be employed in these cases or, for phase protection,supervising distance relays can be used.

If relays are coordinated for high current values, they will usually be cordinated for low-current values also due to their inverse characteristics. But the converse is not true. Hence while coordinating overcurrent relays, generating conditions producing maximum fault currents must be considered to ensure that relays are properly coordinated through the entire range of generations.

10.4 DIRECTIONAL MULTIZONE DISTANCE RELAYS

10.4.1 Characteristics

The conventional distance relay uses three distance measuring units. These relays measure the distance to a fault by measuring line impedance between the fault and relay location. These relays may be of plane impedance, angle impedance *i.e.* ohm or angle admittance *i.e.* mho, offset mho and modified i.e. restricted impedance relay, elliptical characteristic or quadrilateral characteristic type relay.

Multiple zones of protection are achieved by coupling step-time delay units to relay units that measure the distance beyond the first zone with the time delay increasing with zone.

Zones of protection using distance relaying scheme are generally insensitive to system changes with the exception that infeeds and outfeeds will alter the reach.

First -zone which involves instantaneous action, is set to about 0.8 to 0.9 the distance to the end of the protection line for primary protection without any concern for false tripping due to faults beyond the next bus. A time delay second zone of protection is provided to offer primary protection to that section of the protected (*i.e.* end zone) line which is not covered by the first zone. This second zone provides secondary *i.e.* back - up protection to the remote bus (primary protection of the bus being the normal high speed bus differential protection) and also to a portion of the adjacent lines. A time-delay third zone provides back-up protection.

The function of zone-3 is to provide back-up protection in case a relay or breaker in the next bus fails to clear a fault. Inaccuracy due to loads and power infeeds are worse with zone-3 because there are two buses between the relay and cut-off point of the relay. Furthermore, zone-3 becomes susceptible to operation on power swing and also for this relay discrimination between loads and faults becomes poor, if their setting is too long.

Reversing the zone-3 characteristic so that back-up is now provided by the relay at the other end of the protected section, alleviates these problems considerably.

10.4.2 Co.ordination Criteria

Two terminal lines

Desired criteria: Under the normal provision of three zones of protection,one with instantaneous action and two with increasing time delay, both primary and back-up protection are obtained for all phase faults. Faults are to be cleared with a time delay not greater than maximum allowed delay time and sequential breaker action is to be coordinated with a minimum time delay of 0.3 sec., normally. These criteria are to be met when infeeds from all branches within the zones are considered.

Coordination criteria for individual zones are summarised bellow:

Zone 1,used for primary protection, is set to 0.8 to 0.9 times primary line impedance for instantaneous action. For fault in Zone-1, this relay trips instantaneously. This zone never include the adjacent bus.

Zone-2 protects line beyond the range of Zone-1 and also is set to cover remote bus plus some portion of next line (it must not include the next remote bus).

Setting for second zone = 1.25 to1.5 times primary line impedance

It is to be checked that it does not overlap with the second zone of other distance relays.

The relay trips with a time delay referred to as zone-2 time delay T2 for faults in zone-2. Generally, T2 is taken to be 0.3 secs.

Zone-3 is used for back-up protection and it is desirable to set it to the entire length of the longest remote line. However, it should be limited by worst loading conditions. This zone should be properly coordinated with other third zones of relays on the remote lines. Time delay tripping due to fault in this zone *i.e.* T3 should be less than maximum permissible time delay operation for distance relays. This zone always include the last remote bus.

Minimum criteria: In extreme cases, where, due to various infeed effects, the time coordination for second and third zones may not be possible. In these cases, the minimum criteria is to assume a sequence of relay tripping which reduces the infeed effects and eventually isolates the fault. With the help of the example shown in Fig.10.4 minimum criteria requirement will become clear.

Relays 1 and 2 provide back-up for 5. Consider relay 1 which senses faults F1and F2 with its second and third zones when feed from BC was not there. But if this feed is present, then zone-2 and 3 of relay 1 may under reach causing F2 not being sensed and F1 may fall under the zone-3 of this relay. However, if relay 2 detects the fault F1 and F2 in its zone -2 and 3 region and trips,the infeed no longer exists. Now F1 and F2 fall within Zone-2 and 3 of relay 1 which trips. This is especially important for multi-terminal lines.

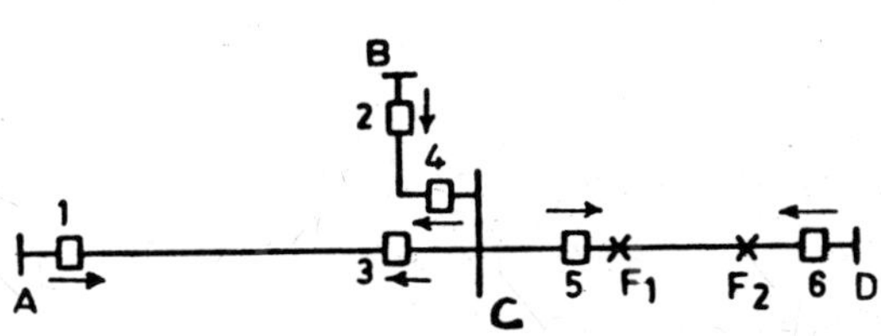

Fig.10.4 General transmission line

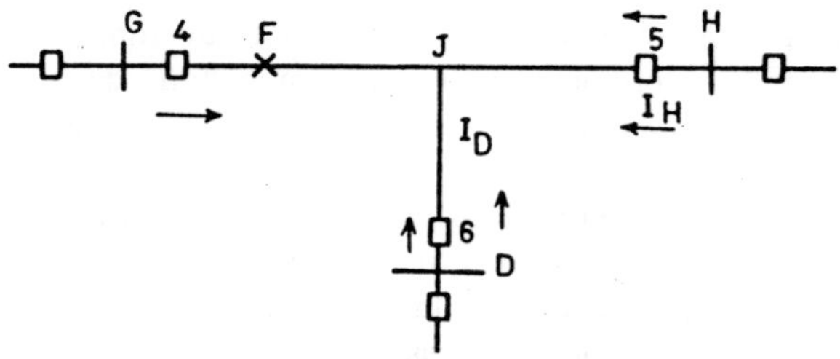

Fig.10.5 Infeed effect

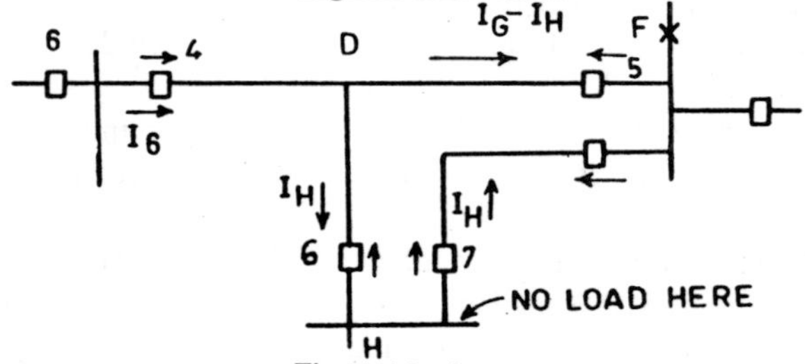

Fig.10.6 Outfeed effect

Enhanced criteria: The desired criteria are to be extended to more than one level of back-up protection (second contingency conditions such as two successive relay/breaker failures) using more than three zones of protection.

Multi-terminal lines : Because of presence of infeed and outfeed, the apparent impedance seen by the relays changes. Let us refer to Fig. 10.5 where an effect of infeed is considered and next to Fig. 10.6 where an effect of outfeed is considered.

Apparent impedance seen by relay 5 and 6 for fault at F with zero fault impedance are

$$Z_{AP}(5) = Z_{HF} + \left(\frac{I_D}{I_H}\right) Z_{JF} \text{ and}$$

$$Z_{AP}(6) = Z_{HF} + \left(\frac{I_H}{I_D}\right) Z_{JF} \tag{10.5}$$

Thus, the apparent impedance seen by the relay will be greater than the actual one. Apparent impedance should not be considered for setting zone-1, since absence of infeed will stretch zone-1 reach beyond next bus. Zone-1 setting should be 0.8 to 0.9 times smallest line length (equivalent impedance) from each relay point. For second zone setting, it must be ensured that all remote buses are included in this zone. Thus, it must be set above the maximum apparent impedance to any remote terminal. The third zone should be set beyond zone-2 to back-up the longest remote line. Considering outfeeds shown in Fig.10.6,

for fault at F;

apparent impedance seen by relay 4

$$Z_{AP}\ (4) = \left(Z_{GD} + Z_{DF}\right) - \left(\frac{I_H}{I_D}\right) Z_{DF} \tag{10.6}$$

Hence apparent impedance is less than actual impedance and thus it tends to overreach.

Here also,zone -1 setting should be 0.8to 0.9 times smallest line length from each relay location. Second zone should be set above the maximum apparent impedance to any remote terminal to ensure that all remote buses are included in this zone. Third zone setting should be above second zone backing up the longest remote line.

Minimum criteria: When unequal lengths are involved in three terminal line and the line is accompanied by short adjacent lines, the second zone setting of maximum apparent impedance may result in poor coordination in zone-2 setting. In this case,zone- 2 setting can be reduced to a smaller length and zone-3 setting may be adjusted to cover all the remote buses of three terminal line.

In the extreme cases,where very long line and a very small line radiate from remote bus, pilot relaying for small line is desirable.

10.5 DISTANCE RELAY SETTING

The fundamental concept concerning distance relay setting is as follows:

The operating zone for each relay element is defined accurately and setting coordination with relays in the forward adjacent stations is established. The optimum setting values are achieved through various load flow and fault analysis covering not only the basic system configuration but also all anticipated changes in system configuration which may influence the relay setting values.

Relays settings are determined using the fault voltages and currents by conducting several studies. Shunt effects and fault resistances are also taken into account for the purpose.

Here,we have have considered directional distance relays (i.e.Mho'srelays) having 3-zones. The first zone is that of instantaneous operation for faults in the primary line. The other two zones protect the main line and adjacent lines with time delays increasing in discrete steps. For each relay, we must find impedance value for setting of each zone and time delay settings for zone-2 and zone-3 such that entire system is perfectly coordinated.

10.5.1 Setting of First Zone

The first zone is that of instantaneous operation for fault on the primary line. It protects the primary line upto 80-90% of its length i.e. it never covers the remote bus.

The setting value for 1st zone is given as,

$$X_I = K_I Z_I \tag{10.7}$$

where X_I : setting value of Ist zone

K_1 : 0.8 to 0.9 for phase relays
: 0.6 to 0.7 for ground relays

Z_1 : positive sequence impedance of the line to which it is connected.

In the case of multi-terminal line, Z_1 should be equal to the minimum value of positive sequence impedance upto the next buses *i.e.*the remote buses.

In case any outfeeds or infeeds are present (particularly for distribution systems) then the Z-1 setting gets affected.

In case of infeeds: (Refer to fig.10.7).Apparent impedance seen is more than actual impedance of line by a factor $\frac{I_3}{I_2}$ (Z_{NF}) (*i..e.*it tends to under reach by this factor).Thus, any absence of infeed will stretch zone-1 reach even beyond the next bus which should be avoided. Because of this ,the relay setting should be equal to 0.8 to 0.9 times, impedance of smallest line length from each relaying point (in absence of infeed).

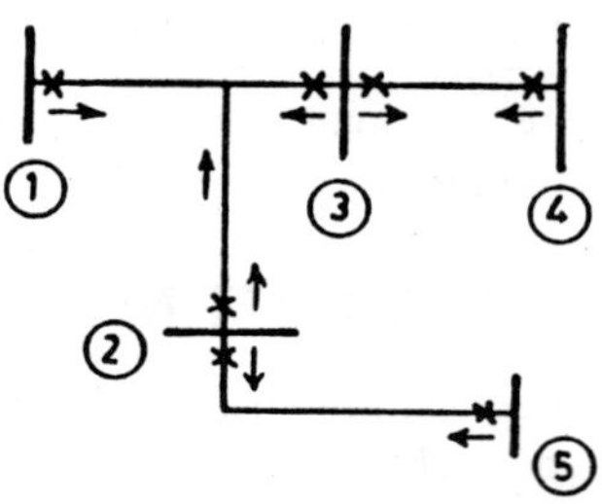

Fig 10.7 Primary tapped: infeed only

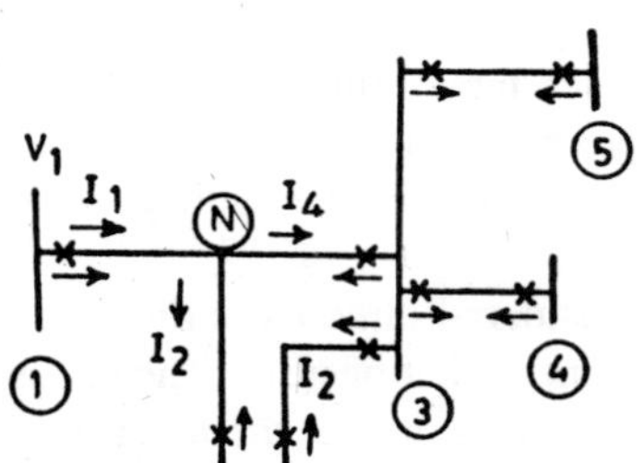

Fig 10.8 Primary tapped: outfeed only

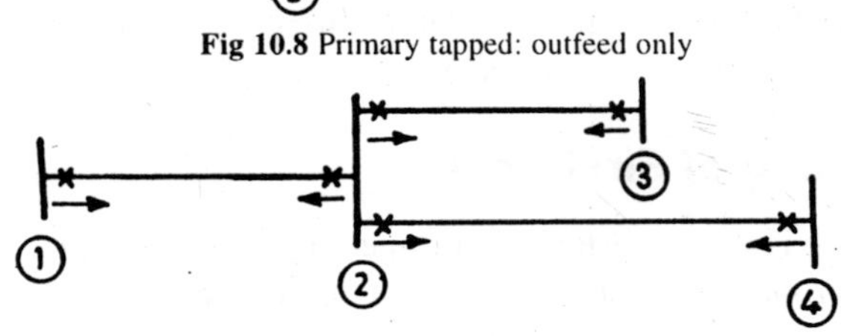

Fig 10.9 General

In case of outfeeds : (Refer to Fig.10.7). Here, apparent impedance seen by relay is less than actual impedance of line. Thus, it tends to overreach by a factor of $\frac{I_2}{I_1}$ (Z_{NF}) in presence of outfeed.In this case, minimum apparent impedance seen upto the next bus with outfeeds present is used to set the Z-1 setting of relays .

10.5.2 Setting of Zone-2

The zone -2 protects the remaining part of the line left unprotected by Z-1 plus remote bus in all conditions and it is desirable to cover as much of the adjacent lines as possible (at least upto 20% of its length) to provide back-up protection, It has timer associated with it (T-2).

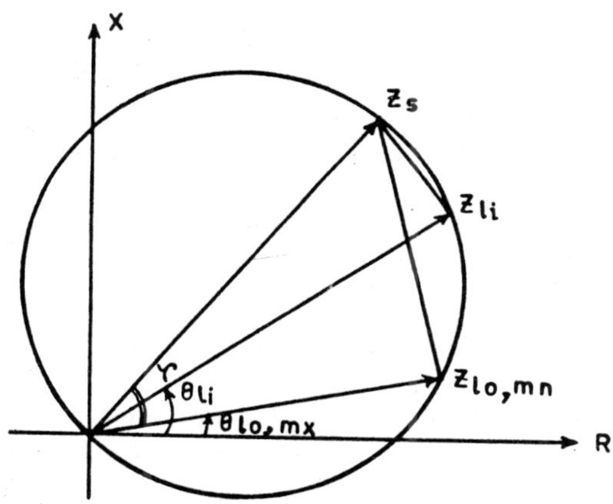

Fig 10.10 Typical Mho Characteristics

For back back-up, the following considerations are taken into account (see Figs,10.7,10.8 and10.9).

Case (i): If more than one line requires back-up protection from the same relay, then impedance tap setting of the relay for back operation is calculated as follows:

(a) Smallest of all the lines requiring back-up operation is considered and fault (LLLG) is created at 50% length of the line. Then apparent impedance seen from relay location for back-up protection of this line is calculated say say it is Z_a.

(b) Longest of all lines requiring back-up protection is considered and fault (LLLG) is created at 20% length of the line.Apprent impedance seen from relay location is calculated, say it is Z_b.

If $Z_a \geq Z_b$, then relay tap for back-up operation is set to Z_a, otherwise, any of the following two criteria may be adopted.

1.pilot relaying for smallest line,or

2. changing of time-delay operation for back-up operation.

The choice of one from the above proposed two schemes depends on coordination criteria of the relay with the others in the system.If (1) is chosen, then impedance tap setting for back-up operation is determined from the consideration of the remaining lines to be protected. If (2) is considered then it is to be ensured that this present value of time-delay is within limit specified for time-delay of back-up.

Case(ii): In this case with the outfeed present,we proceed to determine impedance tap setting value for back-up operation as in case (i).

Case (iii): In this, impedance tap setting for back-operation is determined by proceeding similarly as in case (i) with the infeeds not considered.Case (ii) and case (iii) are usually the case with distribution systems.

It should be ensured that Z-2 does not operate for faults at the next remote bus.

10.5.3 Setting of Z-3

The zone-3 of the distance relay is set to provide back-up protection to the main line as well as all the adjacent lines. It is also used to start the carriers. Thus,they are set to overreach the farthest remote bus. However, it is to be ensured that they do not operate under minimum loading conditions. It is desirable that zone-3 impedance is set to the smaller of (a) minimum load impedance times a safety factor of 0.8 (this factor comes by consideration of overloading the lines by 25% and (b) maximum apparent impedance from the back-up relay to the farthest second remote bus. The limiting load impedance value of each relay is calculated first. The impedance setting should be more than minimum load impedance. Consider the typical Mho characteristics of a distance relay as shown in Fig. 10.10, where,

τ : relay set angle

θ_{li} : line impedance angle

$\theta_{le,mx}$: maximum load angle (representing worst loading condistion)

$Z_{lo,mn}$: minimum load impedance

Z_s : impedance setting of the relay

Z_{li} : minimum load impedance expressed in line quantities.

It should be ensured that zone-3 should not exceed Z_{li};

$$Z_{li} = 0.9\, Z_{lo,mn} \left[\frac{\cos(\tau - \theta_{li})}{\cos(\tau - \theta_{le,mx})} \right] \tag{10.8}$$

Zone-3 impedance setting is chosen to be smaller of

(1) Load impedance given by above equation.

(2) The maximum apparent impedance from the back-up relay to the farthest second remote bus.

In addition to consideration of load impedance,transient and dynamic power swing could also affect the Zone-3 operation of distance relays.

The timer of Z-3 is set equal to timer setting value of Z- 2 plus minimum coordination interval.

The computer based algorithms to carry out the setting process for distance relays are presented in flow diagram 1,2 and3.

10.5.4 Algorithm for Setting Calculation

Setting calculation method is shown in flow diagram 1. For each relay location, worst possible system configuration is determined through a subroutine called WORST. This subroutine determine the possible configuration of system which gives rise to minimum impedance seen from each relay location for a fault, if so happens, on the remote and next remote buses for primary and back-up operations of distance relays and for overcurrent relays setting,it determines the possible system configuration which gives rise to minimum and maximum fault current levels through each relay location.

The impedance so determined is called here, as "Worst impedance' for distance relay and 'maximum current' so determined is called worst current for overcurrent relay.

The maximum fault current is given by LLLG fault with maximum generation and minimum fault current is given by LL fault with minimum generation. This result is useful for overcurrent relay settings.

The number of fault calculations to be carried out is also optimised by recognising the fact that for each relay operation the fault has to be considered only at remote bus and next remote bus. This reduces the number of fault calculations thus reducing the computer time for calculations.

Algorithm - I incorporates above mentioned conditions and calculates voltage and current levels for all relays.

Algorithm- II uses the data generated by Algorithm-I for calculating the impedance tap setting of distance relays.

10.5.5 Overcurrent Relay Setting

The directional overcurrent relays (for phase fault) are assumed to have instantaneous time delay operation. Hence, three parameters for each relay are specified,namely, instantaneous setting, pick up tap setting and time-dial setting.

Ideally, the relay should trip instantaneously for any fault on the primary line.i.e. on the line, the relay provides primary protection. However, it must not trip instantaneously for a fault on an adjacent line.

Instantaneous tap setting : It is specified in terms of maximum possible fault current times a factor 1.2 to 1.3.This maximum current is maximised over worst possible situation arising in the network for the relay to be set. The factor 1.2 to 1.3 is selected to avoid overreaching of the instantaneous operation range to minimise the interruption of power to consumers.

Pick-up tap setting : We first determine the allowaable range and then allow the user to select within this range.

1. *The lower limit* is determined by including the effect of overloading and power swing; and hence,

lower limit = F_p × Maximum load current through relay

where, F_p : factor i.e 1.20 to 1.30

If any relay tap corresponding to this value is not available, then minimum available tap on the relay can be used for this lower limit. At the same time, it should be ensured that minimum remote bus fault current (*i.e.*determined by conducting LL fault with minimum generation) is picked up by this relay, otherwise ti has to be replaced.

The upper limit is smaller value of :

1) minimum remote bus fault current (*i.e.*LL fault with minimum generation) times 0.5 to 0.6. This factor takes into account that the fault in the back up region is cleared.
2) normal remote bus fault current (all lines intact), times a factor of 0.1 to 0.2. Depending on the load level bearing capacity of the line, this factor is selected.

The smaller of the two ensures that minimum fault levels and above is picked up by the relay. For the pick-up tap setting, as determined above, we prefer to set the taps corresponding to the lower of all the values as determined above. This ensures most sensitive back-up relaying.

Time-Dial setting: From Algorithm-I, The maximum fault current possible *i.e.* the worst possible situation which gives maximum current through each relay is determined for all back up operations through steps (7),(8) and (9). Then by using algorithm-IV the time delay settings of the relays are carried out.

Algorithm-III is used to calculate instantaneous and pick-up tap settings. Algorithm-V gives the time- dial setting for each overcurrent relay.

10.6 COORDINATION OF DISTANCE RELAYS

A distance protection scheme comprising directional distance relays of Mho type with three zones of operation is considered. A fully coordinated result for distance relays should indicate the impedance setting values for all the three zones in terms of various impedance taps available on the relays and also the timer setting associated with second and third zone relays.

a) Z-2 timer setting (T-2) and coordination

The coordination issue here is, that, the second zones of all primary/ back-up (P/B) pairs either never interact or if they do, the time delay of backup relay exceed that of the primary relay by a coordination time interval (MCI). The algorithm- IV for setting zone -2 timer is illustrated with flow chart showing coordination of distance relyas.

The coordination is completed at the end of the first round of determining timer setting values if none of the relays have second zone delays greater than minimum coordination interval defined for distance relays. If any of the relays has an increased second zone time delay, we compute second time and modify the delays accordingly to achieve system coordination.

b) Z-3 timer setting (T-3) and coordinaiton

The Z-3 timers of all the P/B paris should coordinate among themselves.

The Z-3 timer (T-3) is set equal to T-2 plus minimum coordination interval. Each P/B pair is taken and checked for coordination, if it does not coordinate,then either Z-3 timer setting is modified or little coordination interval is sacrificed. If still it does not coordinate, then relay parameters are changed or it is replaced with another one.

The algorithm-IV developed for Z-2 timer coordination can be used for Z-3 timer coordination determination with a slight modificaiton in algorithm.

10.7 COORDINATION OF OVERCURRENT RELAY

The coordination of a system of overcurrent relays requires determination of three parameters normally associated with any kind of overcurrent relay, namely, the instantaneous pick-up tap value, the time-delay pick-up tap value and the time-dial setting value for all the relays in the system to satisfy the coordination criteria. The algorithm needed to carry out coordination process is presented here (Algorithm-V).

10.7.1 Coordination algorithm

The instantaneous tap settings and the pick-up tap settings are determined in previous section. The selection of the time dial setting is the most involved portion of the coordination process. Each primary/back-up relay in the system is checked for proper action for various type of faults that affect the current through these relays. The faults considered are the ones which give maximum and minimum possible current through these relays.

All the relays in the system are assigned a time-dial value equal to the minimum tap value available on the relay. Then each back- up relay is set so that it coordinate with all its primary relays for all the fault current pairs fed as input.

The main criteria for the coordination of a given relay pair is that the operating time of a back-up relay should be at least equal to the operating time of the primary relay plus a minimum coordinating time interval (MCI). Algorithm-V detailing the steps involved in calculating the coordination process is shown.

10.8 COMPUTOR GRAPHICS DISPLAY

System control center is designed and built in order to implement advanced ideas relating to system security, control and planning. System control center is dedicated to the operation of generation and transmission systems, distribution system, strictly supervisory control (so called SCADA) or strictly generation dispatch center. In this section, we consider system control center dedicated to generation and transmission system.

For system security and its associated control operations, real time computor applications are required. While for planning purposes, off line or batch processing mode is sufficient. In simple terms, the goal of system control center is the implementation of security control. Security control requires proper integration of both automatic and manual funtions, i.e.,for all operating conditions a total system approach with the human operator being intergral part of the control system. System control center consists of real time data acquisition system,real time control strategy, computor system and man machine interface system.

The totality of real time features and functions of system control center include the following:

i) Several levels of computer system with sufficient memory space and appropriate combination of computer hardware and software requiring minimum time for on line computation.
ii) High speed digital telemetry and data acquisition equipment.
iii) Colour CRT's with graphics for interactive display.
iv) Dynamic wall board group display.
v) Automatic generation control.
vi) Economic dispatch calculation.
vii) Automatic voltage (VAR) control.
viii) Supervisory control (breakers,capacitors transformer taps,generating unit startup and shutdown).
ix) Security monitoring.
x) State estimation.
xi) On line load flow.
xii) Steady state security analysis.
xiii) Optium power flow.
xiv) Automatic system trouble anaylsis.
xv) On line short circuit calculation.
xvi) Emergency control - Automatic load shedding, generator shedding,line tripping,and
xvii) Automatic circuit restoration.

Colour CRT or dynamic wall dispaly are very much helpful for system operation and more speicifically for the system operator.

For a protection engineers, the following functons are predominant.

a) Automatic System Trouble Analysis (ASTA)

ASTA is a logical procedure for analysis circuit breaker tripping and reclosing protective relay operations.

ASTA identifies:

Faulted circuits — permanent and temporary

Primary and backup relay operation

Breaker failure and maloperations

Primary relay failure and maloperations

The protective relay operations are displayed on CRT list or on the wall display.

b) On-line Short Circuit Calculation (OSC)

OSC is run at fixed time interval or on demand, in order to determine maximum short circuit duty at each bus and compare the value with switchgear rating.An alarm is initiated when excessive short circuit duty is found and suitable display is presented to the operators.

c) Automatic Circuit Restoration (ACR)

ACR illustrates the potential of system control centre, for some kind of reactorative action. Restoration of a circuit is not the same as restoring load but clearly system restoration should benefit system security.

d) Supervisory Control (SVC,SBC)

Even though supervisory control is an old concept,its integration in system control center is a new phenomena. Since super through man machine interface or display subsystem.

Supervisory control covers circuit breakers (SBC), voltage regulating device (SVC) or starting or stopping of generating units. SBC gives the operator the ability to open or close circuit breaker for emergency control like load shedding or load restoration.

10.9 THE MAN-MACHINE INTERFACE SUBSYSTEM

In the system control center, the man-machine interface or the display sub-system consists of cathode ray tube (CRT), dynamic wall dislay,trend recorders and alarm devices.

The CRT display

CRT's are in universal use for the system operators, maintenance personnel and programmers. Sharp and effective one-line diagam can be obtained with a full graphic colour CRT. For reduction in cost, roser-type dot addressable colour CRT's can be used.

Rolling Map Technique

In this case, the operator can view any part of the system and then move the picture in any direction to view some other part.

Restospective Display Technique

In this case, the operator can go back in time to any specific minute within some specific time interval and view all the network data and network condition pertaining at that instant.

The Dynamic Wall Display

The dynamic wall display driven by specialised hardware is intended to give an overview of the power system. The overview consists of simplefiied representation, preserving as much geographic orientation as possible. Details can be left to the CRT's. For larger system, the wall display can have less resolution.

10.10 INTEGRATED OPERATION OF NATIONAL POWER SYSTEM

For the purpose of planning and operation, the power system in India has been demarcated into five regions viz. Northern, Souther, Eastern, Western, and North-Eastern. The National Load Display Centre (NLDC) coordinates the activities of the Regional Load Despatch Centers (RLDCs). RLDCs function through State Load Despatch Centres (SLDC).

RLDC has the following functons :

a) short term operation and planning.
b) Coordination and scheduling of maintenance programme.
c) Day to day scheduling of generation and inter system exchange.
d) Real time monitoring of system conditions.
e) Regulation of frequency.
f) Regulaton of inter regional and linear system line flows.
g) Security monitoring and contingency evaluation.

10.11 APPLICATION OF COMPUTER GRAPHICS

System control centre is designed and built in order to implement advanced ideas relating to system security and control and palnning. In simple terms, goal of system control centre is implementation of security control, by proper integration of both manual and automatic functions. Unilke planning studies where offline processing is sufficient, for system security and its associated control operations, real time computer applications are required. The man-machine interface consists of Cathode Ray Tube, Dynamic Wall Display, alarm devices or Computer graphics. Further, the emergency control to a large extent still depends upon human decisions which is in turn are aided by Computer Aided Analysis. This necessitates effective man-machine interface.

Computer graphics is used for following purposes:

a) To obtain one line diagram of the entire test system whcih can be easily modified to accomodate any system changes.It is vrey helpful for system monitoring, particularly from operations point of view. Further, any limit voilations or emergency conditions can be easily displayed using different colours.

b) To dispolay the zone of protection of any particular relay along with its representation for CATPSD (computer aided transmission protection system design) solution and

c) For any particular fault, the associated pair of primary and backup pairs can be easily displayed.

All the above graphic display can be easily stored in memory to avoid repetative calculations. With the availability of real time data, the above algorithm can be easily modified to perform following functons:

a) Relay monitoring to check against relay interactions, interference, maloperations or failures.

b) Possible violations of circuit breaker ratings, circuit breker maloperations.

c) Crossing of upper lower voltage levels,and

d) Overloading/triping of transmisson lines.

REFERENCES

[1] Begian, S.S. et al., 'A computer approach on setting relays in a network', IEEE PICA Conference Record, Vol. 31c 69, May 1964,pp.447-447.

[2] Ramammoorthy, M, 'A nonte on impedance measuring using digital computers',IEE-IERE Proc. (India), Vol.9,Nov/Dec.1971, pp. 243- 247.

[3] Mann, B.J. and Morrison, I.F.,'Digital calculation of impedance for transmission line protection', IEEE Trans on PAS, Vol.PAS-90, Jan/ Feb. 1971, pp.270-279.

[4] Mann, B.J. and Morrison, I.F. 'Relaying a three phase transmission line with a digital computer', IEEE Trans. on PAS, Vol. PAS-90, March/April 1971, pp. 742-750.

[5] Sunak, V.P. and Singh, L.P., 'Microprocessor based protection scheme for EHV/UHV transmission line' Journal of Institute of Engineer (India), Vol. 65, parts EL 2 and 3, Oct/Nov 1984, pp. 89-96

[6] Singh, L.P. and Singh, V.P., 'Coordination and setting of relays : A case study Chukha Transmission System', Proceeding CBIP International Conference, May 1987, Bangalore, pp. 27-32.

[7] Bhàgat, Nitin Sachchidanand and Singh, L.P., 'Setting and Coordination of Distance Relaying scheme using computer graphics : A case study of 400 KV UPSEB sub-system', Proceeding 7th National Power System Conference, Feb.1993, callcutta ,pp. 395-400.

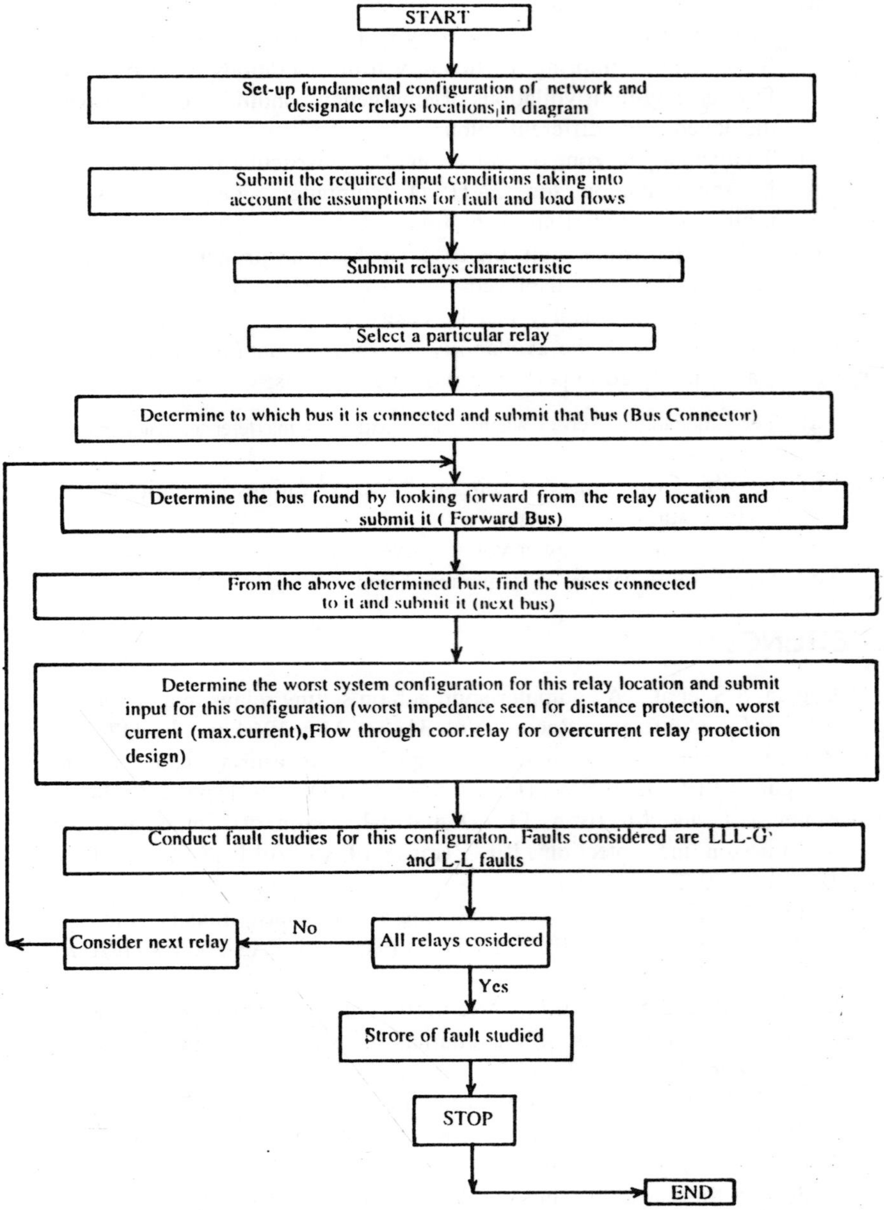

Algorithm : I Fault quantities under worst condition.

(Contd.)

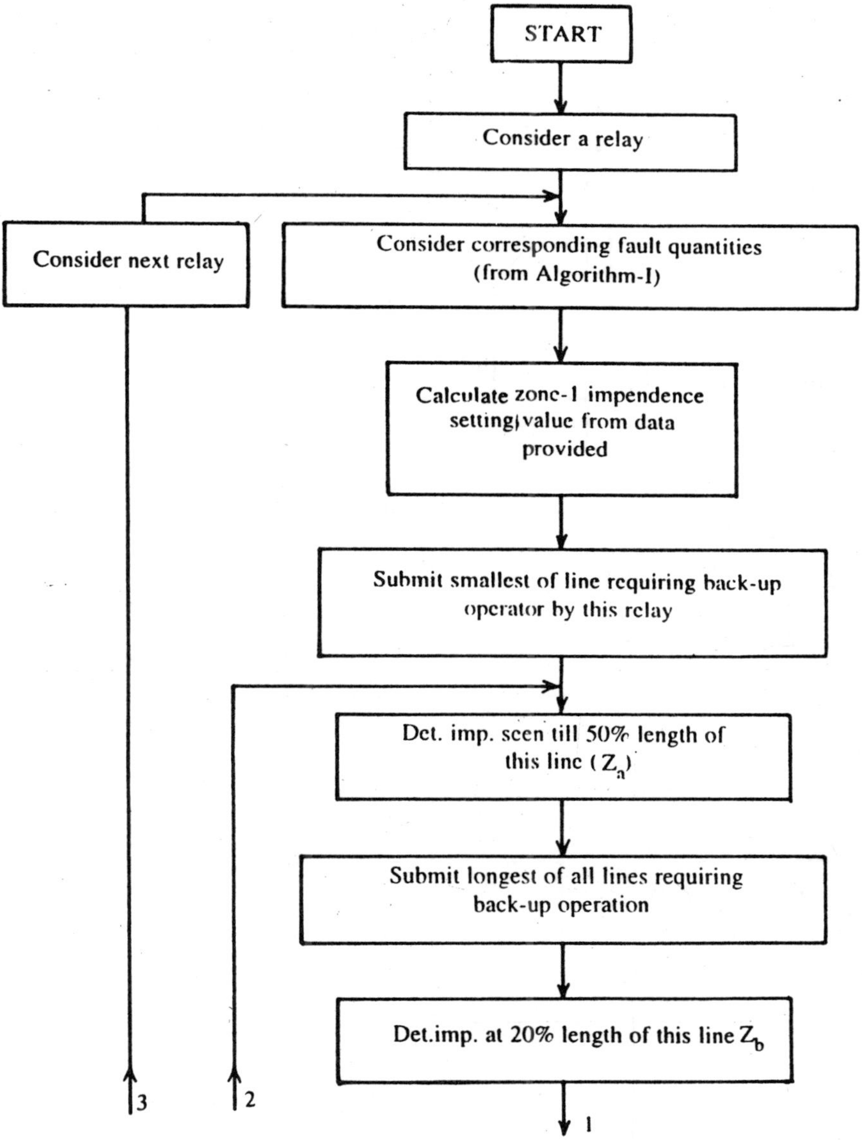
START
Consider a relay
Consider next relay
Consider corresponding fault quantities (from Algorithm-I)
Calculate zone-1 impendence setting value from data provided
Submit smallest of line requiring back-up operator by this relay
Det. imp. seen till 50% length of this line (Z_a)
Submit longest of all lines requiring back-up operation
Det.imp. at 20% length of this line Z_b
3
2
1

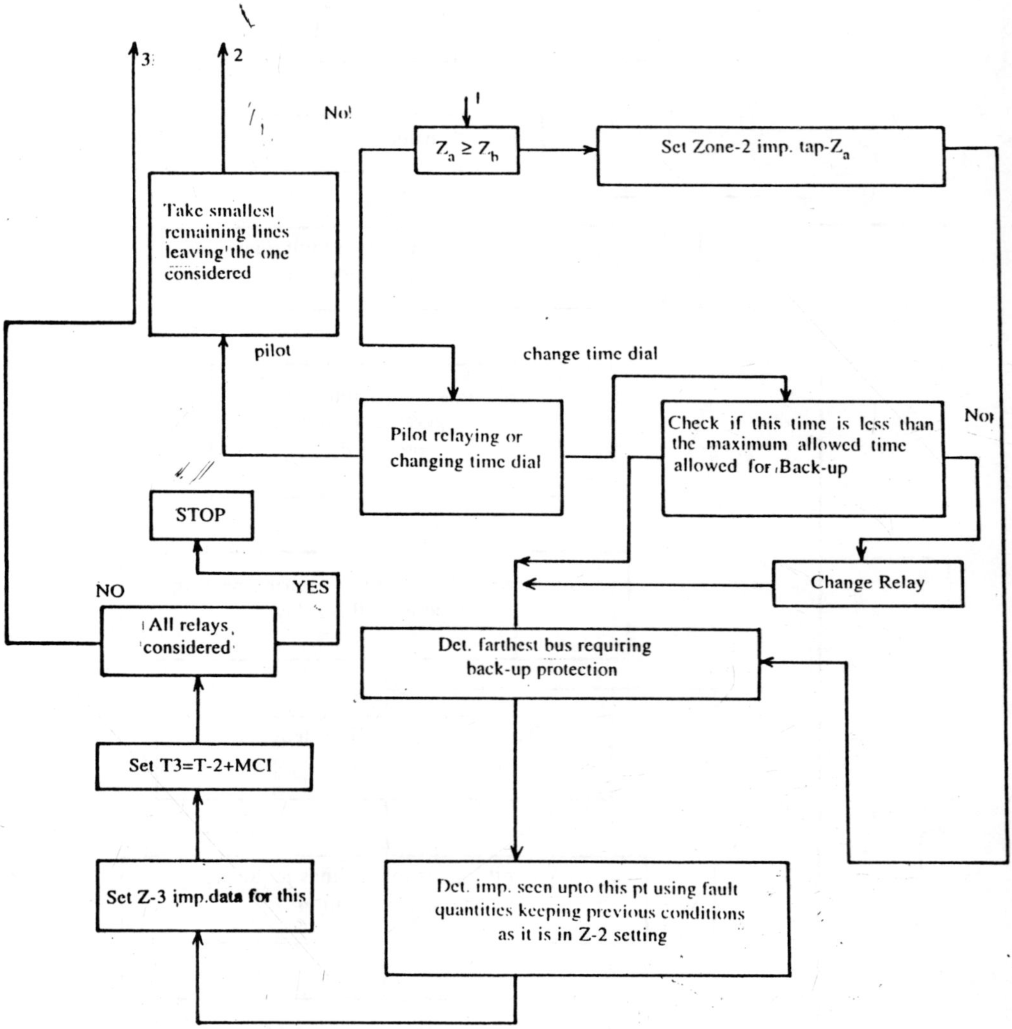

Algorithm : II Impedance tap setting calculations.

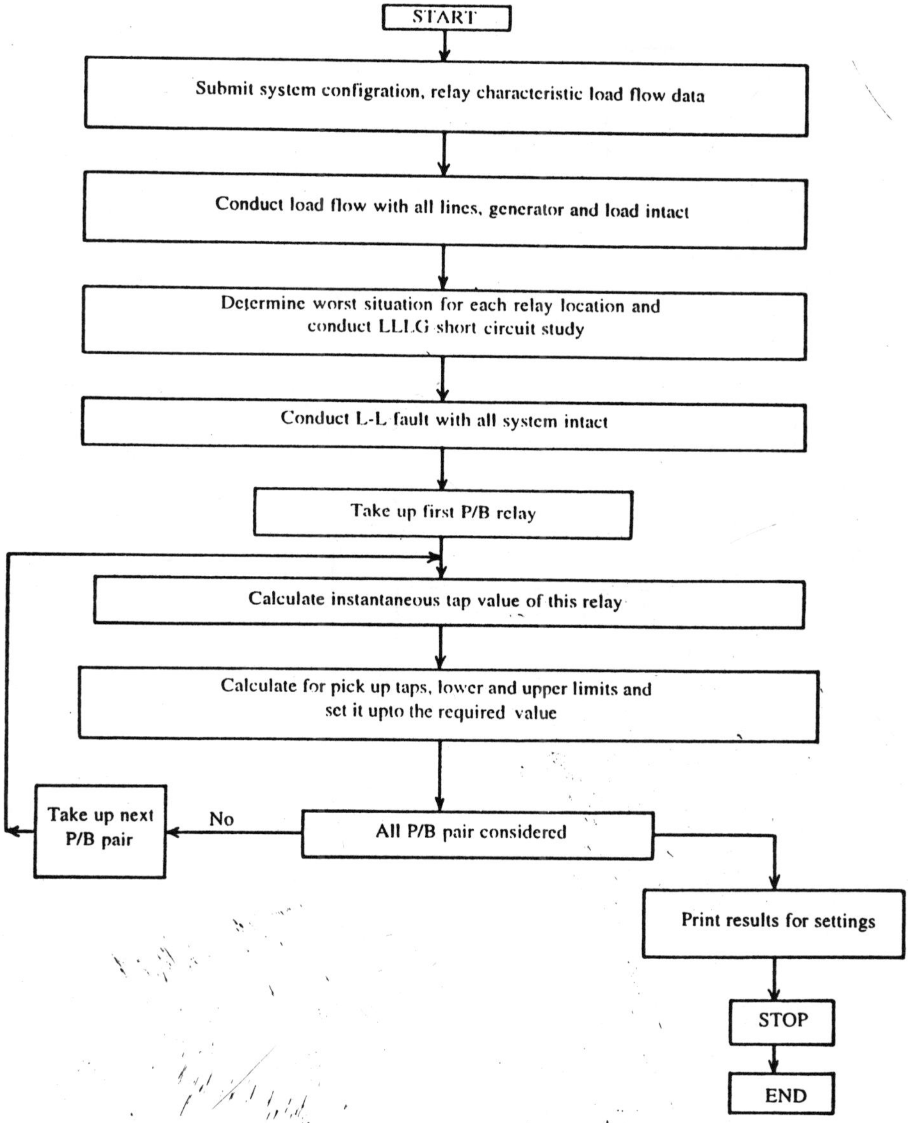

Algorithm : III

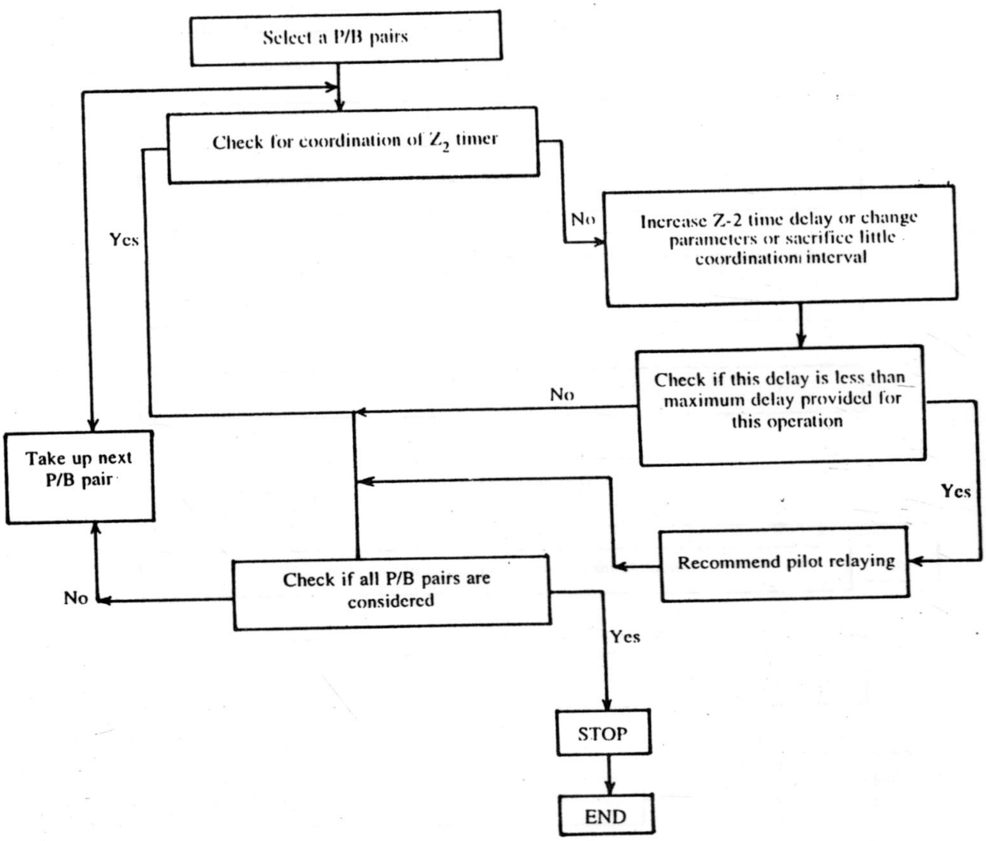

Algorithm : IV

Algorithm : V

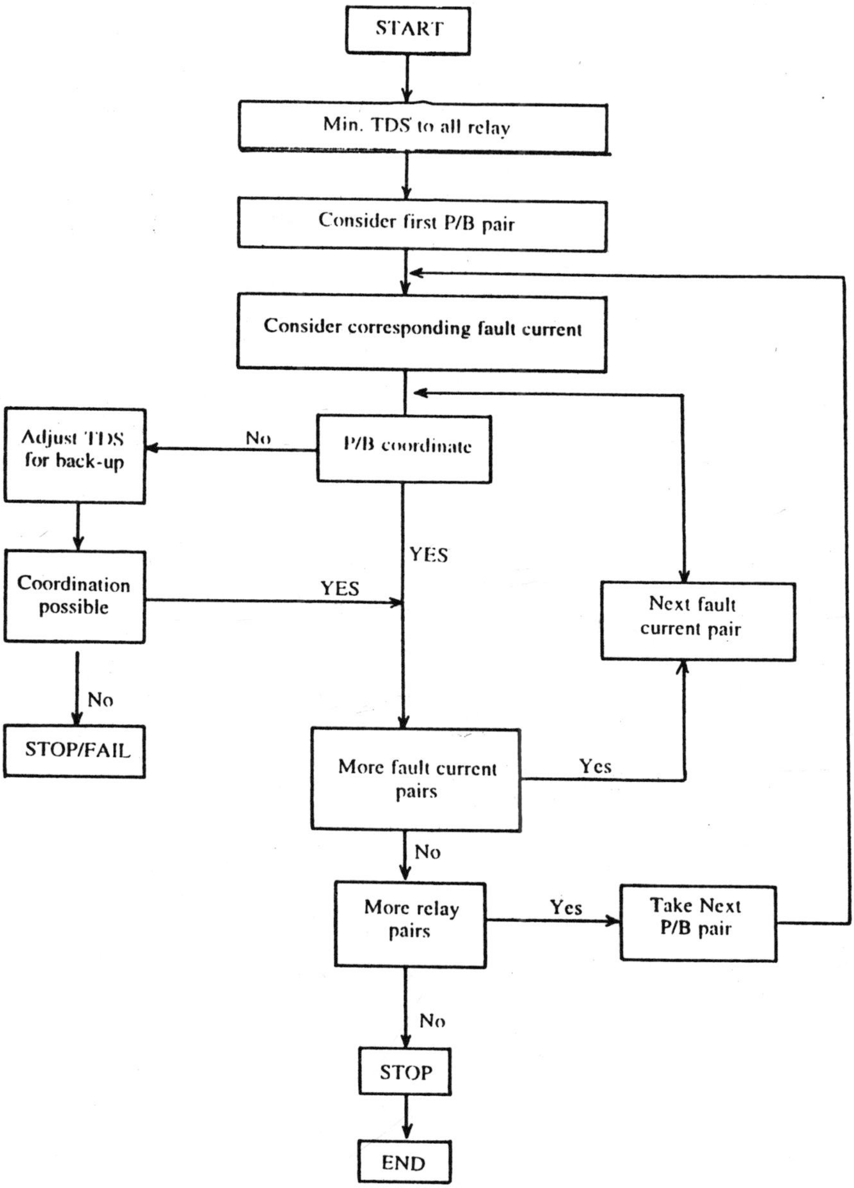

Flow Chart for overcurrent relay coordination

APPENDIX

PC APPLICATIONS IN SHORT CIRCUIT STUDIES FOR DESIGNING RELAYING SCHEME

1 INTRODUCTION

Short circuit studies are important in power system planning because they provide data such as voltages and currents during and after the various types of faults which are necessary in designing the protective schemes of the power system. Current that flows in the power system components just after the occurrence of faults, that flows a few cycles later and the steady state value (i.e. sustained value) of fault currents, differ very much. A protective scheme, basically consists of relays, switch gears such as circuit breakers, etc. The relay which functions as a sensing device is a very important component of the protection scheme as it is the one which senses the fault, determines its location and then sends the command to the proper circuit breaker to operate and thus interrupt the circuit in which the fault has occurred. Thus three intervals of time actually lapse before the circuit breaker is called upon to operate. Therefore in designing the circuit breaker and the protective relay, all the three component currents are important such as the current that flows immediately after the fault and which fixes the momentary rating of the circuit breaker, the current that flows a few cycles later when the circuit breaker actually operates and which fixes the interrupting rating of the circuit breaker and also the steady state value of the fault current.

There are different types of faults in the power system which can broadly be divided into symmetrical and unsymmetrical faults. The currents and voltages resulting from various types of faults occurring at different locations throughout the power system network must be calculated in order to provide sufficient data for designing the protection scheme i.e. both the protective relays and circuit breakers. Because of the extensive calculations of voltages and currents due to different types of faults at different locations of the power system, it becomes necessary to use a suitable computer and today most of the short circuit studies, and hence fault analysis, are performed on the digital computer. However, earlier, network analyzer—especially d.c. network analyzer—was used for the purpose of short circuit studies. However, the d.c. network analyzer has become obsolete because it is restricted to only three-phase fault and also it is not very flexible.

The early approach to the short circuit studies employed the bus frame of reference in the admittance form but this method could not become popular because it was time consuming. Today, most of the short circuit studies of the power system are formulated in the bus frame of reference using bus impedance matrix Z_{bus}, because this method is simpler and less time consuming.

2 TYPES OF FAULTS

The different faults in the power system network can be broadly classified into symmetrical and unsymmetrical faults. These are listed below:

(i) 3-phase direct short circuit or 3-phase fault through finite fault impedance (LLL or LLLG).

(ii) 2-phase to ground fault i.e. double line to ground fault with or without fault impedance (LLG).

(iii) Line to line direct short circuit or short circuit through finite fault impedance (LL), and

(iv) Single phase to ground fault with or without fault impedance (LG).

Out of the above four faults, the first one is a symmetrical fault but the last three are unsymmetrical faults. The three-phase fault is only one in number while the other three faults are each three in number. From this we conclude that in a three-phase system there are four types of faults but they are ten in number. The LLL or LLLG is the most severe fault but it is least common. In the above list of faults, the order of severity decreases as we proceed from top to bottom, i.e. LLG fault is less severe than LLLG fault, similarly LL fault is less severe than LLG fault and finally, LG fault is the least severe. However, the order of frequency of occurrence of fault increases as we proceed from top to bottom i.e. while LLL or LLLG is the least common, the LG fault is the most common.

In addition to the above, there may be several other types of faults such as opening of one or two conductors. We shall derive and discuss the algorithms to calculate the fault currents and voltages etc. due to the above faults. We shall see that in the case of unsymmetrical faults, which is the case of unbalanced excitation in the three-phase balanced network, it becomes simpler to work with component quantities (positive, negative and zero sequence components) since after transformation to component quantities, the different component quantities become uncoupled, i.e. the coefficient matrix describing the system, becomes diagonal after the transformation. Due to this, the different component quantities are such that the 0-sequence current causes only 0-sequence voltage drops; similarly, positive and negative sequence currents cause positive and negative sequence voltage drops only. Thus each sequence current may be assumed to flow in the like sequence impedance only and hence we have sequence networks. Now from the actual power system network, drawing different sequence networks is very simple. For example only positive sequence network will have a voltage source, since excitation voltage of the synchronous generation E_g or prefault voltage V_F are balanced, i.e. these are only positive sequence voltages. There is no voltage source in the negative or 0-sequence network. Moreover, the neutral of the system is the reference for positive and negative sequence networks but ground is the reference for the 0-sequence network and hence only 0-sequence current flows, if the circuit from the neutral to the ground is complete, in the line between the neutral of the power system and the ground.

For a fault at the terminals of an unloaded generator with excitation voltage E_g, the following will be the sequence voltage drop.

$$\begin{bmatrix} V_{a0} \\ V_{a1} \\ V_{a2} \end{bmatrix} = \begin{bmatrix} 0 \\ E_g \\ 0 \end{bmatrix} \begin{bmatrix} Z_0 & & 0 \\ & Z_1 & \\ 0 & & Z_2 \end{bmatrix} \begin{bmatrix} I_{a0} \\ I_{a1} \\ I_{a2} \end{bmatrix} \tag{1}$$

where subscripts 0, 1 and 2 refers respectively to zero, positive and negative sequence quantities. Similarly for a fault in the power system, we have the following relation:

$$\begin{bmatrix} V_{a0} \\ V_{a1} \\ V_{a2} \end{bmatrix} = \begin{bmatrix} 0 \\ V_F \\ 0 \end{bmatrix} \begin{bmatrix} Z_0 & & 0 \\ & Z_1 & \\ 0 & & Z_2 \end{bmatrix} \begin{bmatrix} I_{a0} \\ I_{a1} \\ I_{a2} \end{bmatrix} \tag{2}$$

where V_F is the prefault voltage which is balanced.

3 ASSUMPTION FOR CONDUCTING SHORT CIRCUIT STUDIES OF A LARGE SCALE POWER SYSTEM NETWORK

The following assumptions are made for conducting short circuit studies of a large scale power system network on the digital computer.

(1) Representing each synchronous machine by a constant voltage source behind proper reactances which may be sub-transient, transient or steady state reactance X (because of very fast protection schemes, normally sub-transient reactance is used).

(2) Neglecting all the shunt connections such as static loads, line charging and transformer magnetizing circuits. With this assumption, the power circuit network becomes open circuited and thus the normal load currents (i.e. prefault currents) are automatically neglected and therefore, all the prefault bus voltages will have the same magnitude and phase angle. Thus to work in per unit system, the prefault bus voltages are set equal to $1\angle 0$.

(3) Setting all the transformers to nominal taps (i.e. transformer tappings are neglected). Since we work in per unit system, with this representation, transformers will automatically be out of circuit, i.e. it is represented by its per unit leakage reactance only.

(4) Normally neglecting armature winding effective resistance and transformer winding resistance.

(5) Assuming that the positive sequence impedance is equal to the negative sequence impedance also for 3-phase rotating elements even though these

sequence impedances are equal only in the case of 3-phase stationary elements.

With these assumptions, the performance equation of the power system network in the bus frame of reference using Z_{bus} when fault occurs at any bus p will be given by

$$E_{bus(F)}^{abc} = E_{bus(0)}^{abc} - Z_{bus(F)}^{abc} \, I_{bus(F)}^{abc} \tag{3}$$

where $E_{bus(F)}^{abc}$ is the column vector of the unknown bus voltages after the fault, $E_{bus(0)}^{abc}$ is the column vector of known prefault bus voltages, i.e. open circuit bus voltages and $I_{bus(F)}^{abc}$ are the unknown bus currents when the fault occurs at any bus p.

4 DEVELOPMENT OF ALGORITHM FOR THE SHORT CIRCUIT STUDIES

As discussed earlier, we shall formulate the short circuit studies problem in the bus frame of reference using Z_{bus}. The Z_{bus} matrix is formed by building algorithm including ground node as the reference node. The bus impedance matrix so developed includes the parameters of machines, transformers and transmission system. Actually this representation which is derived by the Thevenin's theorem, include Z_{bus} matrix as defined earlier in series with the open circuit voltages which are actually prefault bus voltages. This is true since all the shunt connections are neglected for the purpose of short circuit studies with the result that the normal load current will automatically be neglected and thus the prefault bus voltages of all the buses will be equal in magnitude and also will have the same phase angle. The performance equation [Eq. (3)] in the expanded form will be as follows;

$$\begin{bmatrix} E_{1\,(F)}^{abc} \\ \cdot \\ \cdot \\ E_{p\,(F)} \\ \cdot \\ \cdot \\ E_{n\,(F)}^{abc} \end{bmatrix} = \begin{bmatrix} E_{1\,(0)}^{abc} \\ \cdot \\ \cdot \\ E_{p\,(0)}^{abc} \\ \cdot \\ \cdot \\ E_{n\,(0)}^{abc} \end{bmatrix} \begin{bmatrix} Z_{11}^{abc} & \cdots & Z_{1p}^{abc} & \cdots & Z_{1n}^{abc} \\ & & & & \\ & & & & \\ Z_{p1}^{abc} & \cdots & \cdots & & Z_{pn}^{abc} \\ & & & & \\ & & & & \\ Z_{n1}^{abc} & \cdots & \cdots & \cdots & Z_{nn}^{abc} \end{bmatrix} \begin{bmatrix} 0 \\ \\ \\ I_{p\,(F)}^{abc} \\ \\ \\ 0 \end{bmatrix} \tag{4}$$

Since prefault currents are neglected, for a fault at bus p, only fault current at the bus p will flow. Equation (4) can be expanded as follows:

$$\begin{aligned} E_{1(F)}^{abc} &= E_{1(0)}^{abc} - Z_{1p}^{abc} \cdot I_{p(F)}^{abc} \\ E_{p(F)}^{abc} &= E_{p(0)}^{abc} - Z_{pp}^{abc} \cdot I_{p(F)}^{abc} \quad \text{and so on.} \end{aligned} \tag{5}$$

Now for a fault at the bus p, the 3-phase voltage vector $E_{p(F)}^{abc}$ is given by

$$E_{p(F)}^{abc} = Z_F^{abc} \, I_{p(F)}^{abc} \tag{6}$$

where Z_F^{abc} is 3×3 fault impedance matrix which depends upon the type of fault. Comparing Eq. (5) with Eq. (6), we get

$$E_{p(F)}^{abc} = E_{p(0)}^{abc} - Z_{pp}^{abc} \; I_{p(F)}^{abc} = Z_F^{abc} \; I_{p(F)}^{abc}$$

$$Z_F^{abc} \; I_{p(F)}^{abc} = E_{p(0)}^{abc} - Z_{pp}^{abc} \; I_{p(F)}^{abc}$$

Solving the above equation, we get

$$I_{p(F)}^{abc} = [Z_F^{abc} \; Z_{pp}^{abc}]^{-1} \; E_{p(0)}^{abc} \tag{7}$$

And also $$E_{p(F)}^{abc} = Z_F^{abc} \; I_{p(F)}^{abc} = Z_F^{abc} \; [Z_F^{abc} + Z_{pp}^{abc}]^{-1} \; E_{p(0)}^{abc} \tag{8}$$

Similarly, the 3-phase bus voltages after the fault at the buses other than the faulted bus p, are

$$E_{i(F)}^{abc} = E_{i(0)}^{abc} - Z_{ip}^{abc} \; [Z_F^{abc} + Z_{pp}^{abc}]^{-1} \; E_{p(0)}^{abc} \tag{9}$$

for $i = 1, \ldots\ldots, n$ and i is not equal to p.

However, in case we are given the fault admittance Y_F^{abc} (fault admittance at the faulted bus p), we have the relation at the faulted bus p,

$$I_{p(F)}^{abc} = Y_F^{abc} \; E_{p(F)}^{abc} \tag{10}$$

Hence for a faulted bus p, we get from Eq. (5),

$$E_{p(F)}^{abc} = E_{p(0)}^{abc} - Z_{pp}^{abc} \; I_{p(F)}^{abc} \tag{11}$$

Substituting from Eq. (10) in Eq. (11), we get

$$E_{p(F)}^{abc} = E_{p(0)}^{abc} - Z_{pp}^{abc} \; Y_F^{abc} \; E_{p(F)}^{abc} \tag{12}$$

Equation (12) will take the following final form after some mathematical manipulations,

$$E_{p(F)}^{abc} = [U + Z_{pp}^{abc} \; Y_F^{abc}]^{-1} \; E_{p(0)}^{abc} \tag{13}$$

And also $$I_{p(F)}^{abc} = Y_F^{abc} [U + Z_{pp}^{abc} \; Y_F^{abc}]^{-1} \; E_{p(0)}^{abc} \tag{14}$$

And for other buses, we have

$$E_{i(F)}^{abc} = E_{i(0)}^{abc} - Z_{ip}^{abc} \; Y_F^{abc} \; [U + Z_{pp}^{abc} \; Y_F^{abc}]^{-1} \; E_{p(0)}^{abc} \tag{15}$$

for $i = 1, 2, \ldots\ldots., n.$ i is not equal to p.

Hence after the fault occurs through the fault impedance/admittance, we calculate first of all the bus voltages after the fault. After this, we calculate the fault current flowing in the elements of power system network. Thus the fault current in any element i-j of the power system network will be

$$i_{ij(F)}^{abc} = y_{ij\rho\sigma}^{abc} \; [E_{\rho(F)}^{abc} - E_{\sigma(F)}^{abc}] \tag{16}$$

Here $E_{\rho(F)}^{abc}$ and $E_{\sigma(F)}^{abc}$ are the bus voltages after the fault for any bus ρ and σ and $y_{ij\rho\sigma}^{abc}$ is the 3-phase element of the power system network (i.e. primitive network).

4.1 Transformation to Symmetrical Components (i.e. Positive, Negative and Zero Sequence Components)

The power system network is symmetric, i.e. balanced, because all its sub-networks such as generation sub-network, transmission sub-network and distribution sub-network are balanced and symmetric. This is because the generation sub-network consisting of three-phases synchronous generators, are designed and constructed to generate balanced set of voltages which are equal in magnitude and displaced in phase by 120 electrical degrees, the 3-phase transmission subnetworks are either arranged symmetrically on the supporting structure or transposed at the regular intervals to balance electrical characteristics with the result that the 3-phase transmission sub-network is also balanced and symmetric. Similarly, the 3-phase distribution sub-network is also balanced and symmetric. From this, we conclude that the entire 3-phase power system network is balanced and symmetric, i.e. it is a case of 3-phase balanced network elements with 3-phase balanced excitation. However, during the fault even though the 3-phase network elements are balanced up to the point of fault, the 3-phase excitation becomes unbalanced. In such cases, if we transform the phasor voltages and phasor currents to the component quantities by means of some linear power-invariant transformation, say symmetrical component transformation, these component quantities obtained after transformation become uncoupled, even though they were coupled in the phasor form. The original coefficient matrix in the phasor form was a full matrix but now after transformation to component quantities, it becomes a diagonal matrix.

It can be shown that Z^{abc}_{phase} can be transformed to $Z^{0,1,2}_{\text{component}}$ with the help of linear, power invarient and complex transformation T_s which is the familiar symmetrical component transformation as shown in the following:

$$T_s = \frac{1}{\sqrt{3}} \begin{bmatrix} 1 & 1 & 1 \\ 1 & \alpha^2 & \alpha \\ 1 & \alpha & \alpha^2 \end{bmatrix}$$

Here $\alpha = 3\sqrt{1} = 1\angle 120 = -0.5 + j\,0.866$

Now $Z^{0,1,2}_{pq}$ (coefficient matrix of the 3-phase power system network in the phasor form) is transformed to $Z^{0,1,2}_{pq}$, as:

$$Z^{0,1,2}_{pq} = T_s^{*T}\, Z^{abc}_{pq}\, T_s = \begin{bmatrix} Z^0_{pq} & 0 & 0 \\ 0 & Z^1_{pq} & 0 \\ 0 & 0 & Z^2_{pq} \end{bmatrix}$$

From the above equation it is clear that after the transformation to the component quantities, the coefficient matrix which was a full matrix in the phasor form has become diagonal in the component form. Now, for 3-phase stationary elements the positive sequence and negative sequence impedances are equal and we assume that for 3-phase rotating elements also the positive and negative sequence impedances are equal, i.e. $Z^1_{pq} = Z^2_{pq}$. Similarly, any element $Y^{abc}_{ij\rho\sigma}$ of the primitive network is transformed to $y_{i\,j\rho\sigma}^{0,1,2}$ which is also diagonal. In the same way each element Z_{ij}^{abc} of the bus impedance matrix can be diagonalized. The fault impedance matrix Z_F^{abc} can also be transformed to $Z_F^{0,1,2}$. However, $Z_F^{0,1,2}$ will only be diagonal if the fault is balanced. Same thing is true for Y_F^{abc} also.

Since we assume that all the bus voltages before the fault are equal in magnitude and have the same phase angle and also since we work in the per unit system, we set all the bus voltages equal to $1\angle 0$. Therefore, three-phase bus voltage for any bus i before fault is $E_{i(0)}^{abc} = 1\angle 0$, i.e.

$$= \begin{bmatrix} E_{i(0)}^{a} \\ E_{i(0)}^{b} \\ E_{i(0)}^{c} \end{bmatrix} = \begin{bmatrix} 1 \\ \alpha^2 \\ \alpha \end{bmatrix}$$

Here $\alpha = 1\angle 120$ and $\alpha^2 = 1\angle 240$.

Transferring the above phasor voltage into the field of component quantities with the help of symmetrical component transformation matrix T_s, we get

$$E_{i(0)}^{0,1,2} = (T_s^{*T})\ E_{i(0)}^{abc}$$

$$= \begin{bmatrix} 0 \\ \sqrt{3} \\ 0 \end{bmatrix} \tag{16a}$$

for $i = 1, \ldots\ldots, n$.

Thus we can transform all the earlier equations into the component quantities. Hence for a faulted bus p, the transformed equations [Eqs. (7), (8), (13), (14)] now become as shown in the following:

$$I_{p(F)}^{0,1,2} = [Z_F^{0,1,2} + Z_{pp}^{0,1,2}]^{-1}\ E_{p(0)}^{0,1,2}$$

$$I_{p(F)}^{0,1,2} = Y_F^{0,1,2}\ [U + Z_{pp}^{0,1,2}\ Y_F^{0,1,2}]^{-1}\ E_{p(0)}^{0,1,2}$$

$$E_{p(F)}^{0,1,2} = Z_F^{0,1,2}[Z_F^{0,1,2} + Z_{pp}^{0,1,2}]^{-1}\ E_{p(0)}^{0,1,2}$$

$$E_{p(F)}^{0,1,2} = [U + Z_{pp}^{0,1,2}\ Y_F^{0,1,2}]^{-1}\ E_{p(0)}^{0,1,2} \tag{17}$$

The bus voltages at the buses other than the faulted p are [Eqs. (9), and (15)]

$$E_{i(F)}^{0,1,2} = E_{i(0)}^{0,1,2} - Z_{ip}^{0,1,2}\ [Z_F^{0,1,2} + Z_{pp}^{0,1,2}]^{-1}\ E_{p(0)}^{0,1,2}$$

$$E_{i(F)}^{0,1,2} = E_{i(0)}^{0,1,2} - Z_{ip}^{0,1,2}\ Y_F^{0,1,2}\ [U + Z_{pp}^{0,1,2}\ Y_F^{0,1,2}]^{-1}\ E_{p(0)}^{0,1,2} \tag{18}$$

The fault current in the 3-phase element $i-j$ from [Eq. (16)] after transformation to component quantities will be:

$$I_{ij(F)}^{0,1,2} = Y_{ij\rho\sigma}^{0,1,2}\ [E_{\rho(F)}^{0,1,2} - E_{\sigma(F)}^{0,1,2}] \tag{19}$$

4.2 Algorithms for Calculating System Conditions after the Occurrence of Faults

We have shown earlier that the different types of faults in a power system network are,

1. 3-phase short circuit or 3-phase to ground fault → one in number
2. Double line to ground fault → Three in number
3. Line to line fault → Three in number
4. Single line to ground fault → Three in number

We shall take up all these cases of faults one by one and develop algorithms to calculate the bus voltages and fault currents and also fault levels at the buses. We shall take up these faults through finite fault impedance Z_f (or finite fault admittance Y_f).

3-Phase to ground fault through fault impedance Z_f per phase. For the faulted bus p, let the fault occur through impedance Z_f, and let there be also a finite ground impedance Z_g, as shown in Fig. A1. For the above case, Z_F^{abc} (i.e. fault

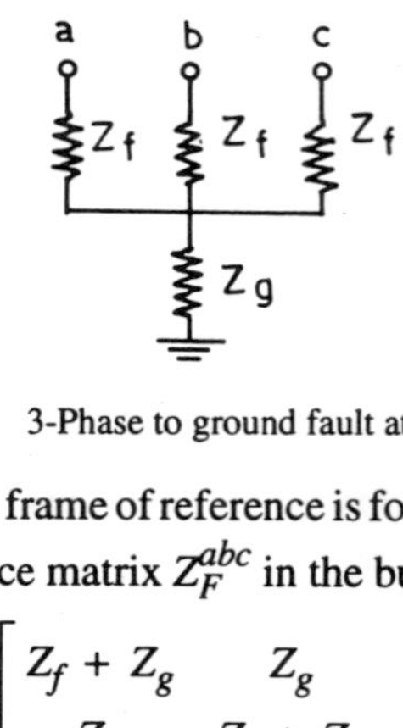

Fig. A 1 3-Phase to ground fault at any bus p

impedance matrix) in the bus frame of reference is found by conducting open circuit test. The final fault impedance matrix Z_F^{abc} in the bus frame of reference is:

$$Z_F^{abc} = \begin{bmatrix} Z_f + Z_g & Z_g & Z_g \\ Z_g & Z_f + Z_g & Z_g \\ Z_g & Z_g & Z_f + Z_g \end{bmatrix}$$

Now, $Z_F^{0,1,2} = T_s^{*T} Z_F^{abc} T_s$ (where T_s is a symmetrical component transformation matrix),

$$= \begin{bmatrix} Z_f + 3Z_g & 0 & 0 \\ 0 & Z_f & 0 \\ 0 & 0 & Z_f \end{bmatrix} \tag{20}$$

From Eq. (17), we get

$$I_{p(F)}^{0,1,2} = [Z_F^{0,1,2} + Z_{pp}^{0,1,2}]^{-1} E_{p(0)}^{0,1,2} \tag{21}$$

Substituting for $Z_F^{0,\,1,\,2}$ from Eq. (20) and for $E_{p(0)}^{0,\,1,\,2}$ from Eq. (16a) in Eq. (21), we get

$$\begin{bmatrix} I_{p(F)}^{0} \\ I_{p(F)}^{1} \\ I_{p(F)}^{2} \end{bmatrix} = \begin{bmatrix} 0 \\ \dfrac{\sqrt{3}}{Z_f + Z_{pp}^{1}} \\ 0 \end{bmatrix}$$

The voltages at the faulted bus p from Eq. (17) after proper substitution come out to be

$$\begin{bmatrix} E_{p(F)}^{0} \\ E_{p(F)}^{1} \\ E_{p(F)}^{2} \end{bmatrix} = \begin{bmatrix} 0 \\ \dfrac{\sqrt{3}\ Z_f}{Z_f + Z_{pp}^{1}} \\ 0 \end{bmatrix}$$

The voltages at the buses other than the faulted bus p from Eq. (18), are as follows:

$$\begin{bmatrix} E_{i(F)}^{0} \\ E_{i(F)}^{1} \\ E_{i(F)}^{2} \end{bmatrix} = \sqrt{3} \begin{bmatrix} 0 \\ 1 - \dfrac{Z_{ip}^{1}}{Z_f + Z_{pp}^{1}} \\ 0 \end{bmatrix}$$

Now we calculate the fault currents in the elements of the power system network. In this case, $Y_{ij\rho\sigma}^{1} = 0$ except for the element

$$\rho\sigma = i\,j$$

Thus the fault current in any element $i - j$, form Eq. (19),

$$\begin{bmatrix} i_{ij(F)}^{0} \\ i_{ij(F)}^{1} \\ i_{ij(F)}^{2} \end{bmatrix} = \begin{bmatrix} 0 \\ Y_{ij,\,ij}^{1}\ [E_{i(F)} - E_{j(F)}] \\ 0 \end{bmatrix}$$

Here 1 refers to the positive sequence component. From this, we concluded that in the case of 3-phase fault, we have only positive sequence network consisting of voltage source and positive sequence parameter. After this, we calculate the fault level at any bus i by summing all the currents in the elements terminating at the bus i when the 3-phase fault has been created at the bus with zero fault impedance.

4.3 Line-to-Line Fault through the Fault Impedance Z_f

Let us take a line-to-line fault at any bus p between any of the two phases b and c through a finite fault impedance Z_f per phase, as shown in Fig. A2.

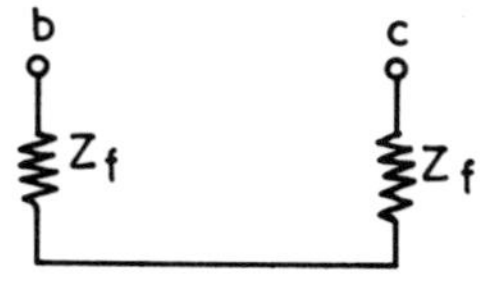

Fig. A2 Line to line fault

In this case Z_F^{abc} is undefined. However, the elements of fault admittance matrix in the bus frame of reference, i.e. Y_F^{abc} are calculated by conducting short circuit test at the bus p. The matrix Y_F^{abc} will be as shown below:

$$Y_F^{abc} = (y_f/2)\begin{bmatrix} 0 & 0 & 0 \\ 0 & 1 & -1 \\ 0 & -1 & 1 \end{bmatrix}$$

Here y_f is the fault admittance per phase and equals $1/Z_f$. After transformation to components, we obtain

$$Y_F^{0,1,2} = T_s^{*T}\ Y_F^{abc}\ T_s$$
$$= (y_f/2)\begin{bmatrix} 0 & 0 & 0 \\ 0 & 1 & -1 \\ 0 & -1 & 1 \end{bmatrix} \qquad (22)$$

Substituting relation (22) into Eq. (17), we get

$$\begin{bmatrix} E_{p(F)}^0 \\ E_{p(F)}^1 \\ E_{p(F)}^1 \end{bmatrix} = \begin{bmatrix} 1 & 0 & 0 \\ 0 & 1+Z_{pp}^1 \frac{y_f}{2} & -Z_{pp}^1 \frac{y_f}{2} \\ 0 & -Z_{pp}^1 \frac{y_f}{2} & 1+Z_{pp}^1 \frac{y_f}{2} \end{bmatrix}^{-1} \begin{bmatrix} 0 \\ \sqrt{3} \\ 0 \end{bmatrix}$$

After calculating $E_{p(F)}^{0,1,2}$ at the faulted bus p, we calculate the current at the faulted bus p from the following equation [Eq. (17)]:

$$I_{p(F)}^{0,1,2} = Y_F^{0,1,2}\ [U + Z_{pp}^{0,1,2}\ Y_F^{0,1,2}]^{-1}\ E_{p(0)}^{0,1,2}$$

After this we calculate, using Eq. (18), the bus voltages at the buses other than the faulted bus p. Finally, we calculate the current in the element i - j of the primitive network. Here only positive and negative sequence components exist and they are connected in parallel.

4.4 Single-phase to Ground Fault

Let us assume that fault has taken place at any bus p with finite fault impedance, The faulted phase is 'a' and fault has taken place through Z_F^{abc}, as shown in Fig. A3. In this case also, we only obtain the fault admittance matrix Y_F^{abc} in the bus frame of reference. After transformation to component quantities, we get

$$Y_F^{0,\,1,\,2} = T_s^{*T}\; T_F^{abc}\; T_s$$

$$= (y_f/3)\begin{bmatrix} 1 & 1 & 1 \\ 1 & 1 & 1 \\ 1 & 1 & 1 \end{bmatrix} \qquad (23)$$

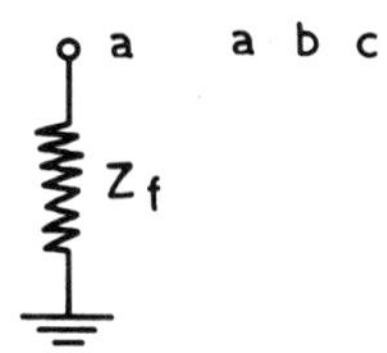

Fig. A3 Single line to ground fault at the phase a

Using Eq. (17) for the faulted bus p, we have after the substitution in Eq. (23).

$$\begin{bmatrix} E^0_{p(F)} \\ E^1_{p(F)} \\ E^2_{p(F)} \end{bmatrix} = \begin{bmatrix} 1 + Z^0_{pp}\dfrac{y_f}{3} & Z^0_{pp}\dfrac{y_f}{3} & Z^0_{pp}\dfrac{y_f}{3} \\ Z^1_{pp}\dfrac{y_f}{3} & 1 + Z^1_{pp}\dfrac{y_f}{3} & Z^1_{pp}\dfrac{y_f}{3} \\ Z^1_{pp}\dfrac{y_f}{3} & Z^1_{pp}\dfrac{y_f}{3} & 1 + Z^1_{pp}\dfrac{y_f}{3} \end{bmatrix}^{-1} \begin{bmatrix} 0 \\ \sqrt{3} \\ 0 \end{bmatrix}$$

After this, using Eqs. (17)–(19) we calculate the bus currents at the faulted bus p, the bus voltages at the other buses and the currents in the elements i - j of the primitive network. Finally, we calculate the fault level. In this case, we have all the three sequence networks viz. positive, negative and zero-sequence networks connected in series.

4.5 Double-Line to Ground Fault

The double line to ground fault at any bus p between any of its phases b and c with the fault impedance Z_f per phase and ground impedance Z_g is shown in Fig. A4.

The elements of the fault impedance matrix Z_F^{abc} in the bus reference frame is found by open circuit test and Y_F^{abc} by finding the inverse Z_F^{abc}. $Y_F^{0,\,1,\,2} = T_s^{*T}\, Y_F^{abc}$ T_s, i.e.

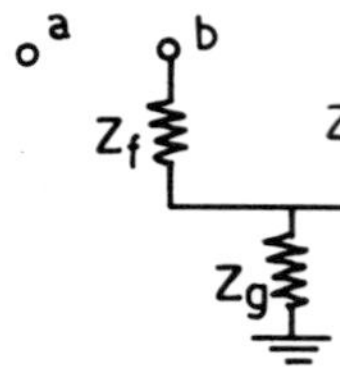

Fig. A4 Double line to ground fault

$$Y_F^{0,1,2} = \frac{1}{3(Z_F^2 + 2Z_f Z_g)} \begin{bmatrix} 2Z_f & -Z_f & -Z_f \\ -Z_f & 2Z_f + 3Z_g & -(Z_f + 3Z_g) \\ -Z_f & -(Z_F + 3Z_g) & 2Z_f + 3Z_g \end{bmatrix} \quad (24)$$

Substituting from Eq. (24) and Eq. (16a) in Eqs. (17)–(19), the bus voltages at the faulted bus p, bus current at the faulted bus p, bus voltages at the other buses, element currents and fault levels at the buses are calculated. In this case, all the three sequence networks are connected in parallel to simulate the double line to ground fault.

4.6 Three-phase Short Circuit without Ground with Fault Impedance Z_f per Phase

The 3-phase short circuit without ground with fault impedance Z_f per phase is shown in Fig. A5. The fault admittance matrix Y_F^{abc} in the bus frame of reference is found by short circuit test as:

$$Y_F^{abc} = \frac{y_f}{3} \begin{bmatrix} 2 & -1 & -1 \\ -1 & 2 & -1 \\ -1 & -1 & 2 \end{bmatrix}$$

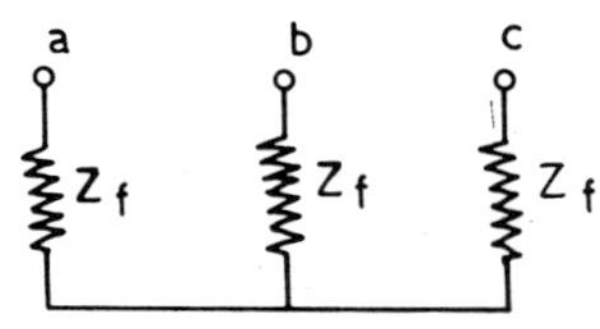

Fig. A5 3-phase fault

After transformation to component quantities, we obtain $Y_F^{0,1,2}$ as:

$$= y_f \begin{bmatrix} 0 & 0 & 0 \\ 0 & 1 & 0 \\ 0 & 0 & 1 \end{bmatrix}$$

In a manner similar to as followed in the case of the other faults dealt with above, we calculate the bus voltages, element currents and fault level at the buses.

5 A PC-BASED INTEGRATED SOFTWARE FOR SHORT CIRCUIT STUDIES

Early work on interactive computing was restricted to mainframe class computers and to some dedicated super-mini and mini class computers. Because of the nature of early computers, the interaction with the user was always hampered by inadequate displays and by low rates of data communication. Today with the advent of microcomputers, problems of slow data transfer rates and deficient displays are almost irrelevant; furthermore, features such as colour graphics and mass data storage devices are more popular and accessible than ever. To put these features to their fullest use, the development of a new generation of PC-oriented interactive programme is necessary.

The digital computer used for solving complex scientific problems is bulky in size and costly. The latest development in computer technology is microprocessor, a device that has all the functions of the central processing unit of a computer, which can fetch instructions from a memory, decode and execute them, perform arithmetical and logical operations, accept data from input devices, and send results to output devices. A microprocessor, together with a memory and input/output elements for communication with the outside world forms a full-fledged computer or microcomputer. Costwise, the microcomputer is much less expensive than the usual digital computer. A microprocessor is an assembly of digital circuits whose circuit connections are determined and controlled by the software program.

There are numerous applications of microprocessor in such fields as, (a) Instrumentation, e.g. calculations on oscilloscope, digital voltmeters, automatic capacitance bridge, X-ray analyzers, blood analyzers, frequency synthesizers, spectrum analyzers etc.; (b) Communications, e.g. microcomputer networks, message switching unit, repeaters, coding and encryption device models, etc.; (c) Computers, e.g. business computers, in minicomputer CPUs and input/output controllers, and in many computer peripherals, including intelligent CRT terminals, magnetic card readers; (d) Industry, e.g. control of d.c. and a.c. motors, automatic weighing, metal stretching and bending process, optical page readers, graphics and drafting systems; (e) Transportation, e.g. traffic signals and controllers, (f) Aerospace and military, e.g. navigation systems, satellite communication systems, mobile communication systems, etc. and (g) Consumers/Commercial, e.g. consumer areas including games, appliances, etc.

5.1 PC-based Formulation

Recent work in Computer Aided Engineering (CAE) and Computer Assisted Instructions (CAI) areas shows a clear trend towards more sophisticated user interfaces. One of the primary goals of any interactive environment is to enhance the bandwidth of communications between the user and the application program. Wider bandwidth of communications means that more information is conveyed to the user in a shorter period of time. The user interface is the aspect of the program that governs the communication between the user and the application. Generally speaking, user interfaces must meet a set of criteria to add to the power of the application program. The user interface must help the user to use the software, display input/output information in an organized and easy-to-understand fashion, allow the user to manipulate the way output information is displayed, activate application programs in the proper context and manage all the needed resources such as data files and memory allocation and this must be carried out with minimum user assistance, supply the user with easy means to enter and modify the data, enhance the effectiveness of trial and error type of studies (this is an immediate result to the simplification of the cycle of modifying data and application, activation and output probing), allow different application programs to share common data basis and help the user make a better understanding of output information. The software package developed at I.I.T. Kanpur is an example of an interactive environment for electrical power engineering studies on microcomputers. This package presents models of electrical power networks graphically.

The user interactively enters models of systems using a graphical editor. Interaction is accomplished through overlaid symbolic menus. When the user completes the graphical description, the graphical editor saves the system on the form of a global data base common to all modules.

To enter numerical data, the user moves to the data editor module. In the data editor, sophisticated tables provide the user with easy and fast means for data entry. Once the user completes data entry, new data are added to the existing data base. Empty slots in the data base designated for numerical data are filled with corresponding values. The user may now apply the needed type of analysis. At the end of the analysis, the package supplies the user with a choice of examining and/or printing the results. This package offers a new dimension in displaying results, the animation module vividly displays the power flow through transmission lines as well as limited violations.

The following modules are discussed briefly:

1. System Configuration
2. System Data
3. Short Circuit Analysis
4. Display and Printout

The system configuration. The graphical editor provides the user with a versatile sketch pad. With this sketch pad, the user can construct the graphical representation of the system. The sketch pad generates one-line diagram models for electrical power network analysis. The graphical editor provides the user with some file-handling functions as well. The following list gives a brief summary of the available functions in this module:

1. Drawing function: Buses, Generators, Loads, Transformers, Capacitors and Phase shifters.
2. Editing function: Delete component, Component temporary outage, Recover component and Move a bus to new location.
3. File management and program control functions: Recall system, Save system, Title system, List of file names, Analyze current file and Exit.

System data. The user enters numerical data associated with the graphical layout of the electrical system using **data editor**. A demand-driven data editor prompts the user for entering no more than the needed data. Tabular representation of data speeds up data entry. Appearing on a portion of the screen is a miniature diagram of the system, it serves as a cross reference between numerical data and system configuration. The first menu level provides the following choices:

Edit data: Bus data, Line data, Transformer data, Phase shifter data and Static capacitor data.

File management and program control: Recall system, Save system and Exit.

The second level of menu is accessible only in data-edit modes and this level provides the following choices:

Fill Automatic: Prompts user for needed data only.

Fill at Mark: Allows the user to choose any field to edit by moving the marker to the field.

Marker Commands: Helps the user to move the marker around or to scroll data windows.

Select Data Set: Allows the user to switch between two different sets of data.

Short circuit analysis. The purpose of this analysis is to find the magnitude of currents flowing through the system's lines in the event of a fault. The load flow analysis is essential in obtaining pre-fault data. The short circuit analysis must be entered after the load flow analysis is successively performed. In the short circuit analysis module, the screen will show the system's one line diagram identically to screens shown earlier.

Before the start of any analysis, the user must provide the data specifying the location of the fault and the transient/sub-transient reactances. As soon as data entry is completed, the analysis is performed and the results are tabulated and displayed. The first step for the fault analysis program is to build the Z-bus impedance matrix. The Z-bus building algorithm (shown by the diagram in Fig. A6) is used here to speed up studies which involve several fault locations. Second, the post-fault currents are calculated using Z-bus matrix. Once current values are calculated, they are displayed in tabular format.

Results display. Included in the software package is a browsing utility with several windows to enhance the accessibility of analyses results. Results are displayed in the form of overlaid windows. The windows display the results of analyses in tabular format specified by the program. In addition to scrolling capability, the user can manipulate the sizes and locations of windows for easier cross-referencing between tables. Moreover, the user may choose to print out the content of windows.

6 TRANSFORMATION TO COMPONENT QUANTITIES

Since after the fault the three-phase excitation becomes unbalanced, even though the three-phase network elements are balanced and symmetric, the analysis is simplified by transferring the phasor quantities to the component quantities because even though in the phasor form the coefficient matrix is a full matrix, after the transformation to the component quantities, it becomes diagonal. In practice, the following types of transformation matrices are used for the analysis of power system networks.

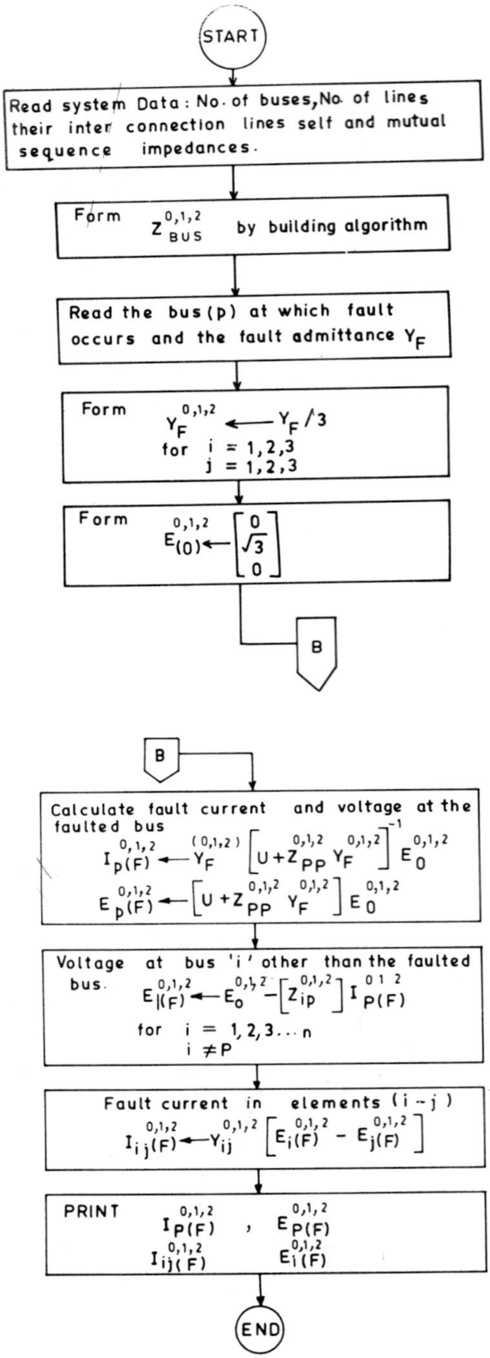

Fig. A6 Flow diagram for single line to ground fault

1. *Symmetrical components transformation "T_S".* This transformation is linear, power-invariant and complex. This transforms the field of phasors to the field of 0, positive and negative sequence components. This is as shown in the following:

$$T_s = \frac{1}{\sqrt{3}} \begin{bmatrix} 1 & 1 & 1 \\ 1 & \alpha^2 & \alpha \\ 1 & \alpha & \alpha^2 \end{bmatrix}$$

The matrix T is a unitary matrix, i.e.

$$T_s^{*T} = T_s^{-1}$$

2. *Clark's component transformation "T_C".* This transformation transforms the field of phasors to the field of 0, α and β components. This is a linear, power-invariant and real transformation and is as follows:

$$T_c = \frac{1}{\sqrt{3}} \begin{bmatrix} 1 & \sqrt{2} & 0 \\ 1 & -\sqrt{1/2} & \sqrt{3/2} \\ 1 & -\sqrt{1/2} & -\sqrt{3/2} \end{bmatrix}$$

This is an othogonal matrix, i.e.

$$T_C^T = T_C^{-1}$$

3. *Park's Component Transformation "T_p".* This transformation matrix which is linear, real and power-invariant, transforms the field of phasors to the field of *o-d-q* components. This is shown in the following:

$$T_p = \frac{1}{\sqrt{3}} \begin{bmatrix} 1 & \sqrt{2}\cos\beta & \sqrt{2}\sin\beta \\ 1 & \sqrt{2}\cos(\beta - 120) & \sqrt{2}\sin(\beta - 120) \\ 1 & \sqrt{2}\cos(\beta + 120 & \sqrt{2}\sin(\beta + 120) \end{bmatrix}$$

This transformation matrix is orthogonal, i.e. $T_p^T = T_p^{-1}$. This transformation matrix is used in the analysis of synchronous machines where, in addition to diagonalizing machine coefficient matrix, it also transforms the machine differential equations having variable coefficients to the differential equations with constant coefficient. However, the first two transformations, i.e. symmetrical components and Clerk's components transformations are used for the analysis of power systems. All the above three transformation have the following common features:

(a) They contain entry of 1 in the column one.
(b) The sum of columns 2 and 3 are zero separately.
(c) All the 3 columns are linearly independent.

7 SHORT CIRCUIT STUDIES OF MULTI-PHASE SYSTEMS

Traditionally, multi-phase transmission has three phases, though higher phase order have been considered for many years. Initially, the idea of adding more phases to the overhead lines was not encouraging, because of complexity and cost involved. However, the demand for electrical energy is increasing day by day and the electric utilities are facing the difficult problem of transmitting more power from generating stations to the far end load centres. The most common solution of increasing power transmission capability by increasing transmission voltages seems to have reached the point of saturation. Also, it has drawbacks of presenting strong electric fields at the ground surface with possible biological effects, visual pollution, audible noise and increasingly difficult problems in acquiring new rights-of-way, etc. High phase order transmission (HPOT), that is, the use of more than the conventional 3-phase, is an important option available today. It can usefully be applied over the full range of transmission voltages, and can be used for uprating (for example, double cicruit 3-phase to 6-phase) or for completely new designs for 6, 9 and 12-phases. The increasingly sophisticated design capabilities, combined with the environmental and cost demands on transmission designers, have made HPOT a unique solution. Several utilitites are now considering it for the future; and research and publications on various design aspects (protection schemes, fault studies and reliability studies, etc.) are rapidly increasing.

An important aspect of planning is the design of adequate protection schemes for the system. This requires a detailed fault analysis from the planning stage. The various types of faults which are likely to occur on a twelve-phase system may be as large as 23 in number, compared to eleven in a six-phase and five in a three-phase system. The 23 types of faults which are likely to occur on a twelve-phase transmission system are twelve-phase to ground fault and twelve-phases fault, eleven-phase to ground fault and eleven-phase fault, ... etc. two phase to ground fault and two-phase fault, and single-phase to ground fault, totalling to $11 \times 2 + 1 = 23$ types.

In the following analysis, it is assumed that the 12-phases system is balanced and unloaded, that is, open circuited during pre-fault stage. To find the various sequence currents and voltage, relationship between phase currents to voltages, and to determine exactly how the sequence networks are interconnected to simulate the different types of fault situations. A similar analysis follows for 6-phase or 9-phase systems.

Single line to ground fault (LG) (For designing ground relay). This is the least severe but the most common fault. The terminal conditions are

$$V_a = 0\,;\; I_b = i_c = I_d = I_e = \dots\; I_k = I_l = 0 \tag{25}$$

The component voltages are found by applying Eq. (25) and it can be shown that

$$V_{a0} + V_{a1} + \dots + V_{a11} = 0$$

The component currents are

$$I_{a0} = I_{a1} = I_{a2} = \dots = I_{a10} = I_{a11} = \frac{1}{\sqrt{12}}\, I_a \tag{26}$$

From Eq. (26), it is clear that the same current is flowing through each sequence network. From Eqs. (25) and (26), it is seen that all sequence networks are connected in series. We have,

$$I_{a1} = \frac{E_{a1}}{Z_0 + Z_1 + Z_2 + \dots + Z_{11}} = \frac{\sqrt{12}\; E_a}{\sum_{i=0}^{11} Z_i} \tag{27}$$

Hence,

$$I_a = \sqrt{12}\; I_{a1} = \frac{12\; E_a}{\sum_{i=0}^{11} Z_i} \tag{28}$$

and

$$I_b = I_c = I_d = I_e = \ldots\; I_k = I_l = 0$$

Twelve Phase to ground fault (for designing phase relays). This is the most severe but least common fault. It is a symmetrical fault.

Under faulted condition the phasor voltages are:

$$V_a = V_b = V_c = \ldots = V_k = V_1 = 0 \tag{29}$$

The component voltages are found by applying the earlier equation,

$$V_{a0} = V_{a1} = V_{a2} = \ldots = V_{a11} = 0$$

Substituting the above result in the equation, as shown

$$E_{\text{comp}} = [Z_{\text{comp}}]\; I_{\text{comp}}$$

we get,

$$\begin{aligned} 0 &= Z_0\; I_{a0} \\ E_{a1} &= Z_1\; I_{a1} \\ 0 &= Z_{a2}\; I_{a2} \\ \vdots\;\; & \;\;\vdots\;\;\;\; \vdots \\ 0 &= Z_{11}\; I_{a11} \end{aligned} \tag{30}$$

or

$$I_{a1} = \frac{E_{a1}}{Z_1} = \frac{\sqrt{12}\; E_a}{Z_1}$$

and

$$I_{a0} = I_{a2} = \ldots. = I_{a10} = I_{a11} = 0.$$

From Eqs. (29) and (30), it is clear that the sequence network will only consist of positive sequence network with positive sequence voltage and current.

From the results of different types of fault, it is clear that in the case of 12-phase fault the system remains symmetrical even after the fault. Therefore, sequence network consists of only the positive sequence impedance. The remaining faults are dual in pairs. For example, the single phase-to-ground and 11-phase-to-ground fault are dual in the sense that all the sequence networks are connected in parallel for 11-phase-to-ground fault while they are connected in series in the case of single phase-to-ground fault. However, in the case of 11-phase fault without involving ground the sequence network connection is similar is 8-phase-to-ground fault except that zero sequence network remains open-circuited. Similar duality exists between LLG fault and 10-phase-to-ground fault, LLLG fault and 9-phase-to-ground fault, LLLLG fault and 8-phase-to-ground fault, 5-phase-to-ground fault and 7-phase-to-ground fault.

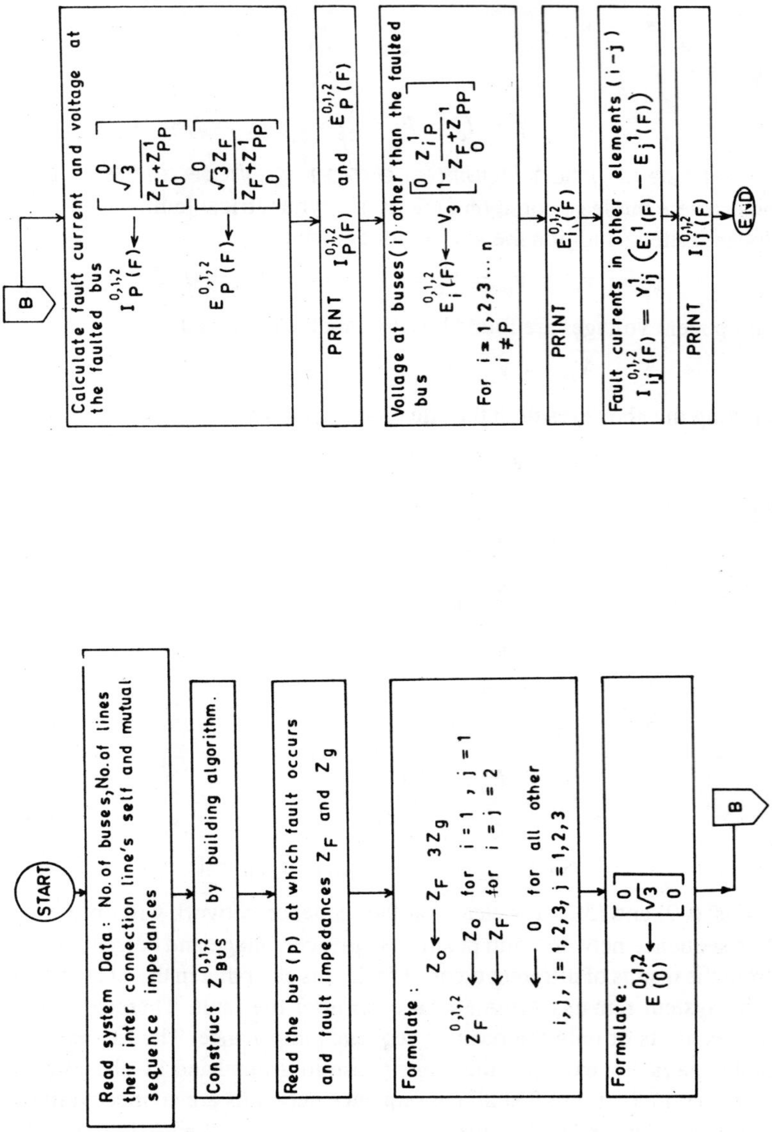

Fig. A7 Flow diagram for 3 P - ground fault

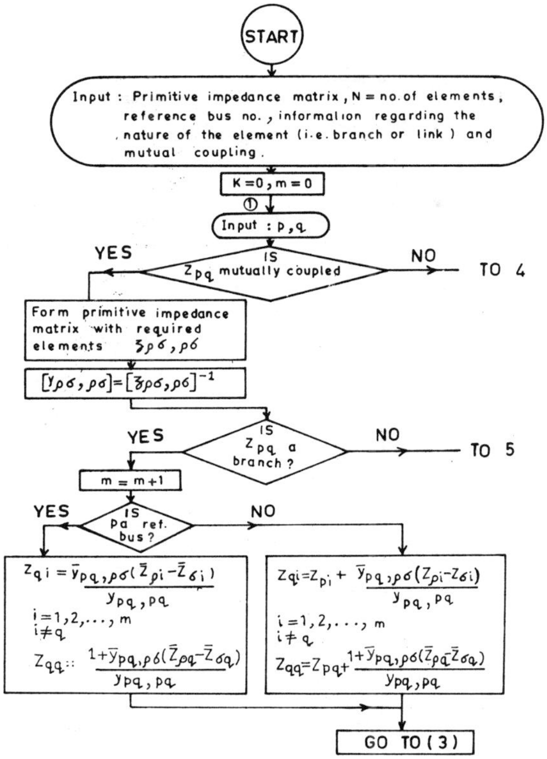

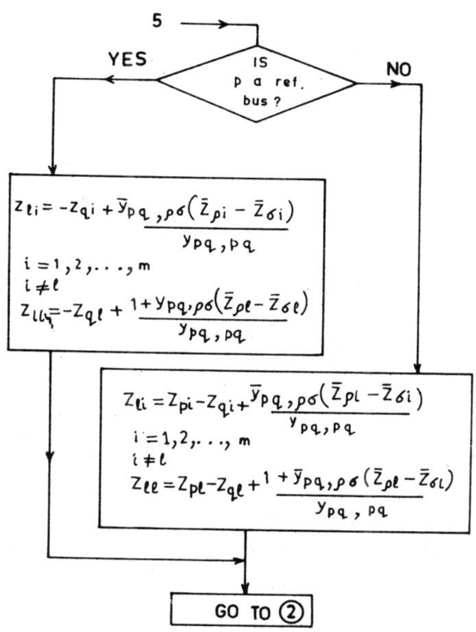

Fig. A8 Flow diagram for building Z_{bus} Algorithm (*contd.*)

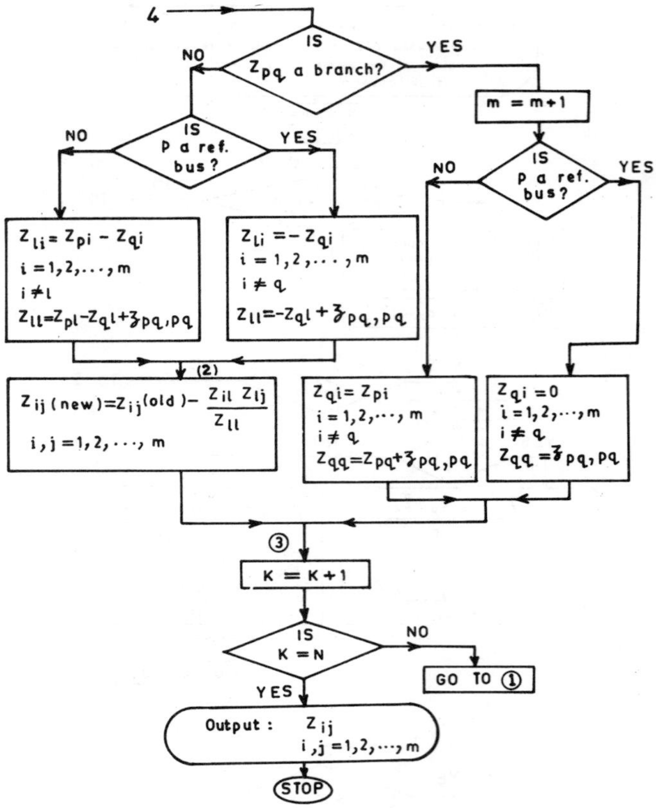

Fig. A8 Flow diagram for building Z_{bus} Algorithm

In all the cases, the zero sequence network will remain open-circuited for a fault not involving ground. Same conclusion is also arrived at for 6-phase and 9-phase systems. The 6-phase system seems to have a bright future. Here also duality is evident, for examples in 5-phase-to-ground fault, all the 6 sequence networks are connected in parallel while in the case of single phase-to-ground fault, they are connected in series. Similar duality holds good between other faults as well. Flow diagrams to conduct single line to ground fault and three phase to ground fault are shown in Figs. 6. and 7 respectively. Elements of Z_{BUS} matrix of a given power system network are obtained with the help of flow diagram shown in Fig. A8.

REFERENCES

1. Ahmad, H. El-Abiad, "Digital Calculation of Line to Ground Short Circuits by Method", *Trans. AIEE,* Vol. 79, Part III, 1960, pp. 323–332.
2. Ahmad, H. El-Abiad *et al.*, "Calculation of Short Circuit Using a High Speed Digital Computer", *Trans. AIEE,* Vol. 80, Part III, 1961, pp. 702–707.
3. Daneshdoost, M., and R. Shaat, " A PC Based Integrated Software for Power System Education", *IEEE Trans. Pwr. Syst.*, Vol. 4, No. 3, Aug. 1989, pp. 1285–1292.
4. Nanda, S.P., S.N. Tiwari and L.P. Singh, "Fault Analysisf Six-phase System", *Electr. Pwr. Syst. Res.*, Vol. 4, 1981, pp. 201–211.
5. Roy, L., "Generalized Polyphase Fault Analysis Program: Calculations of Cross Country Fault", *Proc. IEE,* Vol. 126, No. 10, 1979, pp. 995–1001.
6. Singh, L.P., *Advanced Power System Analysis and Dynamics*, 3rd Edition, Wiley Eastern Ltd. New Delhi, 1992.
7. Stagg, G.W., *et al.*, *Computer Methods in Power System Analysis,* Mc-Graw Hill Co., New York, 1968.
8. Tiwari, S.N. and L.P. Singh, "Mathematical Modeling and Analysis of Multi-phase Systems", *IEEE Trans.*, Vol. PAS-101, 1982, pp. 1784–1793.
9. Tiwari, S.N., and L.P. Singh, "Six-phase (Multi-phase) Power Systems: Some Aspects of Modeling and Fault Analysis", *Electr. Pwr. Syst. Res.*, Vol. 6 1983, pp. 193–202.
10. Umapal and L.P. Singh, "Feasibility and Fault Analysis of Multi-phase (12-phase) Systems", *J. Inst. Engrs.*, (India) Vol. 65, Pt El-4, Feb. 1985, pp. 138–146.

APPENDIX - II

ULTRA HIGH SPEED PROTECTIVE RELAYS FOR HIGH VOLTAGE LONG TRANSMISSION LINE

INTRODUCTORY REMARKS

The ultra high speed clearance of faults improves the transient stability of a power system because the transient rotational kinetic energy introduced into the system is proportional to the square of the fault clearing time. As a matter of fact, the UHS clearing of faults at any location, particularly on EHV/UHV intertie lines and close to large sources of generation, will reduce the system accelaration more than any other form of dynamic control which can be used only after the system is being accelerated. The fault clearing time depends on the speed of both the protective relay and associated circuit breaker. With the development of UHS circuit breakers in the recent past, attention is now focussed on the development of UHS protective relays. The development of UHS protective relays has been possible with the utilization of travelling wave phenomena. Quite a few authors have reported about the development of UHS protective relays based on travelling wave phenomena. After the occurance of a fault, the voltage and current at any point in a power system can be regarded as the sum of prefault and fault generated components. The fault generated components manifest themselves as travelling waves during the first few mili-seconds after the occurance of a fault. The relaying schemes developed so far, utilize these travelling waves for fault detection.

The ASEA (SWEDEN) was the first to develop travelling wave based UHS relaying scheme. This was tested on BPA (USA) 500 kV systems. It needs only the exchange of qualitative information between the ends of protective line. It is basically a directional comparison scheme. In this scheme, the fault generated components of the voltage and current of the first travelling waves reaching the relaying point are used to determine the direction to the fault. These components are of opposite sign for a fault ahead of the relaying point (*i.e.* internal fault) and are of the same sign for a fault behind (*i.e.*. external fault). Thus, only for internal fault, they are of opposite sign at both ends of the protected lines. The present chapter utilizes this feature and further extend it for the protection of a 3-phase line. A novel fault locating relay has also been developed based upon travelling wave phenomena.

TRAVELLING WAVE BASED UHS RELAYING SCHEME

The under line principles of the relay can be best explained by reference to a single phase transmission line interconnecting two large power systems as shown in fig. 1. Their extension to three phase lines is presented later in the next section. After the occurance of a fault, the voltage and current at any point in the system can be regarded as the sum of prefault and fault generated components, i.e.

$$V = V_{pf} + V_f \tag{1}$$

$$i = i_{pf} + i_f \tag{2}$$

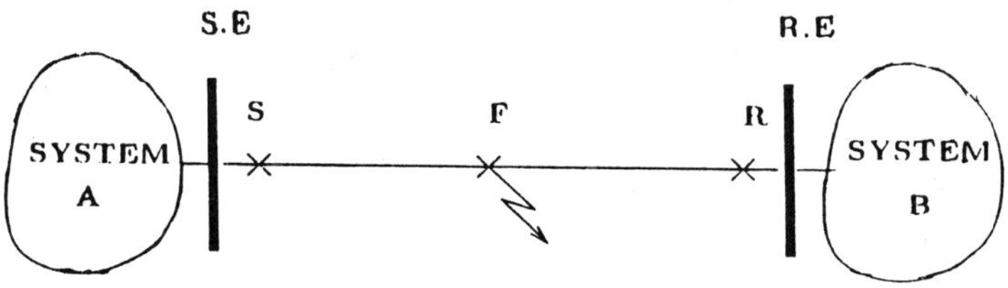

Fig.1 Transmission line interconnecting two power system 'A' and 'B'

where subscripts pf and f refer to the prefault and fault generated components respectively.

For a fault on a transmission line, the fault generated components manifest themselves as travelling waves and travel towards both the ends of the line. Assuming a lossless line, for simplicity, the fault generated components of voltage and current, at any point in line, are given by the solution of the well known wave equation as

$$V_f = f_1\left(t - \frac{x}{u}\right) + f_2\left(t + \frac{x}{u}\right) \tag{3}$$

$$i_f = \frac{1}{Z_0}\left[f_1\left(t - \frac{x}{u}\right) - f_2\left(t + \frac{x}{u}\right)\right] \tag{4}$$

where f_1 and f_2 - arbitrary functions determined by boundary conditions

t — time from the instant of fault occurance

u — velocity of propagation of travelling wave

Z_0 — surge impedance of the line.

From above the equations, it can be seen that, $f_1\left(t-\frac{x}{u}\right)$ represents a forward travelling wave and $f_2\left(t+\frac{x}{u}\right)$, a bachward travelling wave. Also forward travelling wave of voltage and current are of the same sign, whilst the backward travelling waves of voltage and current are opposite sign.

Because of redistribution of energy in the electric and magenetic field in the case of fault on a long line with distributed parameters, travelling waves are created and these travelling waves of the fault -generated components of voltage and current originating at the fault point F travel towards the ends of the line where they undergo refleciton and refraction. If the voltage reflection coefficients at the sending and receiving ends are ρ_s and ρ_r respectively, these events can be depicted by means of lattice diagram shown in Fig.2a where V_{ff} is the fault generated components of the Voltage at fault point. For example, if the fault is bollted one, V_{ff} will be equal to the prefault voltage at the point of fault.

The proposed scheme makes use of signal pair of the form given below for the each of the relays at the ends of protected line. For the sending end relay,the input signals (in p.u.) will be,

$$S_1 = V_{fs} - R_{set}\, i_{fs} \tag{5}$$

$$S_2 = V_{fs} + R_{set}\, i_{fs} \tag{6}$$

where V_{fs} and i_{fs}-fault generated components of voltage and current in p.u.at the sending end Rset is the surge impedance of the line in p.u. which is Z_0 in this case. For a fault on the line (*i.e.*internal fault), the vaules of V_{fs}, i_{fs}, $|S_1|$and $|S_2|$ at various instants, deduced from lattice diagram (Fig.2a) and above equations are given in table 1.τ_1 is the travel time of the waves to travel from the fault point to the sending end. Since ρ_s is always less than 1, except when the sending end is an open circuit, $|S_1| > |S_2|$ from τ_1 till another wave pairs arrive there as seen from Table 1.

Table 1

Relay input signals for internal fault

Time	V_{fs}	i_{fs}	$\lvert S_1\rvert$	$\lvert S_2\rvert$
$t < T_1$	O	O	O	O
$t = T_1^-$	V_{ff}	$-V_{ff} / Z_o$	$2\lvert V_{ff}\rvert$	O
$t \geq T_1^+$	$(1+\rho_s)\, V_{ff}$	$-(1-\rho_s)V_{ff}/Z_0$	$2\lvert V_{ff}\rvert$	$2\lvert \rho_s V_{ff}\rvert$

Next, consider a fault on any of lines feeding the sending end bus as (i.e external fault)shown in Fig.2b. One pair of the travelling waves generated on this line travells towards the sending end bus and undergoes both reflection and refraction at this bus. Due to the refracted wave, we have

$$V_{fs} = \rho_t \, V_{ff} \text{ and } i_{fs} = \rho_t \frac{v_{ff}}{Z_0^1} \tag{7}$$

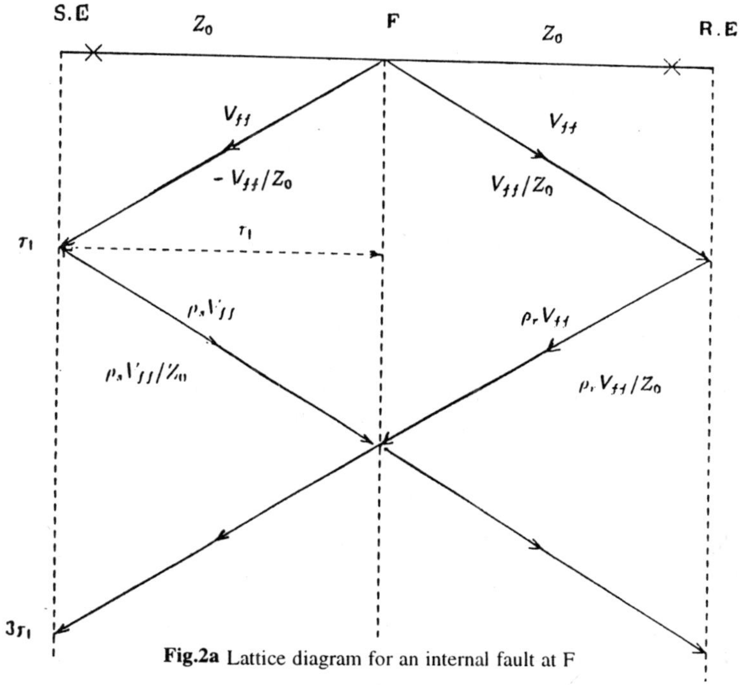

Fig.2a Lattice diagram for an internal fault at F

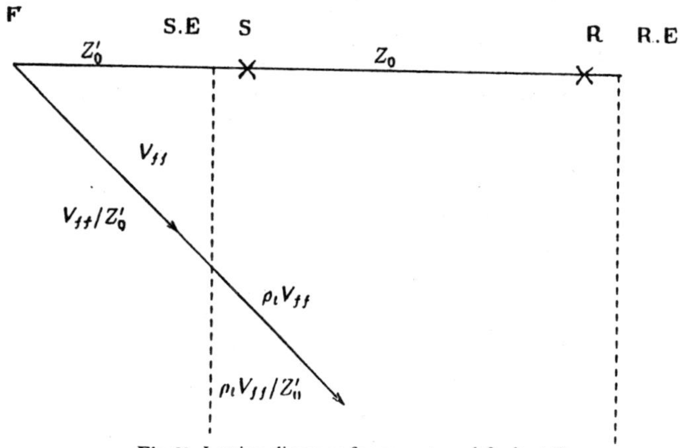

Fig.2b Lattice diagram for an external fault at F

where ρ_t is the refraction coefficient and Z_0^1 is the surge impedance of the faulted line. Then the relay signals as shown are given by

$$S_1 = \rho_t V_{ff} - \frac{R_{set} \rho_t V_{ff}}{Z_0^1}$$

$$= \left(1 - R_{set} / Z_0^1\right) \rho_t V_{ff} \tag{8}$$

$$S_2 = \rho_t V_{ff} + \frac{R_{set} \rho_t V_{ff}}{Z_0^1}$$

$$= \left(1 + R_{set}/Z_0^1\right) \rho_t V_{ff} \tag{9}$$

Therefore, it van be seen from the above equations and Fig. 2b that $|S_1| < |S_2|$ till these waves return after reflection at the remote end of the protected line. Hence, we have

$| S_1 | > | S_2 |$ for internal fault

and $| S_1 | < | S_2 |$ for external fault

An indentical relay arrangement is also provided at the receiving end bus. If $|S_1| > |S_2|$ at both the ends of the transmission line, an internal fault is indicated. The information about this is exchanged between the ends of the protected line through a fast communication channel.

EXTENSION OF THE PRINICIPLE TO THE PROTECTION OF THREE PHASE LINE

A3-phase transmission line with distributed parameters, is described in the frequency domain by the following differential equations,

$$\frac{d^2 \overline{V}^{abc}}{dx^2} = \overline{p}^{abc} \; \overline{V}^{abc}$$

$$\text{and } \frac{d^2 \overline{I}^{abc}}{dx^2} = \left[\overline{p}^{abc}\right]^t \overline{I}^{abc} \tag{10}$$

where $\overline{V}^{abc}$ - Column vector of the transforms of the voltages to earth of the phases abc at a point X on the line.

$\overline{I}^{abc}$ - Column vector of the transforms of the line currents, pertaining to phases a,b,c at X

$\overline{\rho}^{abc} = \overline{ZL}^{abc} \bullet \overline{YL}^{abc}$

$\overline{ZL}^{abc}, \overline{YL}^{abc}$ - transforms of the p.u. lengths series impedance and shunt admittance matrices, respectively of the line

X - distance from sending end.

$\bar{Z}_L^{abc}$ and $\bar{Y}_L^{abc}$ are evaluated by taking into account the presence of earth wire and the frequency dependency of both the resistive and inductive parameters of line and earth. The theory of natural modes enables the above equations to be effectively decoupled by means of voltage and current model transformation matrices S and Q respectively. Using these fransformation matrices, above equations can be rewritten as,

$$\frac{d^2 \bar{V}^{1,2,3}}{dx^2} = S^{-1} \bar{p}^{abc} S\bar{V}^{1,2,3}$$

$$\text{and } \frac{d^2 \bar{I}^{1,2,3}}{dx^2} = Q^{-1} \left[\bar{\rho}^{abc}\right]^t Q\bar{I}^{1,2,3} \qquad (11)$$

where, S - The matrix formed from the eign vectors of $\bar{\rho}^{abc}$

and Q - $[S^{-1}]^t$ i.e. the matrix formed from the eigen vectors of $[\bar{\rho}^{abc}]^t$

$\bar{V}^{1,2,3}$ - $S^{-1}\ \bar{V}^{abc}$ Column vector of model commpenents of phase voltage transforms

$\bar{I}^{1,2,3}$ - $Q^{-1}\ \bar{I}^{abc}$ Column vector of model components of line current transforms

And, $S^{-1}\ [\bar{p}^{abc}]\, S = Q^{-1}\ [\,\bar{p}^{abc}]^t\, Q$

$$= diag\ (\lambda 1\ ,\ \lambda 2 \ldots\ldots\ldots\ldots \lambda 3\ )$$

and $\lambda 1$, $\lambda 2$, $\lambda 3$ *are eigen values of* $\bar{p}^{abc}$ *The above equation can be written as decoupled forms as shown,*

$$\frac{d^2 \bar{V}^{(m)}}{dx^2} = \lambda_m \bar{V}^{(m)} = r_m^2 \bar{V}^{(m)}$$

$$\text{and } \frac{d^2 \bar{I}^{(m)}}{dx^2} = \lambda_m \bar{I}^{(m)} = r_m^2 \bar{I}^{(m)} \qquad (12)$$

for m = 1,2,3

These equations show that the wave propagation in a 3-phase transmission line can be decomposed into three separate and independent components called model components, each possessing its own propagation constant and surge impedance.

Hence, a distributed - parameter 3-phase transmission line can be described in the frequency domain by set of decoupled model differential equations given below,

$$\frac{d^2 \overline{V}^{(m)}}{dx^2} = r_m^2 \overline{V}^{(m)}$$

$$\text{and} \quad \frac{d^2 \overline{I}^{(m)}}{dx^2} = r_m^2 \overline{I}^{(m)} \tag{13}$$

for m= 1,2,3

Here, $\overline{V}^{(m)}, \overline{I}^{(m)}$ – *mth* model components of phase voltage and line current transforms

r^m – propagation constant of mth mode.

These equations show that the wave propagation in a 3-phase line can be considered in terms of three separate and independent components, each possessing its own propagation connstant and surge impedance. Three separate and independent components are called model components and are obtained by modell transformation, using the voltage and the current model transformation matrices S and Q.

It has been the practice to set the protective relays with assumption of an ideally transposed line. With this assumption, S and Q become equal and frequency independent. Here, S and Q are chosen (Karrenbauer model) as,

$$S = Q = \begin{bmatrix} 1 & 1 & 1 \\ 1 & -2 & 1 \\ 1 & 1 & -2 \end{bmatrix} \tag{14}$$

The model surge impedances of the line are given by

$$Z_0^{(1)} = \left\{\left(\overline{Z}_s + 2\overline{Z}_m\right) / \left(\overline{Y}_s - 2\overline{Y}_m\right)\right\}^{1/2} \quad \text{for mode 1}$$

$$\text{and} \quad Z_0^{(2)} = Z_0^{(3)} = \left\{\left(Z_s - Z_m\right) / \left(Y_s + Y_m\right)\right\}^{1/2} \quad \text{for mode 2 \& 3} \tag{15}$$

wher,

$\overline{Z}_s, \overline{Z}_m$ – self and mutual series imedance transforms of the line

$\overline{Y}_s, \overline{Y}_m$ – self and mutual shunt admittance transforms of the line.

Therefore,the results obtained earlier can also be applied to each of the three modes of propagationof travelling waves. Accordingly, three pairs of signals, one for each mode,are employed.For sending end relay, these are given by,

$$S_1^{(m)} = V_{fs}^{(m)} - R_{set}^{(m)} i_{fs}^{(m)}$$

$$\text{and } S_2^{(m)} = V_{fs}^{(m)} + R_{set}^{(m)} i_{fs}^{(m)} \tag{16}$$

for m =1,2,3

Here

$V_{fs}^{(m)}, i_{fs}^{(m)}$ – model components of the fault generated compenent of the sending end phase voltages and line currents, determined by using the model transformation matrix given earlier.

$$R_{set}^{(1)} = R_e\left[\overline{Z}_0^{(1)}\right]$$

$$\text{and } R_{set}^{(2)} = Rset^{(3)} = R_e\left[\overline{Z}_0^{(2)}\right] = R_e\left[\overline{Z}_0^{(3)}\right] \quad (17)$$

The amplitude comparison described earlier is applied to each signal pair. A tripping or blocking signal is issued by the first position outcome of any one of the comparison. We have,

$$\left|S_1^{(m)}\right| > \left|S_2^{(m)}\right| \text{ i.e. } \left|S_1^{(m)}\right| - \left|S_2^{(m)}\right| > 0$$

for fault ahead

$$\text{and } \left|S_1^{(m)}\right| < \left|S_2^{(m)}\right| \text{ i.e. } \left|S_1^{(m)}\right| - \left|S_2^{(m)}\right| < 0 \quad (18)$$

for fault bhind, m =1,2,3

An indentical relay arrangement is provided at the receiving end as well.

FAULT LOCATING RELAY SCHEME

This is the second relaying scheme, which in addition to giving a tripping signal for internal faults, also gives the distance of the fault.

This scheme has the following special features. The tripping on the internal fault takes place without the aid of communication channel. The communication channel is used only for blocking purposes in the event of external fault. Therefore, the operating time of the communication carrier equipments does not come into picture in the case of internal fault. The scheme uses the reflection properties of the travelling waves to determine the fault location.

With regard to this scheme, the underlying principles are explained by considering a lossless 1-phase line as shown in Fig. 1. Two identical relay schemes. located at S and R and with reference direction as shown earlier, are employed for the protection of the line. The discussion is centred on the relay scheme at S. It appllies equally well to that at R. The input signal pair to the relay at S is the same as earlier. However, in the current scheme. S_2 is only used to detect the reverse fault i.e fault behind the relay, whilest S_1 is used not only to detect the fault but also to locate the internal fault.

Reverse fault (behind the relay). Upon the occurrence of a fault on any of other lines connected to the sending end bus, travelling waves of voltage and current are generated. One pair of them travels towards the sending end bus where the waves undergo both reflection and refraction. Due to reflected waves, S_2 increases from zero to $(1+R_{set}/Z_o^{1})\ \rho_t\ V_{ff}$. If $Z_o^{1}=Zo = R_{set}$, as usually the case,then $(1+ R_{set}/Z_{:o}^{1})\ \rho_t\ V_{ff} = 2|\rho_t\ V_{ff}|$. Therefore, if $|S_2| > o$, a reverse fault is indicated. However, there may be measurements and or other types of errors. Hence, the following criterion is adopted for detecting a reverse fault.

$|S_2| >$ a preset level

If $|S_2|$ exceeds the preset level, a transmitter is started after a short time delay T_d. In addition, issue of a trip signal at the local end, by the backwaard waves coming from the remote end bus after reflection, is blockd. The remote end recevier, after the receipt of the transmitter signal, blocks the issue of a trip signal there.

Forward fault. Consider a fault at F (Fig.1) on the protected line. The travelling waves generated at the fault pont, travel between this ponit and ends of the line, for sometime, due to multiple reflections and refractions.

The first travelling wave pair reaching S will be backward and will cause the value of $|S_1|$ to increase suddenly from zero to $2|V_{ff}|$. These waves will also cause $|S_2|$ to increase to $2|\ \rho_s V_{ff}|$ immediately thereafter. This may result in the transmitter being started. However, the starting of the transmitter is delayed by a short interval of time T_d and mean while,the former event is used to block the starting of transmitter.

After a time interval of $2r_1$ there will be a second sudden increase in $|S_1|$ due to the backward reflected wave comming from the fault point. The time interval between the first two sudden increase in $|S_1|$ is measured. This time interval is equal to twice the travel time of the waves between the fault and the relay points. Hence it gives the location of fault. However, if the fault occurs at voltage zero,there will not be any sudden increases in $|S_1|$. This difficulty is surmounted by using sudden increase in $d\,|S_1|\,/\,dt$ in addtion to those in $|S_1|$ for locating the fault. For a close in fault, $|S_1|$ and $d|S_1|\,/\,dt$ builds up rapidly and almost continuously. If rapid and continuous building up takes place over a certain preset time period, then tripping is initiated, and the fault is located as nearby.

In actual practice, the increase in either $|S_1|$ or $d|S_1|/dt$ will not be quite sudden, but will be only fast. This is due to attenuation caused by losses in the line and earth.Also, the magnitude of increase in $|S_1|$ or $d|S_1|/dt$ depends upon the fault resistance which reduces as V_{ff}. Accordingly, $|S_1|$ will have only a finite slope at the instant when the backward waves reach receiving point and not infinite. And,in between the first two rapid increases, $|S_1|$ will have a slope equal to that of $2|V_{ff}|$. If $V_{ff}=V_{ffmax}\ \sin(\omega_0 t+\alpha)$, then the maximum slope of $|S_1|$ between these two instants could be $2\omega_0 V_{ffmax}$ depending upon the fault initiation angle .The maximum value of V_{ff} will be for bolted fault. Then V_{ff} will be equal to V_{pff} the prefault voltage at the fault. And the maximum slope of $|S_1|$ would be equal to $2\omega_0 V_{pffmax}$. When the rapid increase in $|S_1|$ is detected by measuting its slope, the following criterion needs adoption so that no wrong detection of fault occurs, when the slope of $|S_1|$ is maximum or close to it, during the time interval between the two rapid increase in $|S_1|$,

$$\text{i.e} \quad \frac{d|S_1|}{dt} > 2\omega_0 V_{pffmax} \qquad (19)$$

At the instant of second rapid increase in $|S_1|$, V_{ff} gets reduced to $\rho_s V_{ff}$. Hence, the following criterion is adopted for detecting the second rapid increase in $|S_1|$,

$$\frac{d|S_1|}{dt} > 2\rho_s \omega_0 V_{pffmax} \qquad (20)$$

In the similar fashion,the following criterion is adopted to detect the first and second rapid increase in $\frac{d}{dt}|s_1|$

$$\frac{d^2|S_1|}{dt^2} > 2\omega_0^2 V_{pffmax} \qquad (21)$$

$$\text{and} \quad \frac{d^2|S_1|}{dt^2} > 2\rho_s \omega_0^2 V_{pffmax} \qquad (22)$$

For very high fault resistance, the second rapid increase may not be appreciable.

CONCLUSION REMARKS

The ultra high speed fault clearing is certainly a desirable feature for a long heavily loaded EHF/UHV line . The present chapter discusses UHS relaying scheme for a transmission line based upon travelling wave phenomena.The relaying scheme has been extended also for the protection of 3-phase line. A UHS faullt locating relay scheme which gives the distance to the fault has also been presented here.

REFERENCES

[1] Chamia,M.and Liberman, S.,"Ultra High Speed Relay for EHV/UHV Transmission Lines - Development, Design and Applications", IEEE Transactions on Power Apparatus and Systems, Vol. PAS-97, Nov./Dec.1978.1978, pp. 2104-2116.

[2] Esztergalyos, J.Yee,M.T., Chamia,M.and liberman, s, “The Development and operation of an Ultra High Speed Relaying System for EHV Transmission Lines”, CIGRE, Paris, 1878, Paper NO. 34-04.

[3] Johns, A.T., “New Ultra- High- Speed Directional Comparison

Technique for the protection of EHV Transmission Lines", Proc. IEE, Vol.127, Part C, July 1980, PP. 228-239.

[4] Vitins, M.,"A Fundamental Concept for High Speed Relaying', IEEE Transactions on Power Apparatus and systems, Vol. PAS-100, Jan.1981,pp. 163-173.

[5] Desikachar, K.V. and Singh, L.P., "Fault Analysis of Multinode Power System for Designing Ultra High Speed Protective Relays along with a Proposed Relaying Scheme', Electric Power System Research, Vol.6, 1983, pp.13-25.

[6] Desikachar, K.V. and Singh, L.P.," Digital Travelling Wave Protection of 'Transmission Lines', Electric Power System Research, Vol.7, 1984, pp.19-28.

[7] Islam, K.K., Bose, S.K. and Singh,L.P., "On-line Microprocessor Based Relaying Scheme for EHV/UHV Transmission Line - An Exisiting 400 Kv Line", Electric Machines and Power System,1987, PP.313-324.

[8] Islam, K.K.Bose, S.K. and Singh, L.P.,"Digital Protection of EHV/UHV Transmission Line Based upon Travelling Wave Phenomena", Electric Machines and Power System, 1988, PP.413-431.

[9] Singh ,L.P. and Desikachar, K.v., "Ultra High Speed Fault Locating Protective Relay for 3-Phase long heavily loaded EHV/UHV Transmission Line', Journal of Institution of Engineers (India),1996.

OBJECTIVE QUESTIONS

Note: Attempt all questions. All questions carry equal marks. Each question contains four alternatives such as (a), (b), (c) and (d), out of which one is correct/most appropriate. Put tick mark (√) to the correct/most appropriate alternative.

1. Protection scheme consists basically of
   (a) only protective relay
   (b) only circuit breaker
   (c) both the protective relay and circuit breaker
   (d) none of the above
2. For long EHV/UHV transmission line, we normally use
   (a) air circuit breaker
   (b) air blast circuit breaker
   (c) oil circuit breaker
   (d) isolating switch
3. By burden of the relay, we generally mean
   (a) volt-ampere rating of the relay
   (b) current rating of the relay
   (c) voltage rating of the relay
   (d) watt rating of the relay
4. Relay contacts are normally made up of
   (a) silver contact
   (b) copper contact
   (c) platinum contact
   (d) steel contact
5. Relay contacts are usually enclosed in
   (a) an air tight enclosure
   (b) a water tight enclosure
   (c) a moisture proof enclosure

(d) a dust proof enclosure

6. In the case of an electromechanical relay, relay coil is normally designed for
   (a) 1 and 5 amps
   (b) 5 and 10 amps
   (c) 10 and 25 amps
   (d) 50 and 100 amps
7. Relay coil voltage in an electromechanical relay is normally designed for
   (a) 110 and 220 volts
   (b) 220 and 400 volts
   (c) 1100 and 2200 volts
   (d) 2200 and 3300 volts
8. Overcurrent relay is a
   (a) single input comparator
   (b) dual input comparator
   (c) multi-input comparator
   (d) none of the above
9. Phase relays are used to provide protection against
   (a) single phase to ground fault only
   (b) double phase to ground fault only
   (c) phase faults involving two and more phases
   (d) three phase fault only
10. Ground relay is used to provide protection against
    (a) LG fault
    (b) LLG fault
    (c) LL fault
    (d) LLLG fault
11. In the case of transmission line protection, overcurrent relay is used
    (a) only up to 110 kV
    (b) only up to 220 kV
    (c) only up to 50 kV
    (d) only up to 1100 V
12. Zero sequence current is used for relaying purposes only in the case of
    (a) phase overcurrent relay
    (b) phase impedance relay
    (c) ground overcurrent relay
    (d) ground impedance relay
13. Ground fault means
    (a) single line to ground fault
    (b) double line to ground fault
    (c) both single and double line to ground fault
    (d) three line to ground fault
14. Threshold characteristics of a plane impedance relay in a complex *Z*-plane is
    (a) a circle passing through the origin
    (b) a circle with the centre at the origin
    (c) a straight line passing through the origin
    (d) a straight line offset from the origin

15. Circle offset from the origin on the real axis in the complex β-plane, is the threshold characteristic of a
    (a) plane impedance relay
    (b) percentage differential relay
    (c) MHO's relay
    (d) reactance relay
16. Threshold characteristic of an angle admittance (i.e. MHO's) relay in a complex β-plane is a
    (a) circle with the centre at the origin
    (b) straight line offset from the origin
    (c) straight line passing through the origin
    (d) circle passing through origin
17. Directional relay is a dual of
    (a) overcurrent relay
    (b) plane impedance relay
    (c) angle impedance relay
    (d) angle admittance relay
18. Reactance relay characteristic is realized by setting set impedance angle θ of the angle impedance relay
    (a) equal to zero degree
    (b) equal to 90°
    (c) equal to 180°
    (d) equal to 360°
19. The dual of angle impedance relay is
    (a) a plane impedance relay
    (b) an angle admittance relay
    (c) directional relay
    (d) none of the above
20. Impedance (i.e. distance) relay is a
    (a) single input comparator
    (b) dual input comparator
    (c) multi-input comparator
    (d) other than the above
21. Air actuated (i.e. Buchholz) relay is used to provide protection against internal fault
    (a) in the case of a synchronous generator
    (b) in the case of a transformer
    (c) in the case of a bus bar
    (d) in the case of an induction motor
22. Carrier current relaying is required for protection against fault
    (a) in the middle zone of the transmission line
    (b) in the end zones of the transmission line
    (c) both in the central one as well as in the end zones of the transmission line
    (d) other than the above
23. Fault is cleared by the simultaneous tripping of the relays at both the ends of the line if

(a) the fault takes place in the middle zone
(b) the fault takes place in the end zones
(c) the fault takes place in the first half of the line
(d) the fault takes place in the second half of the line

24. Impedance (i.e. distance) relaying scheme uses the
(a) fundamental component of the post-fault current
(b) transient component of the post-fault current
(c) fundamental as well as the transient component of the fault current
(d) other than the above

25. Tripping time of the relay less than a quarter cycle is only possible in the case of a relay
(a) based upon fundamental frequency
(b) based upon travelling wave phenomena
(c) based upon sinusoidal component
(d) based upon cosine component

26. Recursive filters are referred to as
(a) infinite response (impulse) filters
(b) finite response (impulse) filters
(c) both finite as well as infinite response (impulse) filters
(d) other than the above

27. Magnetizing inrush current in a transformer is nearly
(a) 10 to 15 times the normal rate current
(b) 2 to 5 times the normal rated current
(c) 20 to 30 times the normal rated current
(d) half the normal rated current

28. Magnetizing inrush current in a transformer is
(a) rich in 3rd harmonic component
(b) rich in 5th harmonic component
(c) rich in second harmonic component
(d) rich in all odd harmonic components

29. The frequency of the carrier in the case of carrier current pilot scheme is in the range of
(a) 1 kHz to 10 kHz
(b) 10 kHz to 25 kHz
(c) 25 kHz to 50 kHz
(d) 50 kHz to 500 kHz

30. The inrush current due to overvoltage caused by switching in a transformer is rich in
(a) 3rd harmonic component only
(b) 5th harmonic component only
(c) both 3rd harmonic as well as 5th harmonic component
(d) all even harmonic components

31. Multi-input comparator using phase angle criterion produces
(a) conic characteristic
(b) quadrilateral characteristic
(c) circular characteristic

(d) orthogonal characteristic

32. Multi-input comparator using amplitude comparison criterion produces
    (a) circular characteristic
    (b) straight line characteristic
    (c) conic characteristic
    (d) other than the above
33. In the case of carrier current pilot, the line trap connected at the end of the line consists of
    (a) series LC circuit
    (b) series RLC circuit
    (c) parallel LC circuit
    (d) parallel RC circuit
34. The coupling capacitor required for injecting carrier to the transmission line is composed of stack of capacitors of nearly
    (a) 0.1 μF
    (b) 0.25 μF
    (c) 0.001 μF
    (d) 0.01 μF
35. Protective relay based upon travelling wave phenomena operates
    (a) in less than 1/4 cycle
    (b) between 1/4 to 1/2 cycle
    (c) between 1/2 to 1 cycle
    (d) in greater than 1 cycle
36. The second harmonic component current induced in the field circuit of synchronous generator is due to the
    (a) positive sequence stator current
    (b) negative sequence stator current
    (c) zero sequence stator current
    (d) other than the above
37. The single phase to ground (i.e. LG) fault is simulated by connecting
    (a) all the three sequence networks in parallel
    (b) all the three sequence networks in series
    (c) only positive and negative sequence networks in parallel
    (d) only positive and negative sequence in series
38. All the three sequence networks are connected in series to simulate
    (a) LG fault
    (b) LL fault
    (c) LLG fault
    (d) LLLG fault
39. Power swing phenomena is usually caused by
    (a) single phase to ground fault
    (b) momentary overloading in the system
    (c) faults involving two or more phases
    (d) lightning
40. The value of bias factor "*S*" in the unit protection of a synchronous generator
    (a) lies between 0.05 to 0.1 pu

(b) is less than 0.05 pu
(c) lies between 0.1 to 0.25 pu
(d) is greater than 0.25 pu

41. The unit protection scheme provides
(a) primary protection
(b) backup (i.e. secondary) protection
(c) simultaneous protection
(d) remote protection

42. Interturn fault in the winding is caused by
(a) short circuit between turns of the same phase
(b) short circuit between turns of two adjacent phases
(c) short circuit between turns of all the three phases
(d) short circuit between turns of the ground i.e. core

43. Symmetrical components method is applicable when the
(a) three phase elements are unbalanced but the three phase excitation is balanced
(b) three phase elements are balanced but three phase excitation is unbalanced
(c) three phase elements and also three phase excitation is unbalanced
(d) other than the above

44. The frequency of carrier transmitted by microwave pilot is in the range of
(a) 100 kHz to 1500 kHz
(b) 2000 kHz to 5000 kHz
(c) 900 MHz to 6000 MHz
(d) 10,000 MHz to 15,000 MHz

45. The microwave pilot scheme
(a) needs both the line trap and coupling capacitor
(b) needs only line trap
(c) needs only coupling capacitor
(d) does not need either line trap or coupling capacitor

46. In addition to operating coil (or operating signal), there is also restraining coil (i.e. restraining signal)
(a) in the case of only differential relaying scheme
(b) in both differential as well as percentage differential relaying scheme
(c) in only percentage differential relaying scheme
(d) in neither differential relaying scheme nor percentage differential relaying scheme

47. The main purpose of using digital relaying scheme is that it provides
(a) only self checking feature
(b) only flexibility
(c) both self checking feature as well as flexibility
(d) neither flexibility nor self checking features

48. In order to quench the arc quickly and also optimize the dimensions, generally
(a) oil circuit breaker is preferred
(b) airblast circuit breaker is preferred
(c) minimum oil circuit breaker is preferred

(d) SF_6 breaker is preferred.

49. Relaying scheme based upon travelling wave phenomena is used only in the case of
    (a) synchronous generator
    (b) medium length transmission line
    (c) long EHV/UHV transmission line
    (d) transformer
50. For relaying purposes the second harmonic content of the inrush magnetising current in the transformer is
    (a) less than 5%
    (b) less then 10% but more than 5%
    (c) at least 16%
    (d) at least 25%
51. Buchholz relay is used for the protection against internal faults in the case of
    (a) a transformer
    (b) a synchronous generator
    (c) a bus bar
    (d) an induction motor
52. For the protection of EHV/UHV transmission line, the protective relay used is
    (a) OC relay
    (b) plane impedance relay
    (c) MHO's relay
    (d) differential relaying scheme
53. The threshold characteristics of reactance relay is a
    (a) circle passing through the origin
    (b) circle with the centre at the origin
    (c) straight line passing through the origin
    (D) straight line offset from the origin and parallel to R axis
54. The dual of plane impedance relay is
    (a) a directional relay
    (b) an angle admittance (MHO's) relay
    (c) an angle impedance (OHM) relay
    (d) an overcurrent relay
55. For ground fault, the relaying scheme preferred is
    (a) plane impedance relay
    (b) directional relay
    (c) reactance relay
    (d) OC relay
56. For the protection of feeder, the protective relay used is
    (a) percentage differential relaying scheme
    (b) plane impedance relay
    (c) MHO's relay
    (d) reactance relay
57. The threshold characteristic of a directional relay is a
    (a) circle with the centre at the origin

(b) straight line offset from the origin
(c) straight line passing through the origin
(d) circle passing through the origin

58. The dual of angle admittance (MHO's) relay is
(a) overcurrent relay
(b) angle impedance relay
(c) directional relay
(d) plane impedance relay

59. For phase fault involving two or more phases in a long heavily loaded transmission line, the relaying scheme preferred is
(a) MHO's relay
(b) plane impedance relay
(c) OC relay
(d) percentage differential relay

60. For the purpose of designing adequate protection scheme, we usually conduct
(a) load flow study
(b) short circuit study
(c) stability study
(d) none as above

61. The most severe fault on a 3-phase transmission line is a
(a) single phase to ground fault
(b) phase to phase fault
(c) double line (i.e. phase) to ground fault
(d) three-phase fault

62. The zero sequence quantity is used in the case of
(a) ground OC relay
(b) ground impedance relay
(c) phase OC relay
(d) phase impedance relay

63. In the protection scheme, the relay functions as a
(a) switching device
(b) sensing device
(c) breaking device
(d) none as above

64. Main purpose of using oil in oil circuit breaker is to
(a) provide insulation between oil circuit breaker contacts
(b) provide cooling of contacts
(c) quenching arc
(d) none as above

65. The inrush current due to overvoltage caused by switching in a transformer is rich in
(a) third harmonic component only
(b) fifth harmonic component only
(c) both third and fifth harmonic components
(d) second harmonic component

66. Plane impedance relay is a

(a) dual input comparator
(b) single input comparator
(c) multi-input comparator
(d) none as above

67. For the protection of transformer we normally prefer
(a) unit protection scheme
(b) MHO's relay
(c) plane impedance relay
(d) OC relay

68. The inrush magnetizing current in a transformer is maximum when
(a) the switch is closed at the voltage zero
(b) the switch is closed at the voltage maximum
(c) the switch is closed at half the voltage
(d) the switch is closed at twice the voltage

69. The inrush magnetizing current in a transformer is rich in
(a) second harmonic component
(b) third harmonic component
(c) odd harmonic components
(d) none as above

70. The impedance relaying scheme is used for the protection of
(a) transformer
(b) synchronous generator
(c) bus bar
(d) transmission line

71 Duality between phase and amplitude comparison scheme is only possible
(a) in the case of single input comparator
(b) in the case of dual input comparator
(c) in the case of multi input comparator
(d) none as above

72 The multi input comparator uses
(a) only one input signal
(b) only two input signal
(c) only three input signal
(d) more than two input signal

73 The multi input comparator using amplitude comparison principle, produces
(a) quadrilateral characteristics
(b conic characteristics
(c) circular characteristics
(d) straight line characteristics

74 The multi-input comparator using phase comparison principle produces
(a) conic characteristics
(b) circular characteristics
(c) quadrilateral characteristics
(d) none as above

75 If the threshold characteristics is a circle with the centre at the origin in the complex Z-plane (*i.e.* complex β-plane). then in the complex Y-plane (*i.e.* complex α-plane)
(a) it will also be circle with the centre at the origin
(b) it will be a circle passing through the origin
(c) it will be a circle offset from the origin
(d) none of the above

76 If the threshold characteristics is a circle passing through the origin in the complex Z-plane (*i.e.* complex β-plane), then in the complex Y-plane (*i.e.* complex α-plane)
(a) it will also be a circle with the centre at the origin
(b) it will be a circle passing through the origin
(c) it will be a circle offset from the origin
(d) it will be straight line offset from the origin

77 If the threshold characteristics is a straight line offset from the origin in the complex Z-plane (*i.e.* complex β-plane). then in the complex Y-plane (*i.e.* complex α-plane)
(a) it will be circle with the centre at the origin
(b) it will be a circle passing through the origin
(c) it will be circle offset from the origin
(d) it will be a straight line offset from the origin

78 The tripping zone is within the circle in the complex Z-plane, but in the complex Y-plane
(a) the tripping zone is outside the circle
(b) the tripping zone is within the circle
(c) the tripping zone is at the boundary of the circle
(d) none as above

79 Recursive filters are
(a) infinite impulse response filters
(b) finite impulse response filters
(c) definite impulse response filters
(d) none as above

80 Overcurrent relay relay for the protection of the transmission line is normally is used
(a) upto 33 kV
(b) upto 50 kV
(c) upto 100 kV
(d) beyond 10 kV

81 The reach of the protective relay will not change with the change in the type of fault, change in the generation or switching operation, in case of
(a) overcurrent relay
(b) IDMT relay
(c) directional overcurrent relay
(d impedance relay (*i.e.* distance relay)

INDEX